I broke a bone for the first time in my life.
Here's *World Trigger* 4.

—Daisuke Ashihara, 2014

Daisuke Ashihara began his manga career at the age of
27 when his manga *Room 303* won second place in the
75th Tezuka Awards. His first series, *Super Dog Rilienthal*,
began serialization in *Weekly Shonen Jump* in 2009.
World Trigger is his second serialized work in *Weekly
Shonen Jump*. He is also the author of several shorter
works, including the one-shots *Super Dog Rilienthal*,
Trigger Keeper and *Elite Agent Jin*.

WORLD TRIGGER VOL. 4
SHONEN JUMP Manga Edition

STORY AND ART BY DAISUKE ASHIHARA

Translation/Lillian Olsen
Touch-Up Art & Lettering/Annaliese Christman
Design/Sam Elzway
Editor/Hope Donovan

WORLD TRIGGER © 2013 by Daisuke Ashihara/SHUEISHA Inc.
All rights reserved.
First published in Japan in 2013 by SHUEISHA Inc., Tokyo.
English translation rights arranged by SHUEISHA Inc.

Printed in the U.S.A.

Published by VIZ Media, LLC
P.O. Box 77010
San Francisco, CA 94107

10 9 8 7 6 5 4 3 2 1
First printing, February 2015

www.shonenjump.com

www.viz.com

WORLD TRIGGER

4

DAISUKE ASHIHARA

SHONEN JUMP MANGA EDITION

WORLD TRIGGER DATA BASE

NEIGHBOR

Invaders from another dimension that enter Mikado City through Gates. Most "Neighbors" here are Trion soldiers built for war. The Neighbors who actually live on the other side of the Gates are human, like Yuma.

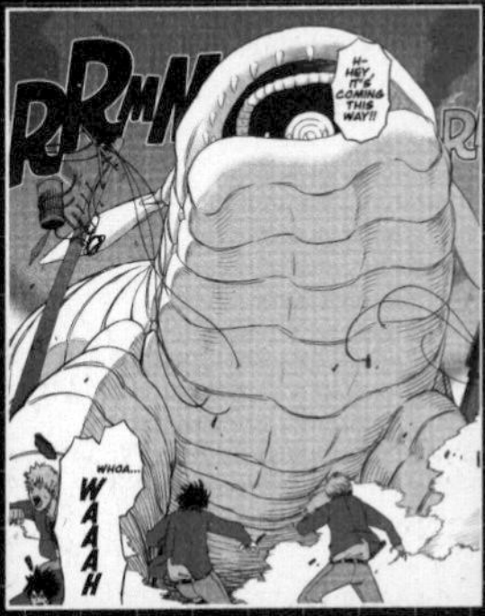
H-HEY! IT'S COMING THIS WAY!!
RRMN
WHOA...
WAAAH

Trion solider built for war. ▶

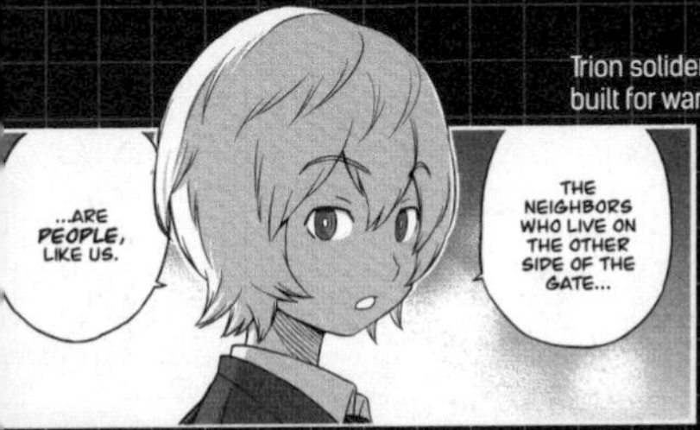
THE NEIGHBORS WHO LIVE ON THE OTHER SIDE OF THE GATE...
...ARE PEOPLE, LIKE US.

Invasion ▽ BORDER △ Resistance

Its official name is Border Defense Agency, or "Border" for short. Its purpose is to research Neighbor technology and protect the city from Neighbors. Agents are classified as follows: C-Rank for trainees, B-Rank for main forces and A-Rank for elites.

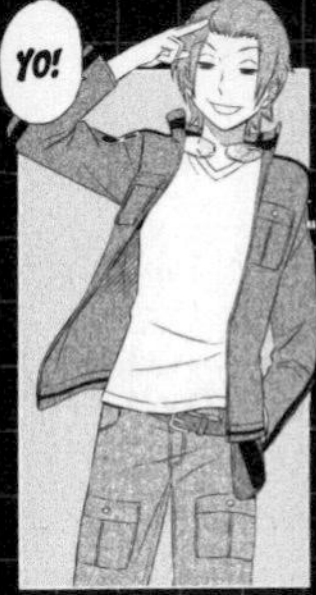
YO!

◀ Jin, with his Black Trigger, is S-Rank.

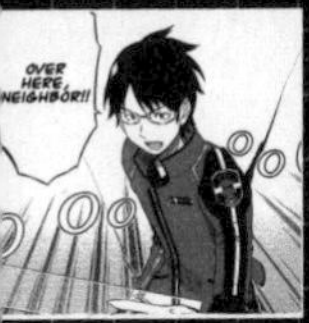
OVER HERE, NEIGHBOR!!

B-Rank: Osamu

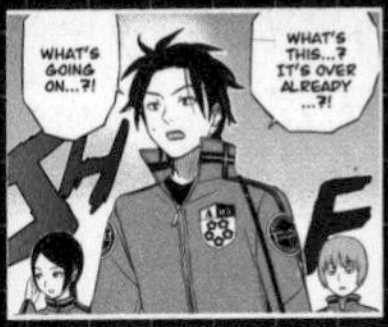
WHAT'S GOING ON...?!
WHAT'S THIS...? IT'S OVER ALREADY ...?!

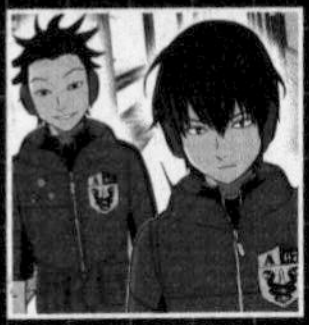

A-Rank: Arashiyama Squad, Miwa Squad

S-Rank: Yuichi Jin

Trigger

A technology created by Neighbors to manipulate Trion. Used mainly as weapons, Triggers come in various types. Border classifies them into three groups: Attacker, Gunner and Sniper.

▶ Attacker Trigger

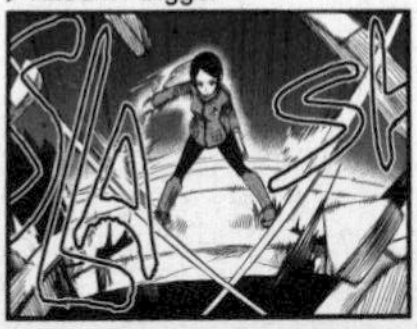

▶ Gunner Trigger

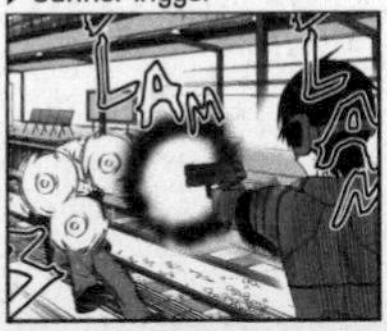

▶ Sniper Trigger

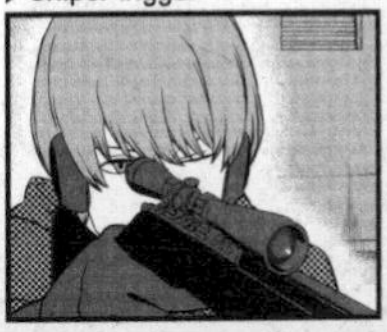

Black Trigger

A special Trigger created when a skilled user pours their entire life force and Trion into a Trigger. Outperforms regular Triggers, but the user must be compatible with the personality of the creator, meaning only a few people can use any given Black Trigger.

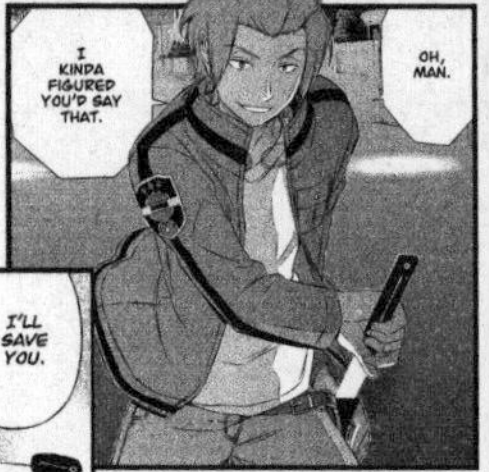
OH, MAN.
I KINDA FIGURED YOU'D SAY THAT.

▲ What can Jin's Trigger do?

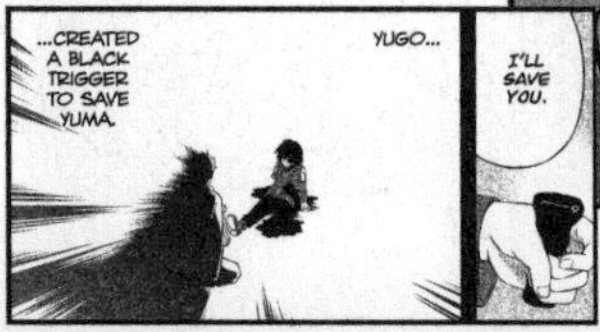
I'LL SAVE YOU.
YUGO...
...CREATED A BLACK TRIGGER TO SAVE YUMA.

▶ Yuma's father Yugo sacrificed his life to create a Black Trigger and save Yuma.

Trion

Energy supply for Triggers. Everyone has a Trion gland, but there is individual variation. Two people using the same Trigger may get different results.

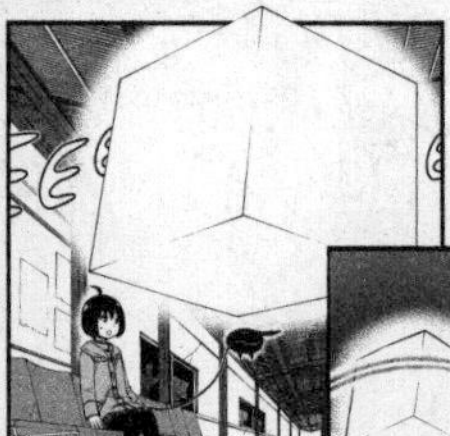

◀ Chika's Trion level

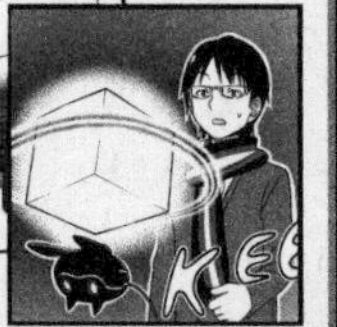

▶ Osamu's Trion level

Side Effect

Term for extrasensory perception abilities manifested by rare individuals with high Trion levels. A Side Effect is not a supernatural ability; rather, it is an extension of a human ability.

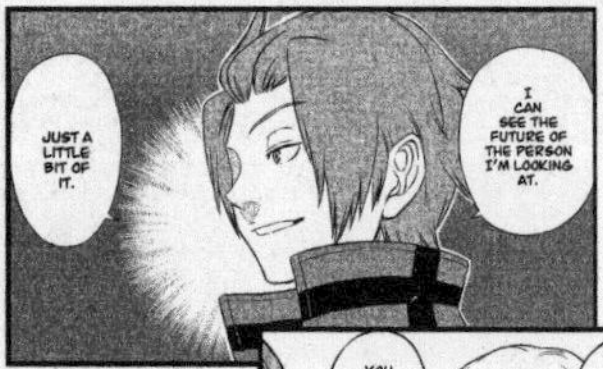
I CAN SEE THE FUTURE OF THE PERSON I'M LOOKING AT.
JUST A LITTLE BIT OF IT.

▲ Jin sees the future.

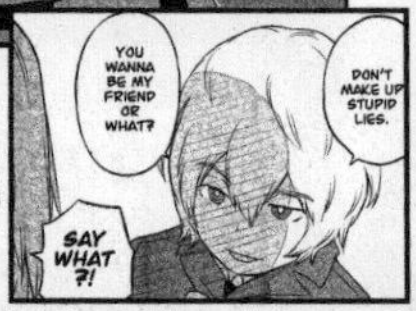
DON'T MAKE UP STUPID LIES.
YOU WANNA BE MY FRIEND OR WHAT?
SAY WHAT ?!

▶ Yuma detects lies

STORY

About four years ago, a Gate connecting to another dimension opened in Mikado City leading to the appearance of invaders called Neighbors. After the establishment of the Borde Defense Agency, people were able to return to their normal lives.

Osamu Mikumo is a C-Rank trainee and junior high student who finds out that transfe student Yuma Kuga is a Neighbor. Yuma is friendly, but Border HQ orders his capture! S-Ran agent Yuichi Jin is appointed to the task, but instead he asks Yuma to join Border's Tamakom Branch. There, Yuma learns that the man he was looking for on Earth, his father's friend Soicl Mogami, has passed away. Yuma loses all motivation, but Osamu gives him purpose again b asking him to help Chika Amatori and find her missing brother and friend. The three of ther decide to join Tamakoma in order to make A-Rank and travel to the Neighbor World! Ther members from HQ's top squads come to steal Yuma's Black Trigger and clash with Jin an

WORLD TRIGGER CHARACTERS

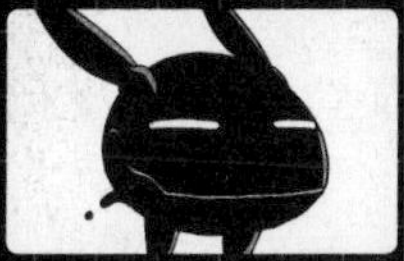

REPLICA

Yuma's chaperone.

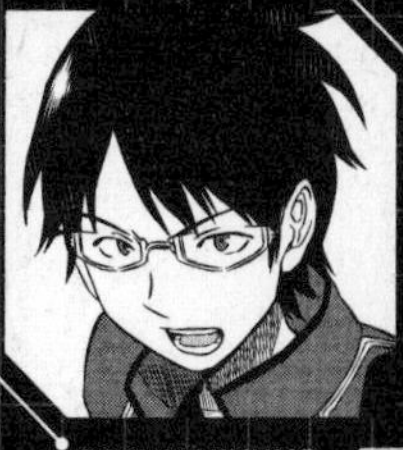

OSAMU MIKUMO

Ninth-grader who's compelled to help those in trouble. Border agent.

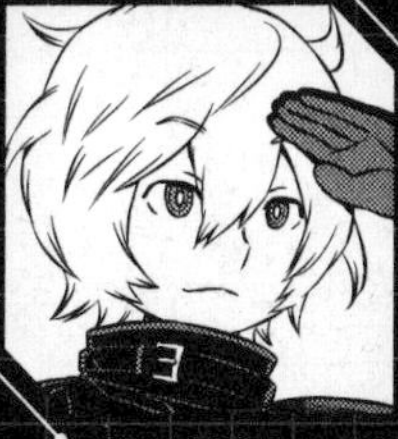

YUMA KUGA

Since he's a Neighbor, he lacks common sense. Has a Black Trigger.

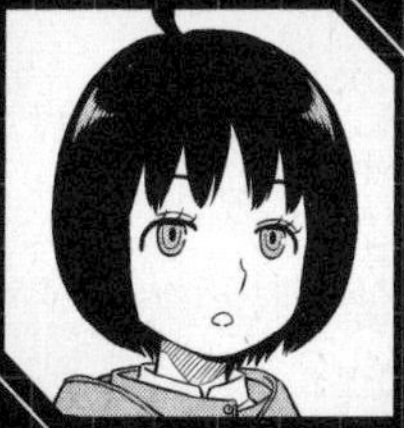

CHIKA AMATORI

Targeted by Neighbors because of her high Trion levels.

ENLISTMENT/ TRANSFER

TAMAKOMA BRANCH

Understanding toward Neighbors. Considered divergent from Border's main philosophy.

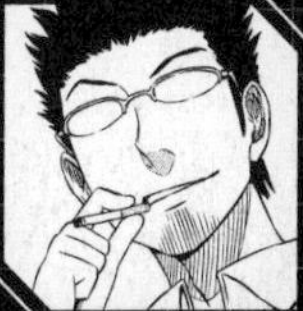

TAKUMI RINDO

Tamakoma Branch Director

TAMAKOMA-1

Tamakoma's A-Rank squad.

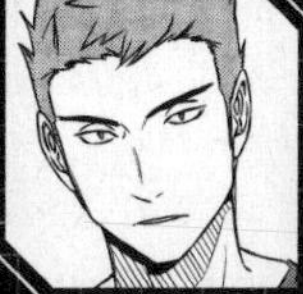

REIJI KIZAKI

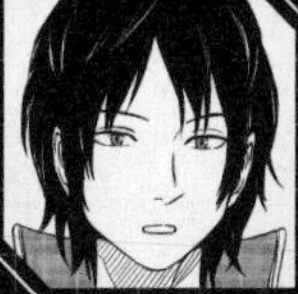

KYOSUKE KARASUMA

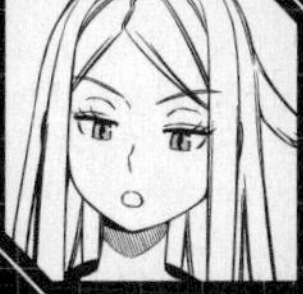

KIRIE KONAMI

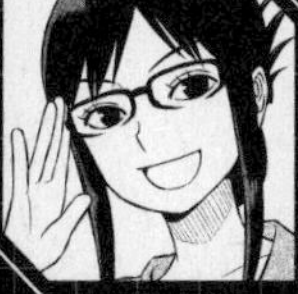

SHIORI USAMI

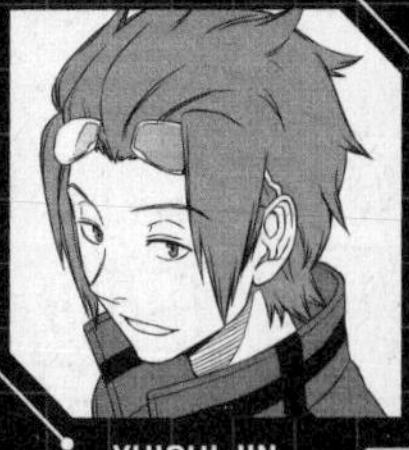

YUICHI JIN

S-Rank Border agent with a Black Trigger. His Side Effect lets him see the future.

TION

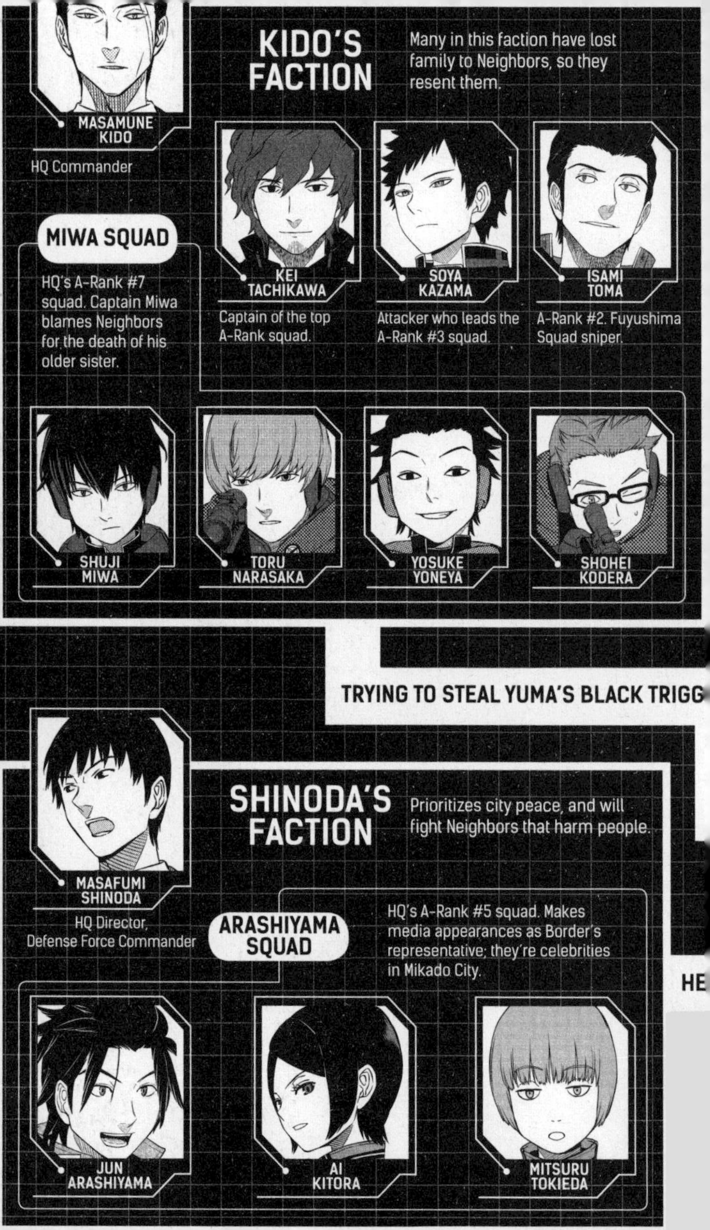
KIDO'S FACTION
Many in this faction have lost family to Neighbors, so they resent them.
MASAMUNE KIDO
HQ Commander
KEI TACHIKAWA
Captain of the top A-Rank squad.
SOYA KAZAMA
Attacker who leads the A-Rank #3 squad.
ISAMI TOMA
A-Rank #2. Fuyushima Squad sniper.
MIWA SQUAD
HQ's A-Rank #7 squad. Captain Miwa blames Neighbors for the death of his older sister.
SHUJI MIWA
TORU NARASAKA
YOSUKE YONEYA
SHOHEI KODERA
TRYING TO STEAL YUMA'S BLACK TRIGG
SHINODA'S FACTION
Prioritizes city peace, and will fight Neighbors that harm people.
MASAFUMI SHINODA
HQ Director, Defense Force Commander
ARASHIYAMA SQUAD
HQ's A-Rank #5 squad. Makes media appearances as Border's representative; they're celebrities in Mikado City.
JUN ARASHIYAMA
AI KITORA
MITSURU TOKIEDA
HE

WORLD TRIGGER

4

CONTENTS

DEFENSE ORGANIZATION
BORDER
MIKADO CITY

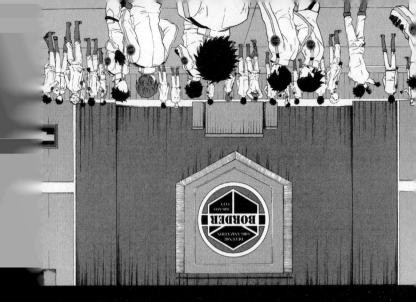

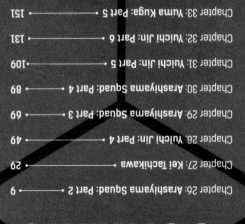

Chapter 26 Arashiyama Squad: Part 2

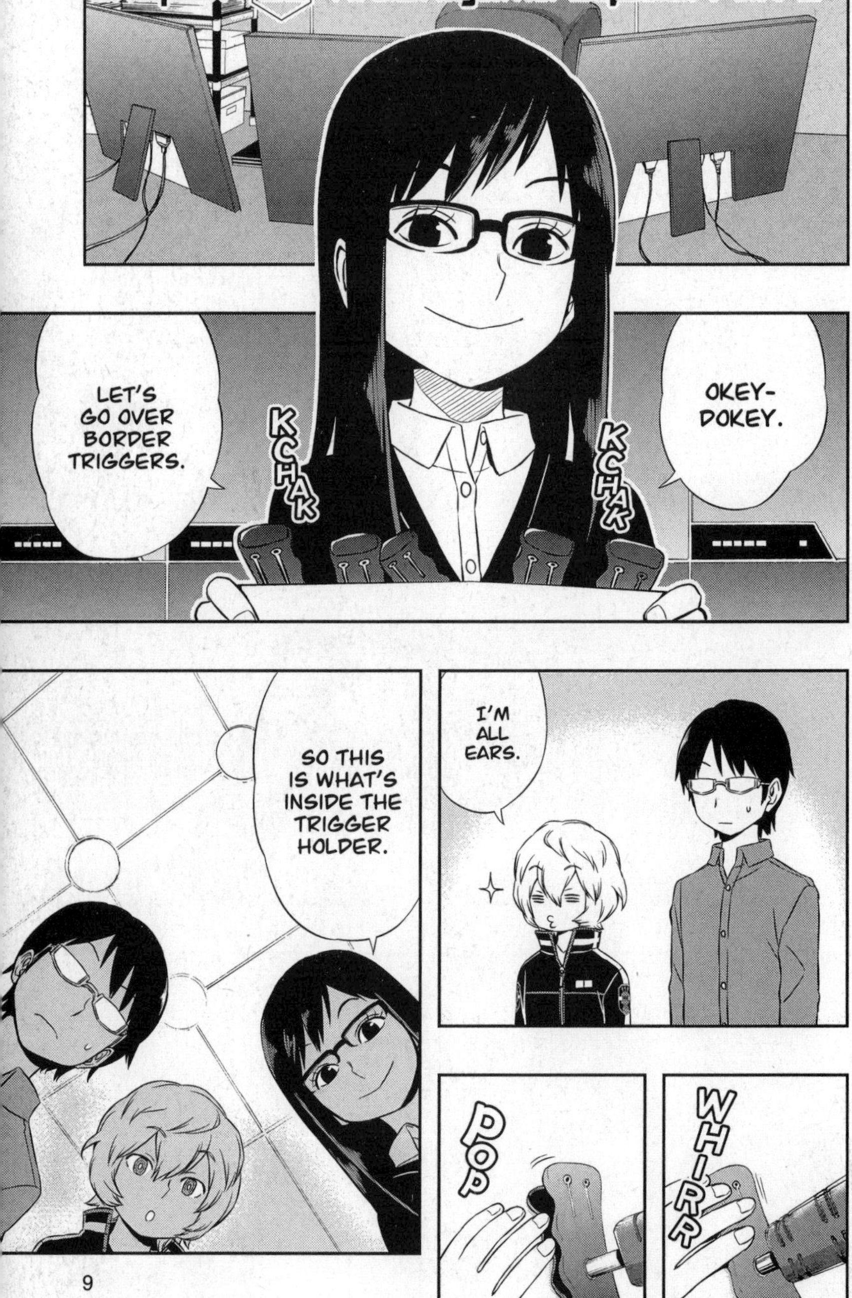
OKEY-DOKEY.
KCHAK
KCHAK
LET'S GO OVER BORDER TRIGGERS.
I'M ALL EARS.
SO THIS IS WHAT'S INSIDE THE TRIGGER HOLDER.
WHIRR
POP

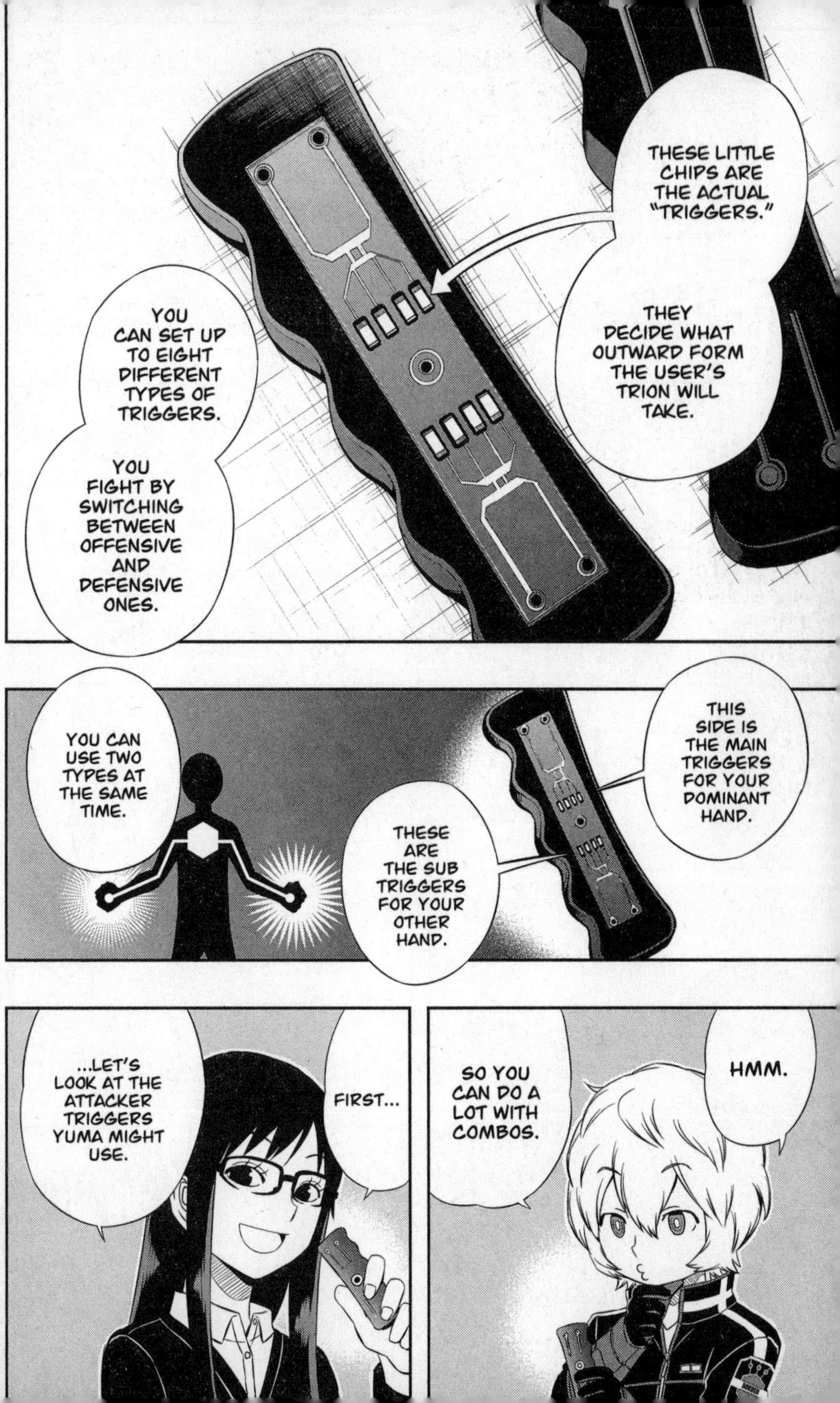
THESE LITTLE CHIPS ARE THE ACTUAL "TRIGGERS."
THEY DECIDE WHAT OUTWARD FORM THE USER'S TRION WILL TAKE.
YOU CAN SET UP TO EIGHT DIFFERENT TYPES OF TRIGGERS.
YOU FIGHT BY SWITCHING BETWEEN OFFENSIVE AND DEFENSIVE ONES.
THIS SIDE IS THE MAIN TRIGGERS FOR YOUR DOMINANT HAND.
THESE ARE THE SUB TRIGGERS FOR YOUR OTHER HAND.
YOU CAN USE TWO TYPES AT THE SAME TIME.
HMM.
SO YOU CAN DO A LOT WITH COMBOS.
FIRST...
...LET'S LOOK AT THE ATTACKER TRIGGERS YUMA MIGHT USE.

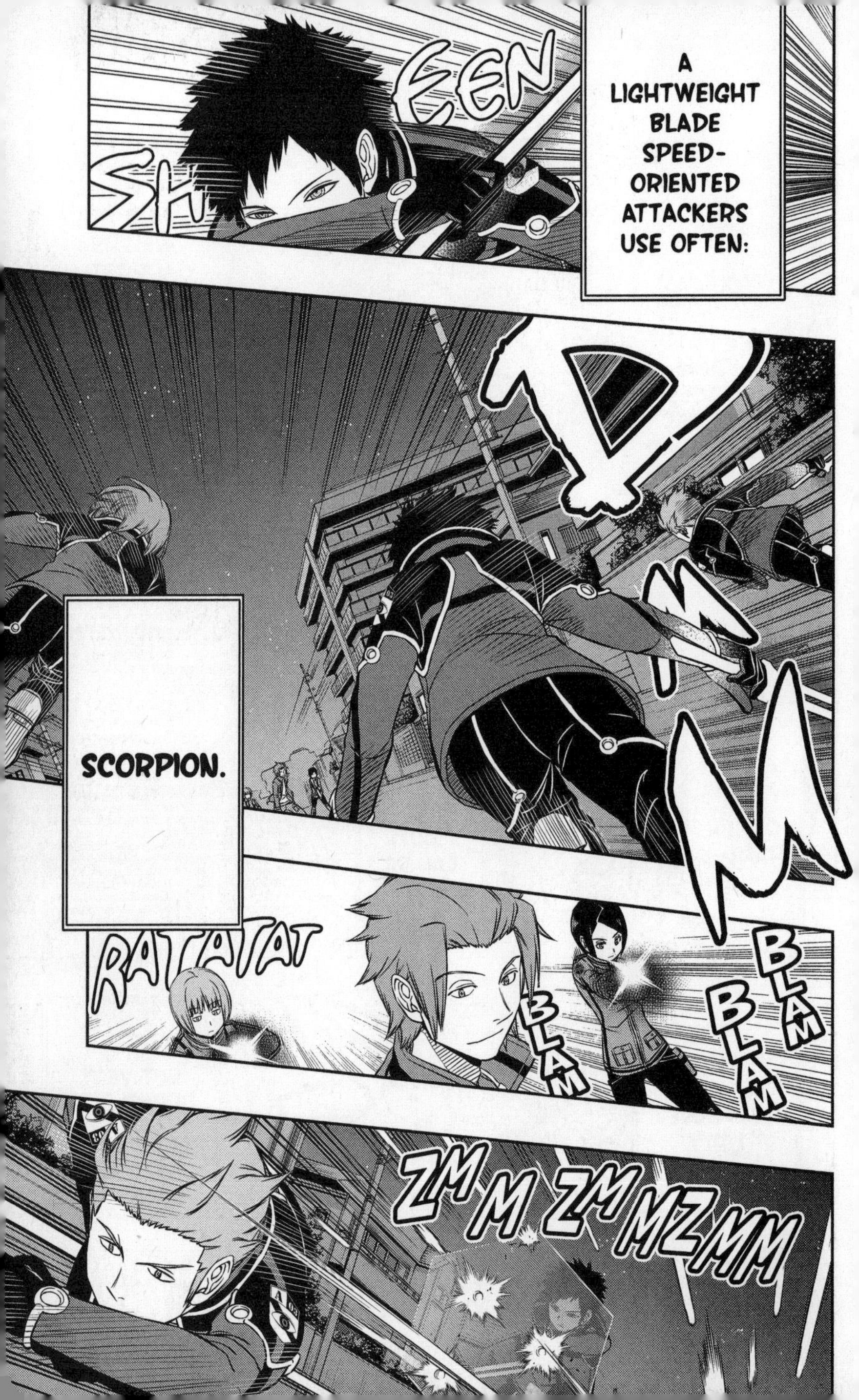
A LIGHTWEIGHT BLADE SPEED-ORIENTED ATTACKERS USE OFTEN:
SHEEN
VM
SCORPION.
BLAM BLAM
BLAM
RATATAT
ZM M ZM MZMM

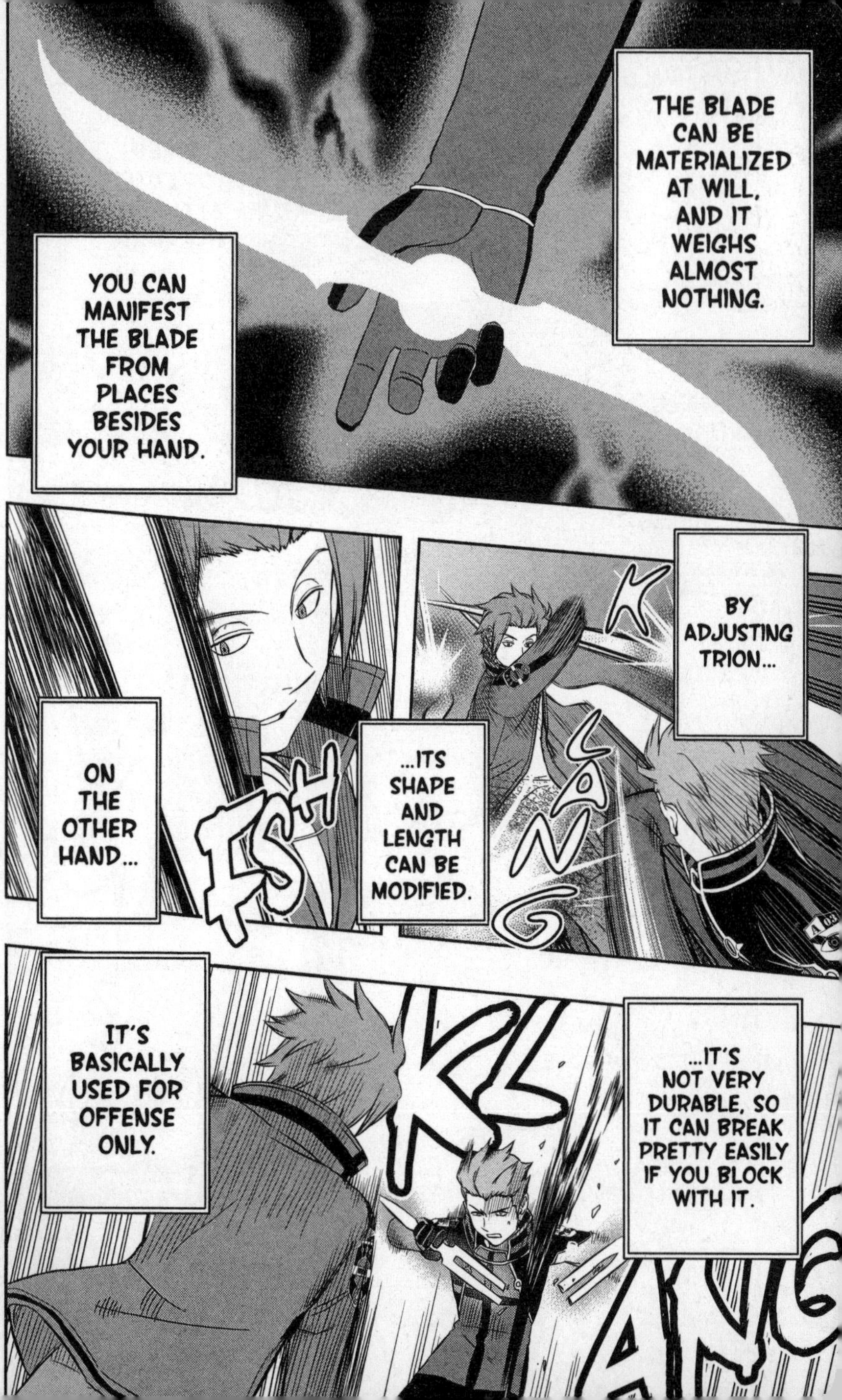
THE BLADE CAN BE MATERIALIZED AT WILL, AND IT WEIGHS ALMOST NOTHING.
YOU CAN MANIFEST THE BLADE FROM PLACES BESIDES YOUR HAND.
BY ADJUSTING TRION...
K
LANG
...ITS SHAPE AND LENGTH CAN BE MODIFIED.
FSH
ON THE OTHER HAND...
...IT'S NOT VERY DURABLE, SO IT CAN BREAK PRETTY EASILY IF YOU BLOCK WITH IT.
KL
ANG
IT'S BASICALLY USED FOR OFFENSE ONLY.

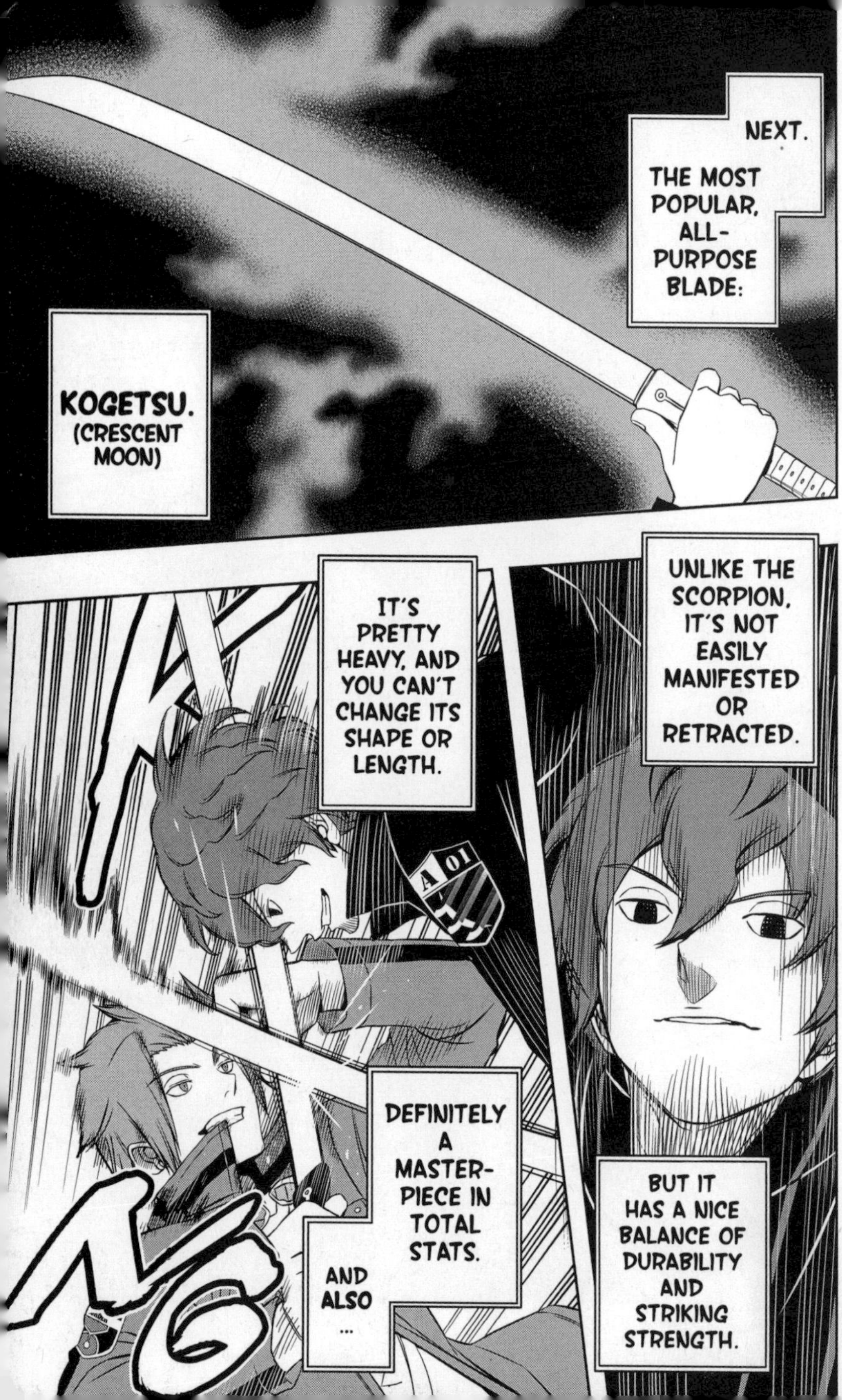
NEXT.
THE MOST POPULAR, ALL-PURPOSE BLADE:
KOGETSU. (CRESCENT MOON)
UNLIKE THE SCORPION, IT'S NOT EASILY MANIFESTED OR RETRACTED.
BUT IT HAS A NICE BALANCE OF DURABILITY AND STRIKING STRENGTH.
IT'S PRETTY HEAVY, AND YOU CAN'T CHANGE ITS SHAPE OR LENGTH.
DEFINITELY A MASTER-PIECE IN TOTAL STATS.
AND ALSO ...

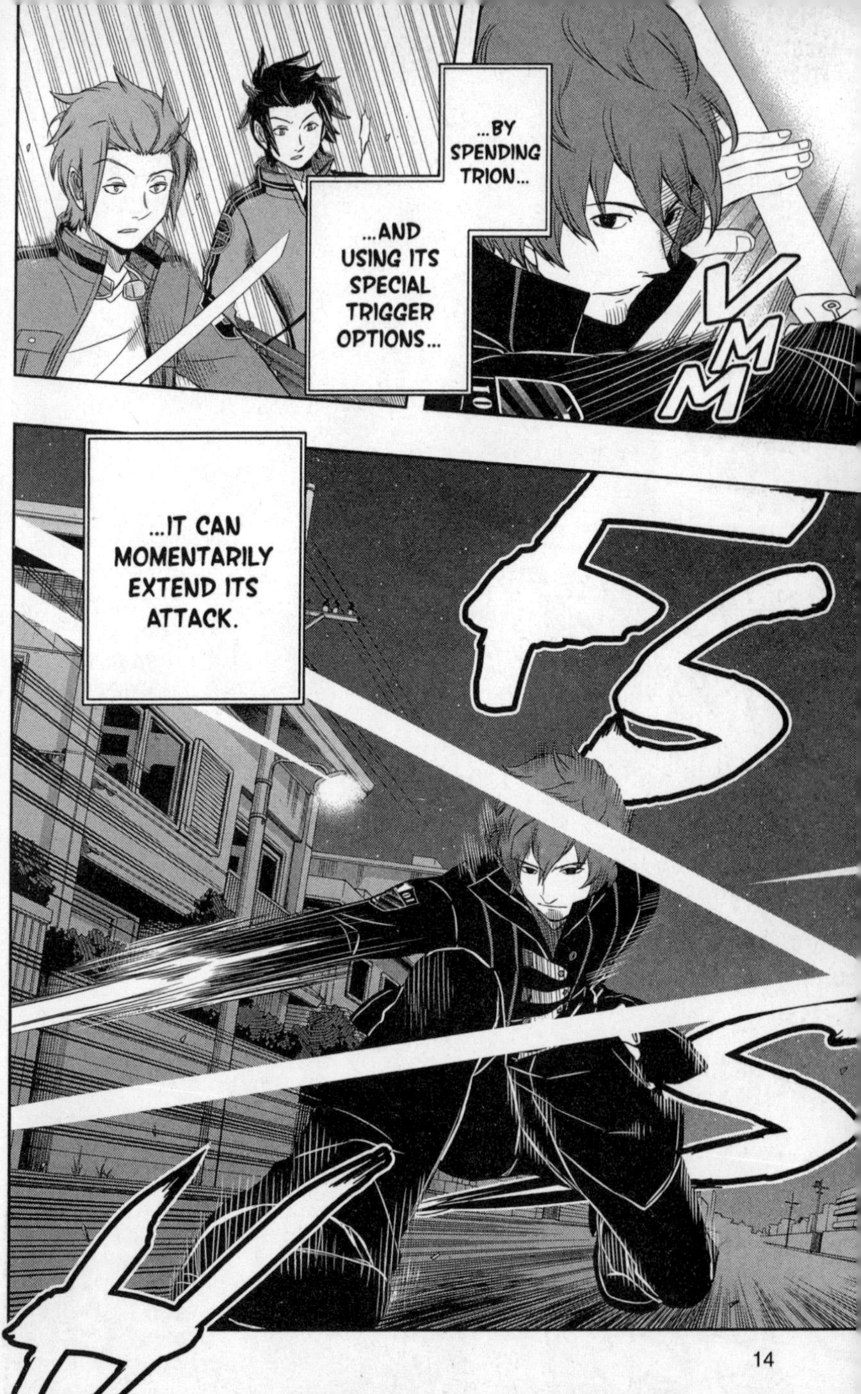
VMM
...BY SPENDING TRION...
...AND USING ITS SPECIAL TRIGGER OPTIONS...
...IT CAN MOMENTARILY EXTEND ITS ATTACK.

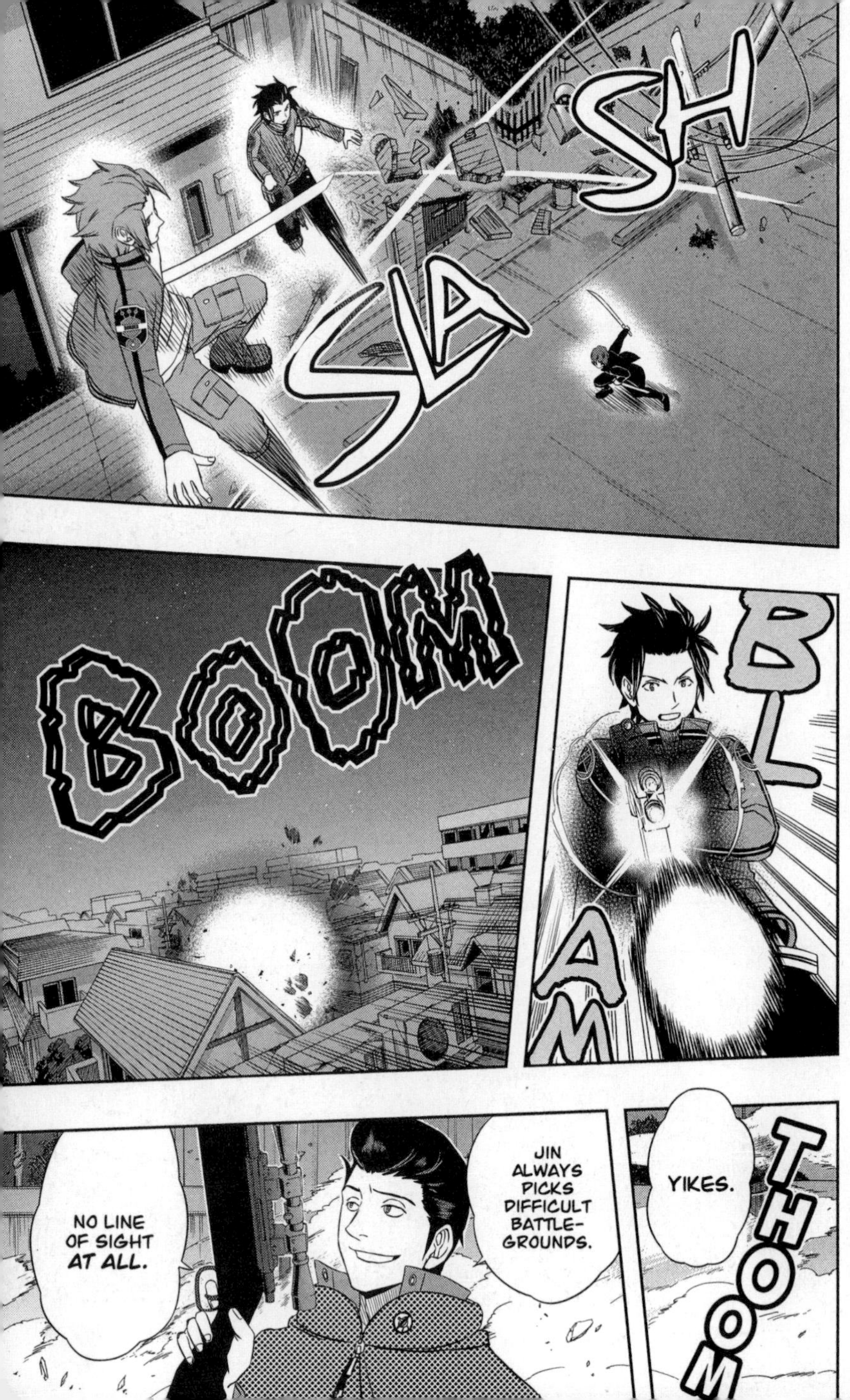
SLASH
BLAM
BOOM
THOOM
YIKES.
JIN ALWAYS PICKS DIFFICULT BATTLE-GROUNDS.
NO LINE OF SIGHT AT ALL.

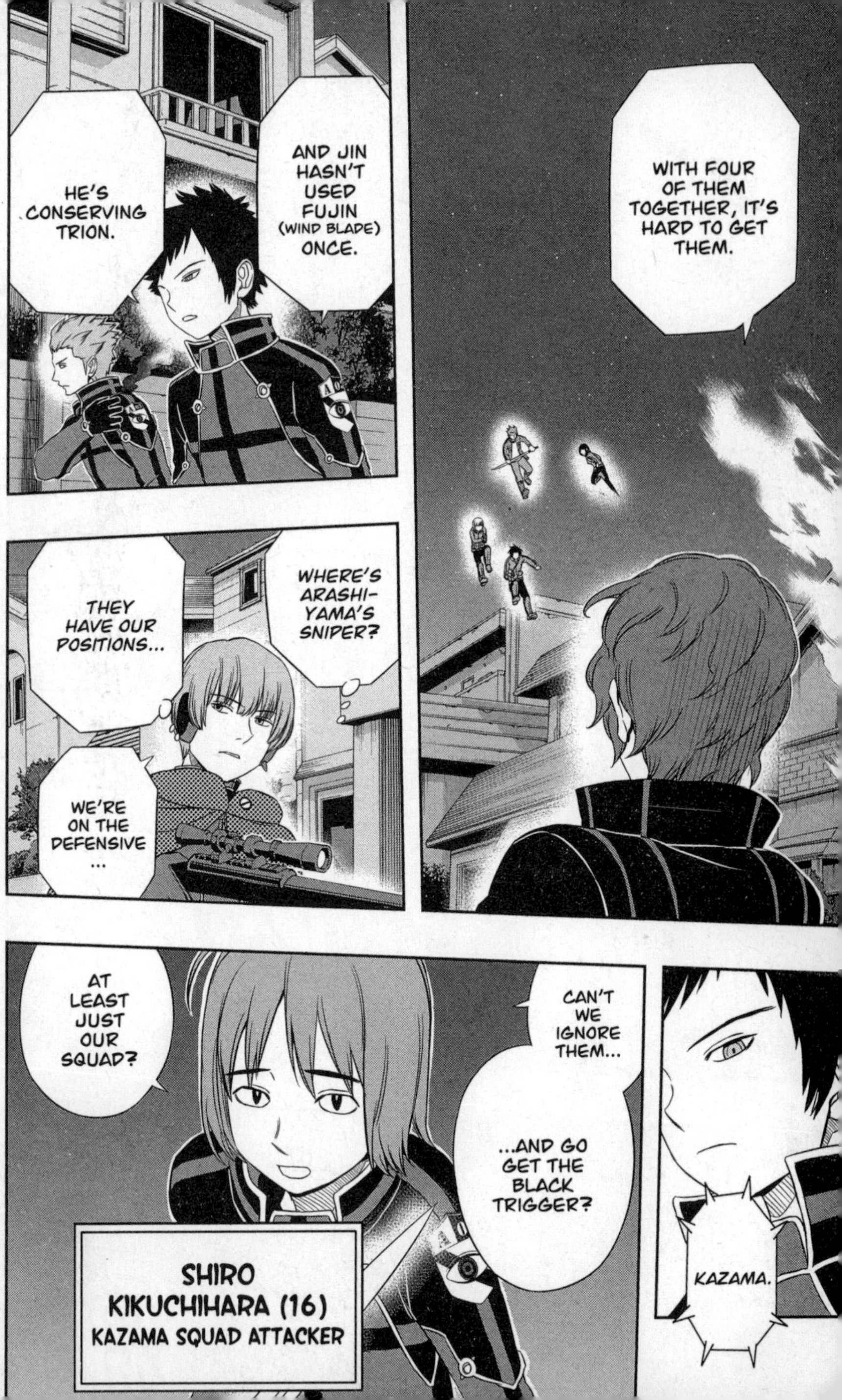
WITH FOUR OF THEM TOGETHER, IT'S HARD TO GET THEM.
AND JIN HASN'T USED FUJIN (WIND BLADE) ONCE.
HE'S CONSERVING TRION.
WHERE'S ARASHIYAMA'S SNIPER?
THEY HAVE OUR POSITIONS...
WE'RE ON THE DEFENSIVE...
KAZAMA.
CAN'T WE IGNORE THEM...
...AND GO GET THE BLACK TRIGGER?
AT LEAST JUST OUR SQUAD?
SHIRO KIKUCHIHARA (16)
KAZAMA SQUAD ATTACKER

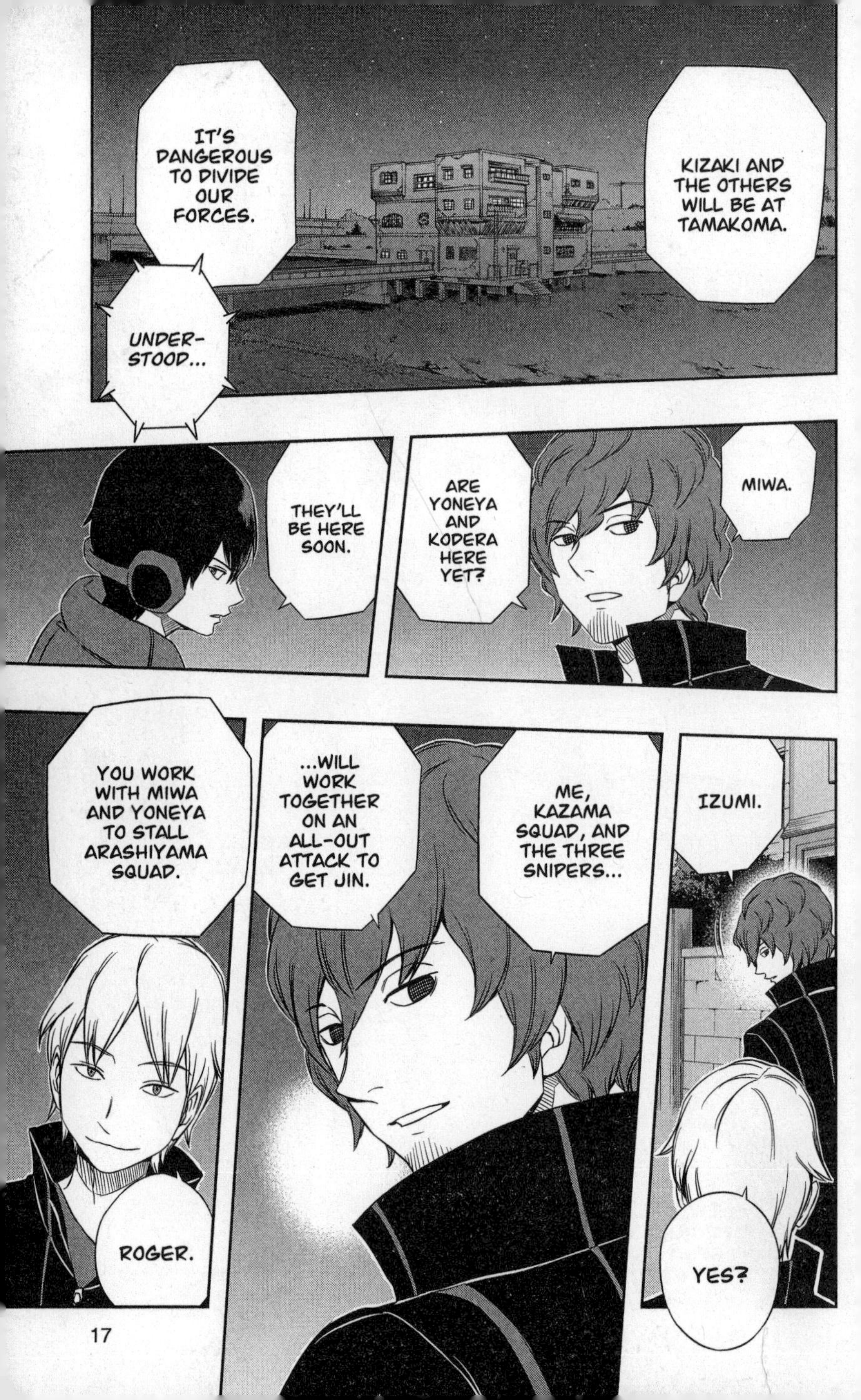
KIZAKI AND THE OTHERS WILL BE AT TAMAKOMA.
IT'S DANGEROUS TO DIVIDE OUR FORCES.
UNDER-STOOD...
MIWA.
ARE YONEYA AND KODERA HERE YET?
THEY'LL BE HERE SOON.
IZUMI.
YES?
ME, KAZAMA SQUAD, AND THE THREE SNIPERS...
...WILL WORK TOGETHER ON AN ALL-OUT ATTACK TO GET JIN.
YOU WORK WITH MIWA AND YONEYA TO STALL ARASHIYAMA SQUAD.
ROGER.

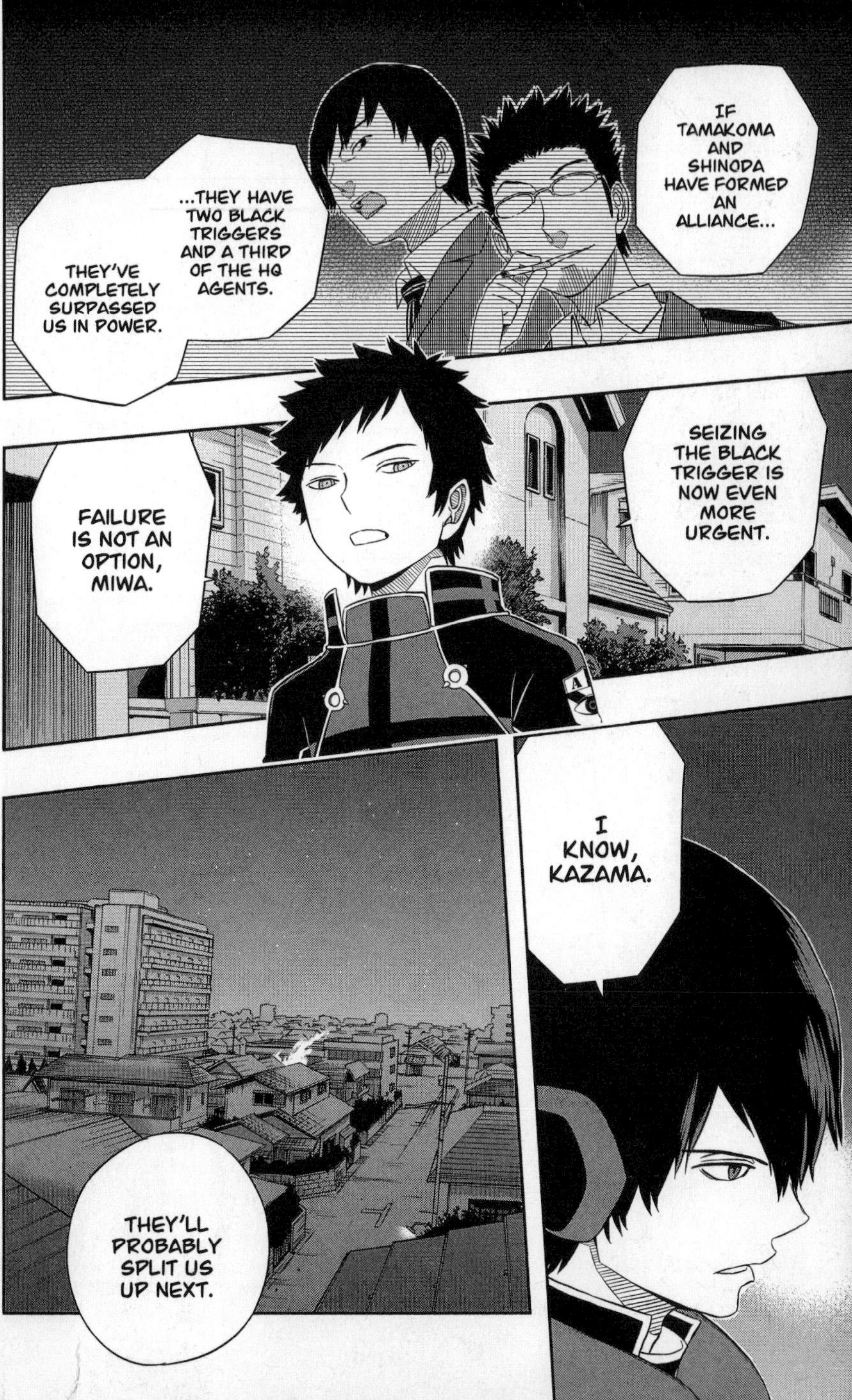
IF TAMAKOMA AND SHINODA HAVE FORMED AN ALLIANCE...
...THEY HAVE TWO BLACK TRIGGERS AND A THIRD OF THE HQ AGENTS.
THEY'VE COMPLETELY SURPASSED US IN POWER.
SEIZING THE BLACK TRIGGER IS NOW EVEN MORE URGENT.
FAILURE IS NOT AN OPTION, MIWA.
I KNOW, KAZAMA.
THEY'LL PROBABLY SPLIT US UP NEXT.

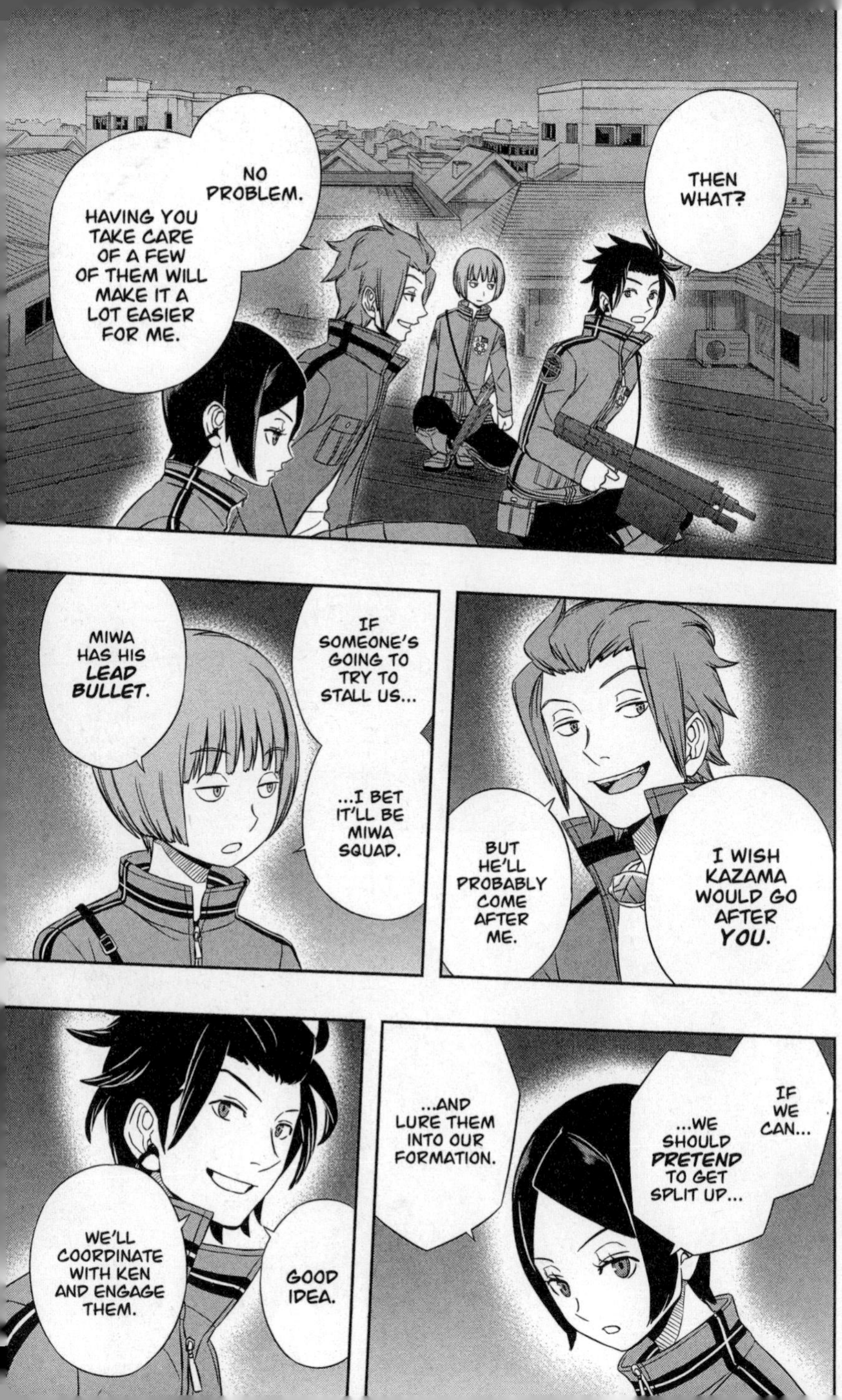
THEN WHAT?
NO PROBLEM.
HAVING YOU TAKE CARE OF A FEW OF THEM WILL MAKE IT A LOT EASIER FOR ME.
I WISH KAZAMA WOULD GO AFTER YOU.
BUT HE'LL PROBABLY COME AFTER ME.
IF SOMEONE'S GOING TO TRY TO STALL US...
...I BET IT'LL BE MIWA SQUAD.
MIWA HAS HIS LEAD BULLET.
IF WE CAN...
...WE SHOULD PRETEND TO GET SPLIT UP...
...AND LURE THEM INTO OUR FORMATION.
GOOD IDEA.
WE'LL COORDINATE WITH KEN AND ENGAGE THEM.

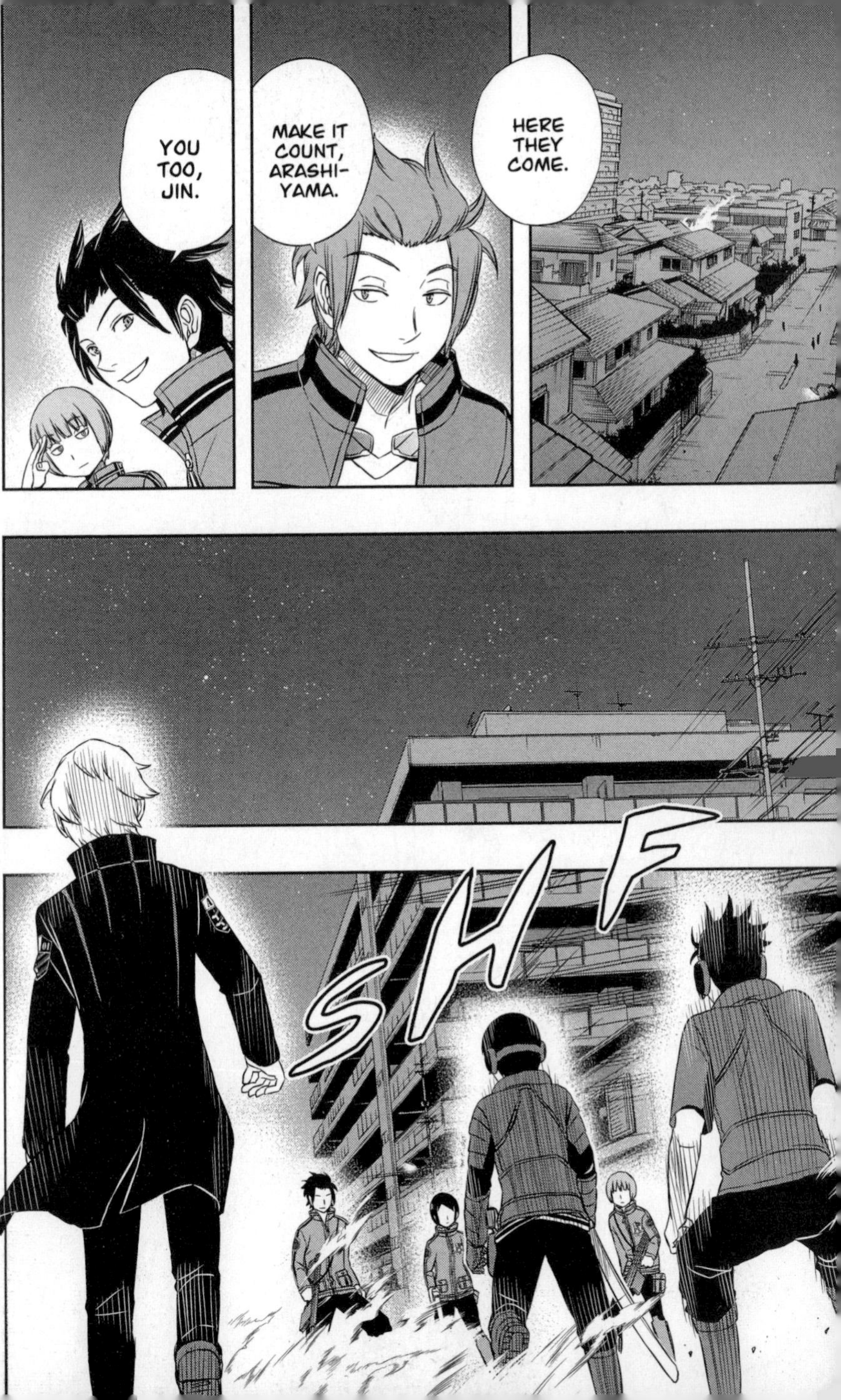
HERE THEY COME.
MAKE IT COUNT, ARASHI-YAMA.
YOU TOO, JIN.
SHF

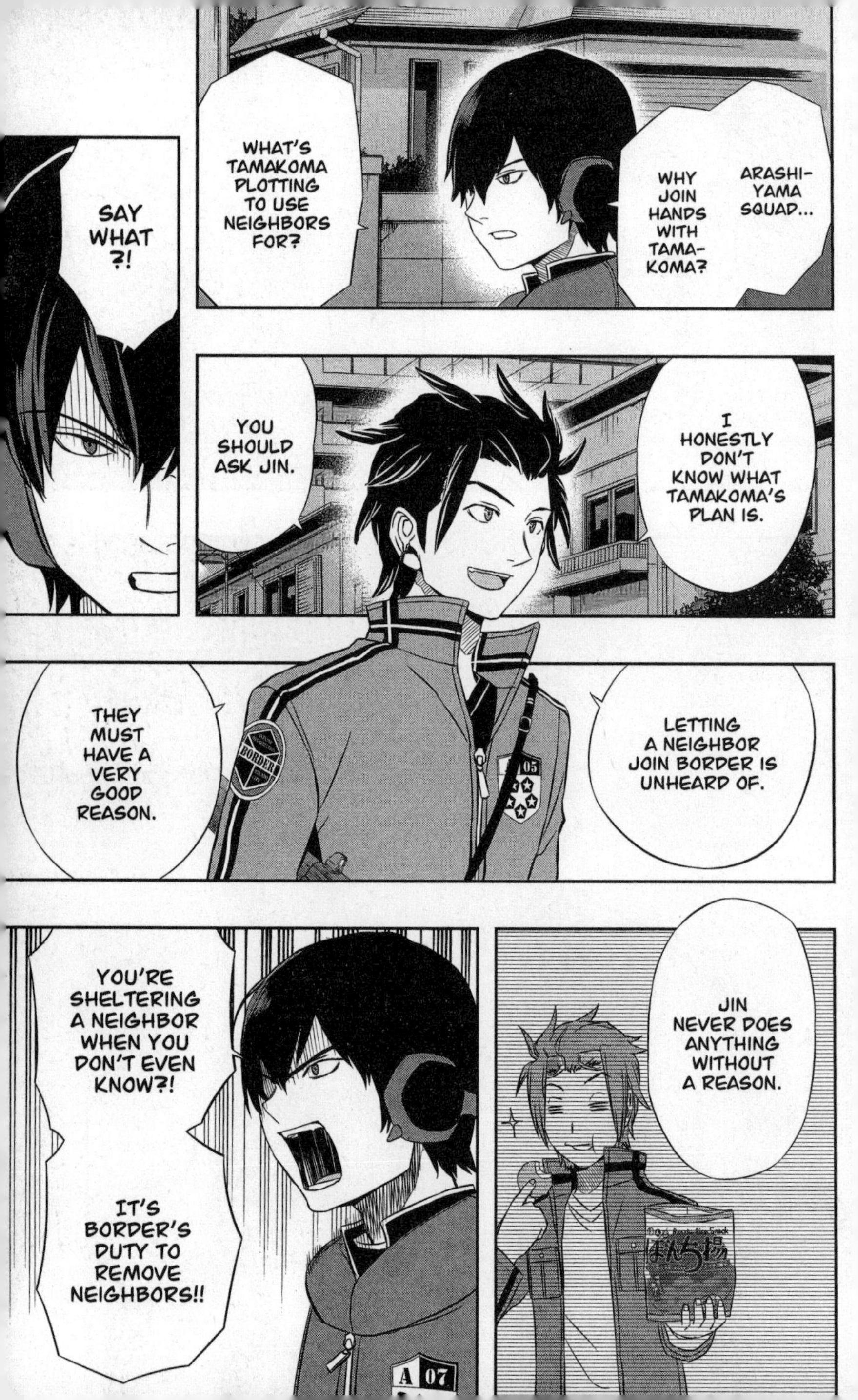
ARASHI-YAMA SQUAD...
WHY JOIN HANDS WITH TAMA-KOMA?
WHAT'S TAMAKOMA PLOTTING TO USE NEIGHBORS FOR?
SAY WHAT?!
I HONESTLY DON'T KNOW WHAT TAMAKOMA'S PLAN IS.
YOU SHOULD ASK JIN.
LETTING A NEIGHBOR JOIN BORDER IS UNHEARD OF.
THEY MUST HAVE A VERY GOOD REASON.
BORDER
05
JIN NEVER DOES ANYTHING WITHOUT A REASON.
YOU'RE SHELTERING A NEIGHBOR WHEN YOU DON'T EVEN KNOW?!
IT'S BORDER'S DUTY TO REMOVE NEIGHBORS!!
A 07

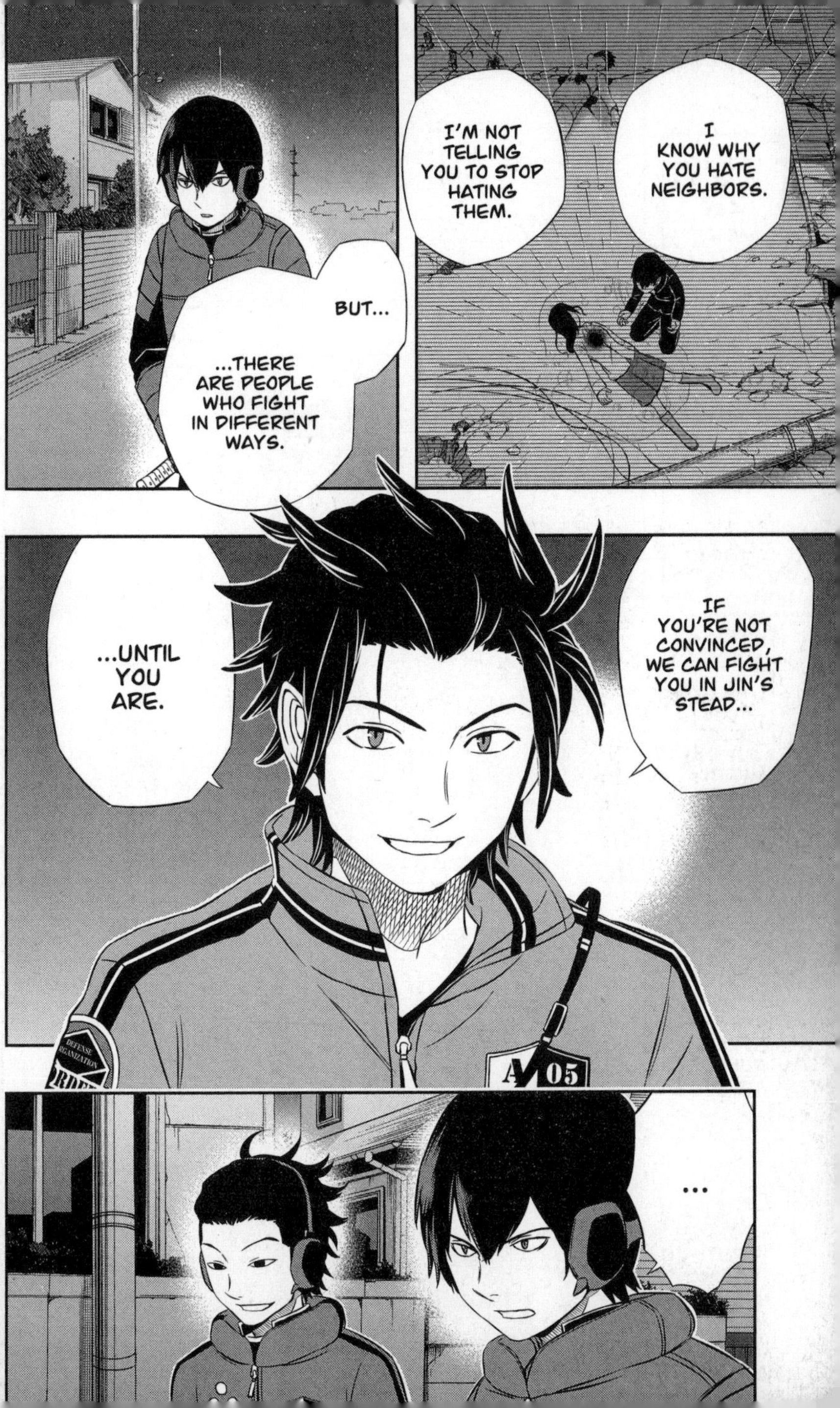
I KNOW WHY YOU HATE NEIGHBORS.
I'M NOT TELLING YOU TO STOP HATING THEM.
BUT...
...THERE ARE PEOPLE WHO FIGHT IN DIFFERENT WAYS.
IF YOU'RE NOT CONVINCED, WE CAN FIGHT YOU IN JIN'S STEAD...
...UNTIL YOU ARE.
A 05
...

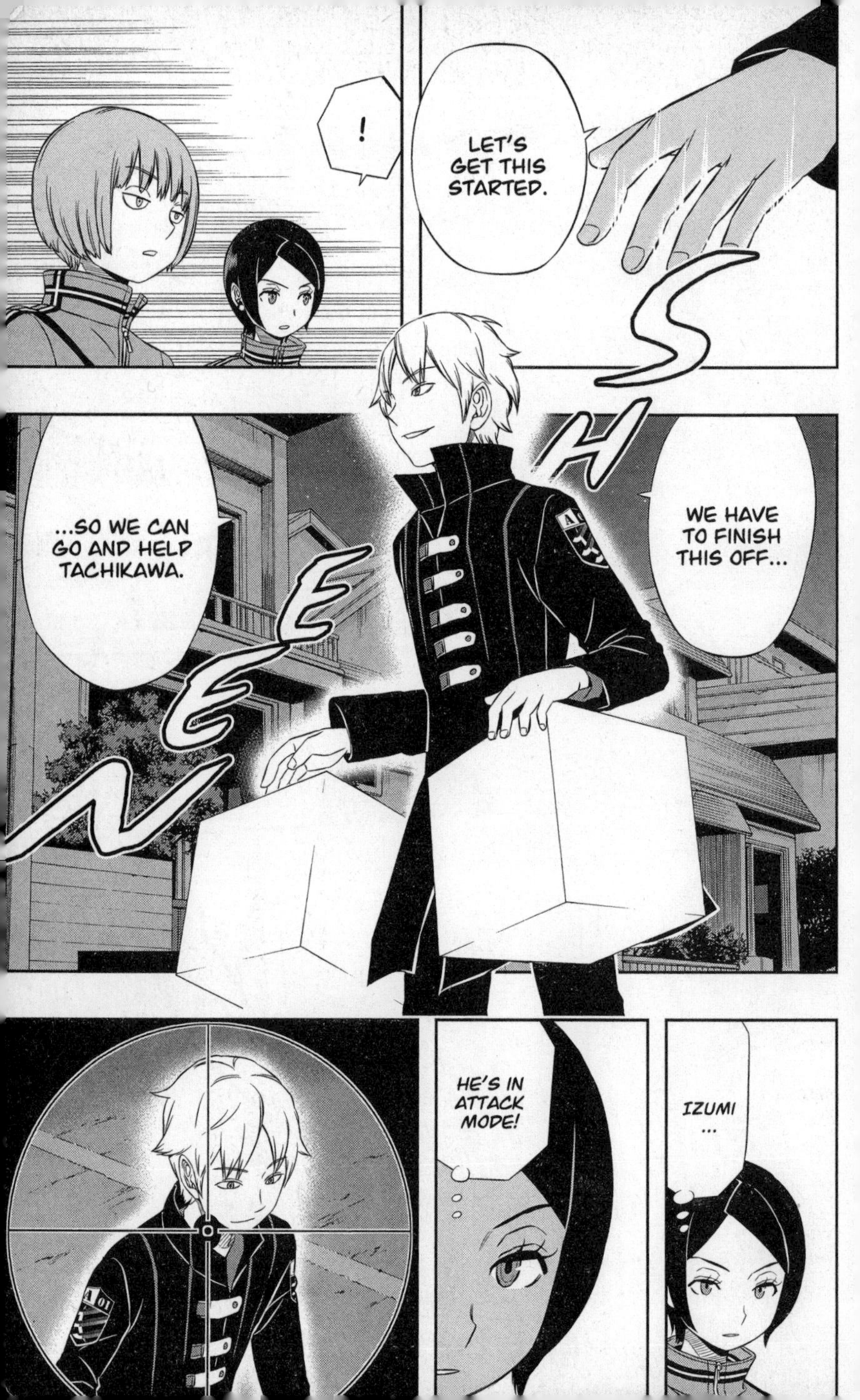
LET'S GET THIS STARTED.
!
SHHNEEN
WE HAVE TO FINISH THIS OFF...
...SO WE CAN GO AND HELP TACHIKAWA.
IZUMI ...
HE'S IN ATTACK MODE!

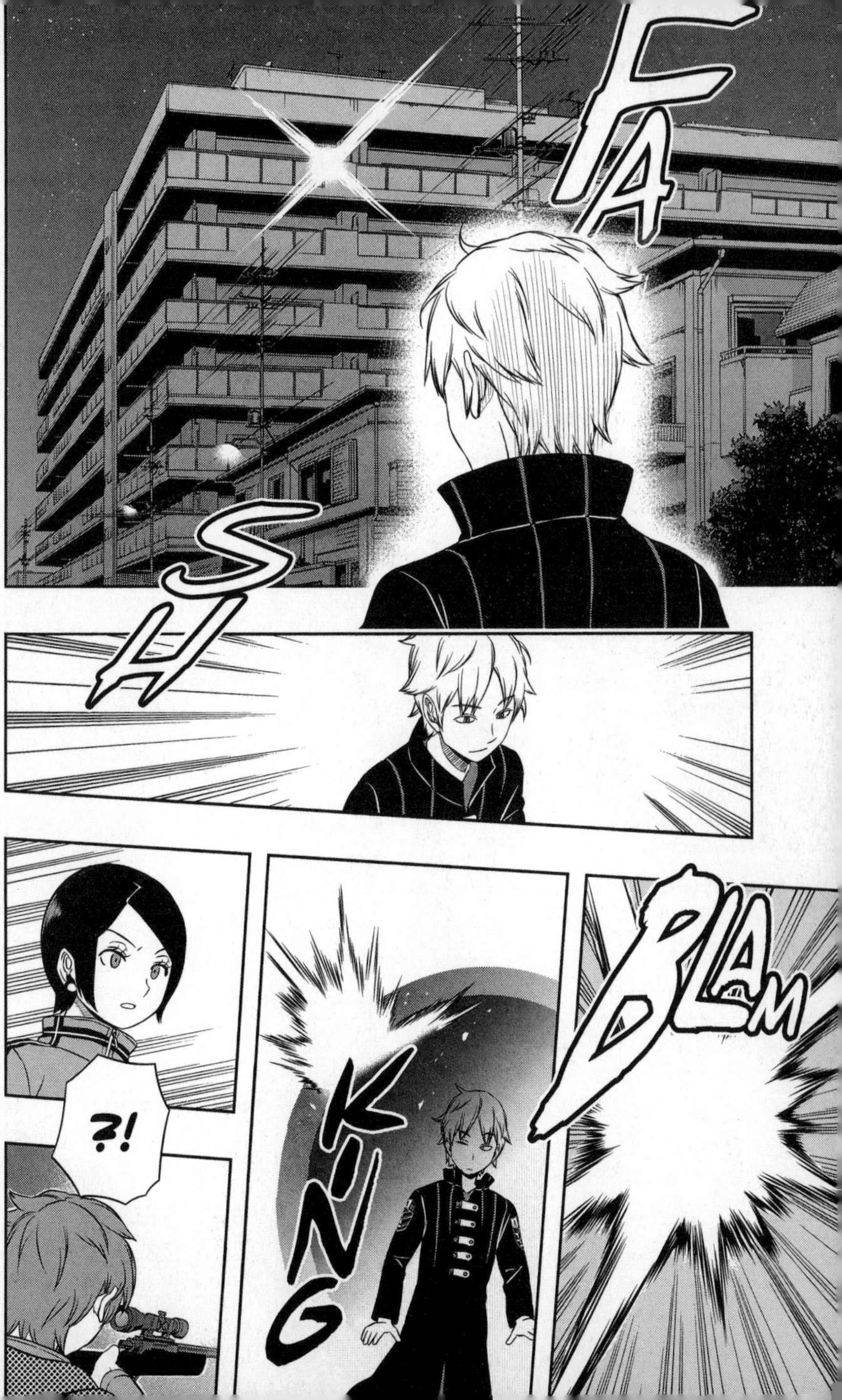
FA
SH
BLAM
KING
?!

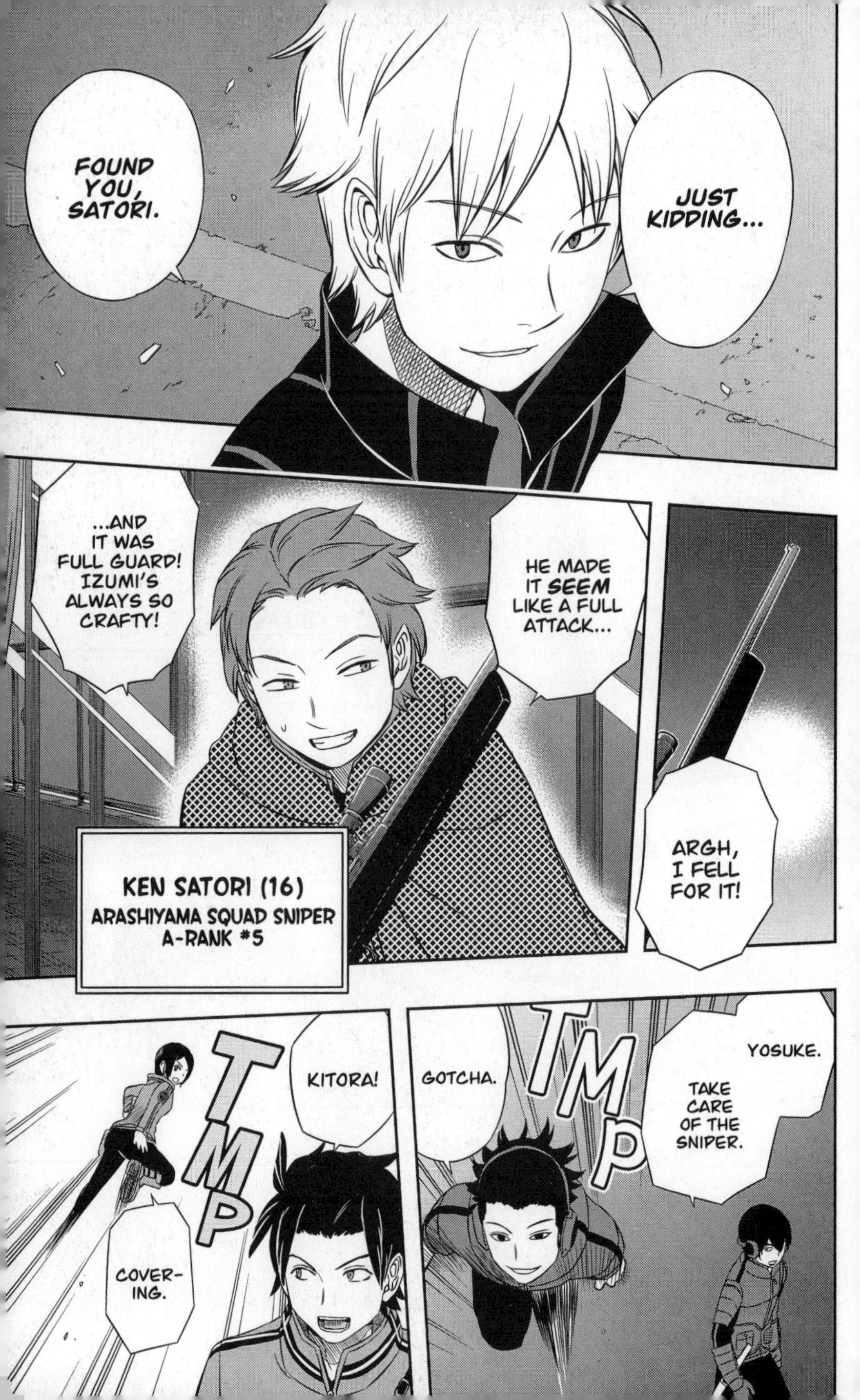
JUST KIDDING...
FOUND YOU, SATORI.
ARGH, I FELL FOR IT!
HE MADE IT SEEM LIKE A FULL ATTACK...
...AND IT WAS FULL GUARD! IZUMI'S ALWAYS SO CRAFTY!
KEN SATORI (16)
ARASHIYAMA SQUAD SNIPER
A-RANK #5
YOSUKE.
TAKE CARE OF THE SNIPER.
TMP
GOTCHA.
KITORA!
TMP
COVERING.

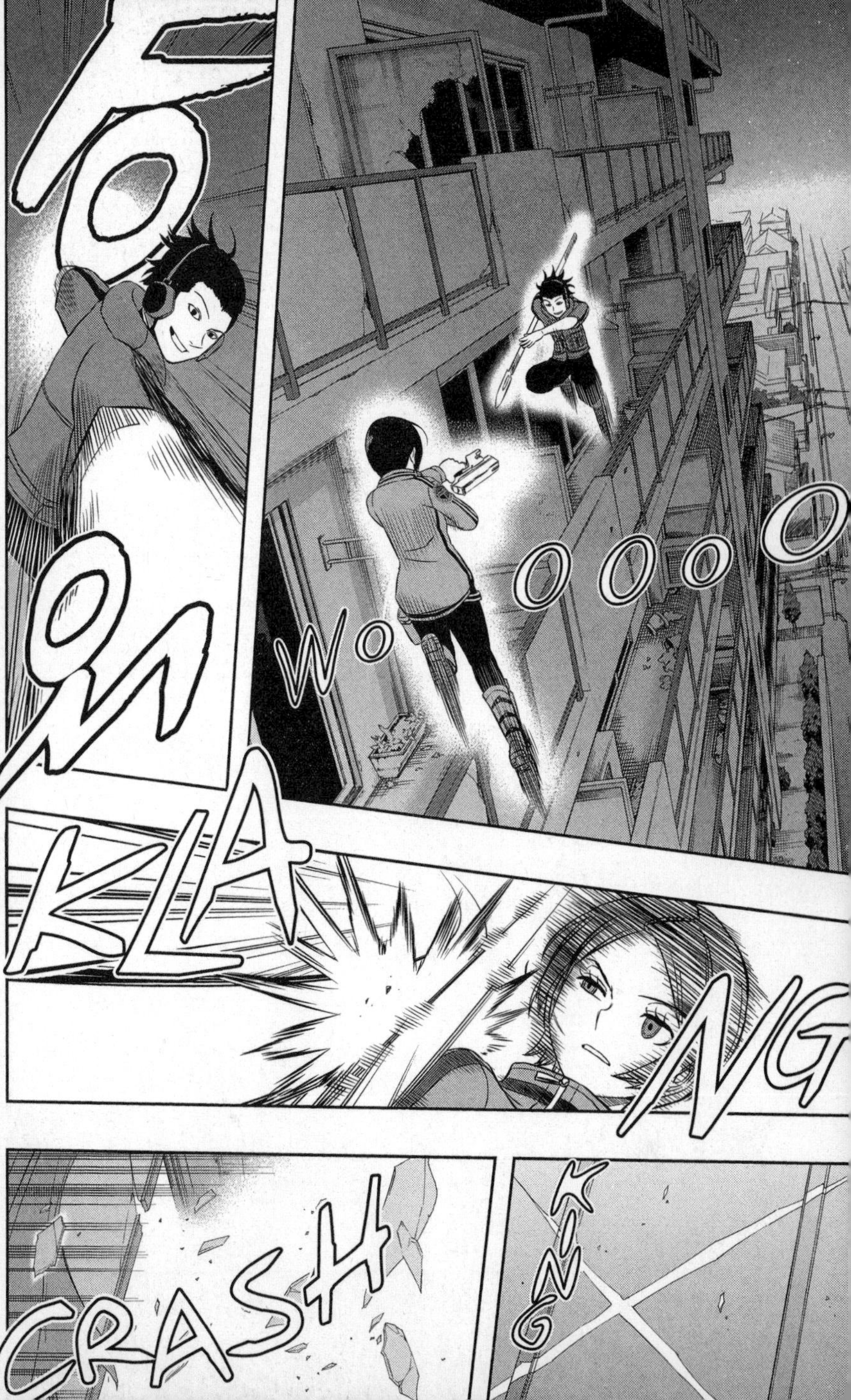
WOOOOO
KLANG
KING
CRASH

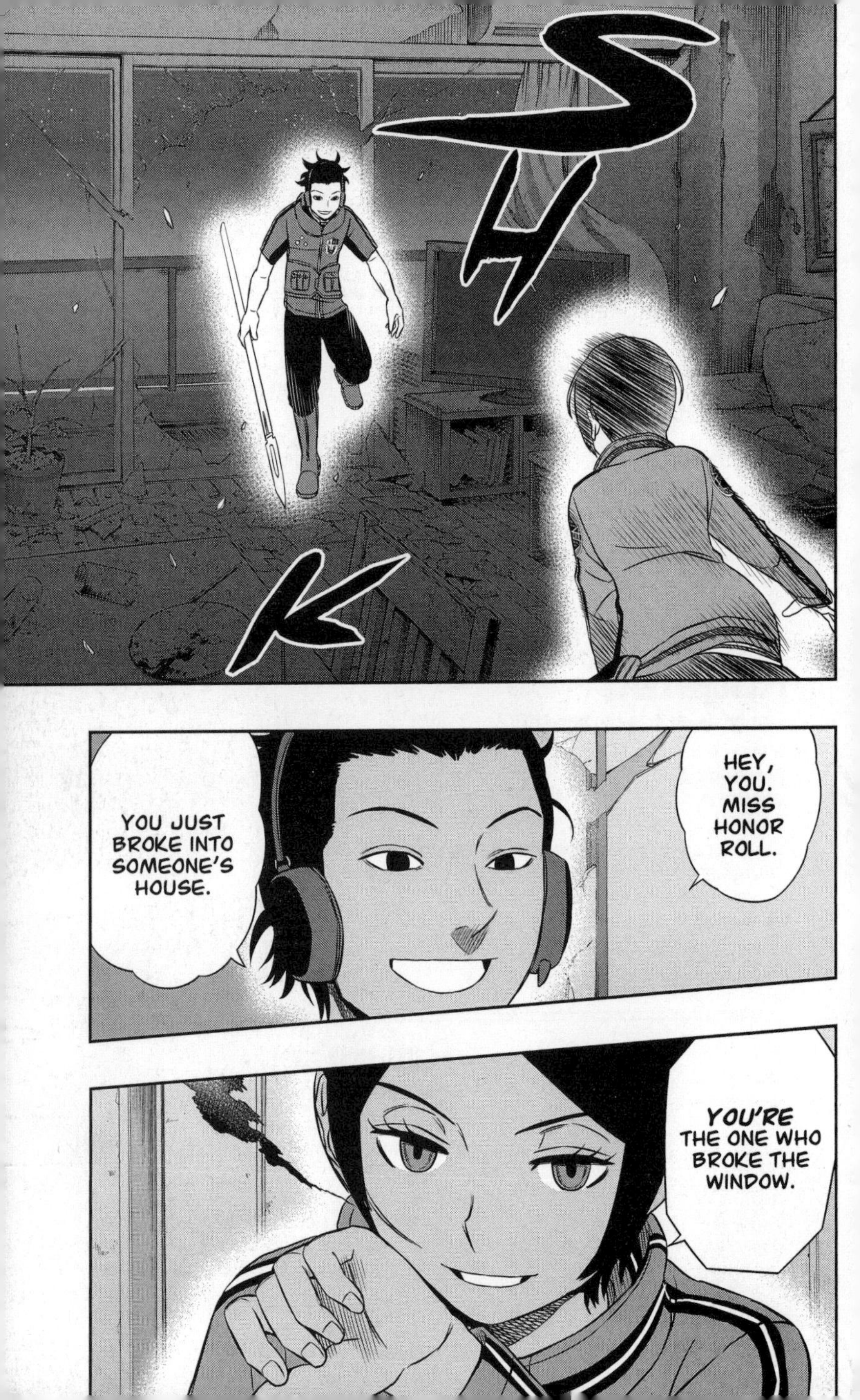
SHK
HEY, YOU. MISS HONOR ROLL.
YOU JUST BROKE INTO SOMEONE'S HOUSE.
YOU'RE THE ONE WHO BROKE THE WINDOW.

Attacker Triggers

Close-range, powerful Triggers for hand-to-hand combat. Good Trion cost-performance ratio.

Scorpion
Emphasis on offense and surprise attacks

Attack: A
Durability: D (longer blade = more fragile)
Weight: A

A lightweight blade that can be materialized at will from any part of the body. Shape and length can be modified. Often used as the main weapon for lightweight Attackers or the secondary weapon of All-Rounders.

Kogetsu
Emphasis on balance and utility

Attack: A
Durability: A
Weight: C

The most popular all-purpose blade. Doesn't change shape, but its good basic stats make it useful for aggressive Attackers or All-Rounders. A separate optional Trigger is required to transform or extend the blade.

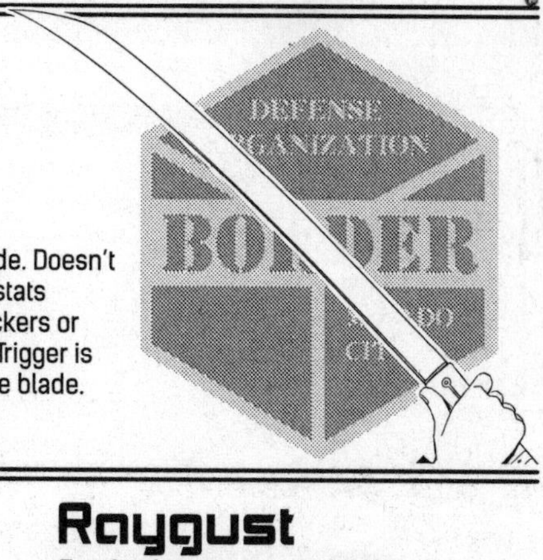

Raygust
Emphasis on armor and defense

Attack: B (Shield mode: E)
Durability: B (Shield mode: SS)
Weight: D

The blade can transform at will, and Shield Mode sacrifices attack strength for durability. It also has a separate optional thruster that uses a jet of Trion to accelerate the blade.

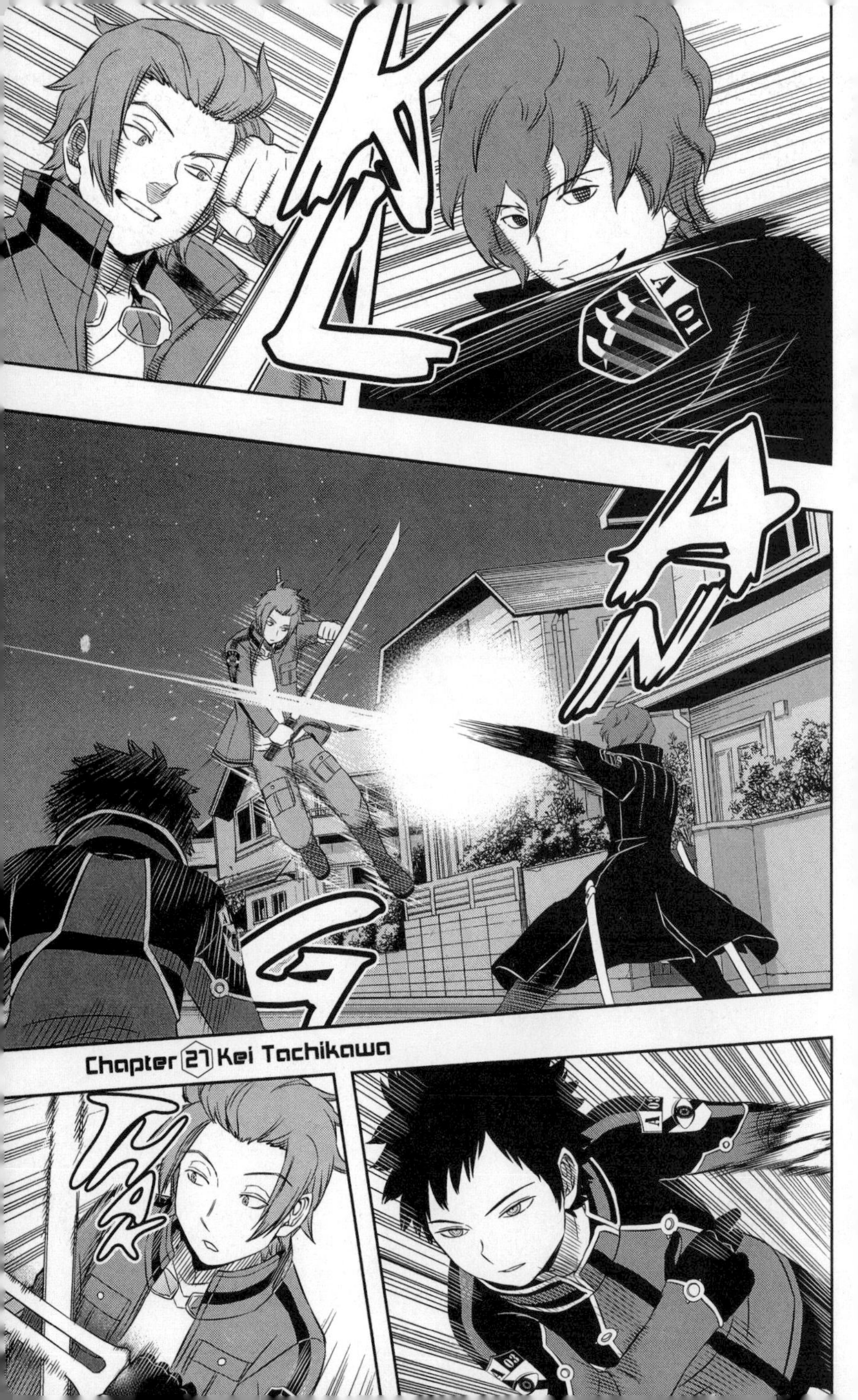
Chapter 27 Kei Tachikawa

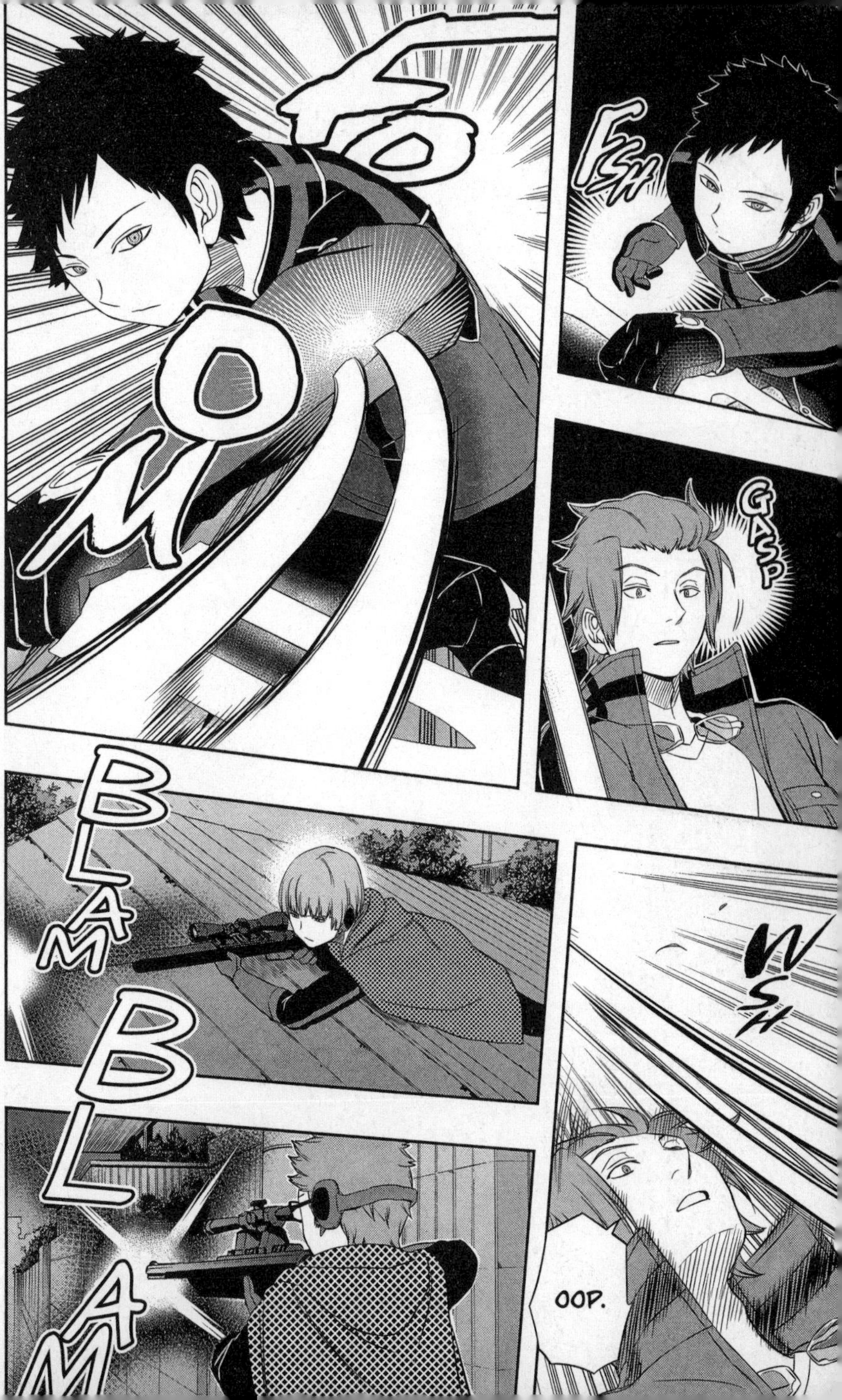
FSH
GASP
VWOOM
WSH
OOP.
BLAM
BLAM

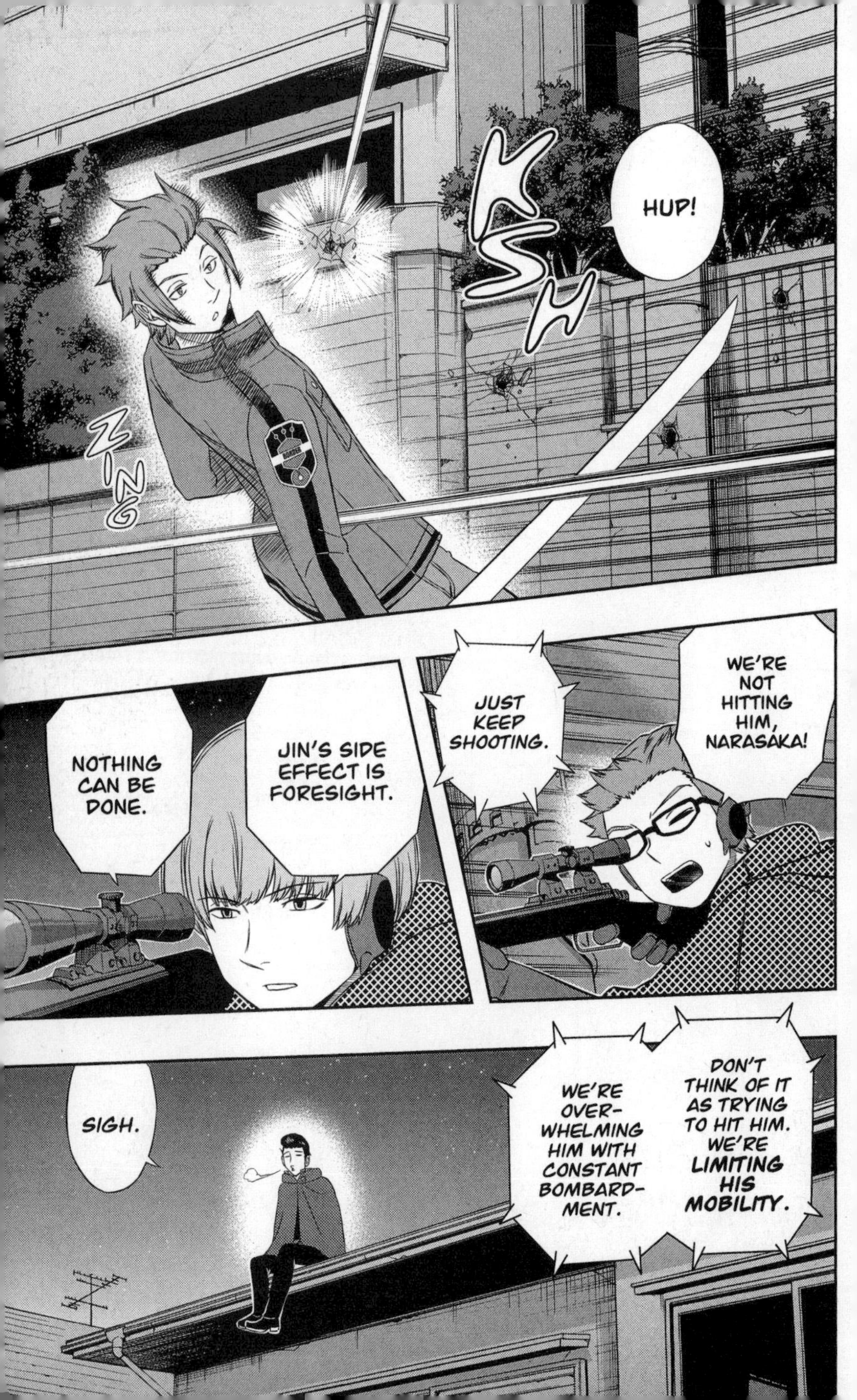
HUP!
KSH
ZING
WE'RE NOT HITTING HIM, NARASAKA!
JUST KEEP SHOOTING.
JIN'S SIDE EFFECT IS FORESIGHT.
NOTHING CAN BE DONE.
DON'T THINK OF IT AS TRYING TO HIT HIM. WE'RE LIMITING HIS MOBILITY.
WE'RE OVER-WHELMING HIM WITH CONSTANT BOMBARD-MENT.
SIGH.

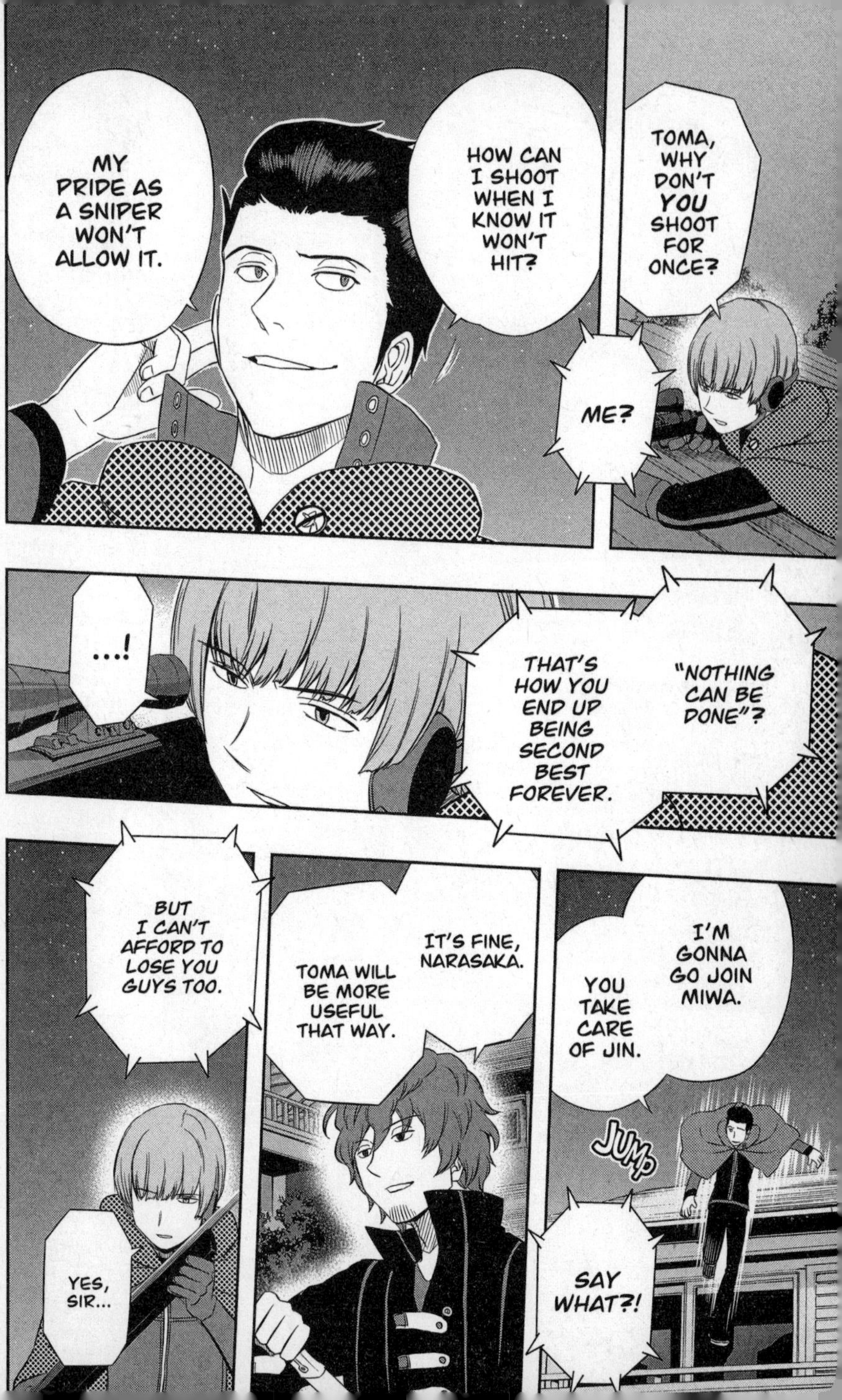
TOMA, WHY DON'T YOU SHOOT FOR ONCE?
ME?
HOW CAN I SHOOT WHEN I KNOW IT WON'T HIT?
MY PRIDE AS A SNIPER WON'T ALLOW IT.
"NOTHING CAN BE DONE"?
THAT'S HOW YOU END UP BEING SECOND BEST FOREVER.
...!
I'M GONNA GO JOIN MIWA.
YOU TAKE CARE OF JIN.
JUMP
SAY WHAT?!
IT'S FINE, NARASAKA.
TOMA WILL BE MORE USEFUL THAT WAY.
BUT I CAN'T AFFORD TO LOSE YOU GUYS TOO.
YES, SIR...

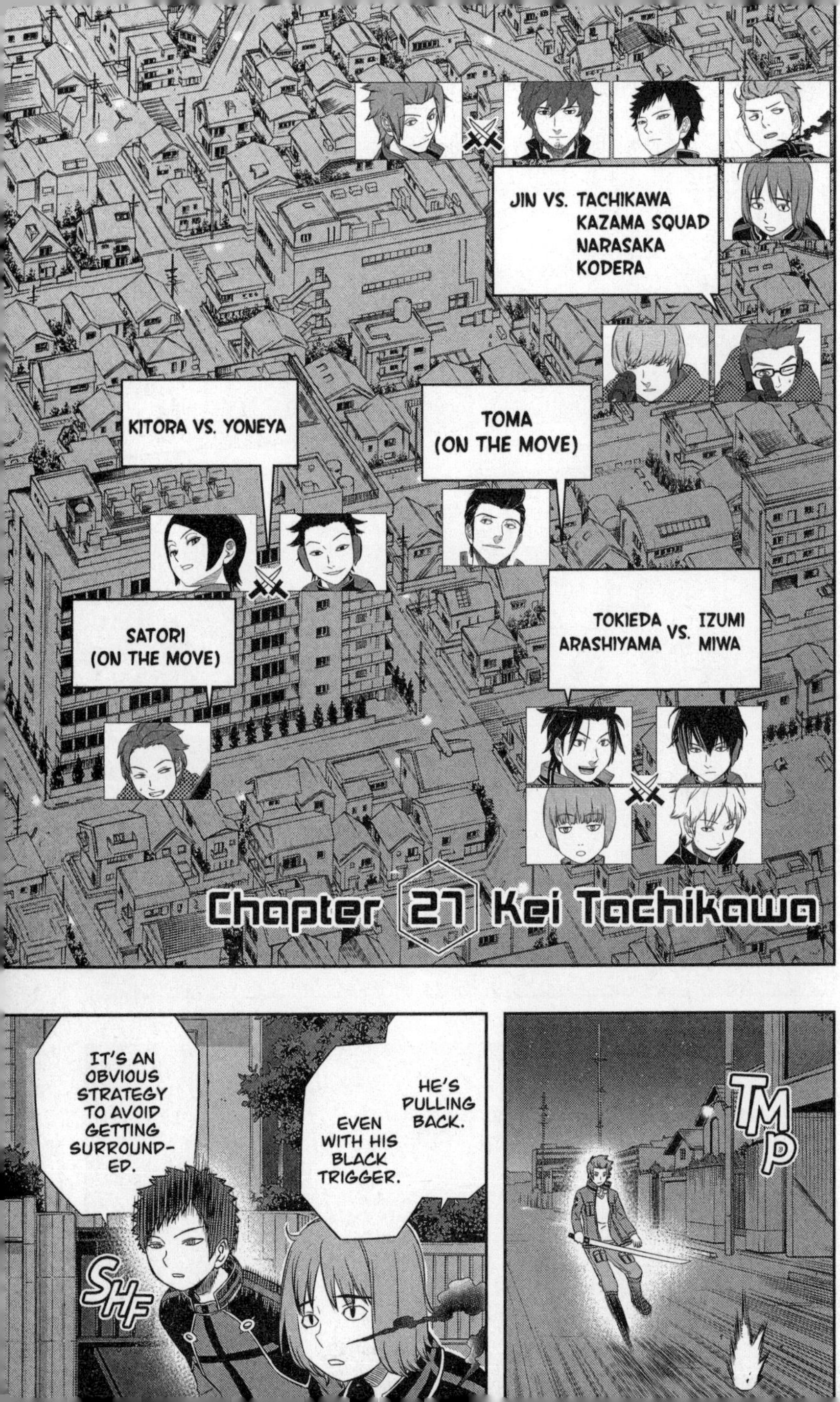
JIN VS. TACHIKAWA
KAZAMA SQUAD
NARASAKA
KODERA
TOMA
(ON THE MOVE)
KITORA VS. YONEYA
TOKIEDA
ARASHIYAMA
VS.
IZUMI
MIWA
SATORI
(ON THE MOVE)
Chapter 21 Kei Tachikawa
TMP
HE'S PULLING BACK.
EVEN WITH HIS BLACK TRIGGER.
IT'S AN OBVIOUS STRATEGY TO AVOID GETTING SURROUND-ED.
SHF

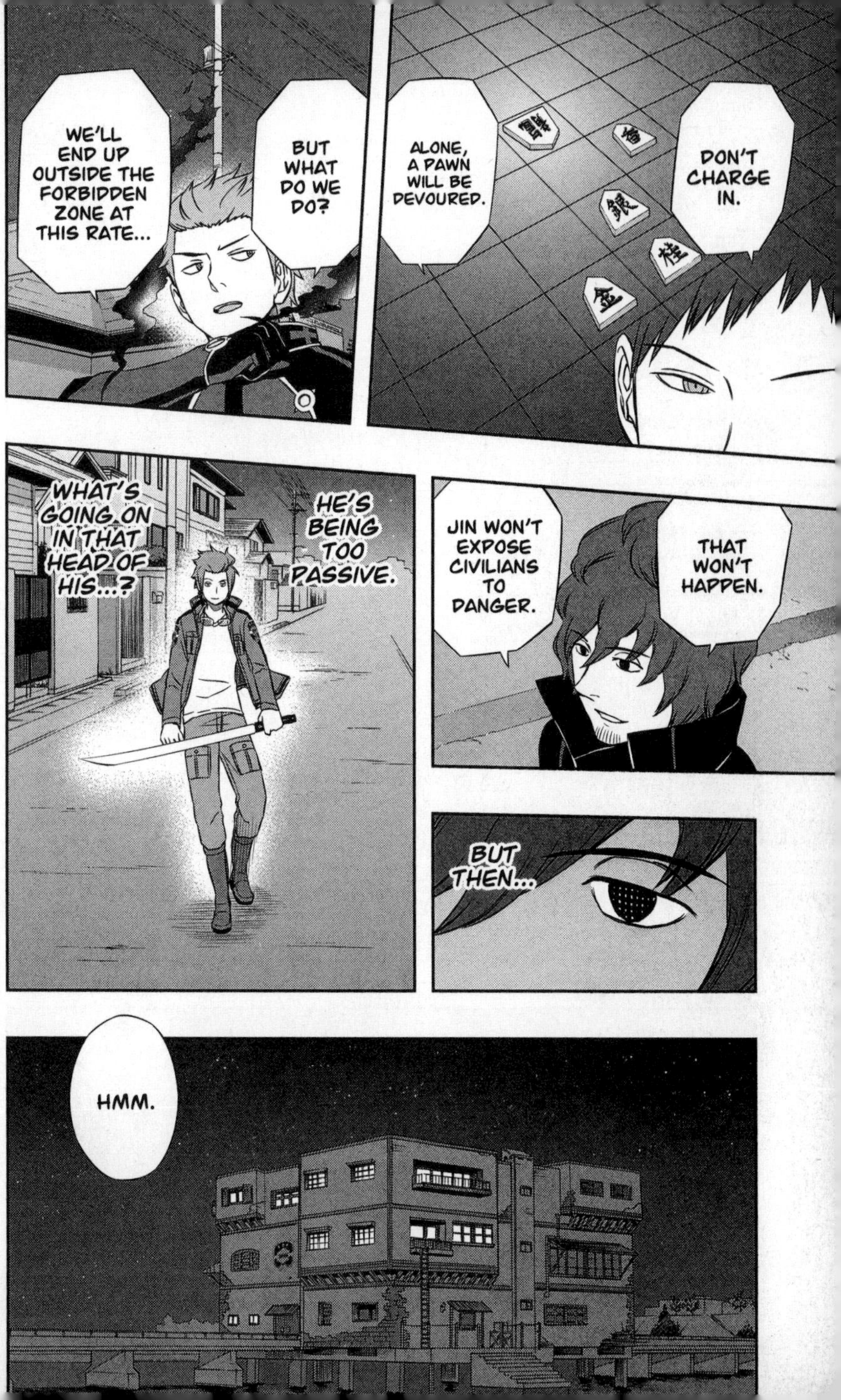
DON'T CHARGE IN.
ALONE, A PAWN WILL BE DEVOURED.
BUT WHAT DO WE DO?
WE'LL END UP OUTSIDE THE FORBIDDEN ZONE AT THIS RATE...
THAT WON'T HAPPEN.
JIN WON'T EXPOSE CIVILIANS TO DANGER.
BUT THEN...
HE'S BEING TOO PASSIVE.
WHAT'S GOING ON IN THAT HEAD OF HIS...?
HMM.

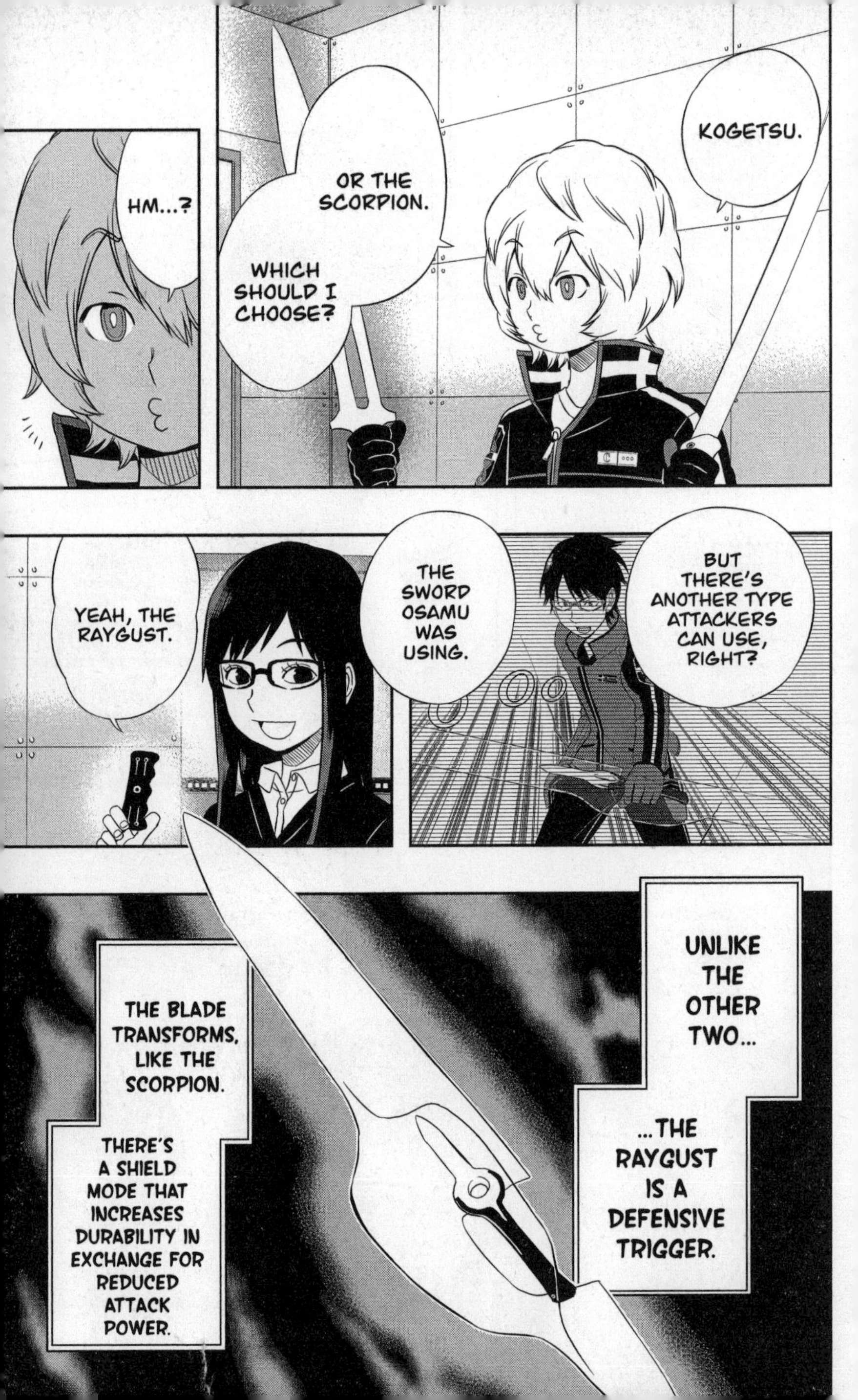
KOGETSU.
OR THE SCORPION.
WHICH SHOULD I CHOOSE?
HM...?
BUT THERE'S ANOTHER TYPE ATTACKERS CAN USE, RIGHT?
THE SWORD OSAMU WAS USING.
YEAH, THE RAYGUST.
UNLIKE THE OTHER TWO...
...THE RAYGUST IS A DEFENSIVE TRIGGER.
THE BLADE TRANSFORMS, LIKE THE SCORPION.
THERE'S A SHIELD MODE THAT INCREASES DURABILITY IN EXCHANGE FOR REDUCED ATTACK POWER.

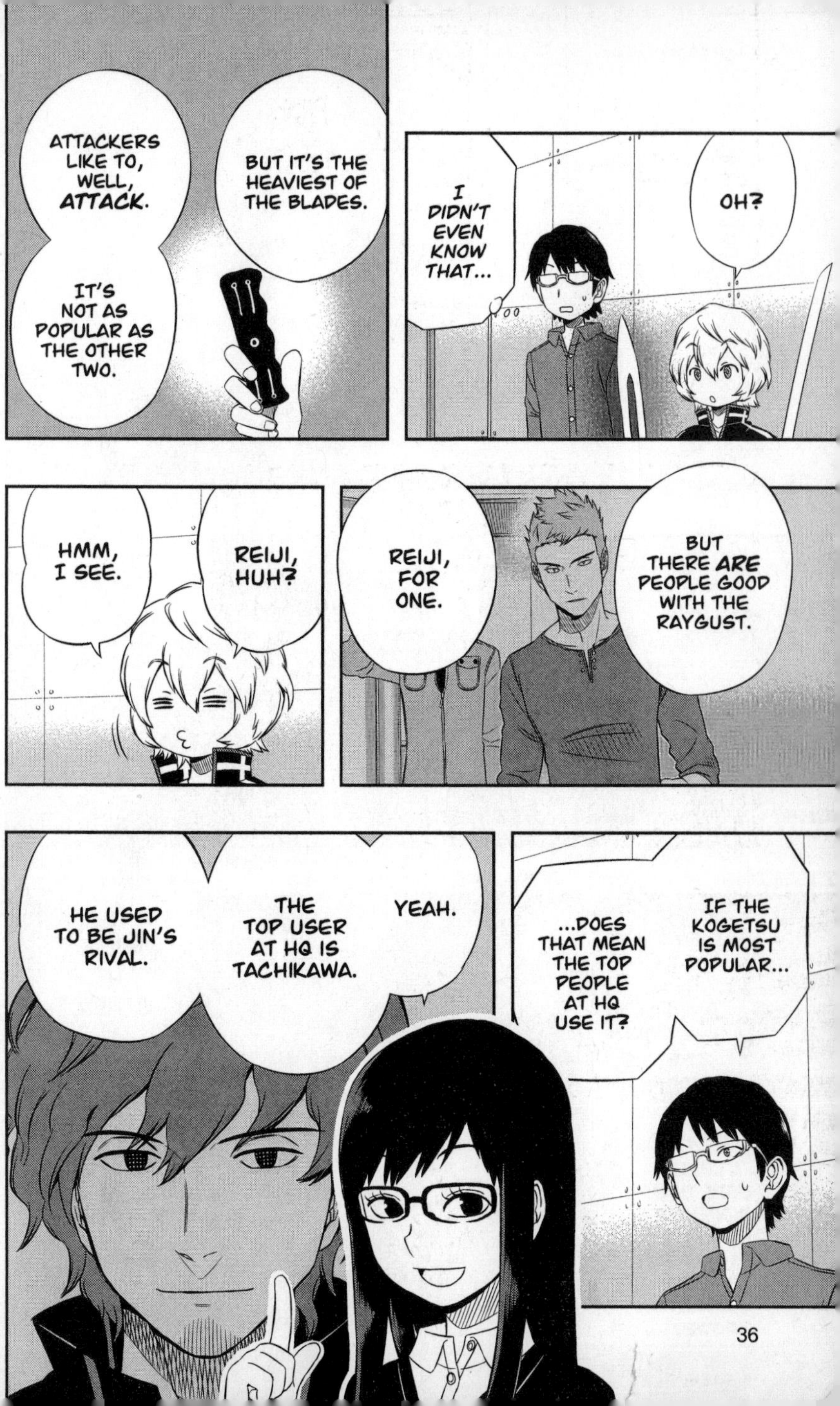
OH?
I DIDN'T EVEN KNOW THAT...
BUT IT'S THE HEAVIEST OF THE BLADES.
ATTACKERS LIKE TO, WELL, ATTACK.
IT'S NOT AS POPULAR AS THE OTHER TWO.
BUT THERE ARE PEOPLE GOOD WITH THE RAYGUST.
REIJI, FOR ONE.
REIJI, HUH?
HMM, I SEE.
IF THE KOGETSU IS MOST POPULAR...
...DOES THAT MEAN THE TOP PEOPLE AT HQ USE IT?
YEAH.
THE TOP USER AT HQ IS TACHIKAWA.
HE USED TO BE JIN'S RIVAL.

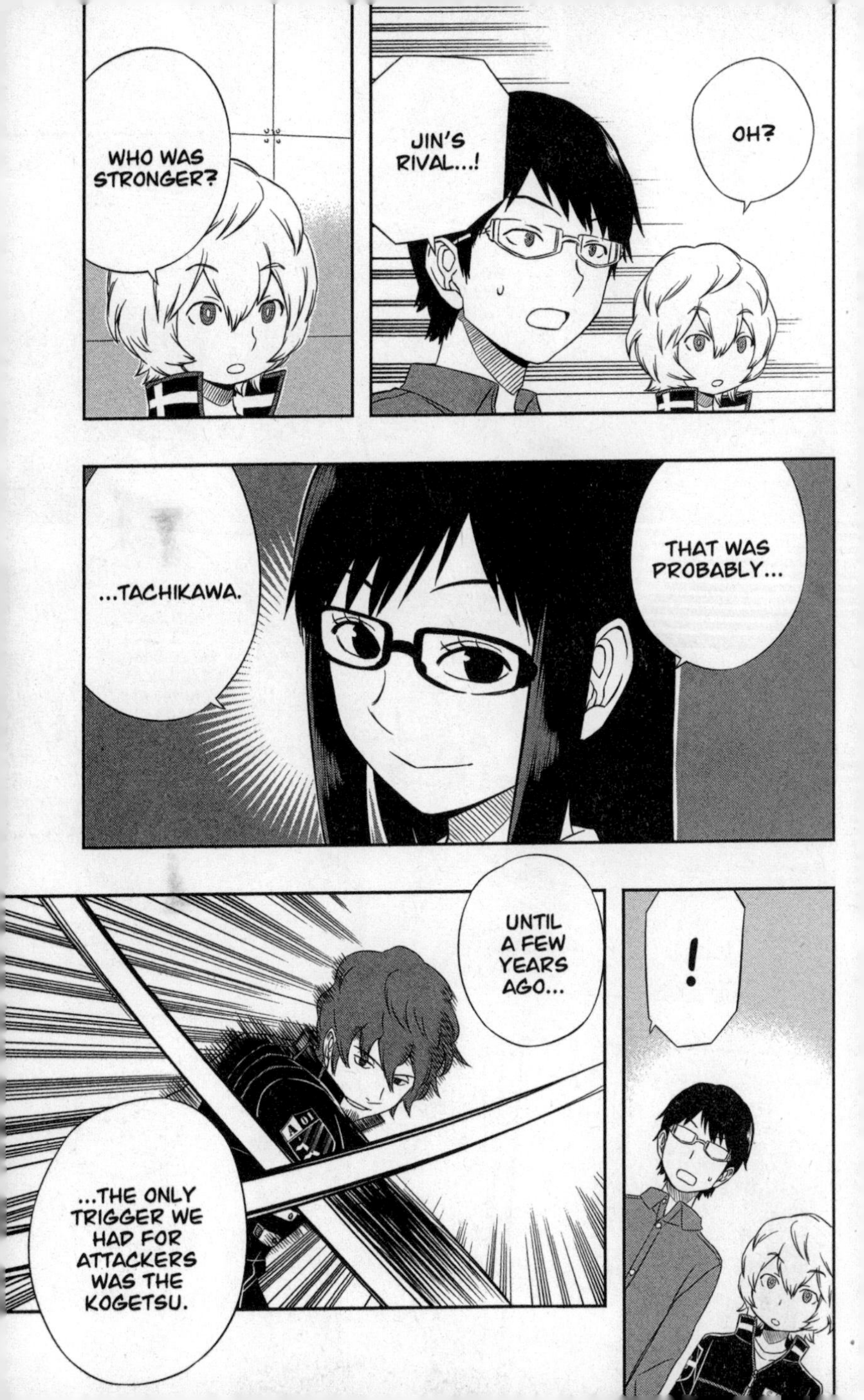
OH?
JIN'S RIVAL...!
WHO WAS STRONGER?
THAT WAS PROBABLY...
...TACHIKAWA.
!
UNTIL A FEW YEARS AGO...
...THE ONLY TRIGGER WE HAD FOR ATTACKERS WAS THE KOGETSU.

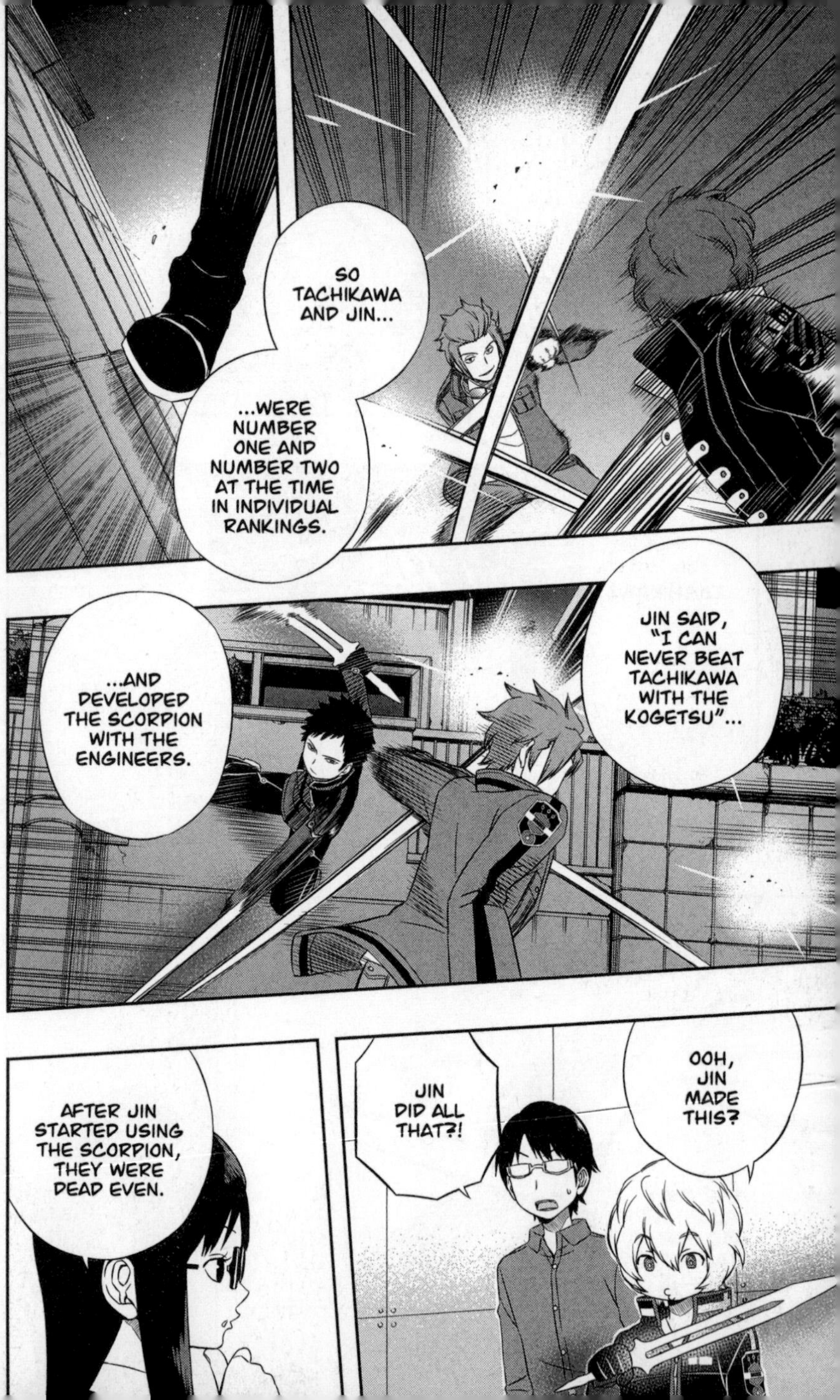
SO TACHIKAWA AND JIN...
...WERE NUMBER ONE AND NUMBER TWO AT THE TIME IN INDIVIDUAL RANKINGS.
JIN SAID, "I CAN NEVER BEAT TACHIKAWA WITH THE KOGETSU"...
...AND DEVELOPED THE SCORPION WITH THE ENGINEERS.
OOH, JIN MADE THIS?
JIN DID ALL THAT?!
AFTER JIN STARTED USING THE SCORPION, THEY WERE DEAD EVEN.

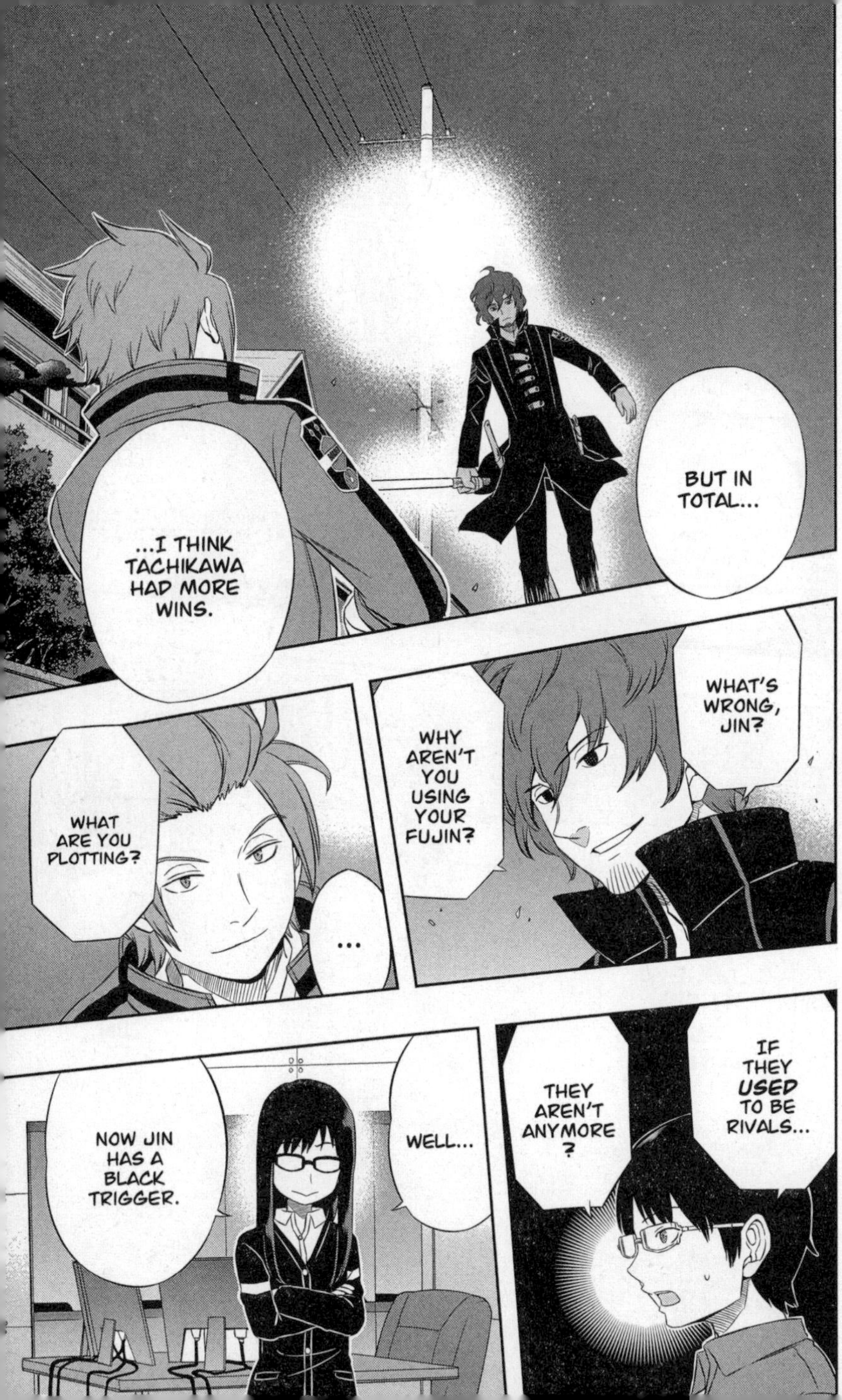
BUT IN TOTAL...
...I THINK TACHIKAWA HAD MORE WINS.
WHAT'S WRONG, JIN?
WHY AREN'T YOU USING YOUR FUJIN?
...
WHAT ARE YOU PLOTTING?
IF THEY USED TO BE RIVALS...
THEY AREN'T ANYMORE?
WELL...
NOW JIN HAS A BLACK TRIGGER.

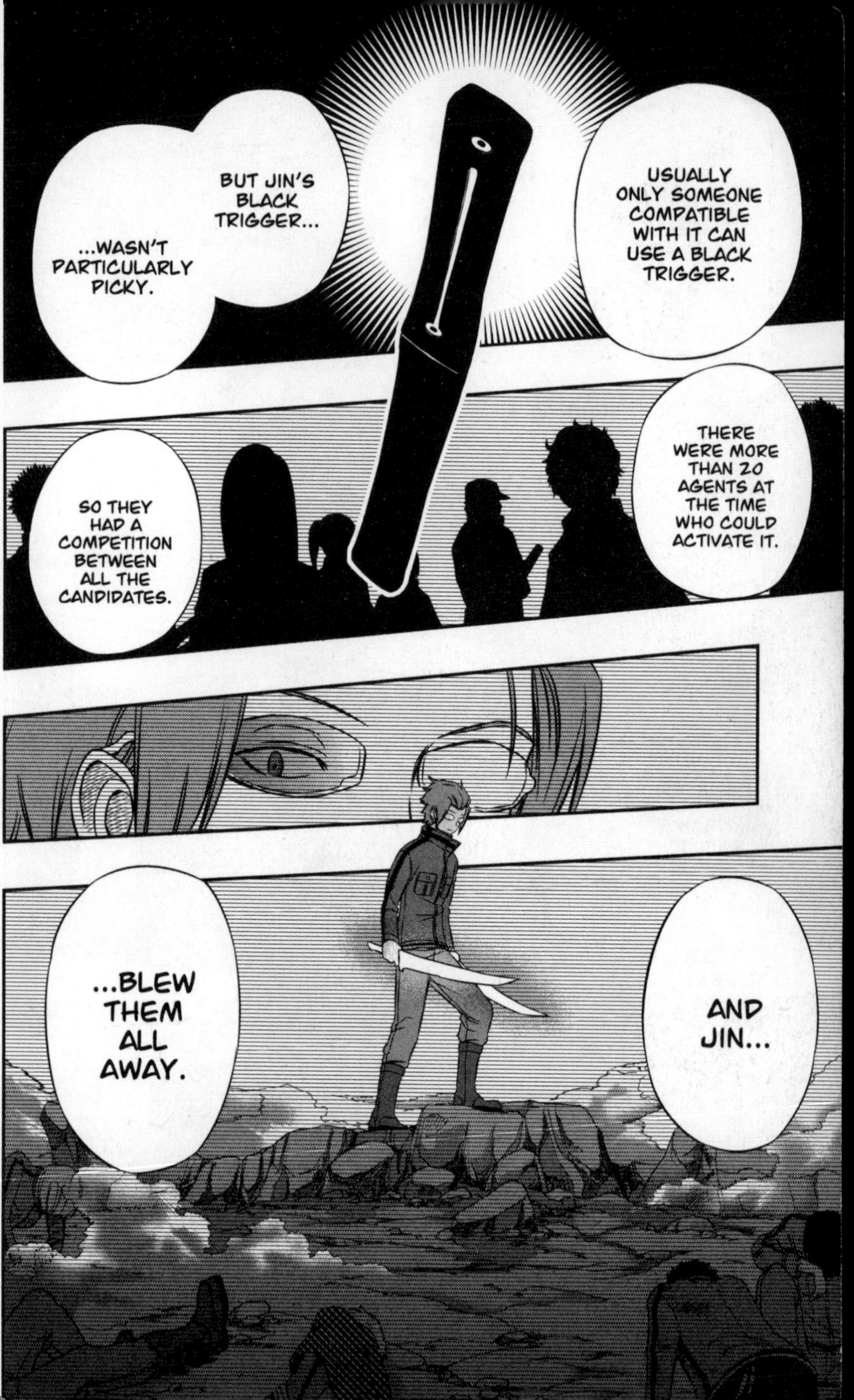
USUALLY ONLY SOMEONE COMPATIBLE WITH IT CAN USE A BLACK TRIGGER.
BUT JIN'S BLACK TRIGGER...
...WASN'T PARTICULARLY PICKY.
THERE WERE MORE THAN 20 AGENTS AT THE TIME WHO COULD ACTIVATE IT.
SO THEY HAD A COMPETITION BETWEEN ALL THE CANDIDATES.
AND JIN...
...BLEW THEM ALL AWAY.

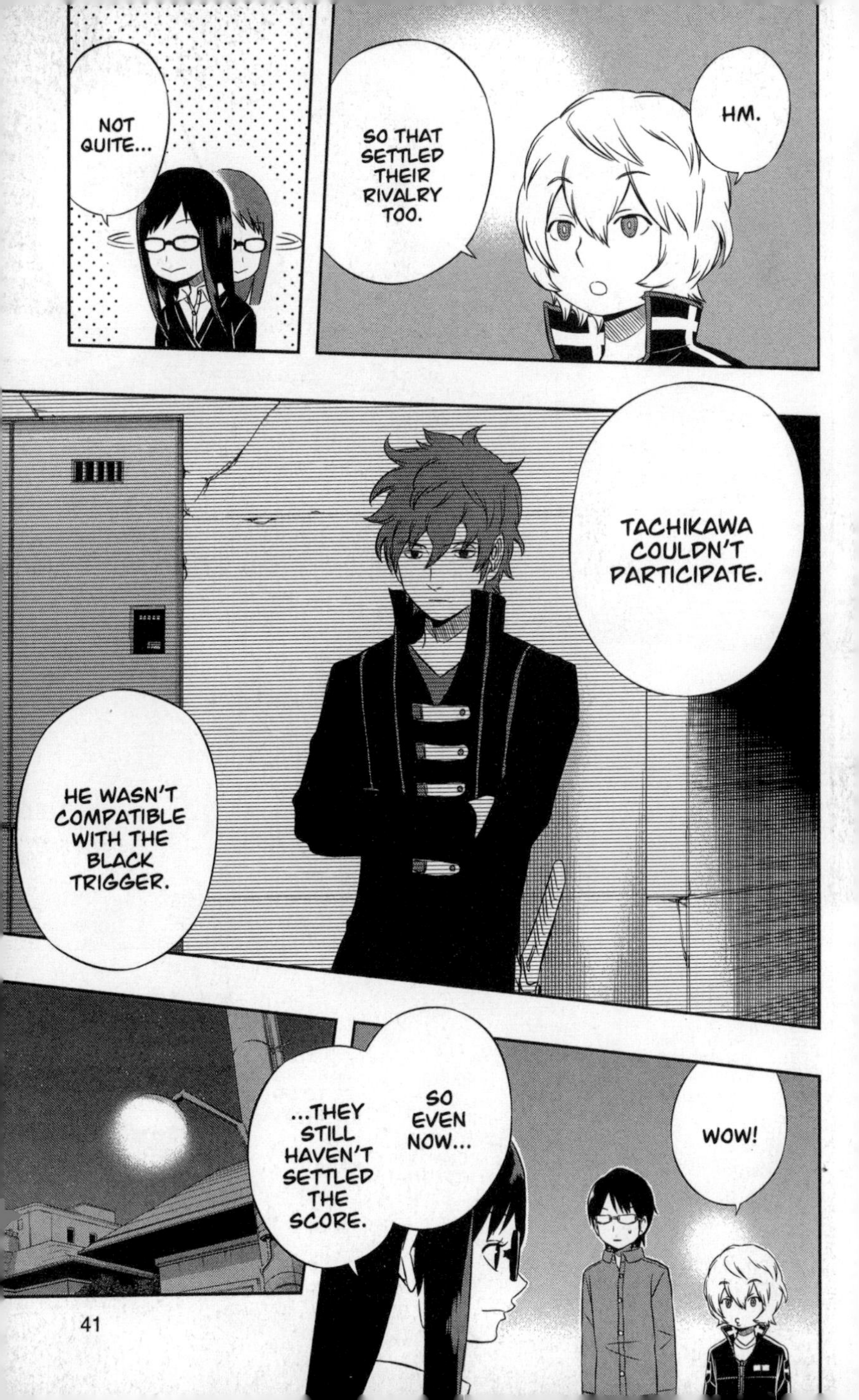
HM.
SO THAT SETTLED THEIR RIVALRY TOO.
NOT QUITE...
TACHIKAWA COULDN'T PARTICIPATE.
HE WASN'T COMPATIBLE WITH THE BLACK TRIGGER.
WOW!
SO EVEN NOW...
...THEY STILL HAVEN'T SETTLED THE SCORE.

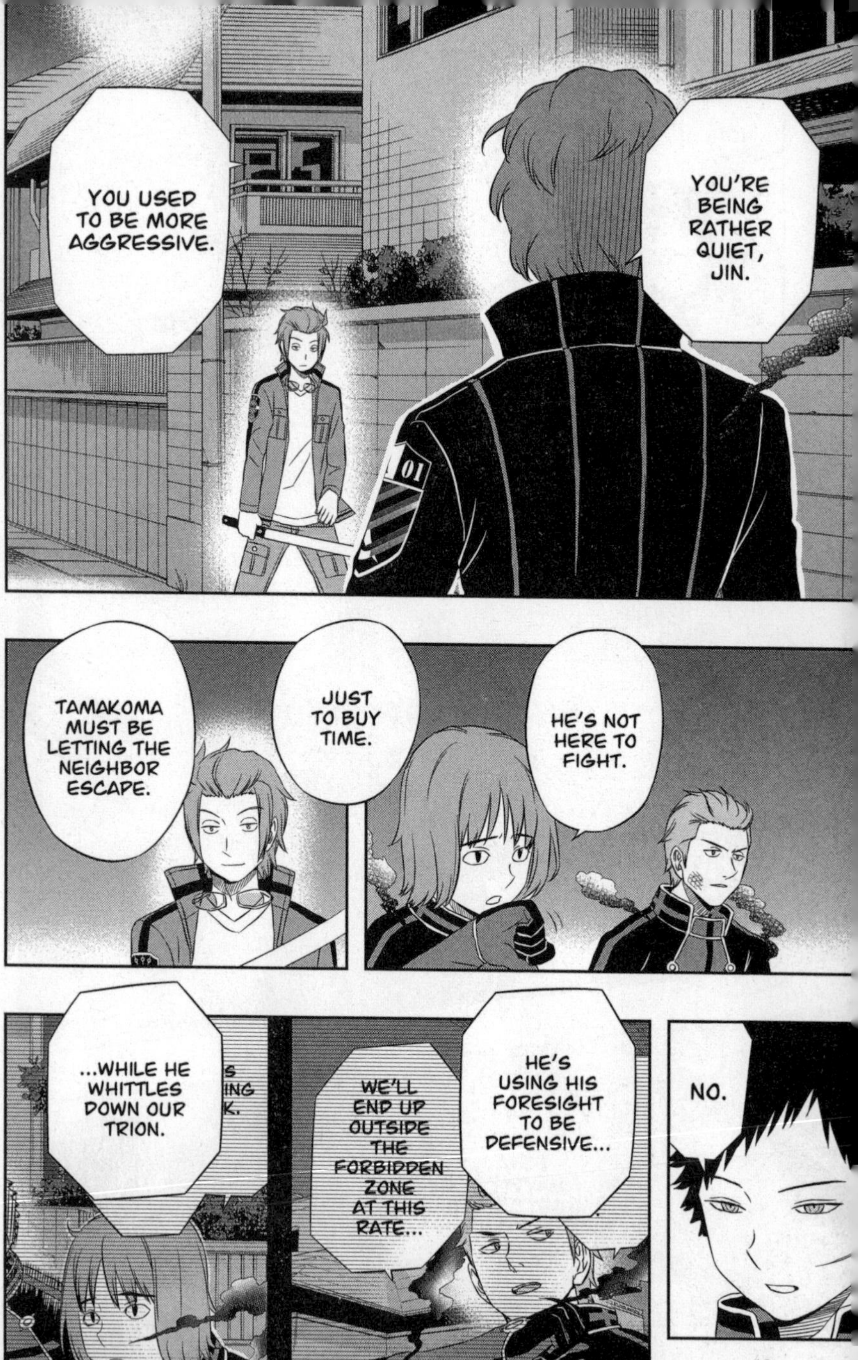
YOU'RE BEING RATHER QUIET, JIN.
YOU USED TO BE MORE AGGRESSIVE.
HE'S NOT HERE TO FIGHT.
JUST TO BUY TIME.
TAMAKOMA MUST BE LETTING THE NEIGHBOR ESCAPE.
NO.
HE'S USING HIS FORESIGHT TO BE DEFENSIVE...
WE'LL END UP OUTSIDE THE FORBIDDEN ZONE AT THIS RATE...
...WHILE HE WHITTLES DOWN OUR TRION.

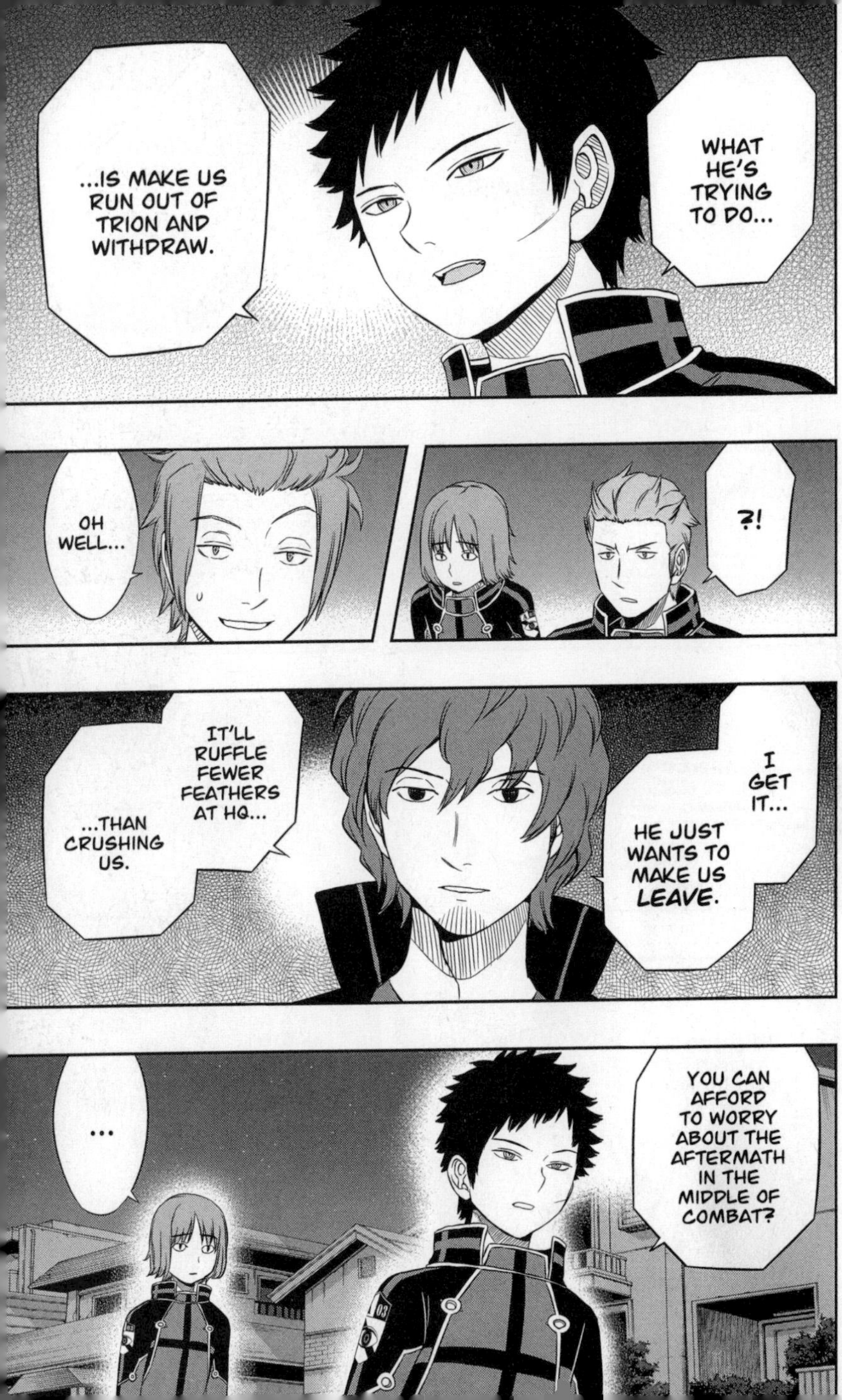
WHAT HE'S TRYING TO DO...
...IS MAKE US RUN OUT OF TRION AND WITHDRAW.
?!
OH WELL...
I GET IT...
HE JUST WANTS TO MAKE US LEAVE.
IT'LL RUFFLE FEWER FEATHERS AT HQ...
...THAN CRUSHING US.
YOU CAN AFFORD TO WORRY ABOUT THE AFTERMATH IN THE MIDDLE OF COMBAT?
...

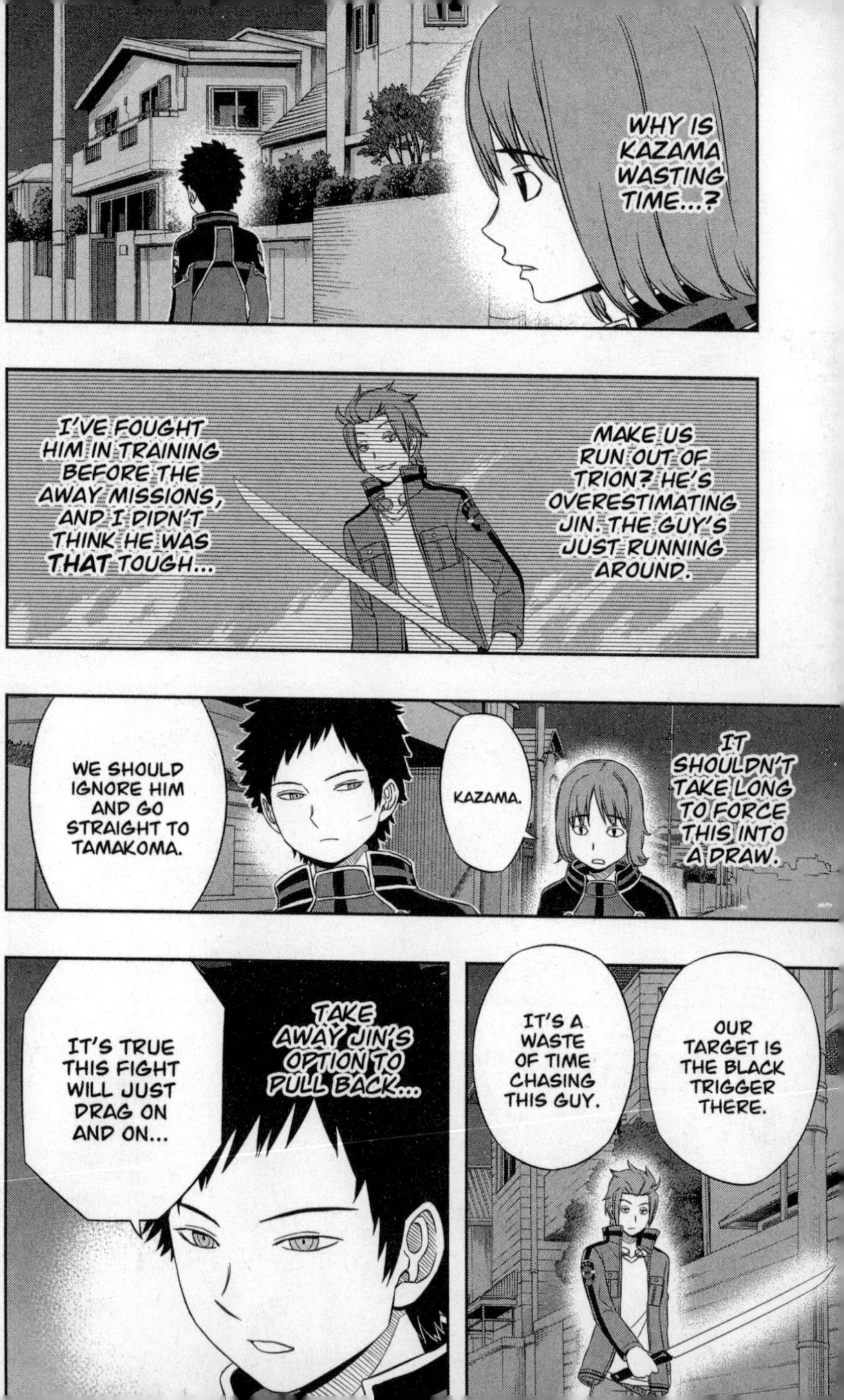
WHY IS KAZAMA WASTING TIME...?
MAKE US RUN OUT OF TRION? HE'S OVERESTIMATING JIN. THE GUY'S JUST RUNNING AROUND.
I'VE FOUGHT HIM IN TRAINING BEFORE THE AWAY MISSIONS, AND I DIDN'T THINK HE WAS THAT TOUGH...
IT SHOULDN'T TAKE LONG TO FORCE THIS INTO A DRAW.
KAZAMA.
WE SHOULD IGNORE HIM AND GO STRAIGHT TO TAMAKOMA.
OUR TARGET IS THE BLACK TRIGGER THERE.
IT'S A WASTE OF TIME CHASING THIS GUY.
TAKE AWAY JIN'S OPTION TO PULL BACK...
IT'S TRUE THIS FIGHT WILL JUST DRAG ON AND ON...

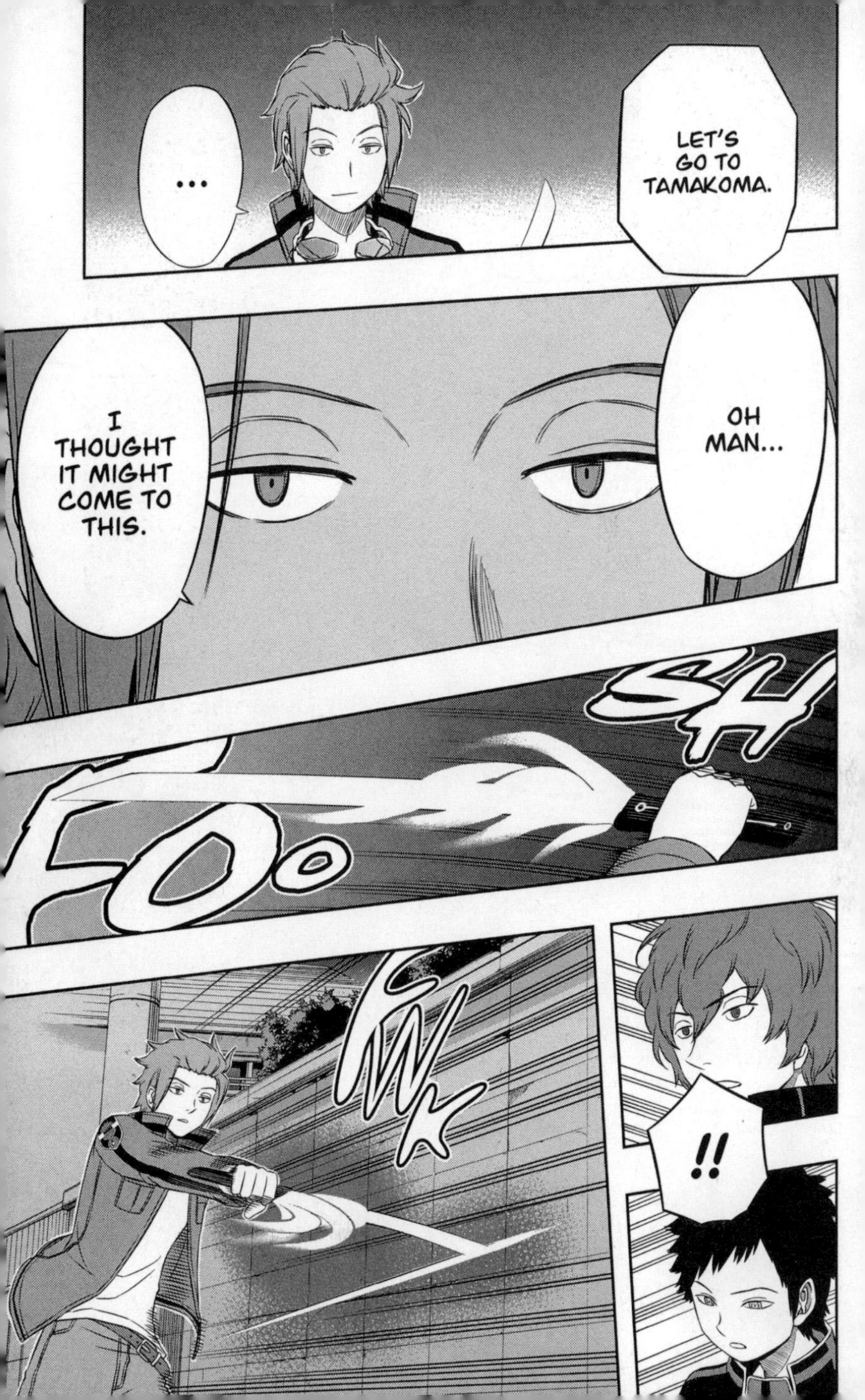
LET'S GO TO TAMAKOMA.
...
OH MAN...
I THOUGHT IT MIGHT COME TO THIS.
SH
OO
!!

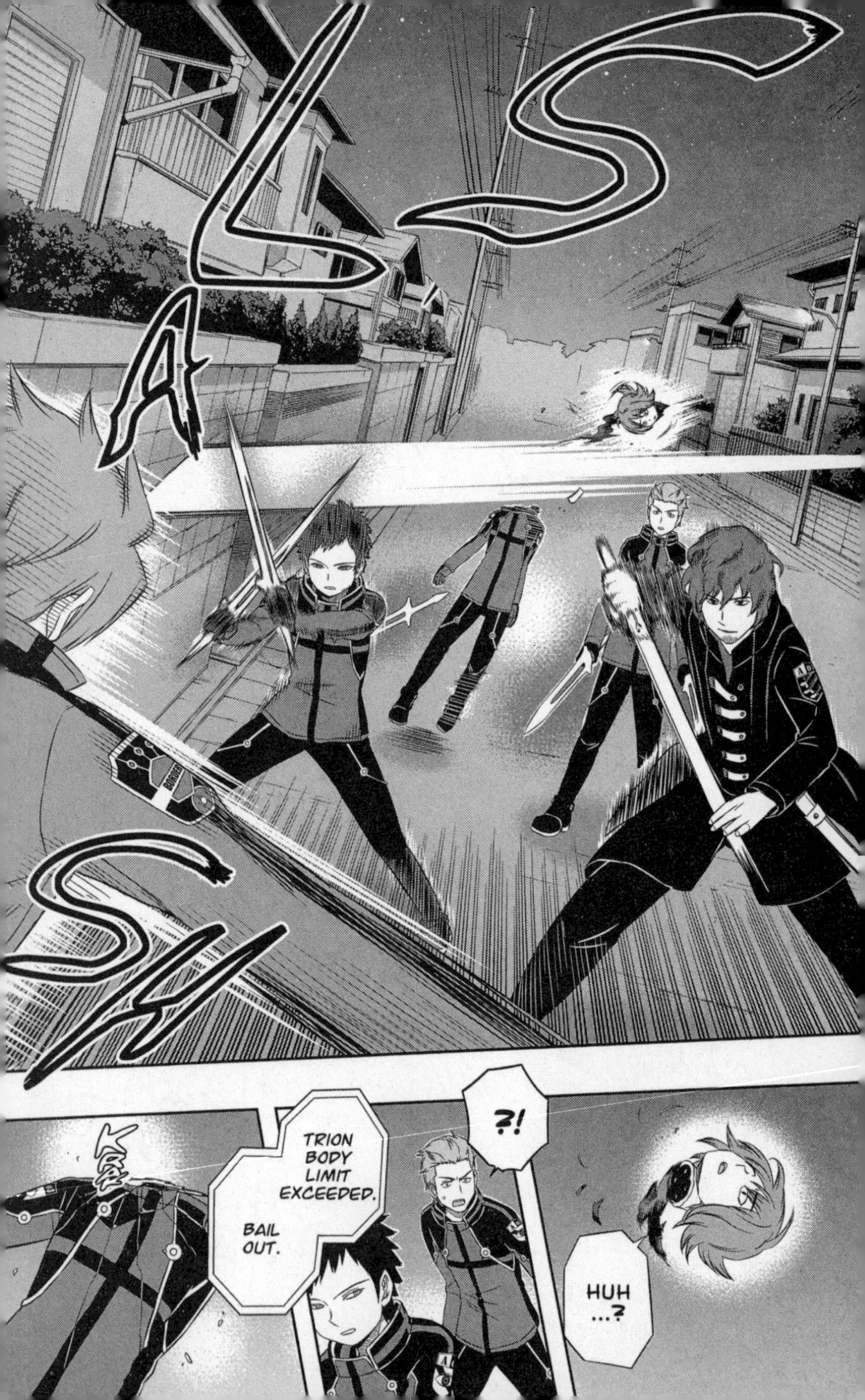
SLASH
?!
HUH ...?
TRION BODY LIMIT EXCEEDED.
BAIL OUT.

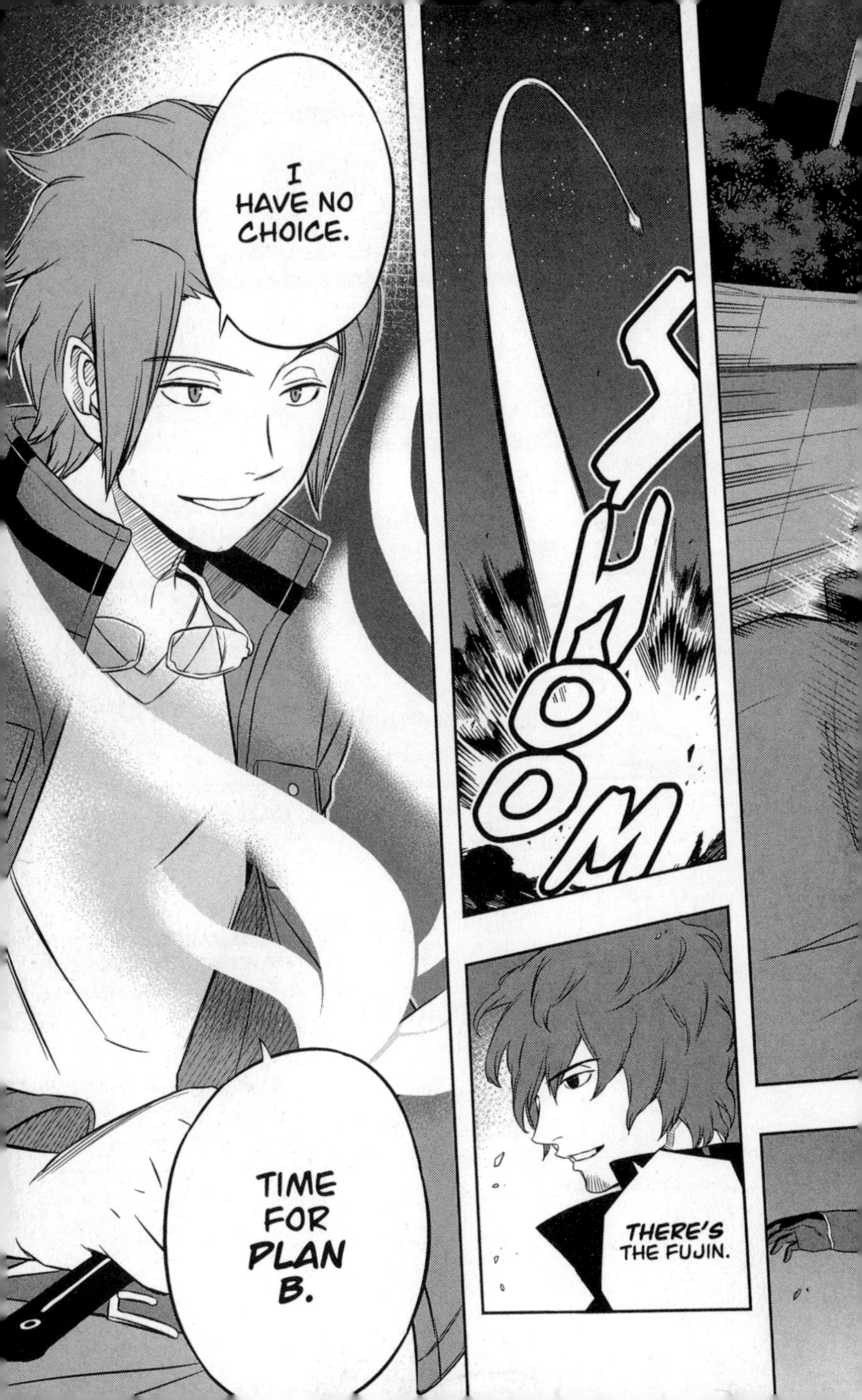
WHOOM
THERE'S THE FUJIN.
I HAVE NO CHOICE.
TIME FOR PLAN B.

Kazama Squad
Border HQ A-Rank #3

Soya Kazama
Captain, Attacker

- 21 years old (college student)
- Born Sept. 24

- Luna Falcata, Blood type A
- Height: 5'2"
- Likes: Pork cutlet with curry, milk, discipline

Ryo Utagawa
All-Rounder

- 16 years old (high school student)
- Born June 10

- Lepus, Blood type A
- Height: 5'8"
- Likes: Dogs, yakitori, sports

Shiro Kikuchihara
Attacker

- 16 years old (high school student)
- Born Dec. 14

- Cetacea, Blood type O
- Height: 5'5"
- Hates: Tomatoes, green peppers, boiled fish, oysters, people who look like overachievers

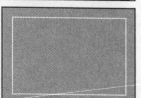

Kaho Mikami
Operator

- 16 years old (high school student)
- Born Feb. 23

- Apis, Blood type A
- Height: 5'
- Likes: tonkotsu (pork bone broth) ramen, daifuku sweets, manga

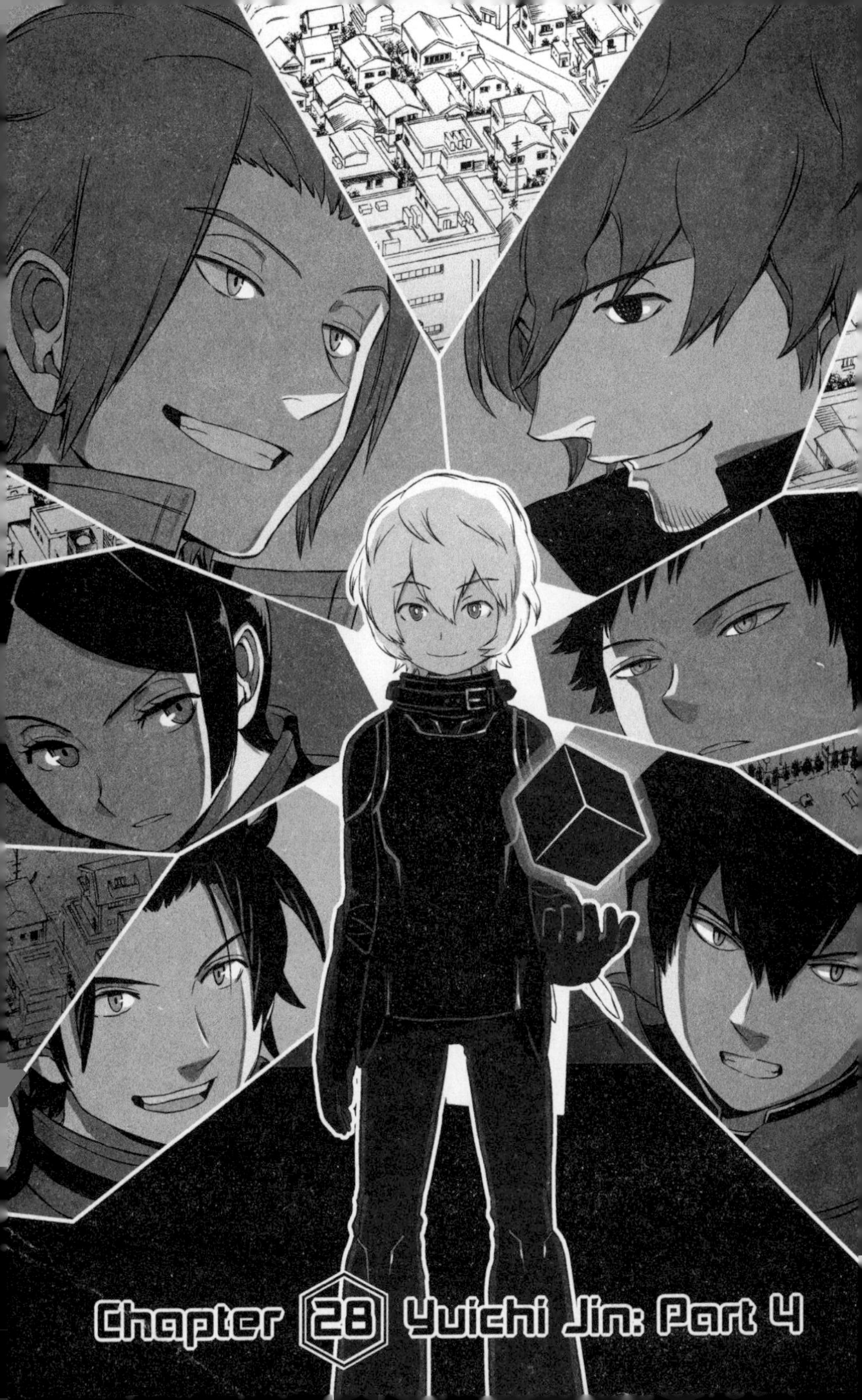
Chapter 28 Yuichi Jin: Part 4

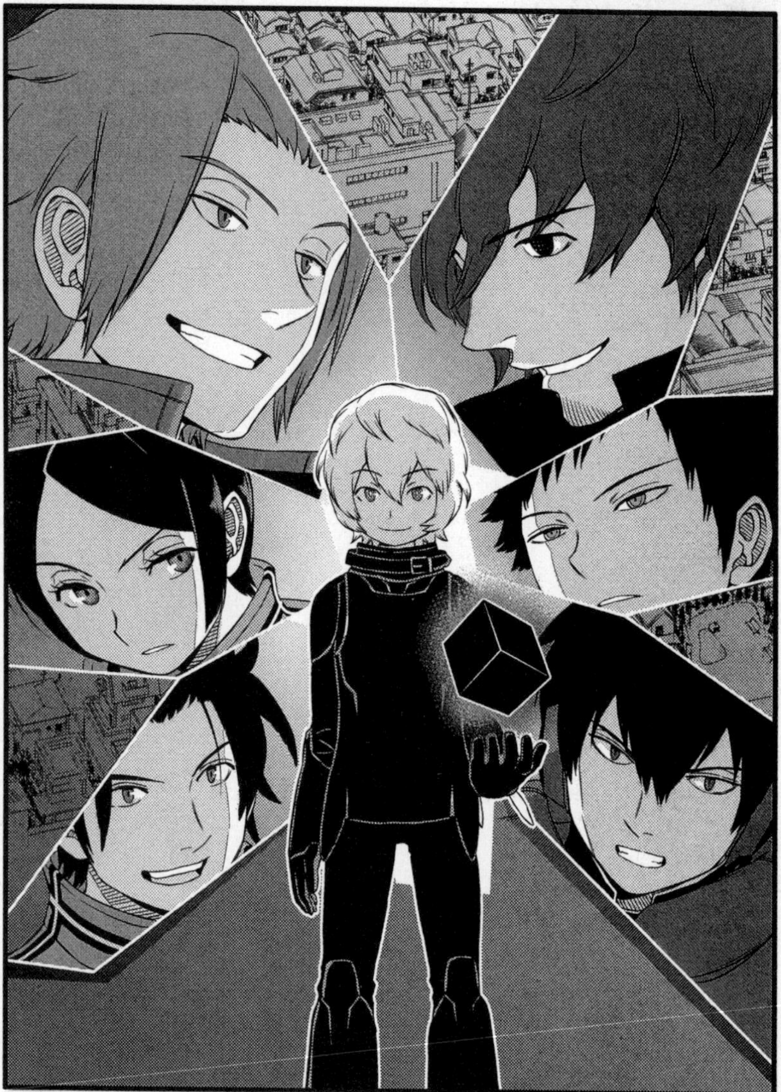

■ 2013 *Weekly Shonen Jump* issue 40, center color page (fifth one)

I used backlighting to make it look cool. I like how evil Tachikawa looks. I feel that my techniques for color art solidified around this time.

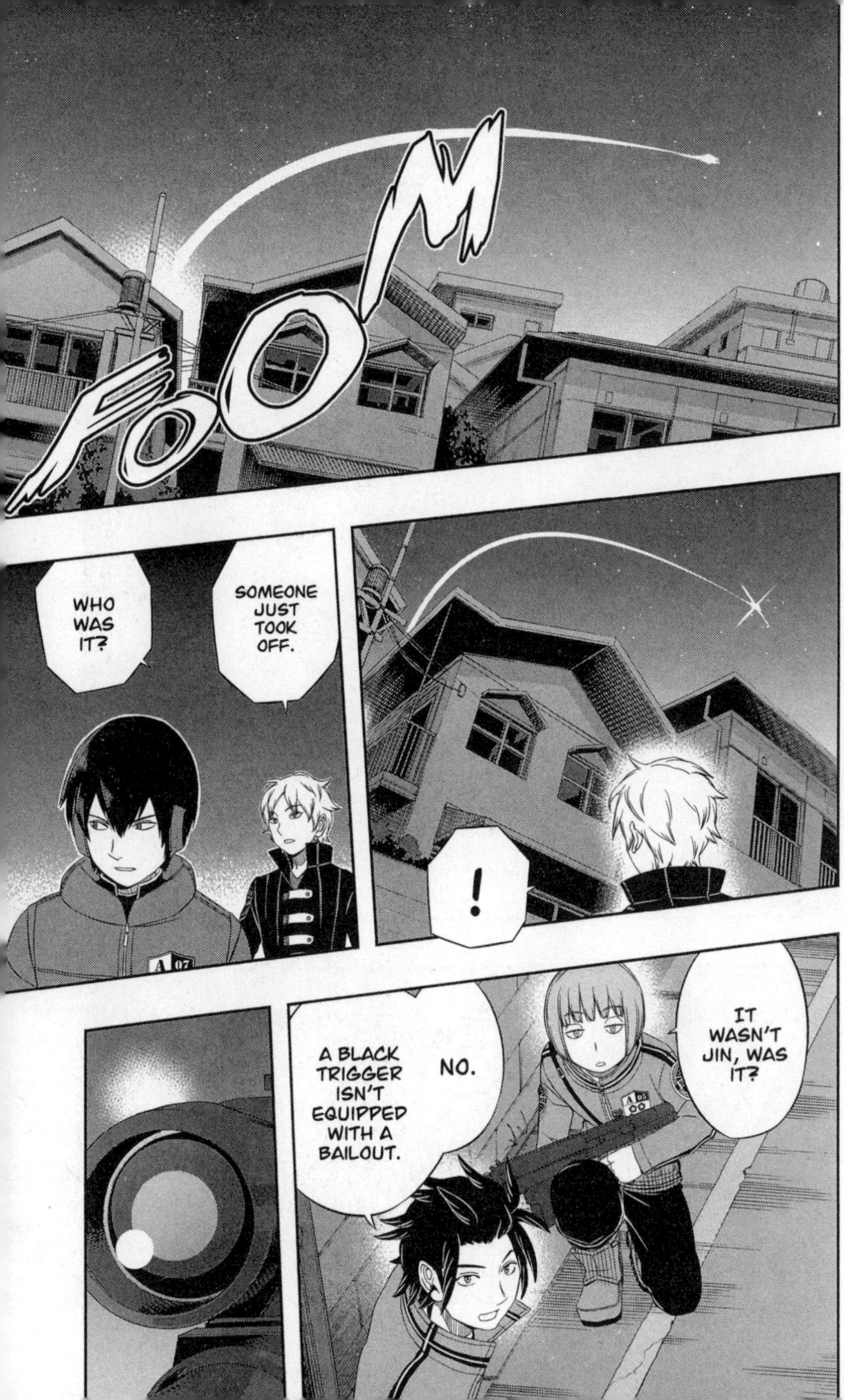
FOOOM
SOMEONE JUST TOOK OFF.
WHO WAS IT?
!
IT WASN'T JIN, WAS IT?
NO.
A BLACK TRIGGER ISN'T EQUIPPED WITH A BAILOUT.

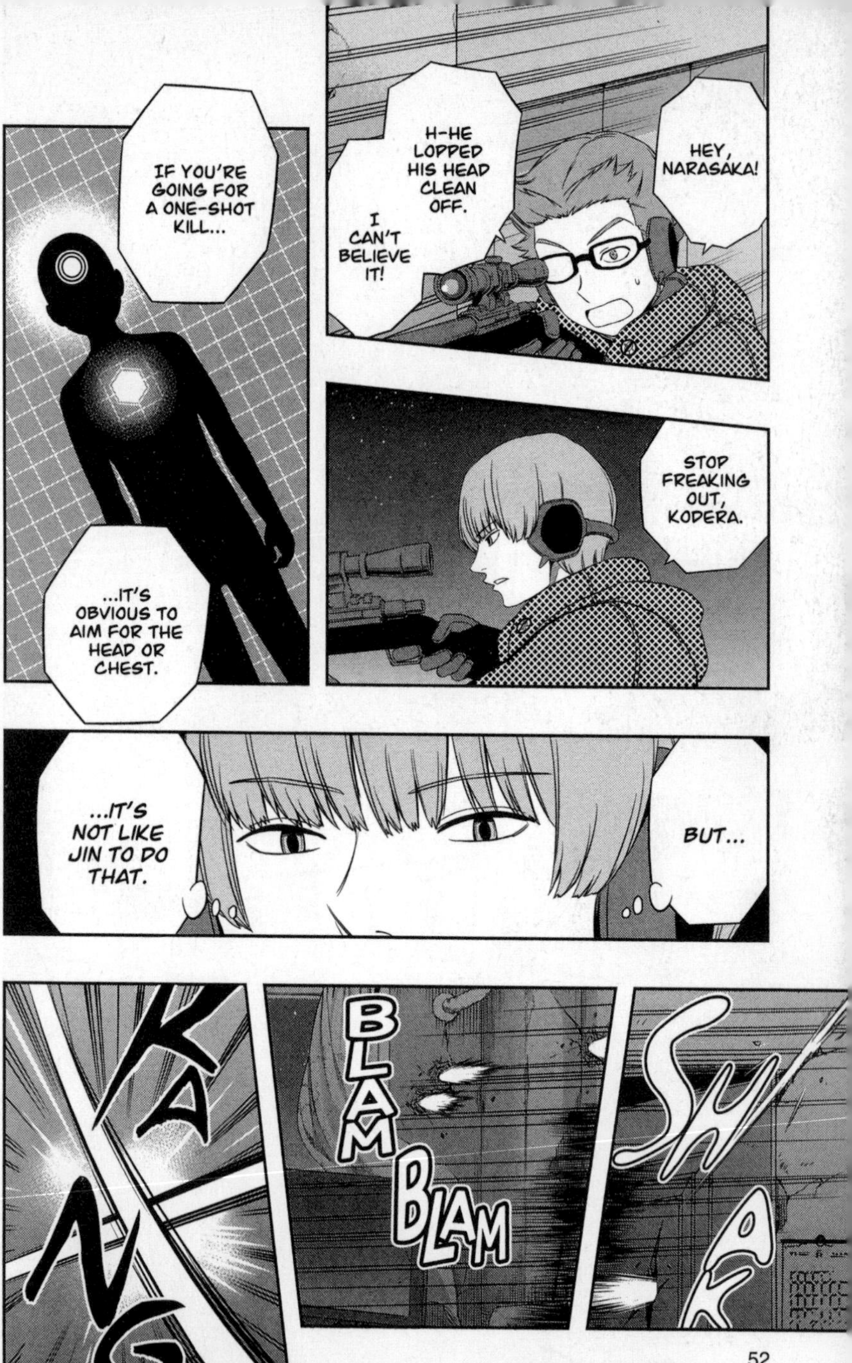
HEY, NARASAKA!
H-HE LOPPED HIS HEAD CLEAN OFF.
I CAN'T BELIEVE IT!
STOP FREAKING OUT, KODERA.
IF YOU'RE GOING FOR A ONE-SHOT KILL...
...IT'S OBVIOUS TO AIM FOR THE HEAD OR CHEST.
BUT...
...IT'S NOT LIKE JIN TO DO THAT.
SHAK
BLAM
BLAM
KANG

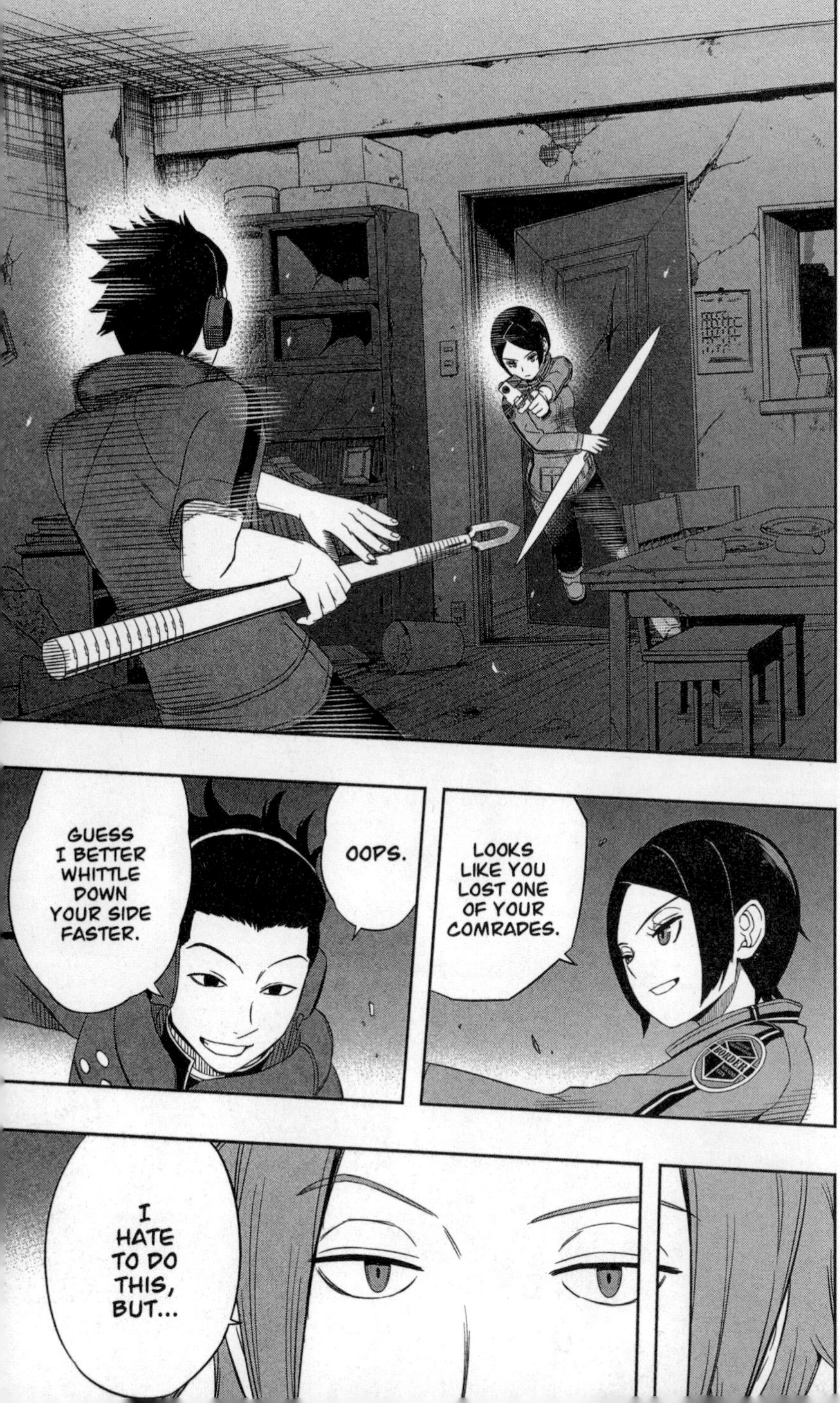
LOOKS LIKE YOU LOST ONE OF YOUR COMRADES.
OOPS.
GUESS I BETTER WHITTLE DOWN YOUR SIDE FASTER.
I HATE TO DO THIS, BUT...

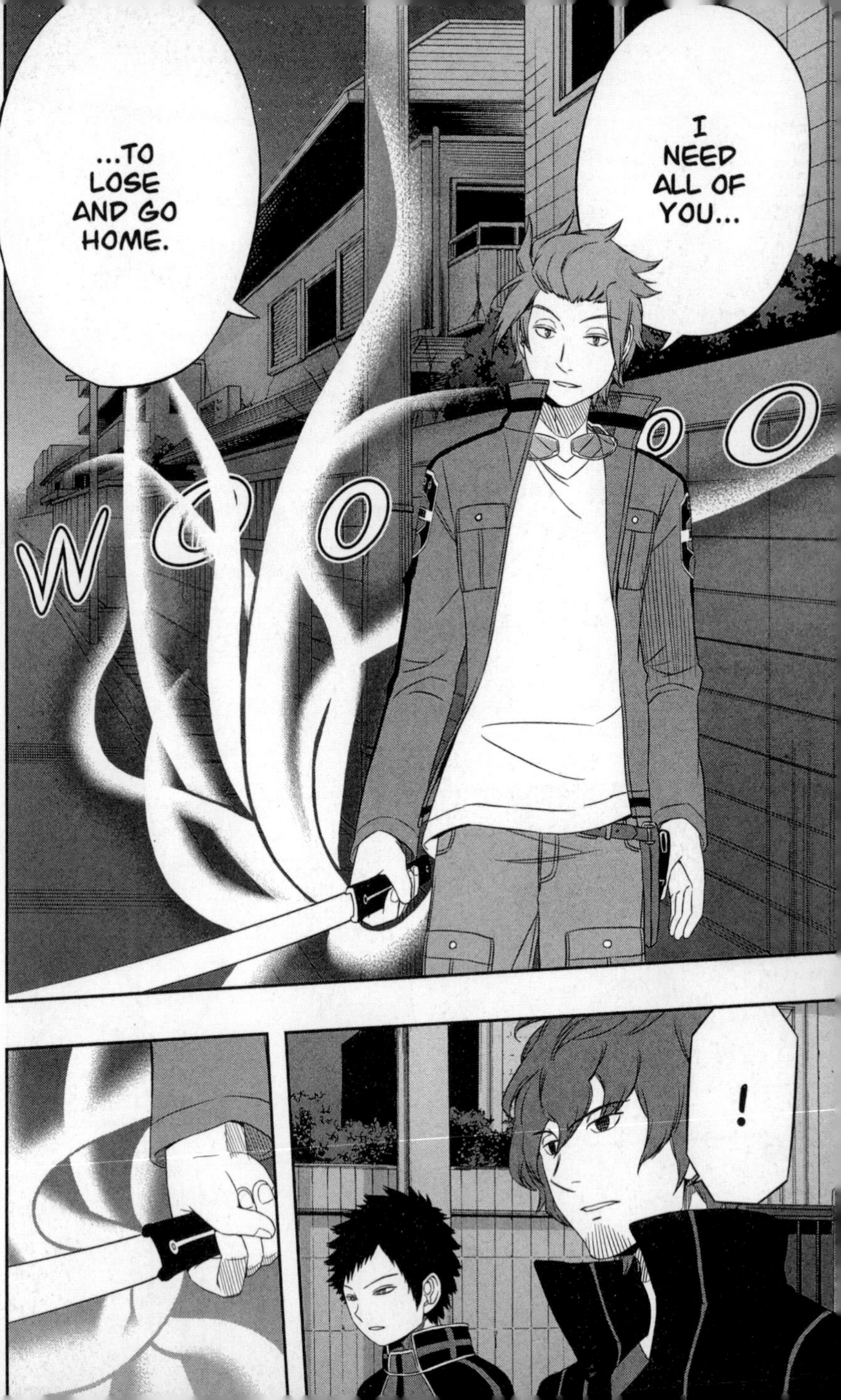
I NEED ALL OF YOU...
...TO LOSE AND GO HOME.
WOOOOO
!

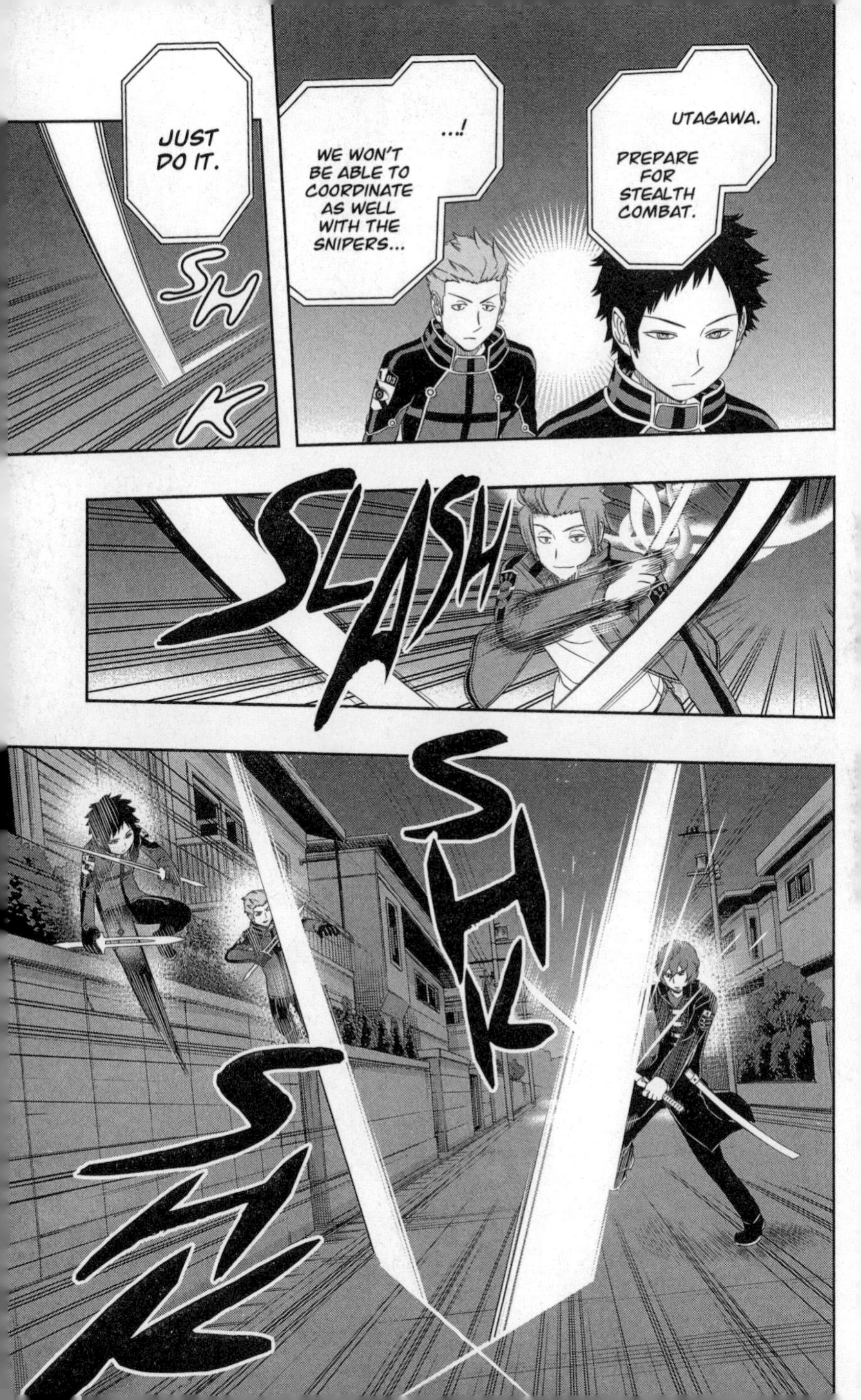
UTAGAWA.
PREPARE FOR STEALTH COMBAT.
...!
WE WON'T BE ABLE TO COORDINATE AS WELL WITH THE SNIPERS...
JUST DO IT.
SHK
SLASH
SHK
SHK

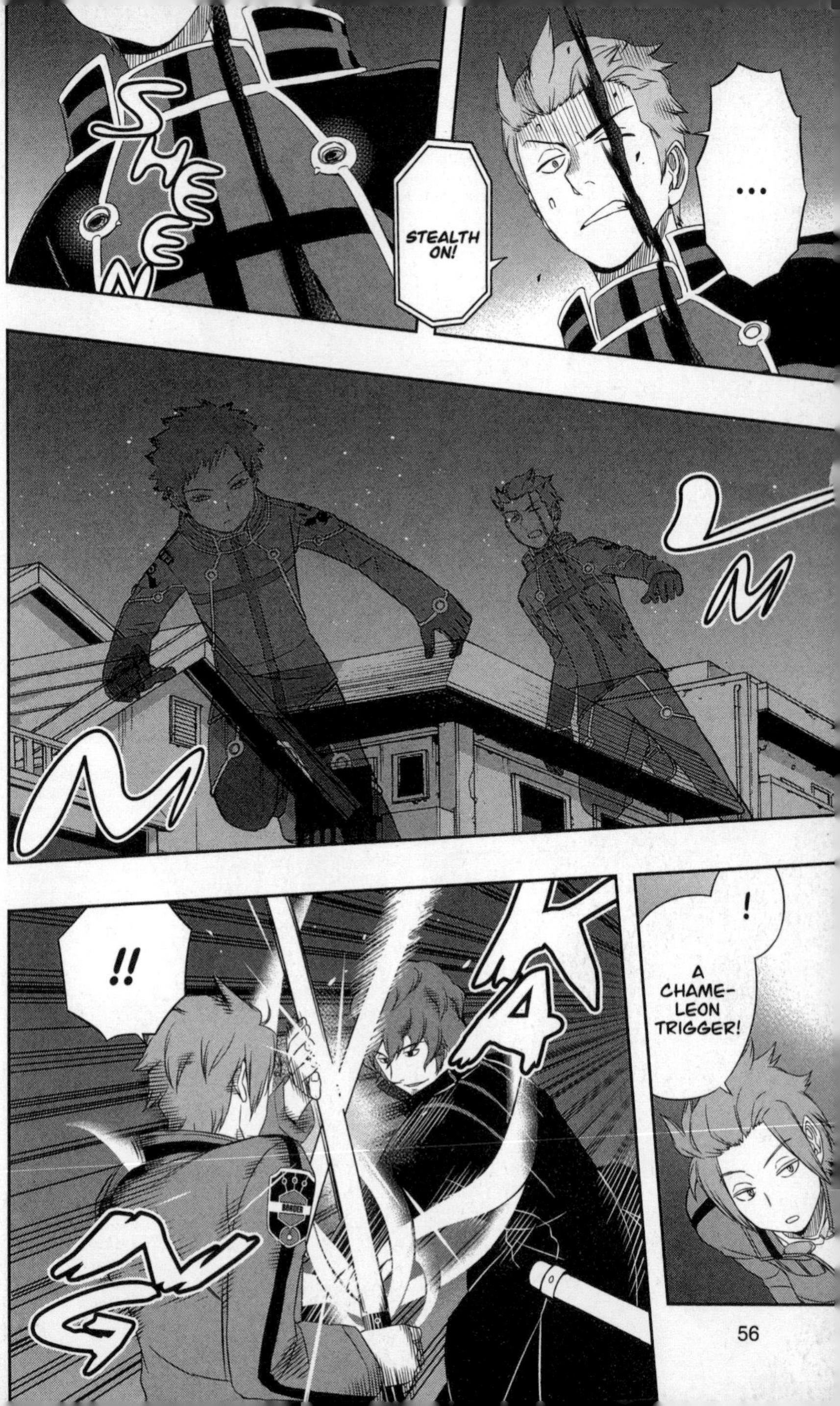
...
STEALTH ON!
SHEEN
!
A CHAME-LEON TRIGGER!
!!
KA

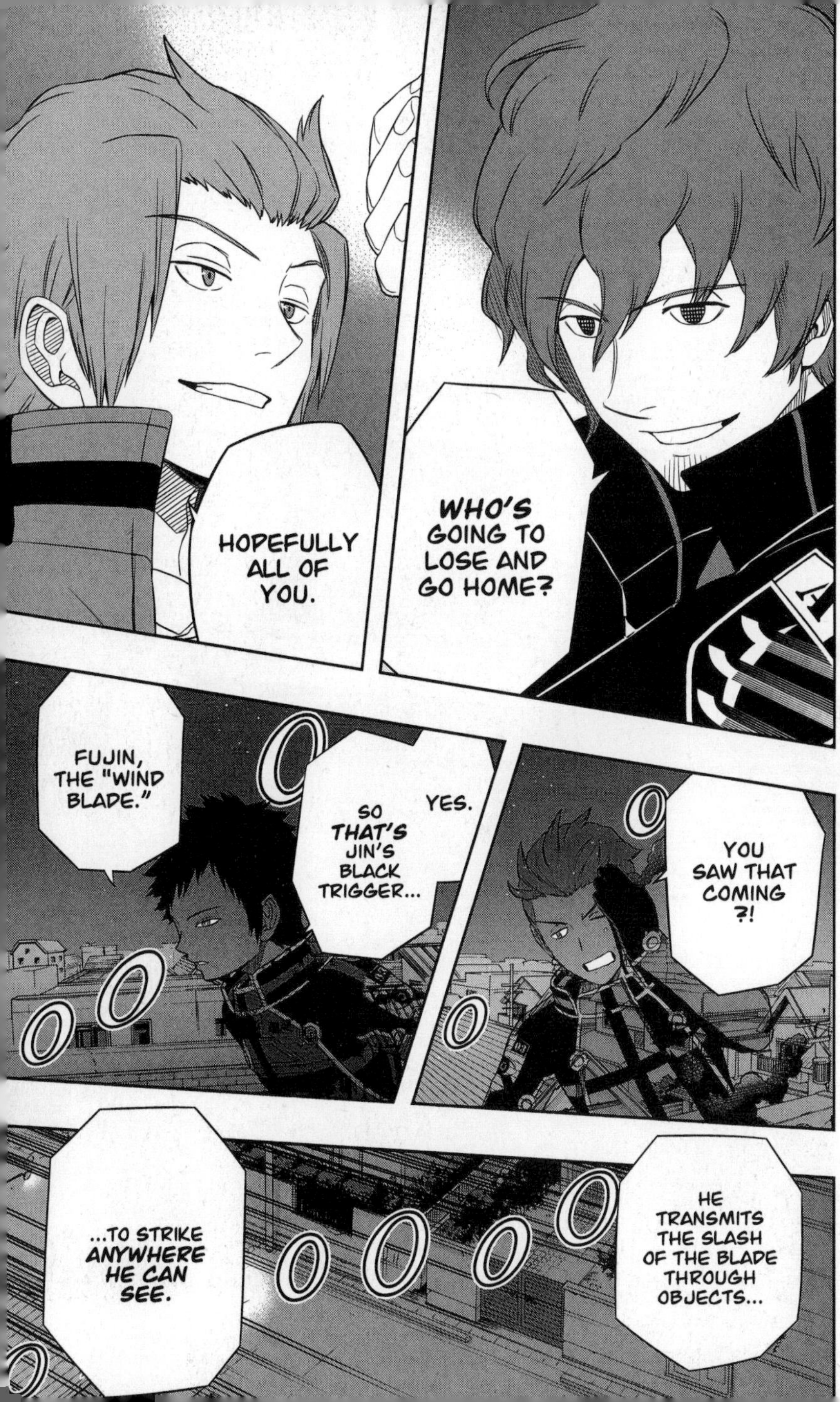
WHO'S GOING TO LOSE AND GO HOME?
HOPEFULLY ALL OF YOU.
YOU SAW THAT COMING ?!
YES.
SO THAT'S JIN'S BLACK TRIGGER...
FUJIN, THE "WIND BLADE."
HE TRANSMITS THE SLASH OF THE BLADE THROUGH OBJECTS...
...TO STRIKE ANYWHERE HE CAN SEE.

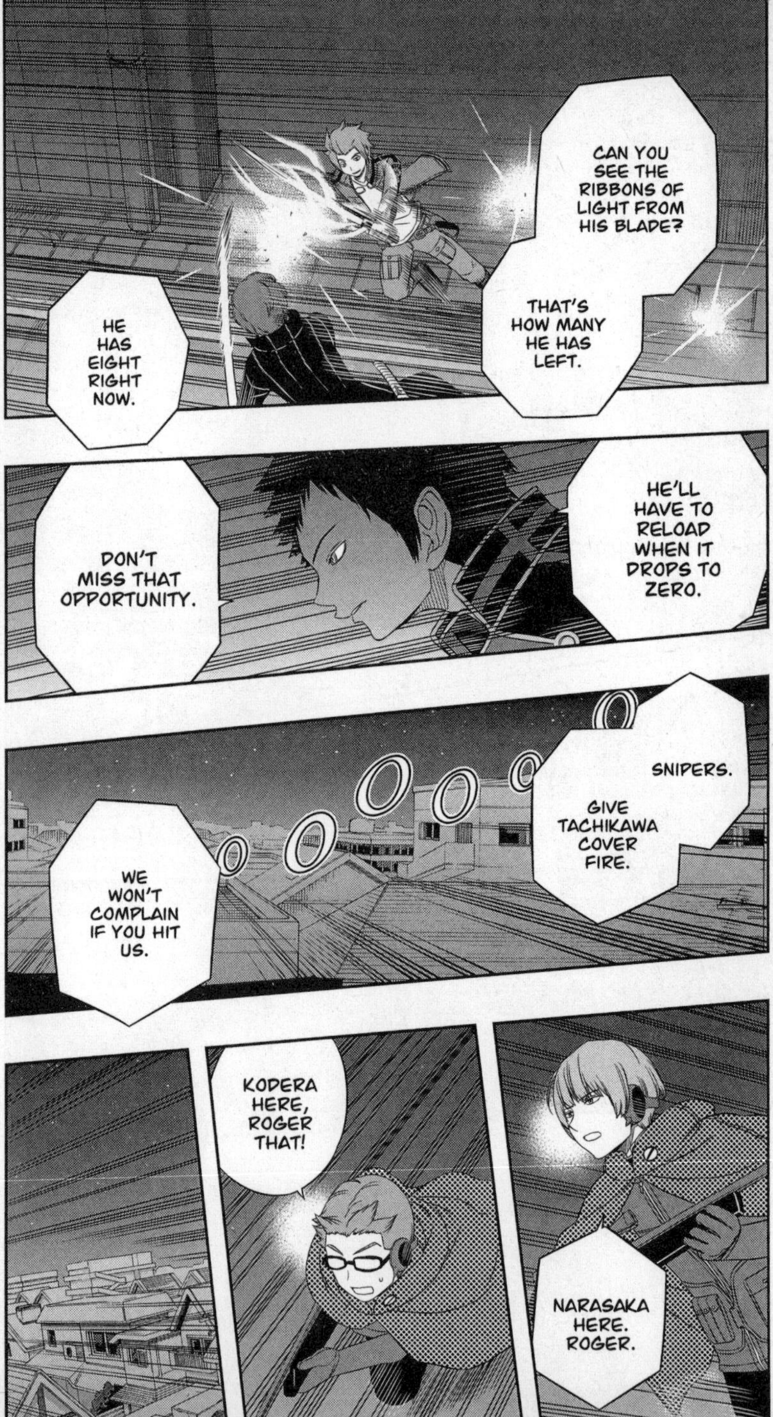
CAN YOU SEE THE RIBBONS OF LIGHT FROM HIS BLADE?
THAT'S HOW MANY HE HAS LEFT.
HE HAS EIGHT RIGHT NOW.
HE'LL HAVE TO RELOAD WHEN IT DROPS TO ZERO.
DON'T MISS THAT OPPORTUNITY.
SNIPERS.
GIVE TACHIKAWA COVER FIRE.
WE WON'T COMPLAIN IF YOU HIT US.
NARASAKA HERE. ROGER.
KODERA HERE, ROGER THAT!

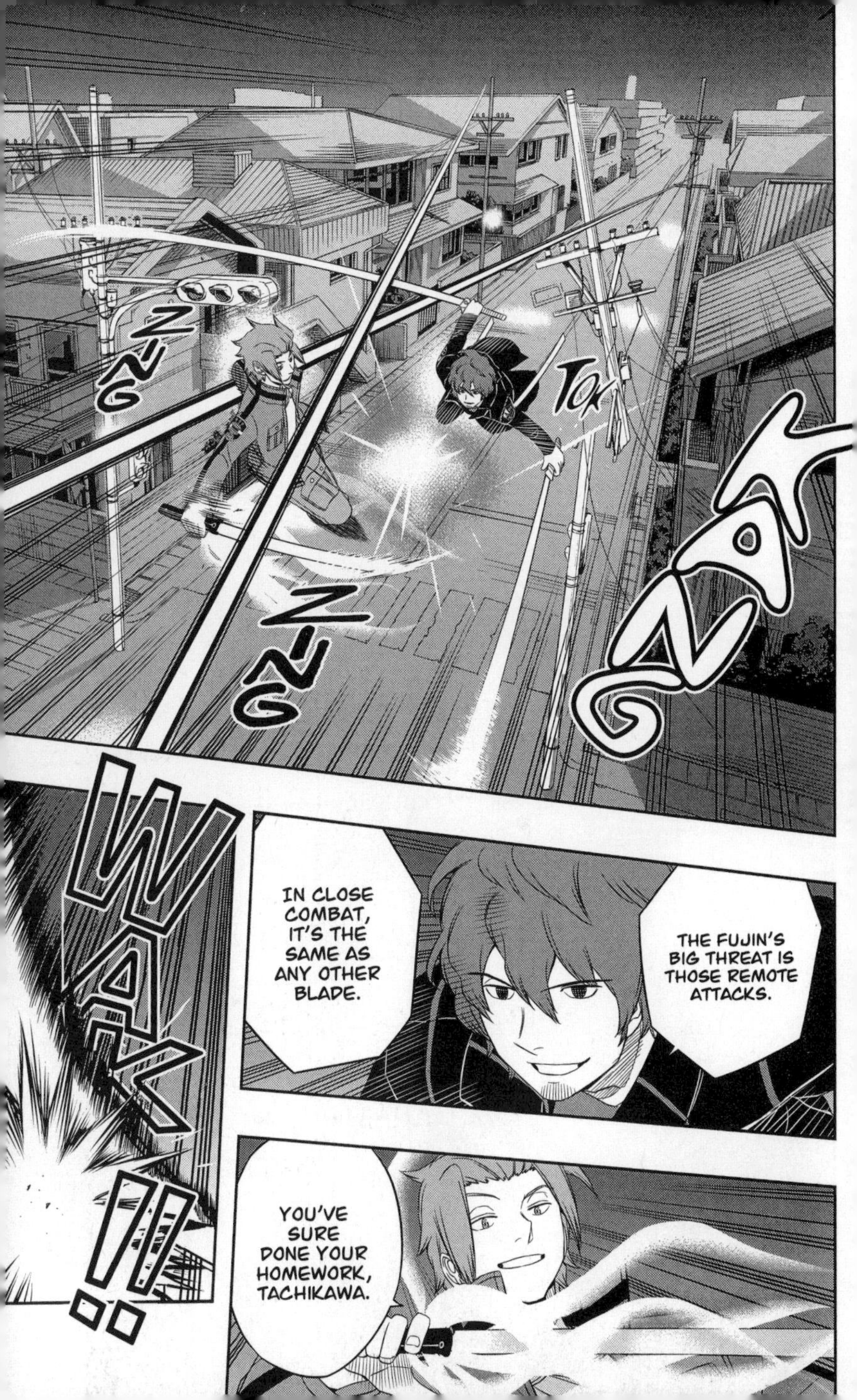
GZAT
TOK
ZING
ZING
THE FUJIN'S BIG THREAT IS THOSE REMOTE ATTACKS.
IN CLOSE COMBAT, IT'S THE SAME AS ANY OTHER BLADE.
YOU'VE SURE DONE YOUR HOMEWORK, TACHIKAWA.
WAK!!

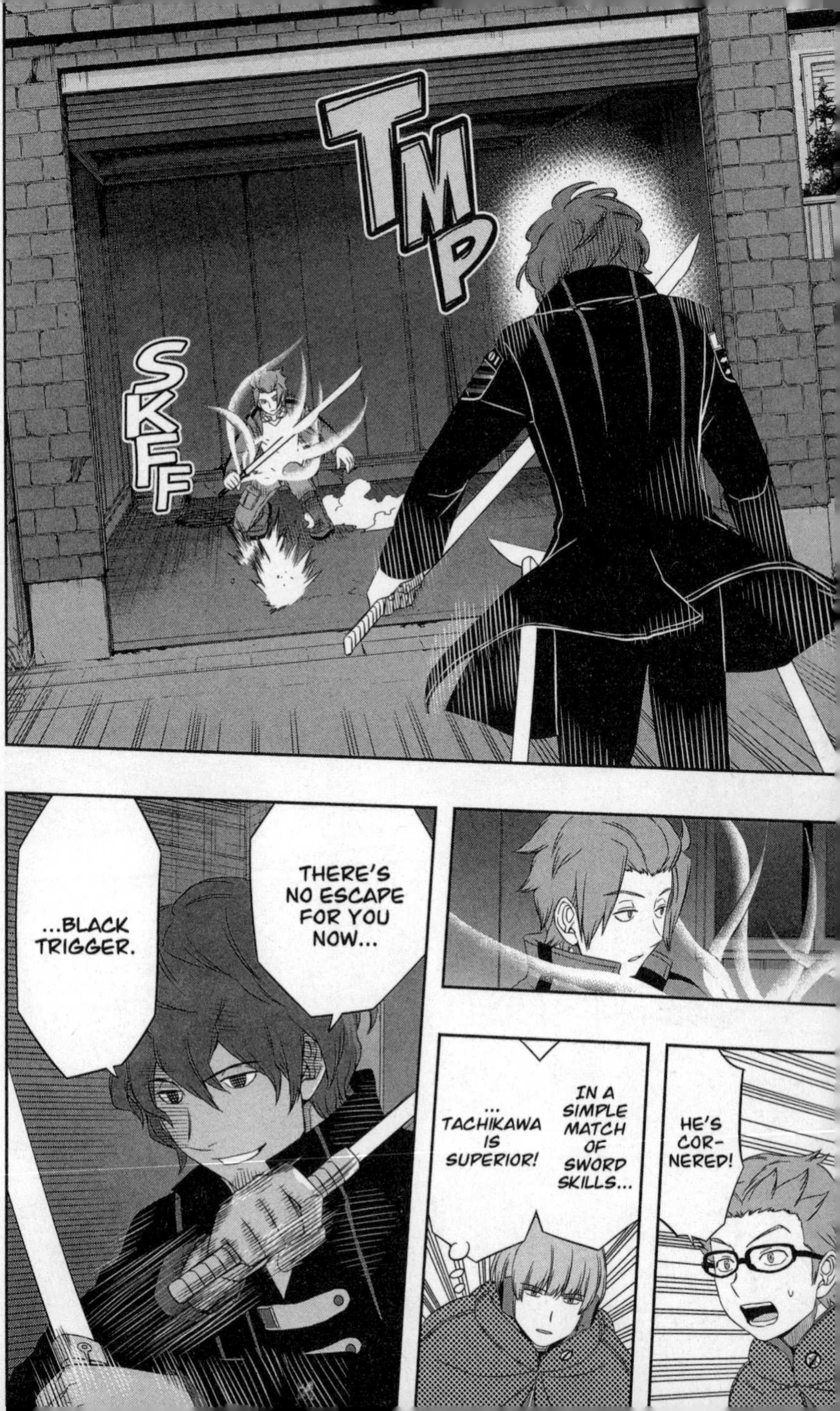

TMP
SKFF
HE'S COR-NERED!
IN A SIMPLE MATCH OF SWORD SKILLS...
...TACHIKAWA IS SUPERIOR!
THERE'S NO ESCAPE FOR YOU NOW...
...BLACK TRIGGER.

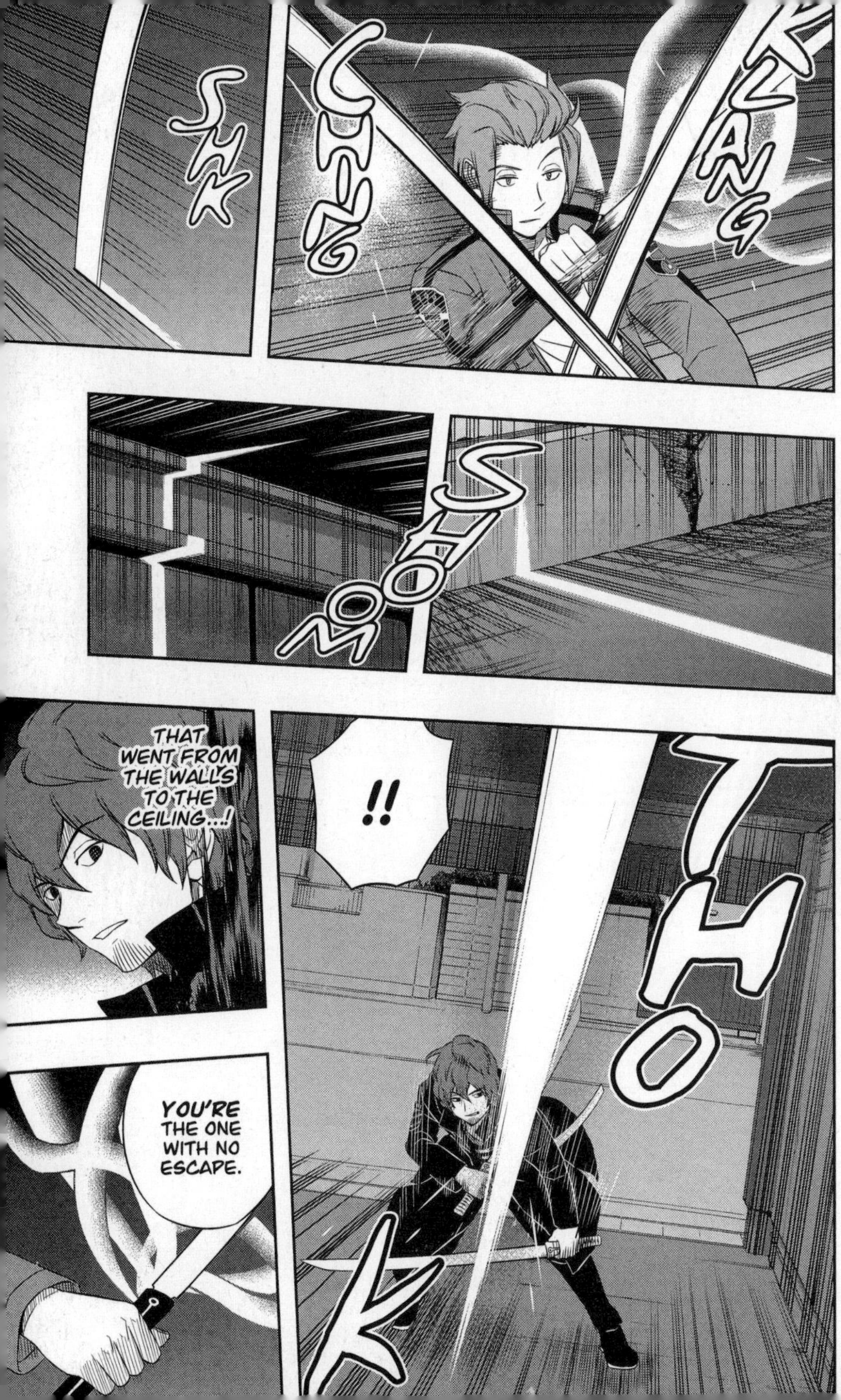
KLANG
CHING
SHK
SHOOM
THOK
!!
THAT WENT FROM THE WALLS TO THE CEILING...!
YOU'RE THE ONE WITH NO ESCAPE.

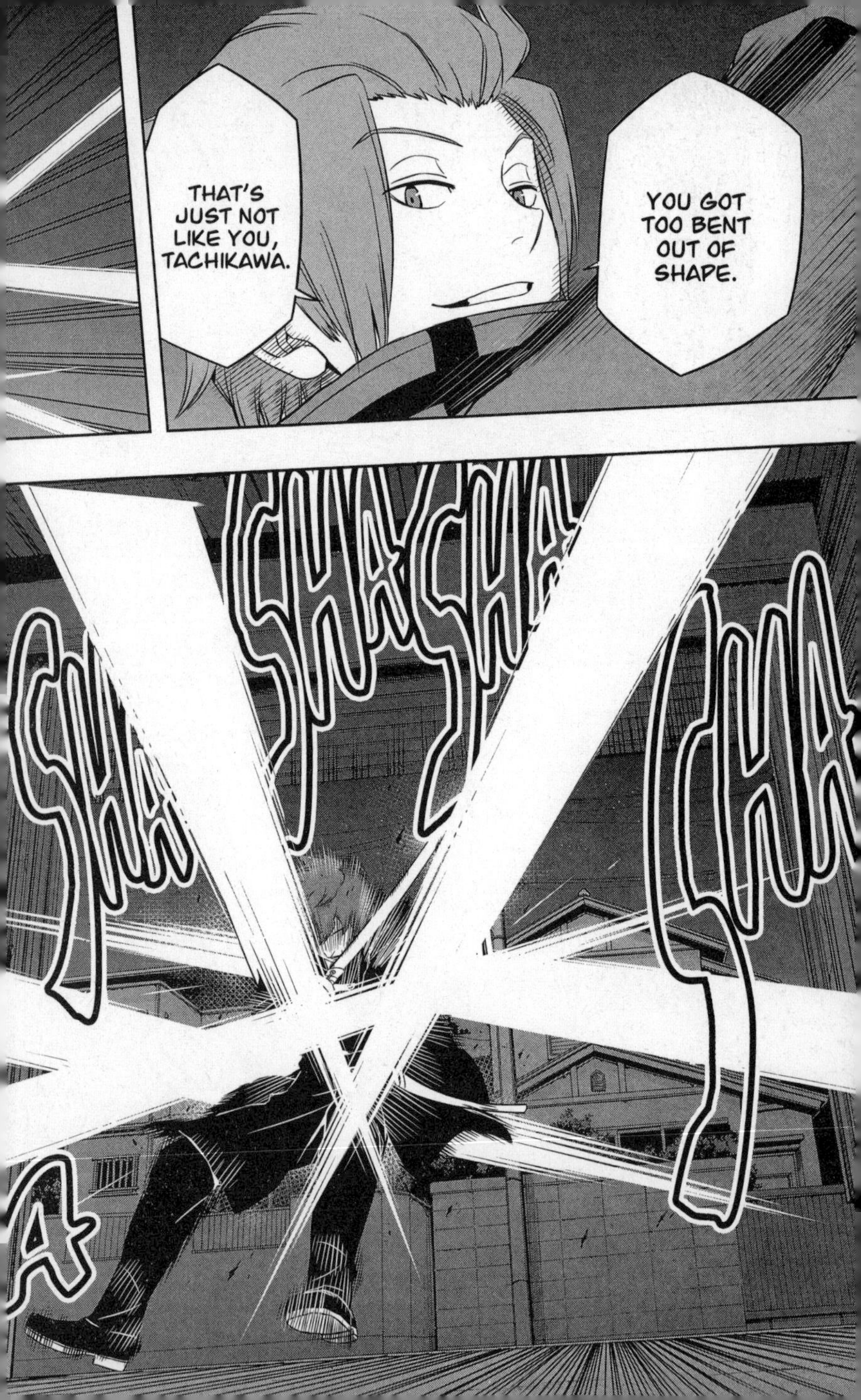
YOU GOT TOO BENT OUT OF SHAPE.
THAT'S JUST NOT LIKE YOU, TACHIKAWA.

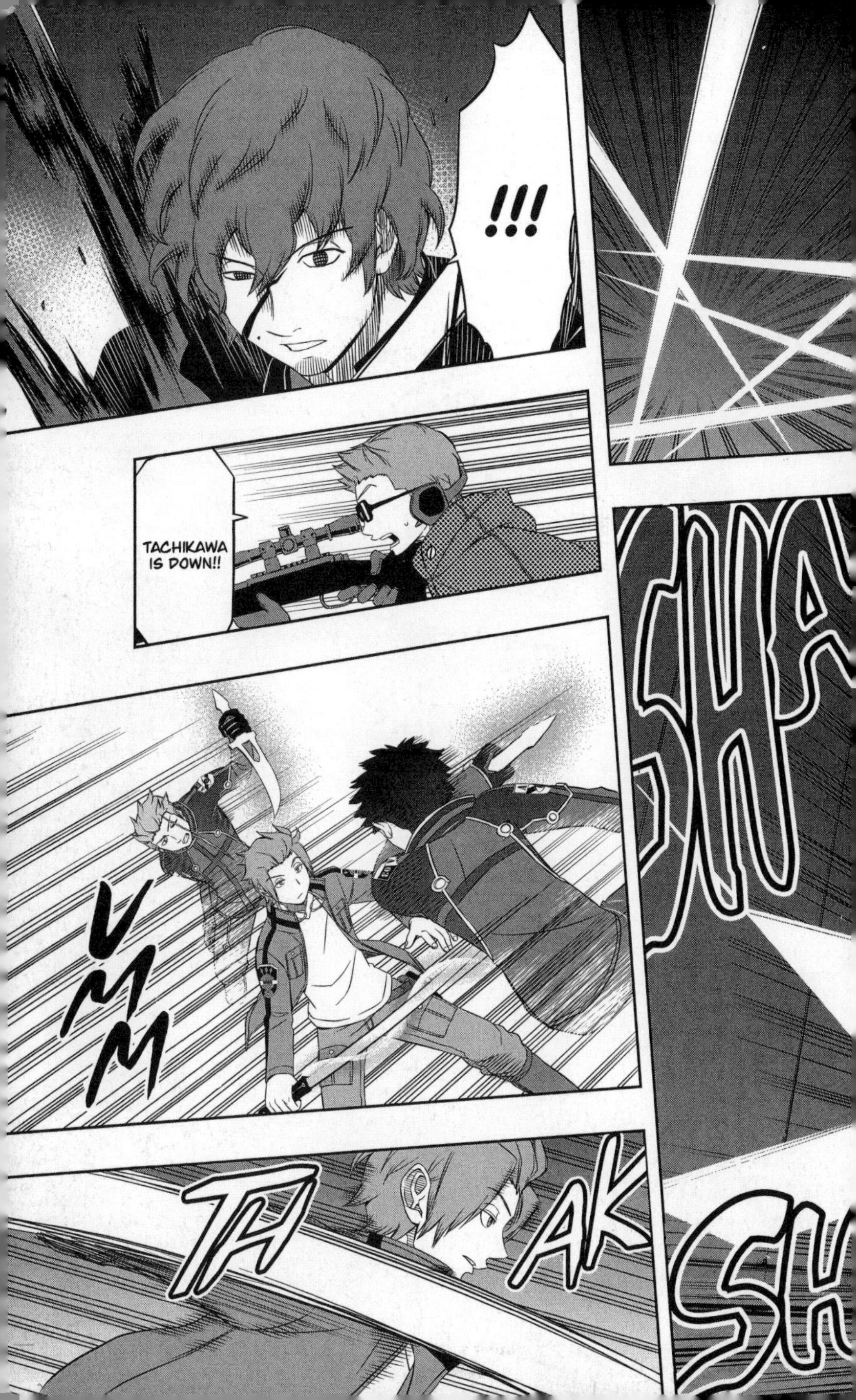
!!!
SHA
TACHIKAWA IS DOWN!!
VMMM
THAK
SH

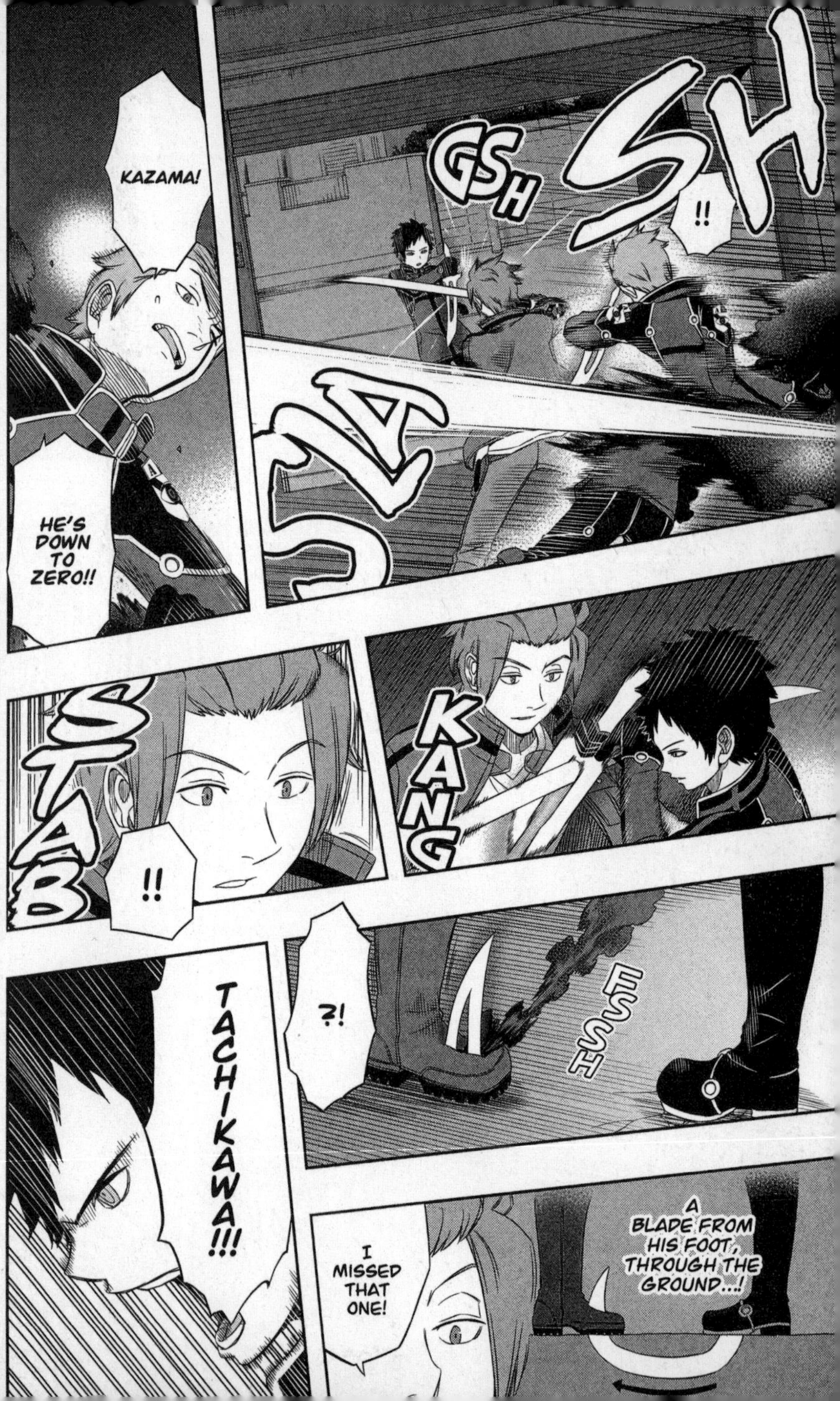
GSH
SH
!!
KAZAMA!
HE'S DOWN TO ZERO!!
KANG
STAB
!!
?!
FSSH
A BLADE FROM HIS FOOT, THROUGH THE GROUND...!
I MISSED THAT ONE!
TACHIKAWA!!!

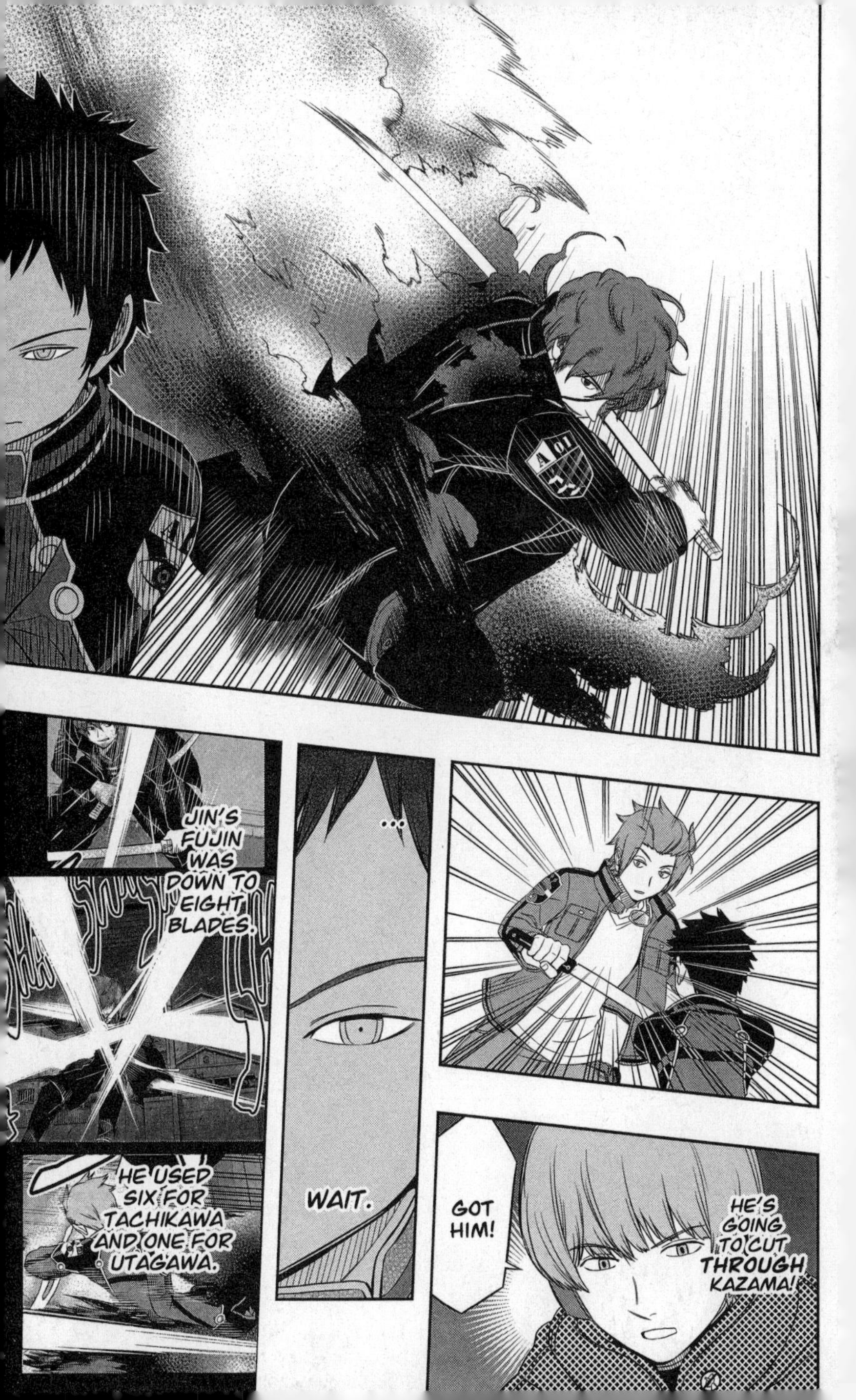
HE'S GOING TO CUT THROUGH KAZAMA!
GOT HIM!
...
WAIT.
JIN'S FUJIN WAS DOWN TO EIGHT BLADES.
HE USED SIX FOR TACHIKAWA AND ONE FOR UTAGAWA.

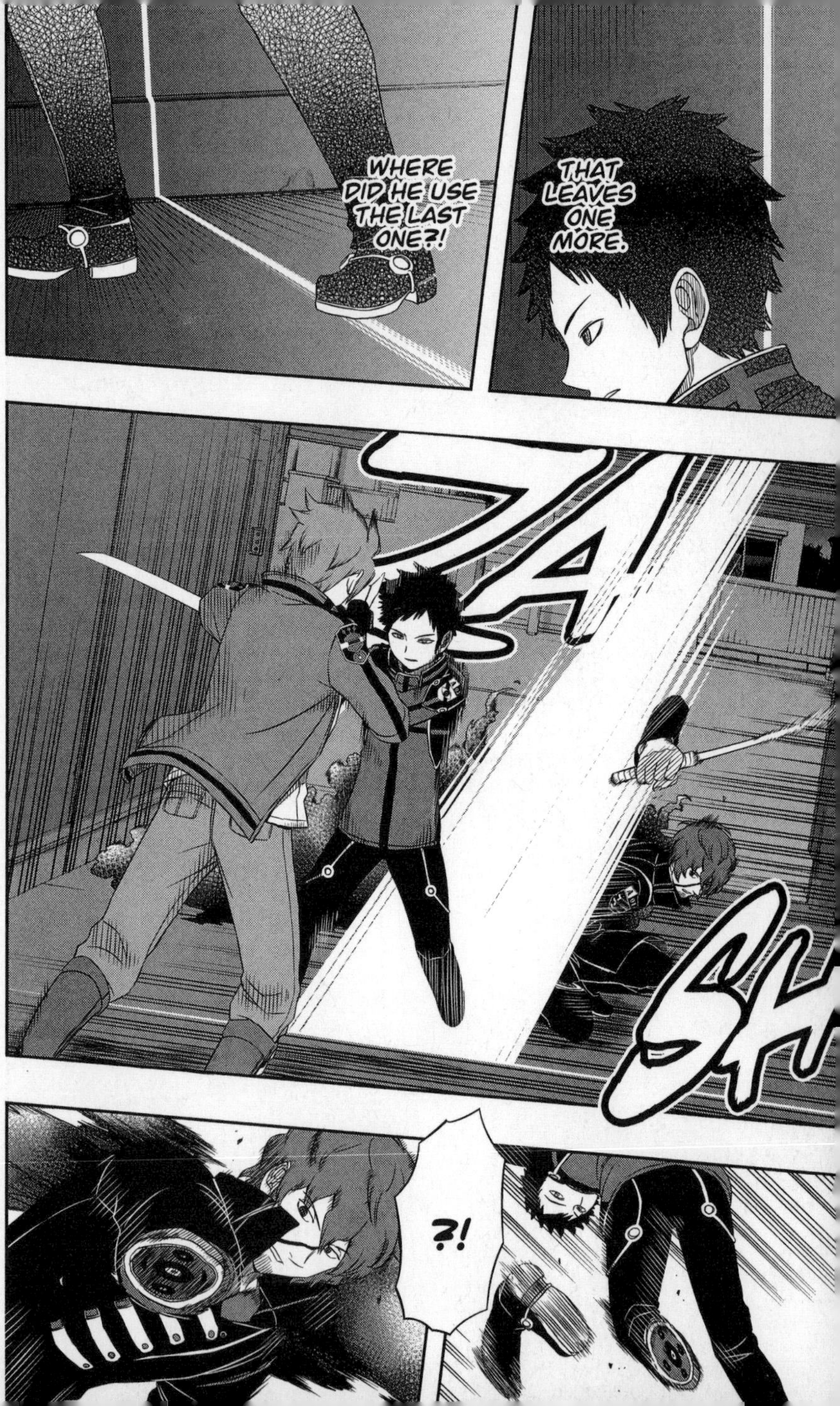
THAT LEAVES ONE MORE.
WHERE DID HE USE THE LAST ONE?!
ZA
?!

READ THIS WAY

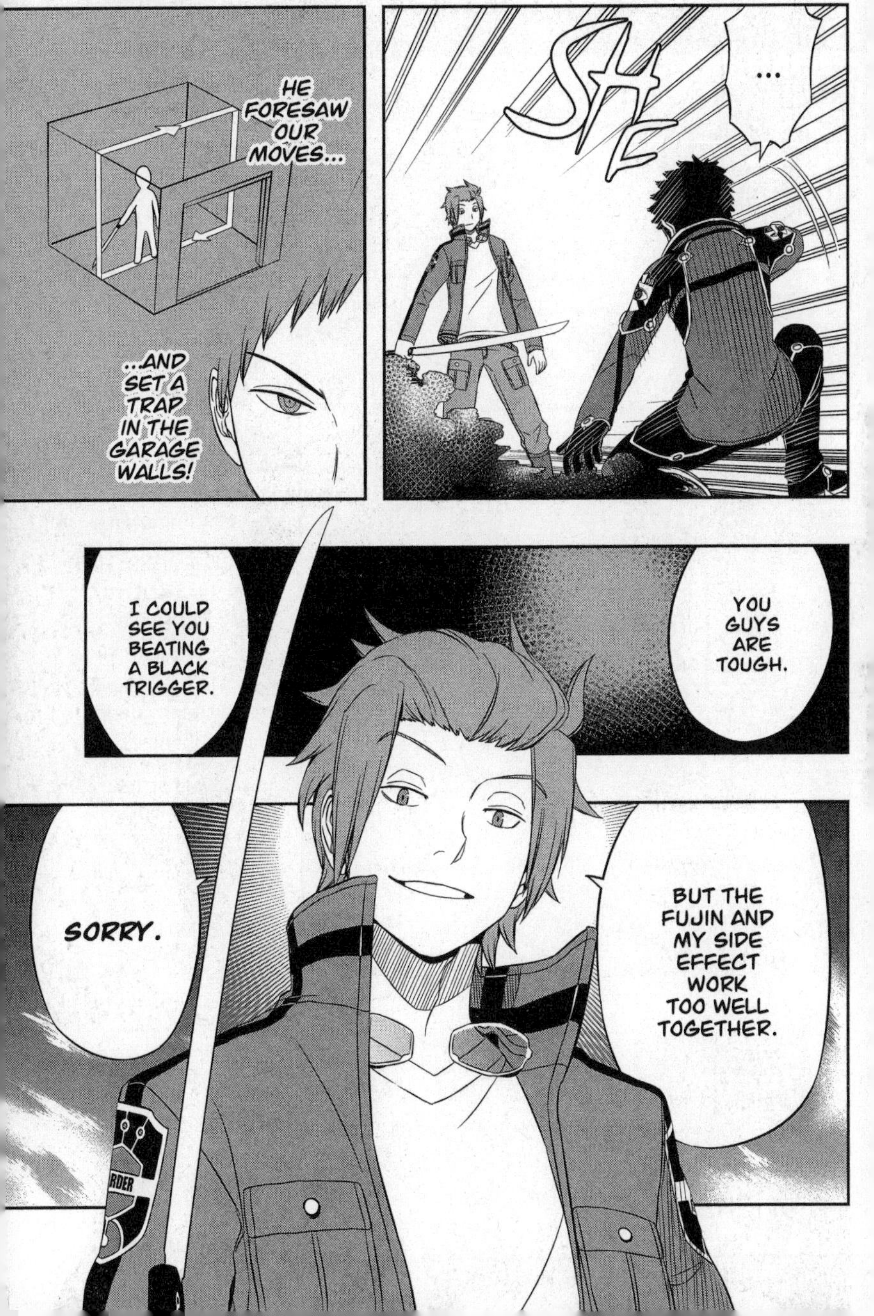

SH
...
HE FORESAW OUR MOVES...
...AND SET A TRAP IN THE GARAGE WALLS!
YOU GUYS ARE TOUGH.
I COULD SEE YOU BEATING A BLACK TRIGGER.
BUT THE FUJIN AND MY SIDE EFFECT WORK TOO WELL TOGETHER.
SORRY.

Rejected Storyboard

Following unsteady footprints

Chapter 4 Reject

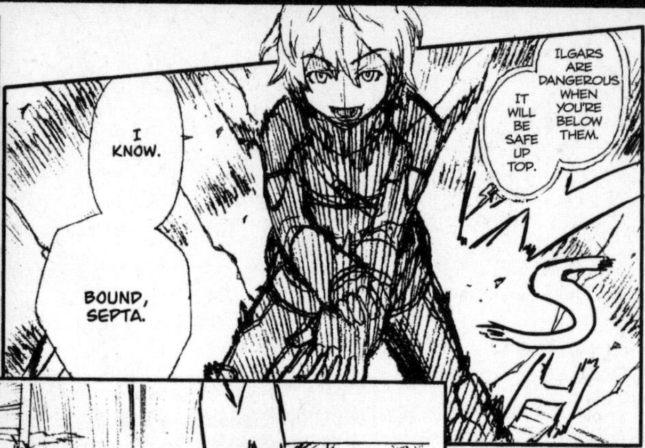
ILGARS ARE DANGEROUS WHEN YOU'RE BELOW THEM.
IT WILL BE SAFE UP TOP.
I KNOW.
BOUND, SEPTA.

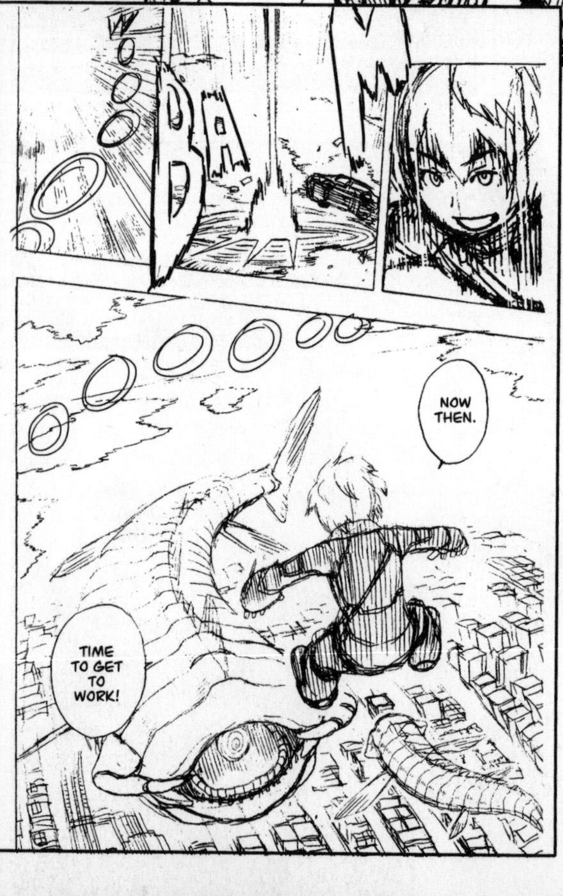
NOW THEN.
TIME TO GET TO WORK!

Another first draft, just like last volume. An Ilgar was supposed to show up at the end of chapter 3 and get defeated in chapter 4. Since Kitora hadn't appeared yet, Yuma did the aerial combat. The way Osamu helps civilian evacuation was the same. I had Jin show up at the end of this chapter. There was a lot of action and twists, and my editor liked it. But there was too much action and not enough character development, so it was rejected. The ideas and layouts were used later, so it wasn't a total waste.

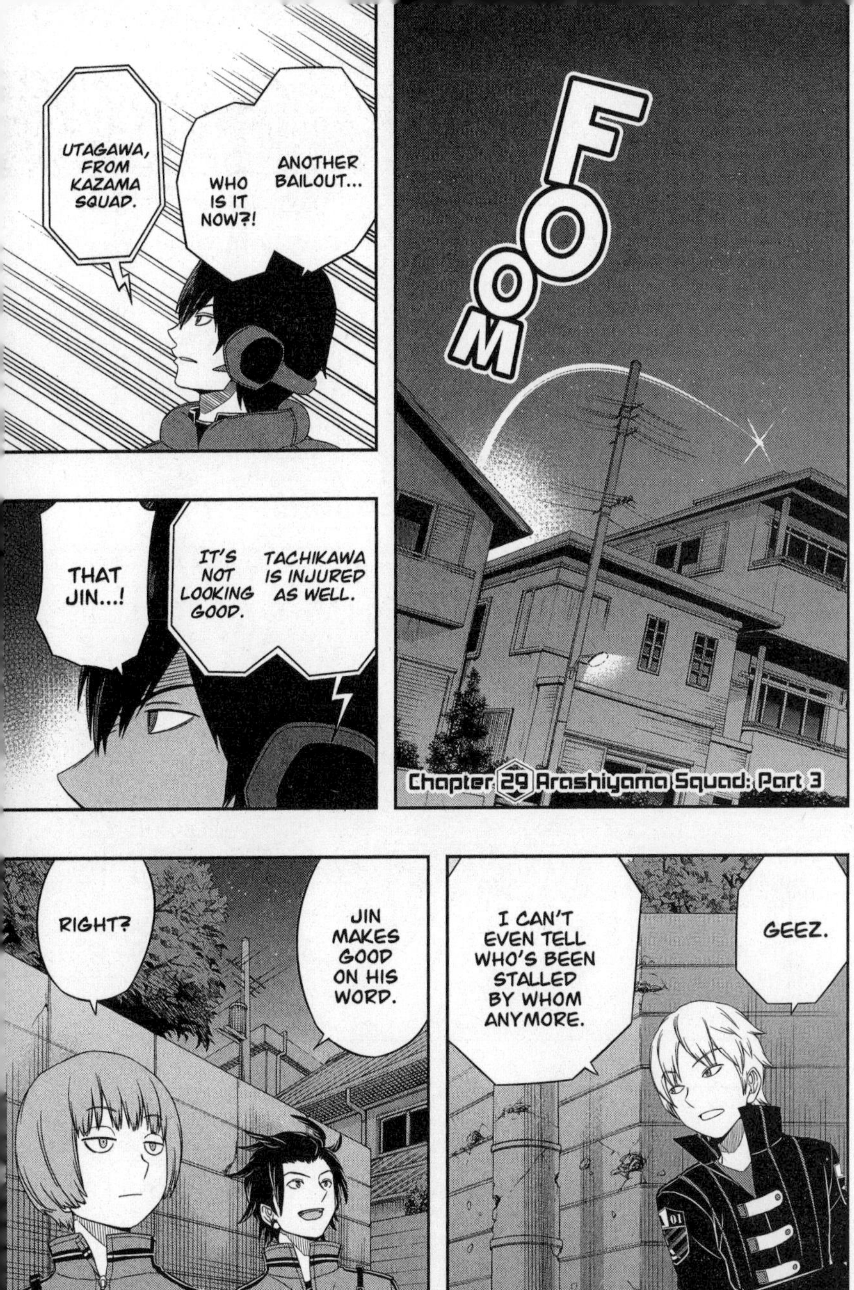
FOOM
Chapter 29 Arashiyama Squad: Part 3
ANOTHER BAILOUT... WHO IS IT NOW?!
UTAGAWA, FROM KAZAMA SQUAD.
TACHIKAWA IS INJURED AS WELL. IT'S NOT LOOKING GOOD.
THAT JIN...!
GEEZ.
I CAN'T EVEN TELL WHO'S BEEN STALLED BY WHOM ANYMORE.
JIN MAKES GOOD ON HIS WORD.
RIGHT?

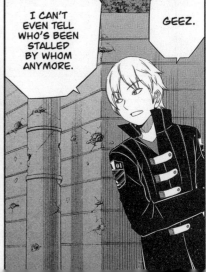

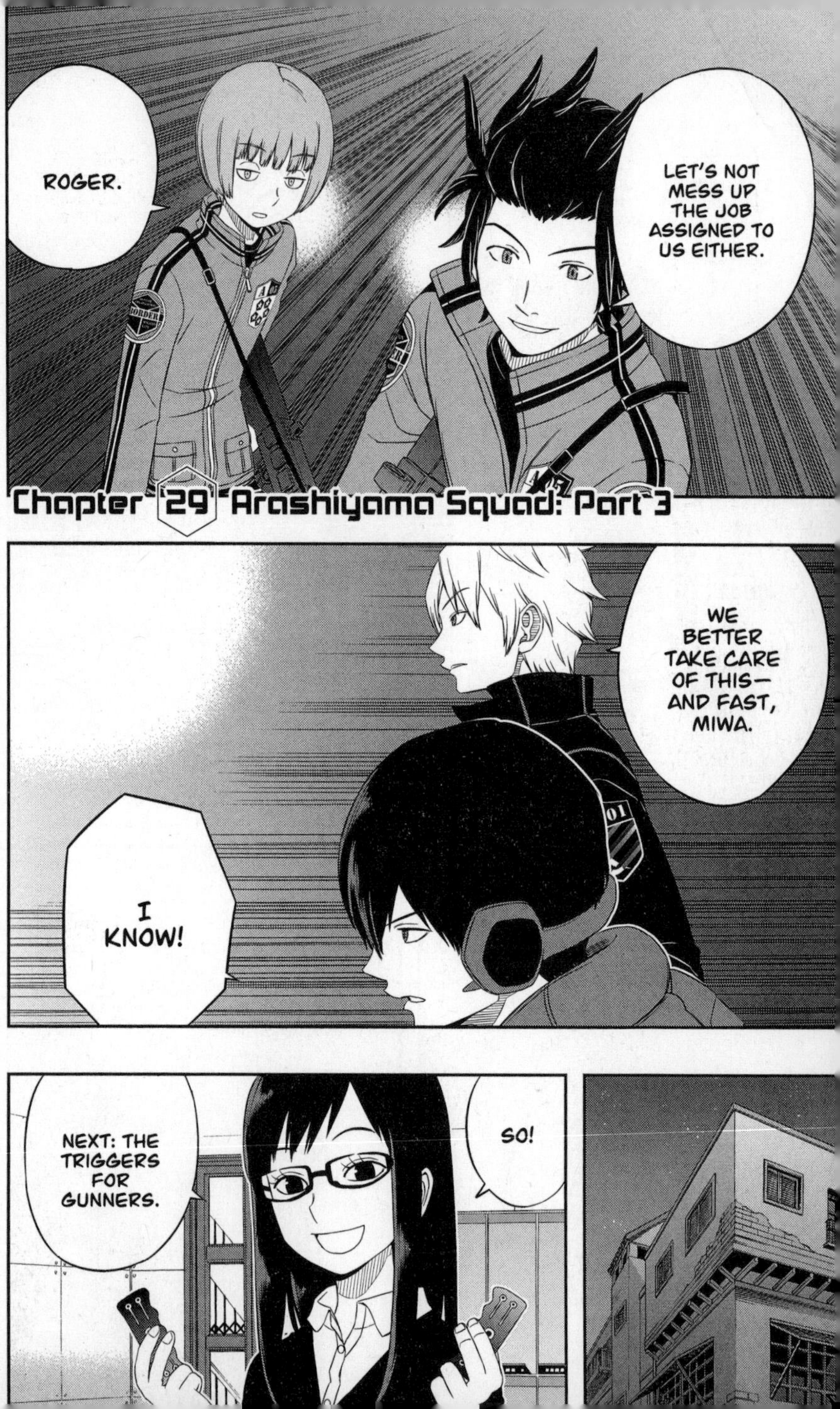
LET'S NOT MESS UP THE JOB ASSIGNED TO US EITHER.
ROGER.
Chapter 29 Arashiyama Squad: Part 3
WE BETTER TAKE CARE OF THIS—AND FAST, MIWA.
I KNOW!
SO!
NEXT: THE TRIGGERS FOR GUNNERS.

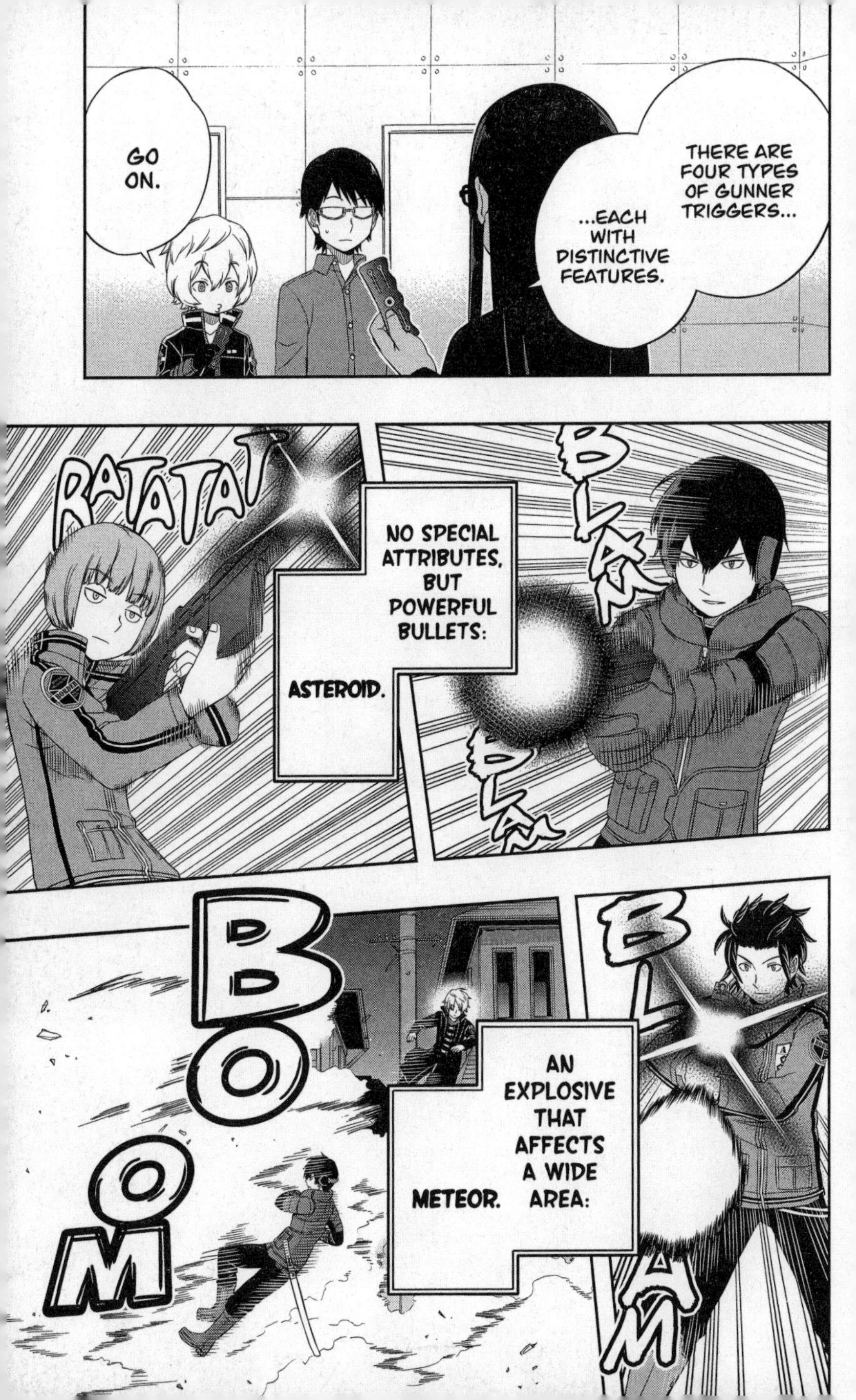
THERE ARE FOUR TYPES OF GUNNER TRIGGERS...
...EACH WITH DISTINCTIVE FEATURES.
GO ON.
BLAM
BLAM
NO SPECIAL ATTRIBUTES, BUT POWERFUL BULLETS:
ASTEROID.
RATATAT
BLAM
AN EXPLOSIVE THAT AFFECTS A WIDE AREA:
METEOR.
BOOOM

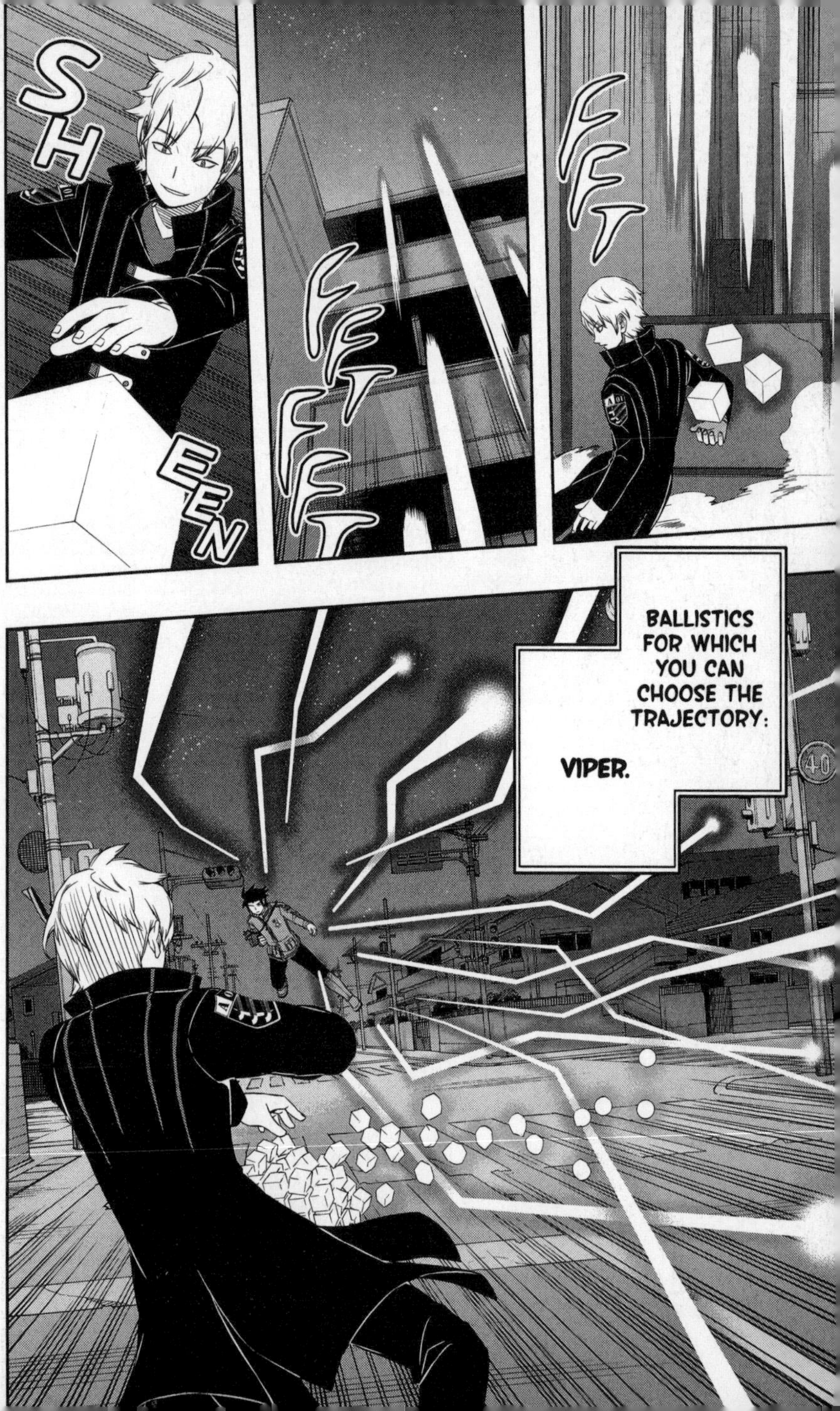
FFT
FFT
FFT
SHEEN
BALLISTICS FOR WHICH YOU CAN CHOOSE THE TRAJECTORY:
VIPER.

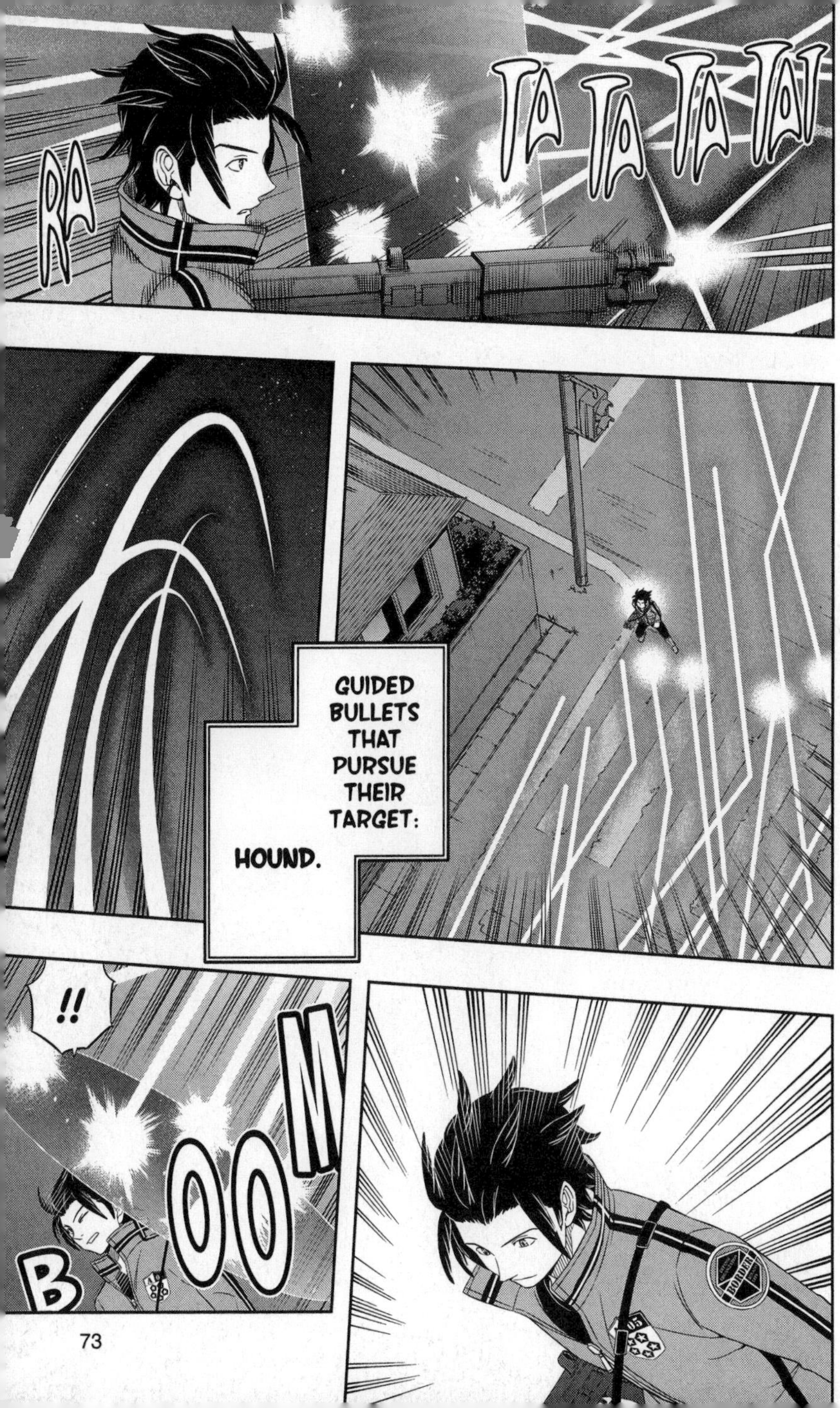
RA
TA TA TA TAT
GUIDED BULLETS THAT PURSUE THEIR TARGET:
HOUND.
BOOM
!!

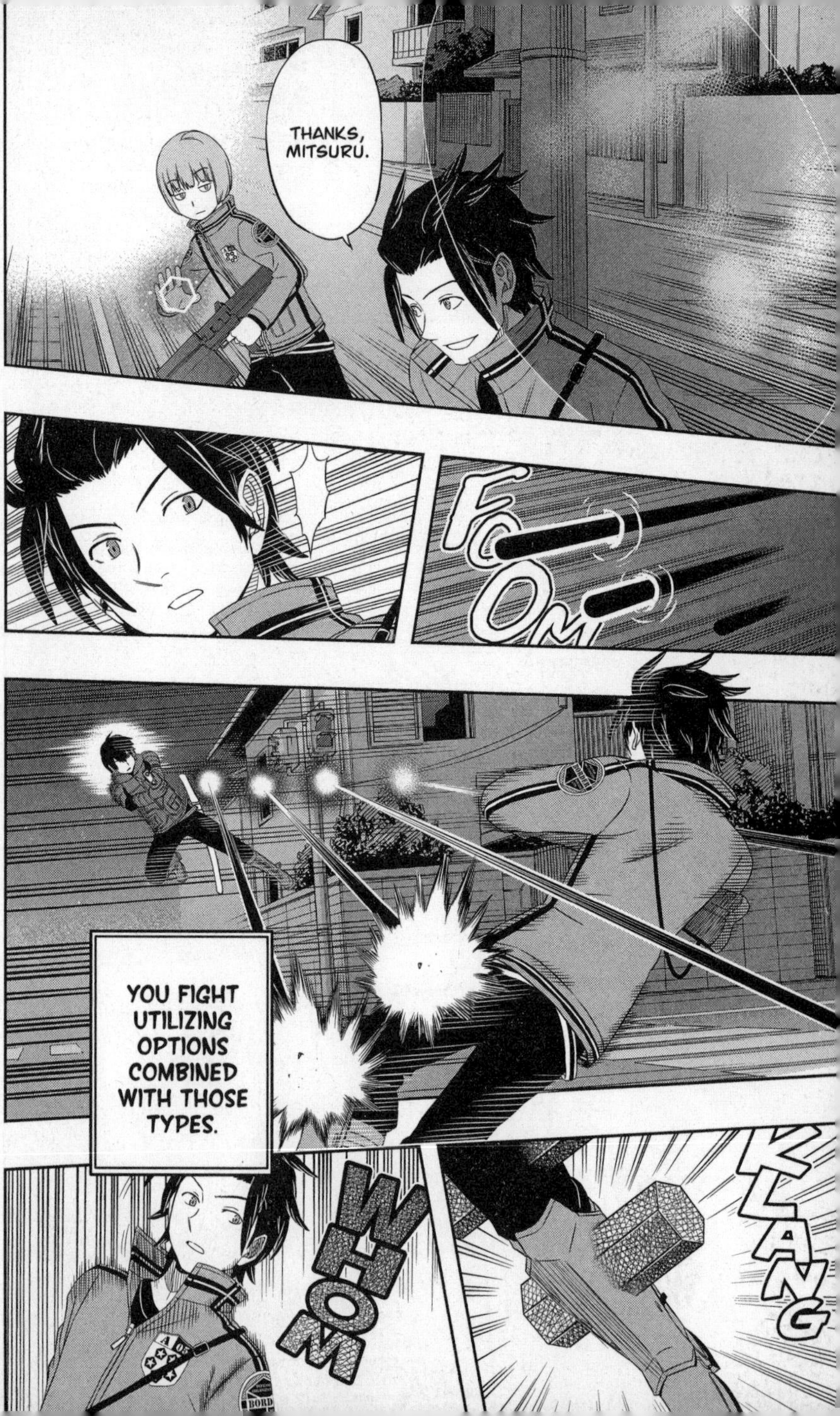
THANKS, MITSURU.
FOOM
YOU FIGHT UTILIZING OPTIONS COMBINED WITH THOSE TYPES.
KLANG
WHOM

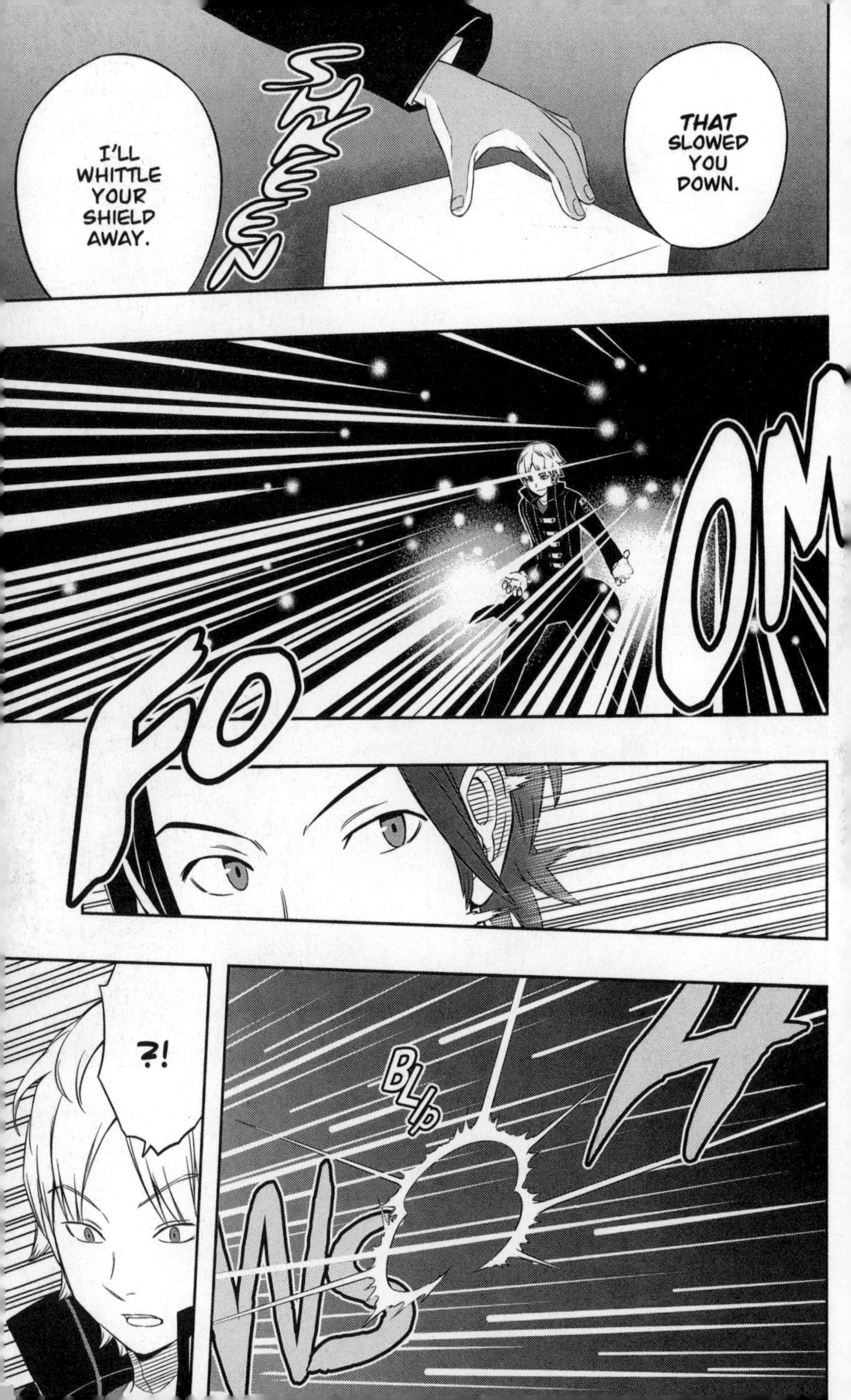
THAT SLOWED YOU DOWN.
SHEEEEN
I'LL WHITTLE YOUR SHIELD AWAY.
FOOM
BLIP
?!

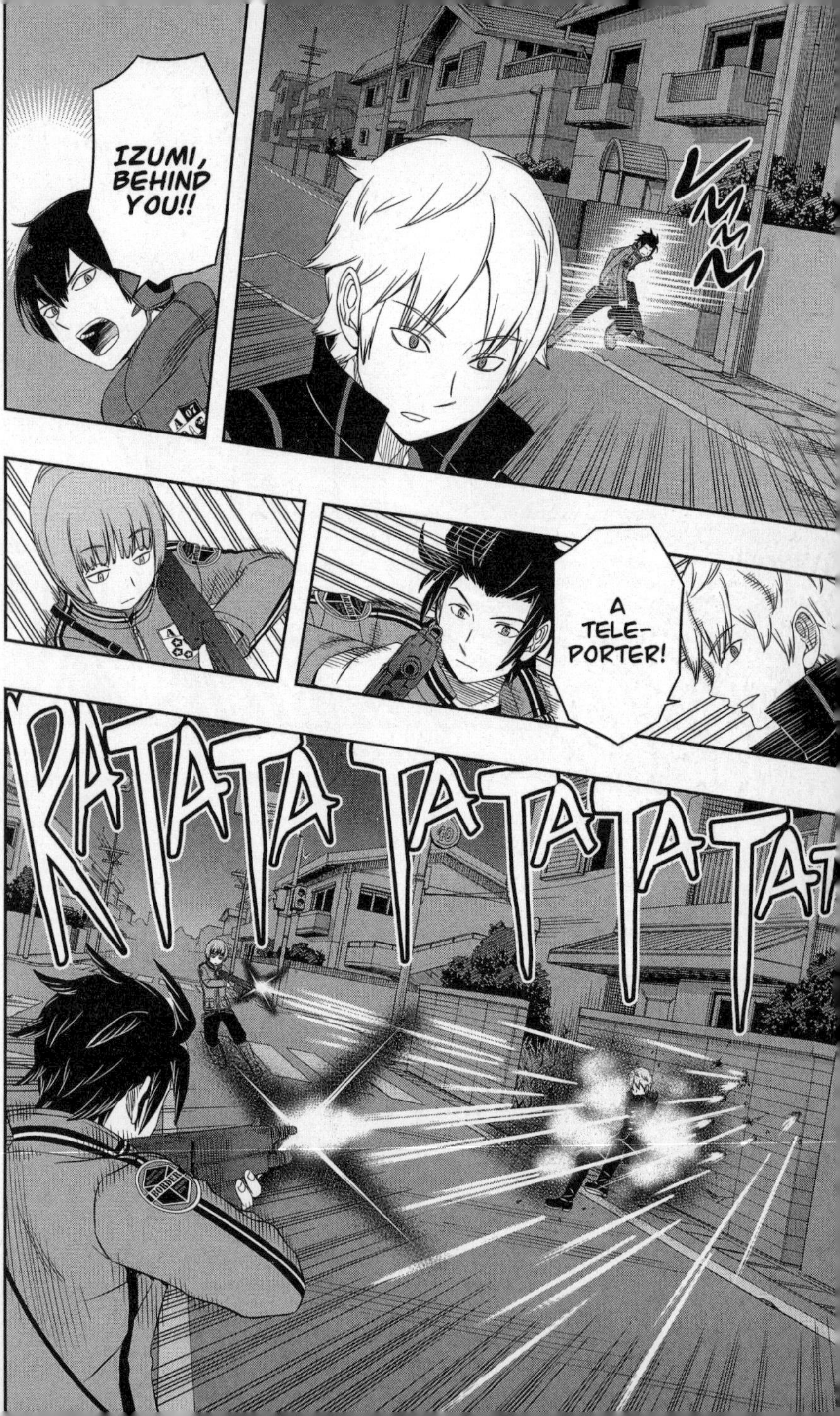
VMMM
IZUMI, BEHIND YOU!!
A TELE-PORTER!
RATATA TA TATATAT

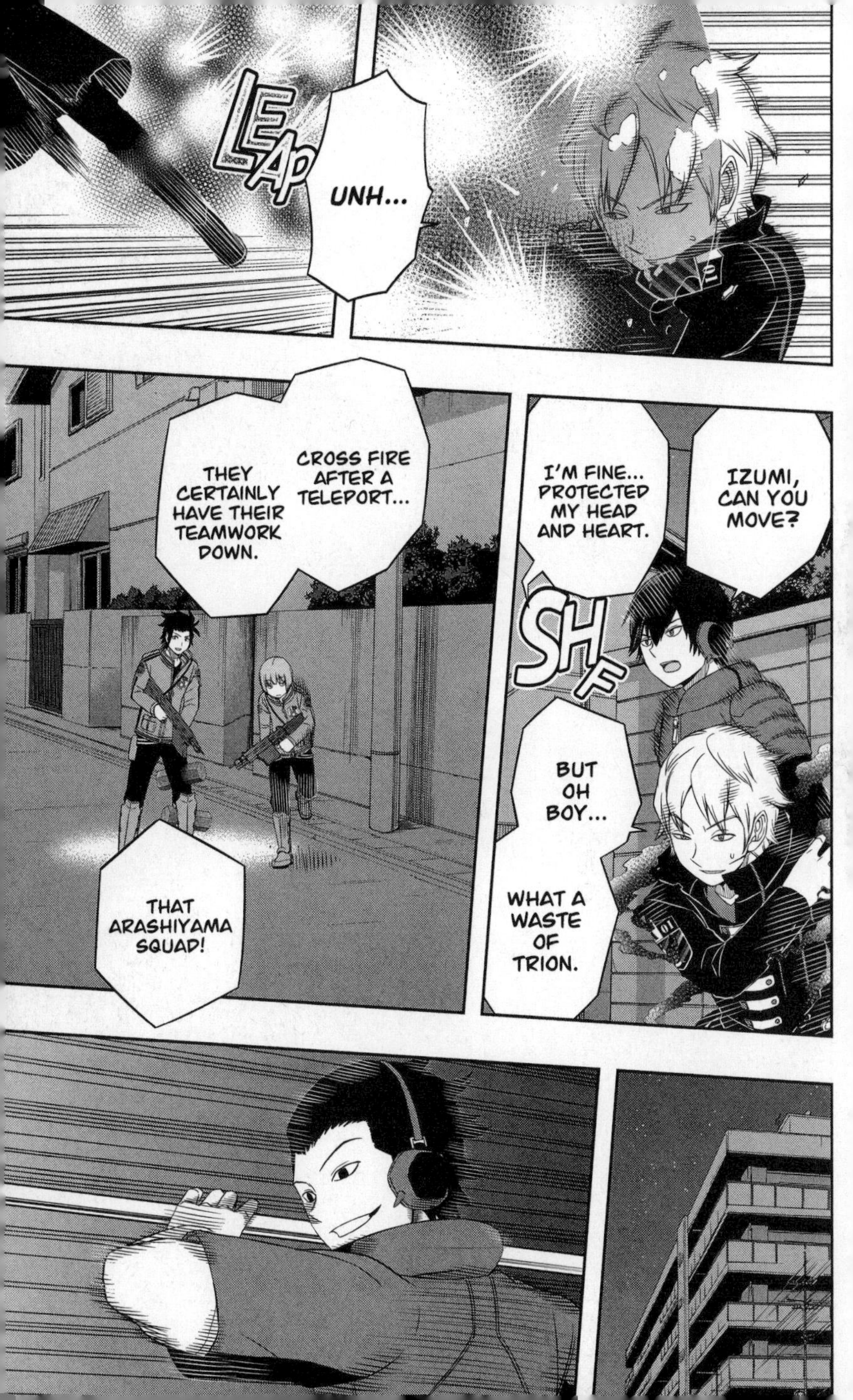
UNH...
LEAP
IZUMI, CAN YOU MOVE?
I'M FINE... PROTECTED MY HEAD AND HEART.
SHF
BUT OH BOY...
WHAT A WASTE OF TRION.
CROSS FIRE AFTER A TELEPORT...
THEY CERTAINLY HAVE THEIR TEAMWORK DOWN.
THAT ARASHIYAMA SQUAD!

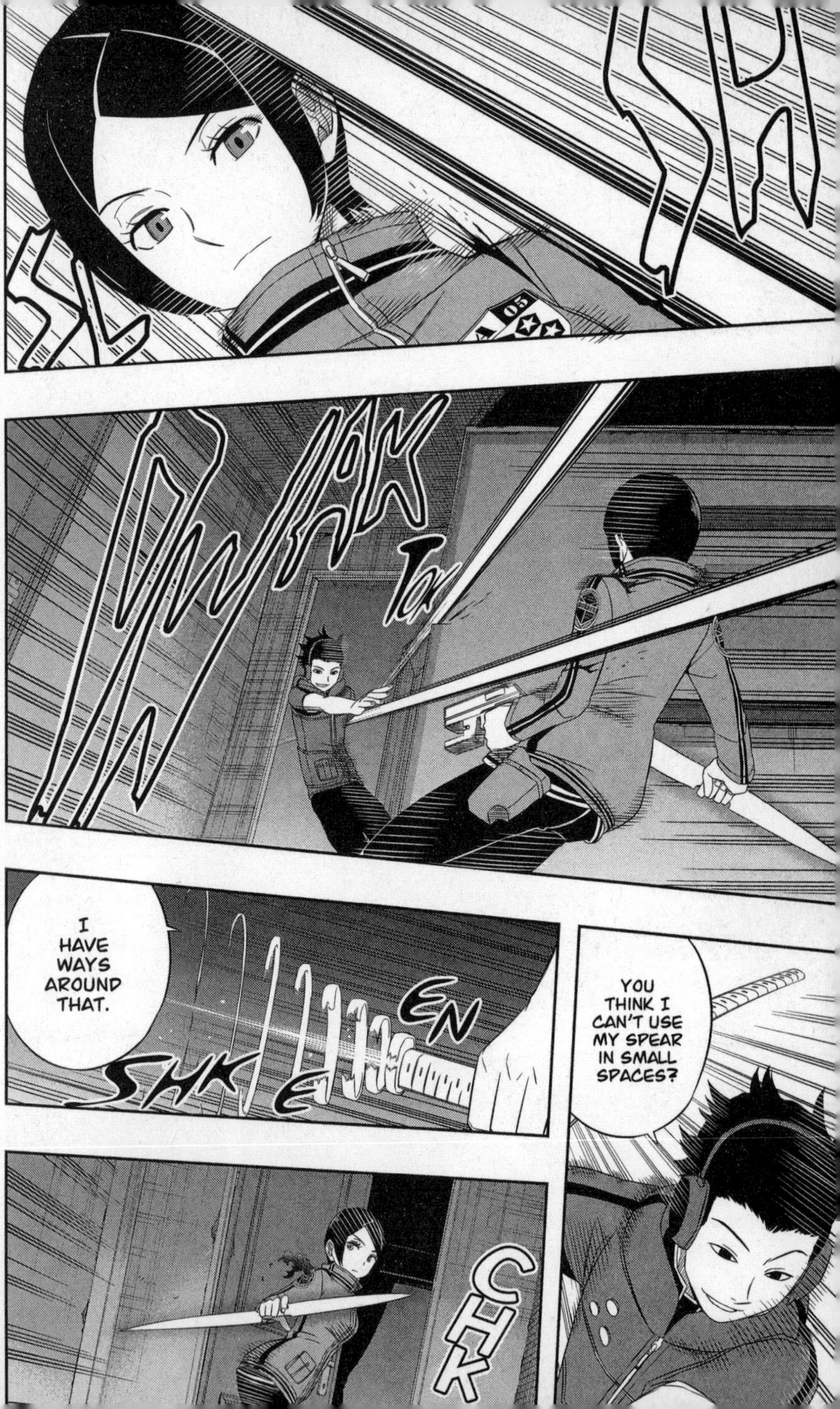
YOU THINK I CAN'T USE MY SPEAR IN SMALL SPACES?
I HAVE WAYS AROUND THAT.
CHK

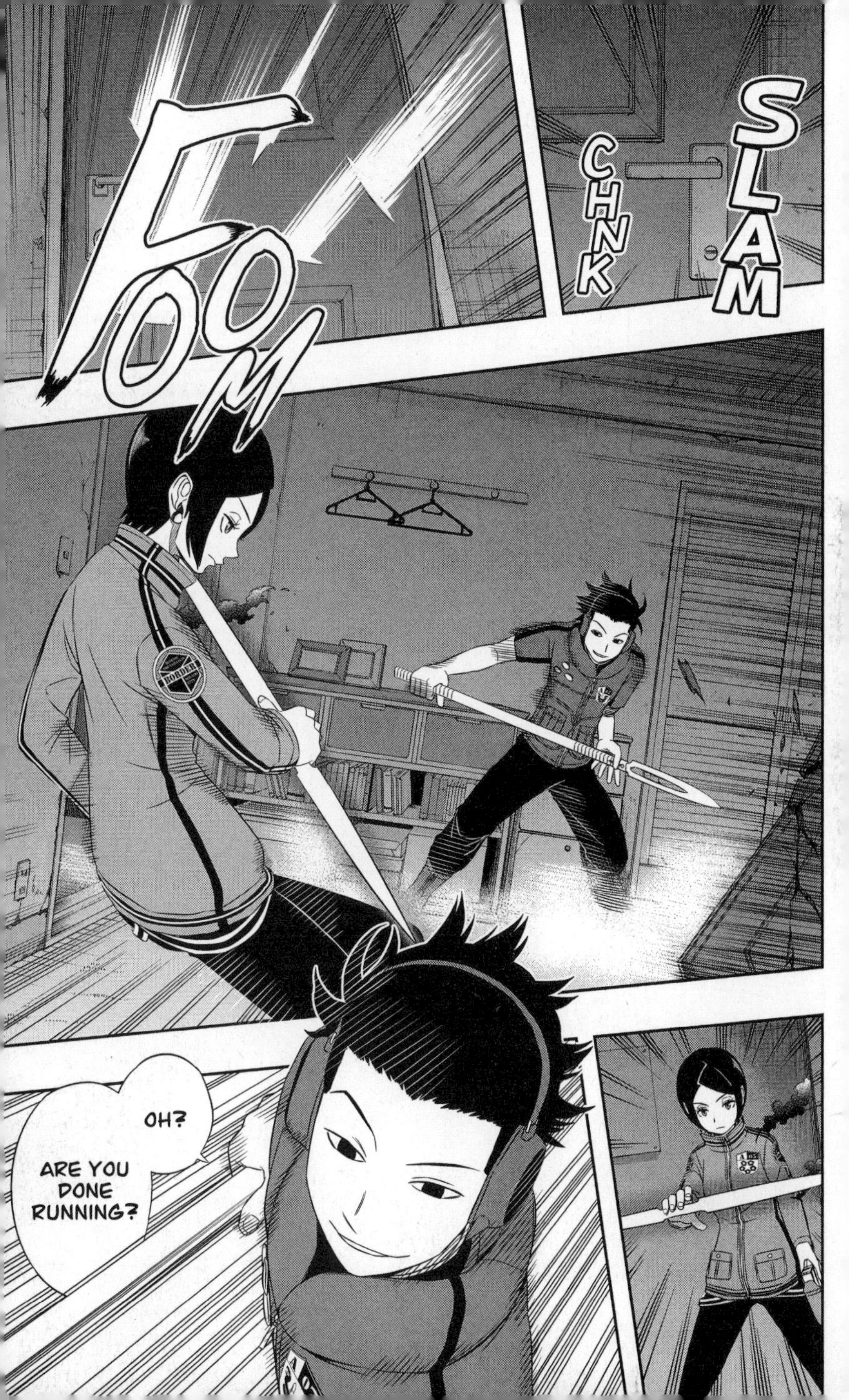
SLAM
CHNK
ZOOM
OH?
ARE YOU DONE RUNNING?

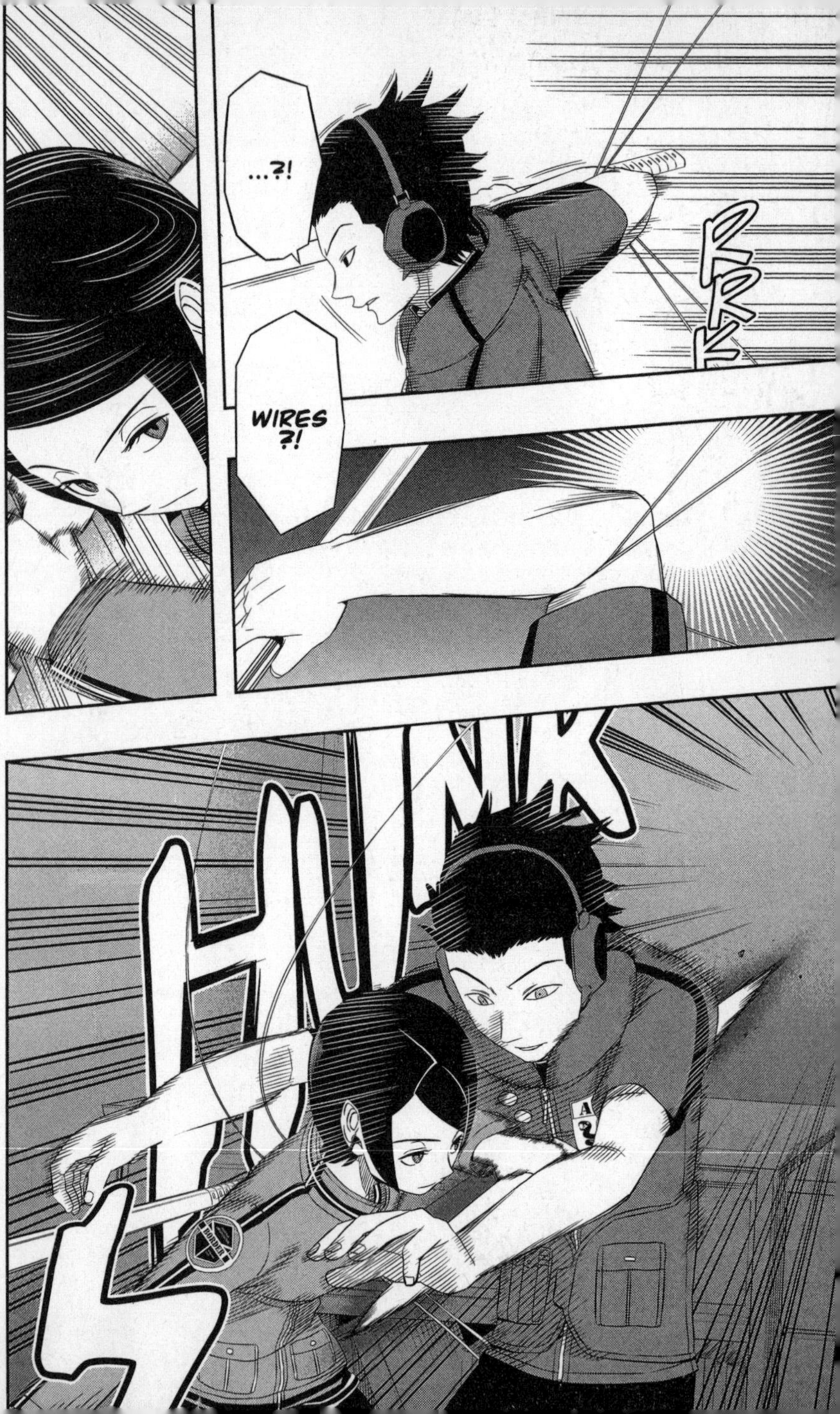
RRK
...?!
WIRES ?!
CHINK

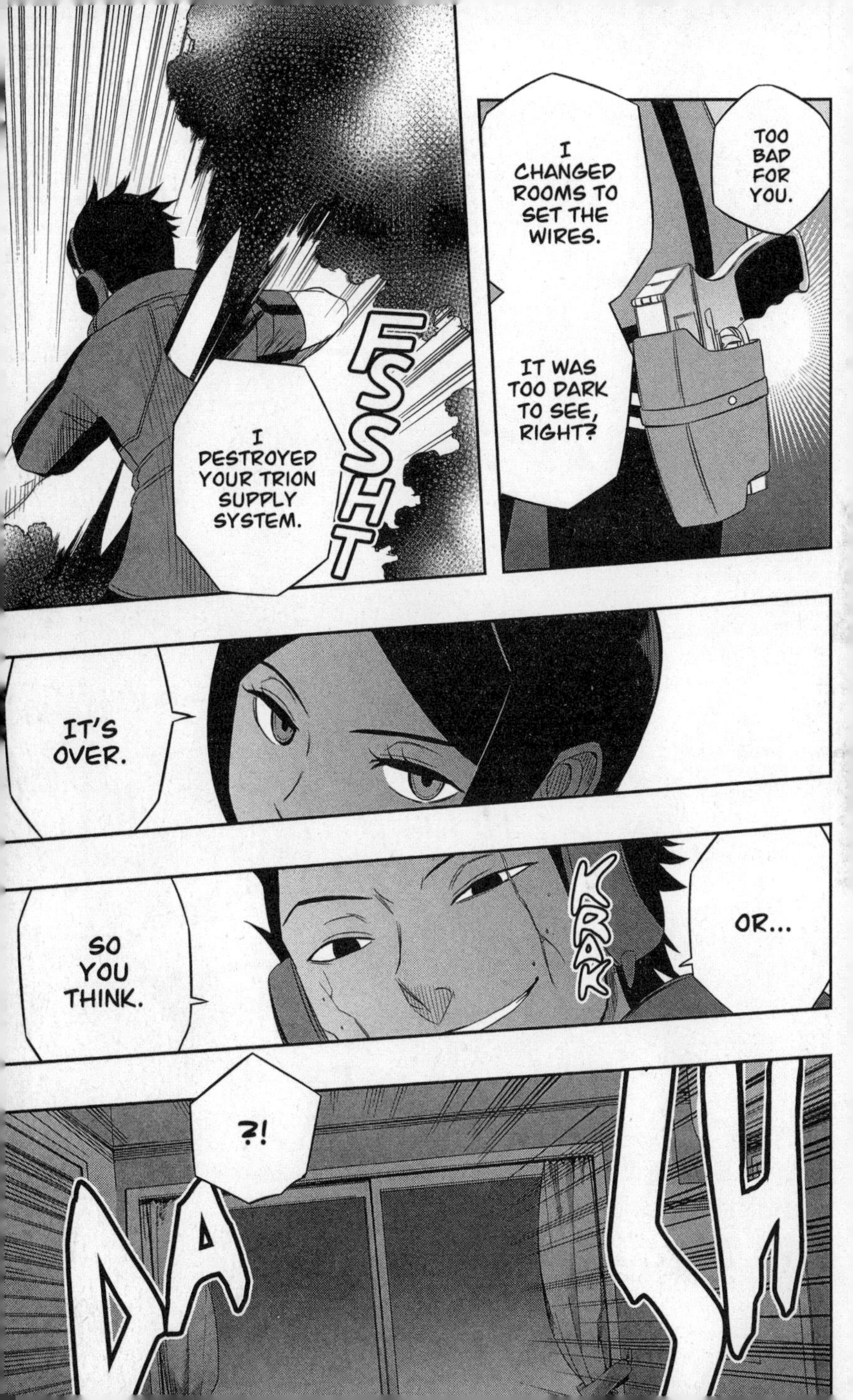
TOO BAD FOR YOU.
I CHANGED ROOMS TO SET THE WIRES.
IT WAS TOO DARK TO SEE, RIGHT?
FSSHT
I DESTROYED YOUR TRION SUPPLY SYSTEM.
IT'S OVER.
OR...
KRAK
SO YOU THINK.
?!
DASH

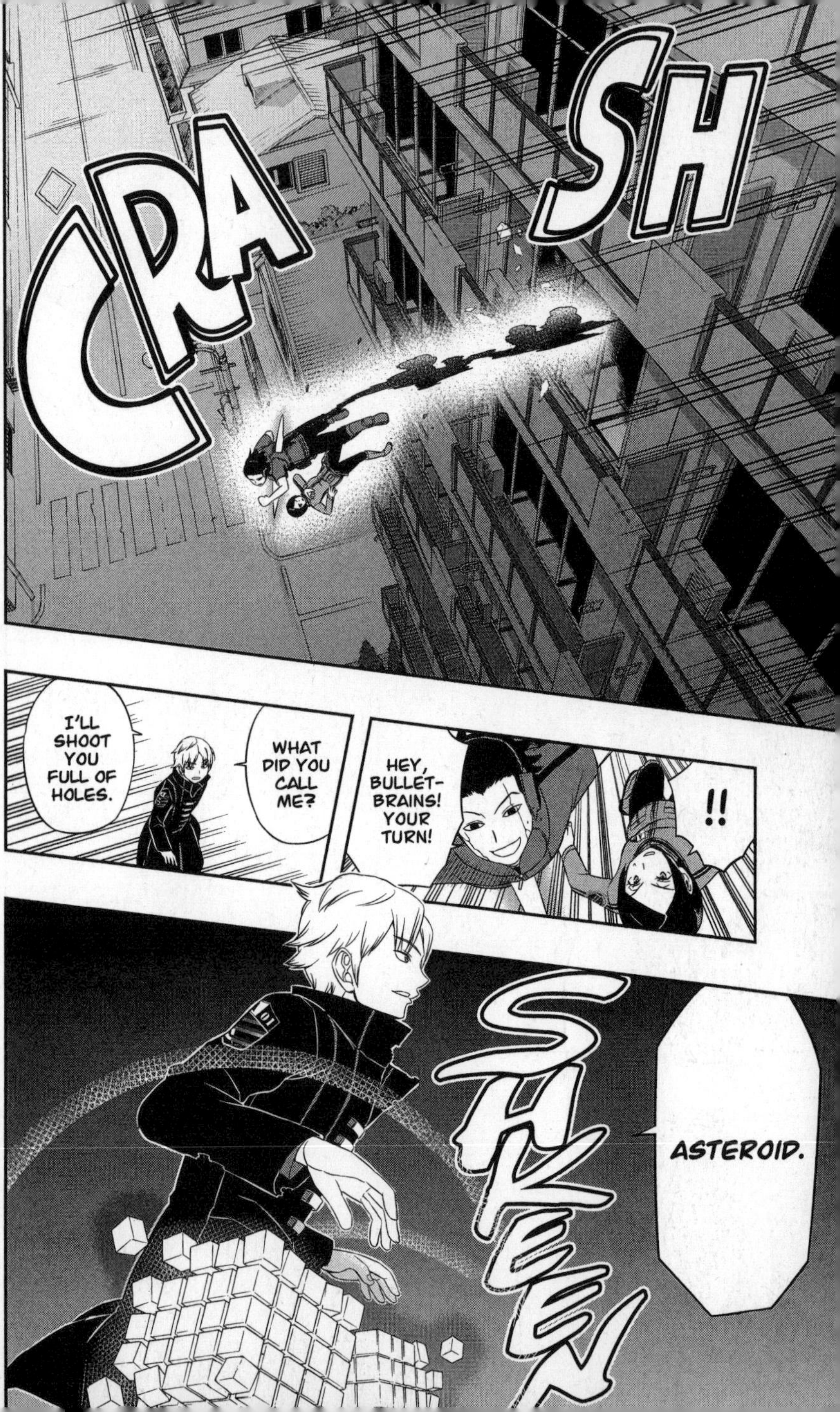
CRASH
!!
HEY, BULLET-BRAINS! YOUR TURN!
WHAT DID YOU CALL ME?
I'LL SHOOT YOU FULL OF HOLES.
ASTEROID.
SHKEEN

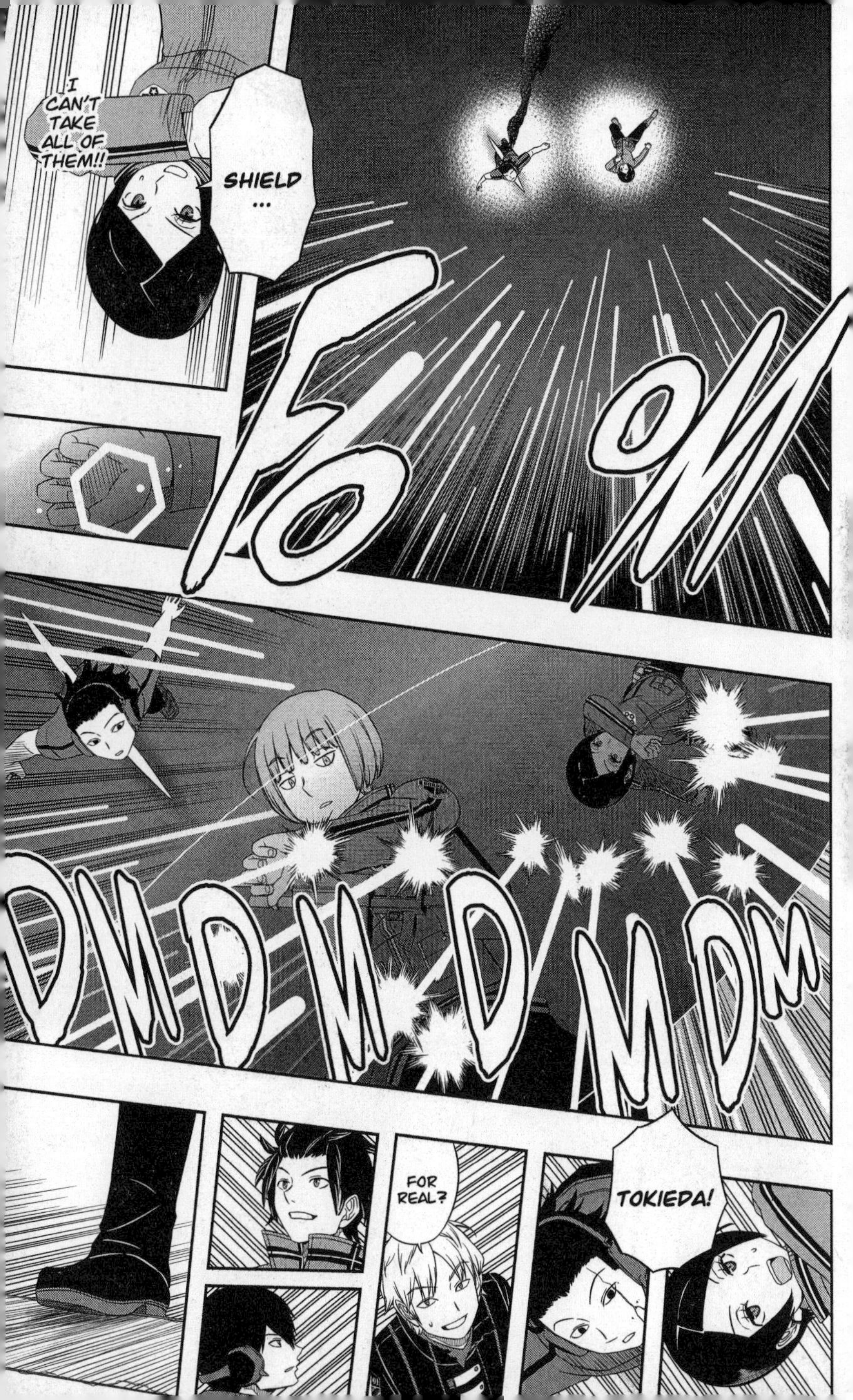
SHIELD ...
I CAN'T TAKE ALL OF THEM!!
DMDMDMDMDM
TOKIEDA!
FOR REAL?

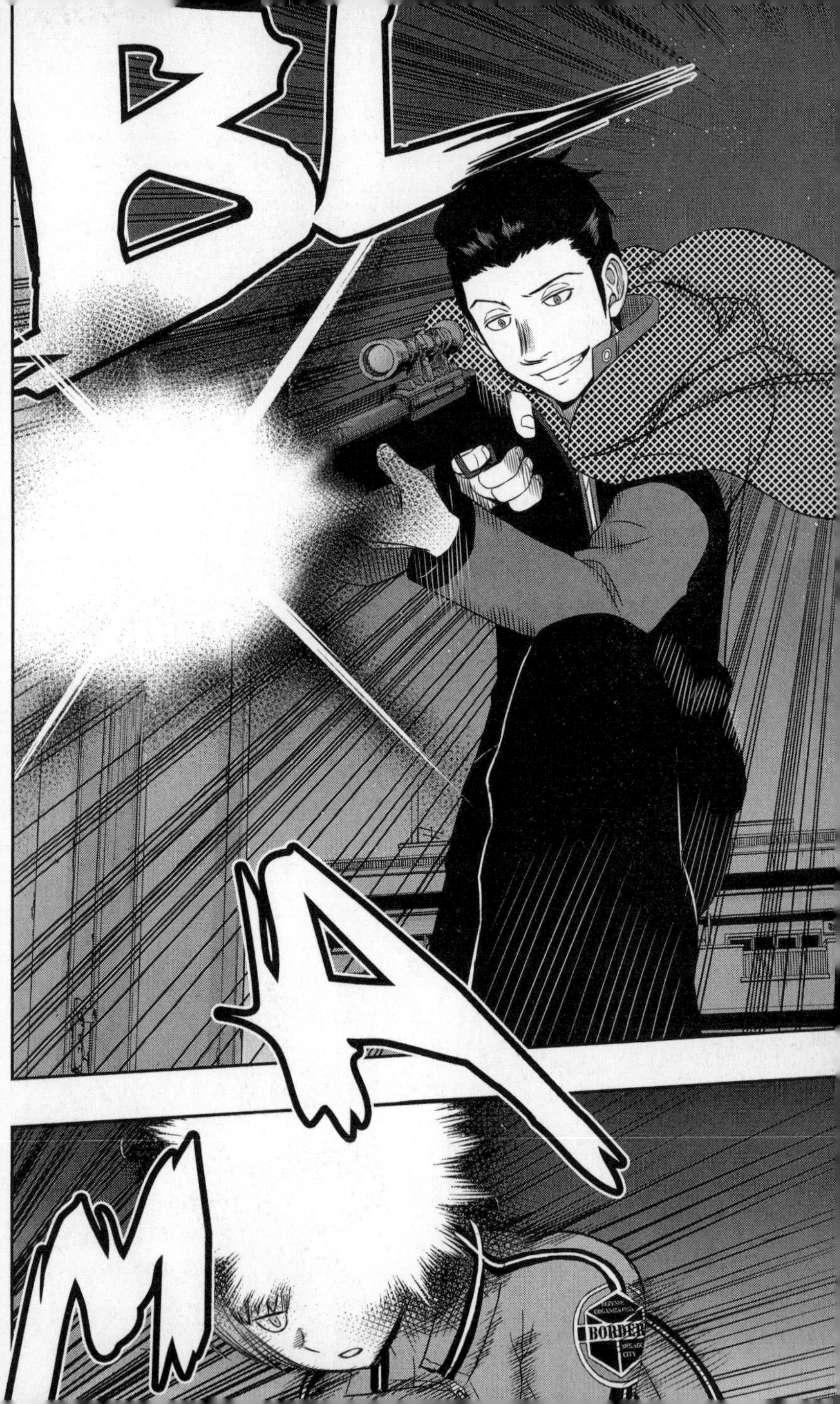
BLAM
BORDER

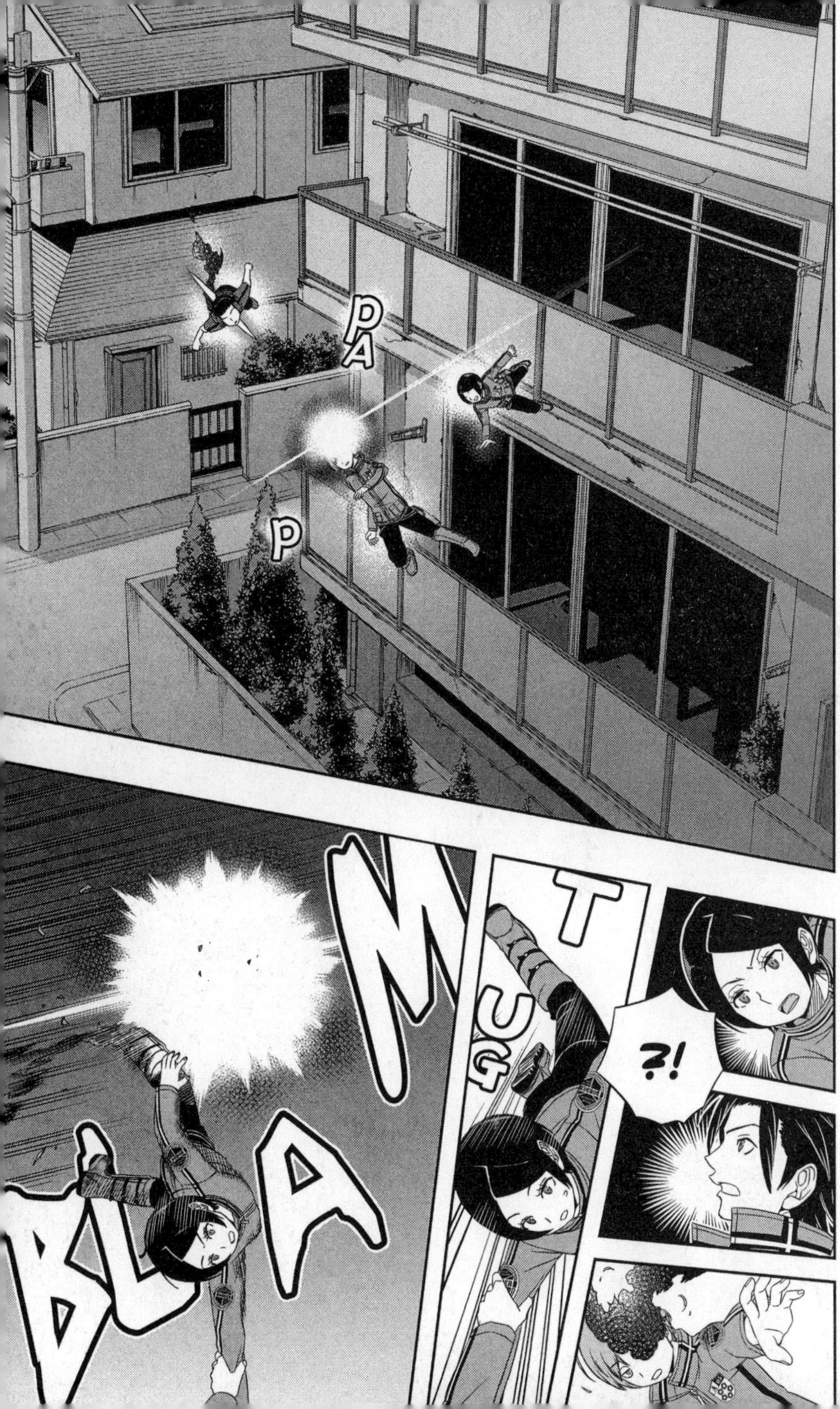
PA
P
?!
TUG
BLAM

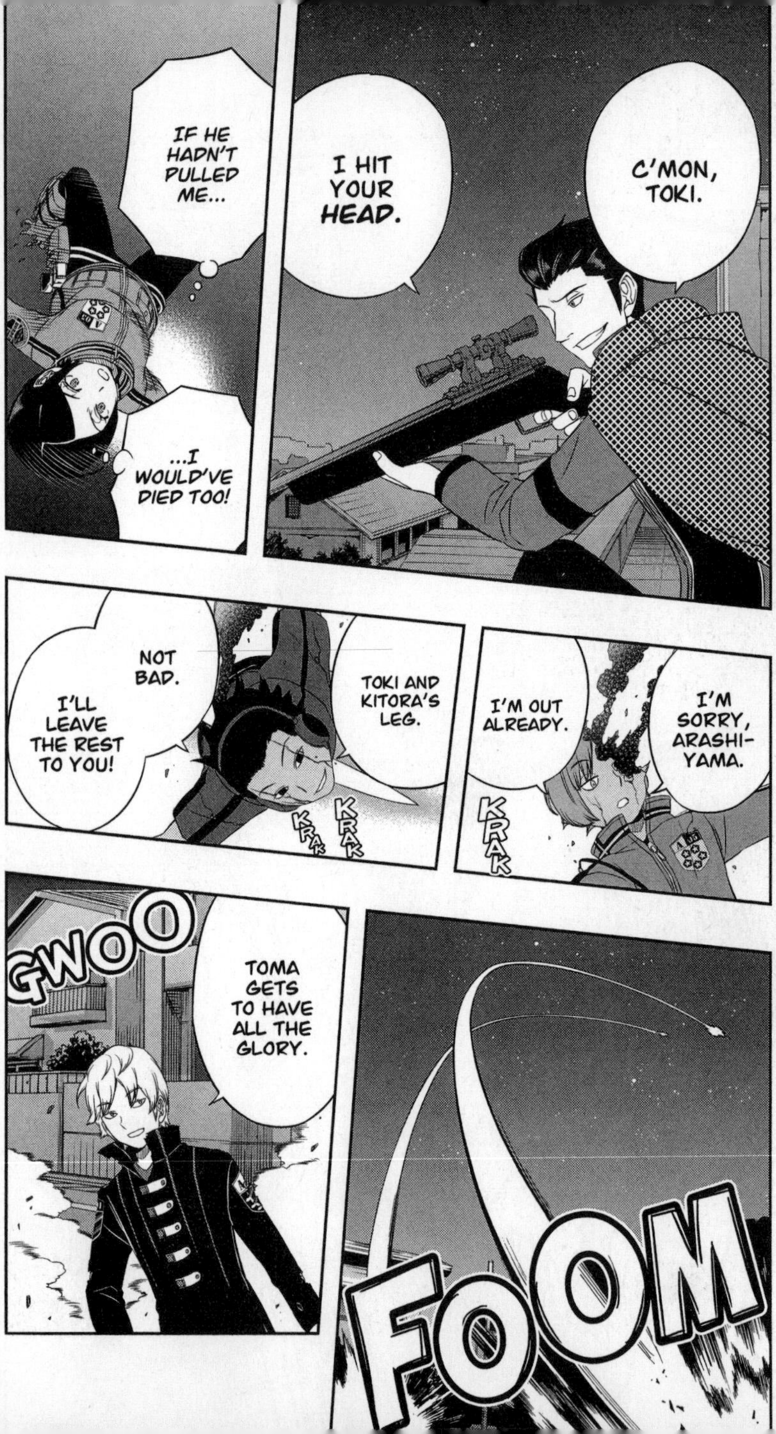
C'MON, TOKI.
I HIT YOUR HEAD.
IF HE HADN'T PULLED ME...
...I WOULD'VE DIED TOO!
I'M SORRY, ARASHI-YAMA.
I'M OUT ALREADY.
KRAK
TOKI AND KITORA'S LEG.
NOT BAD.
I'LL LEAVE THE REST TO YOU!
KRAK
KRAK
FOOM
GWOO
TOMA GETS TO HAVE ALL THE GLORY.

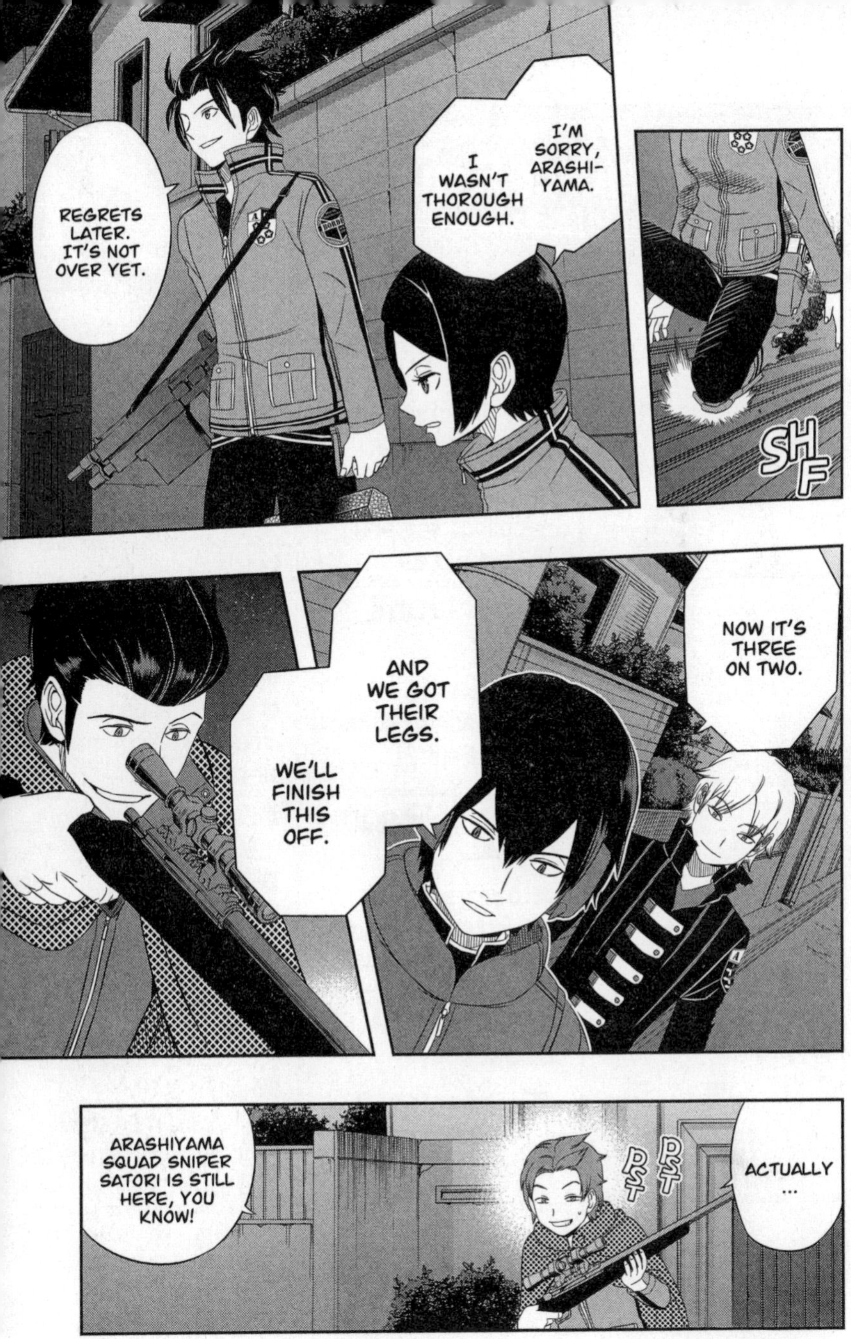
SHF
I'M SORRY, ARASHIYAMA.
I WASN'T THOROUGH ENOUGH.
REGRETS LATER. IT'S NOT OVER YET.
NOW IT'S THREE ON TWO.
AND WE GOT THEIR LEGS.
WE'LL FINISH THIS OFF.
ACTUALLY ...
PST PST
ARASHIYAMA SQUAD SNIPER SATORI IS STILL HERE, YOU KNOW!

Tachikawa Squad

Border HQ A-Rank #1

Kei Tachikawa
Captain, Attacker

■20 years old
(college student)
■Born Aug. 29

■Lupus,
Blood type A
■Height: 5'11"
■Likes: Udon noodles,
mochi, croquettes, winning
Rank Wars

Kohei Izumi
Shooter

■17 years old
(high school student)
■Born Sept. 21

■Lupus,
Blood type B
■Height: 5'9"
■Likes: Breaded shrimp,
croquettes, clementines,
all-out attacks

Takeru Yuiga
Gunner

■16 years old
(high school student)
■Born June 30

■Gladius,
Blood type O
■Height: 5'7"
■Likes: Expensive
French cuisine, to be
admired

Yu Kunichika
Operator

■17 years old
(high school student)
■Born Feb. 2

■Amphibious,
Blood type B
■Height: 5'4"
■Likes: Salmon stew,
buttered potatoes, any
kind of game

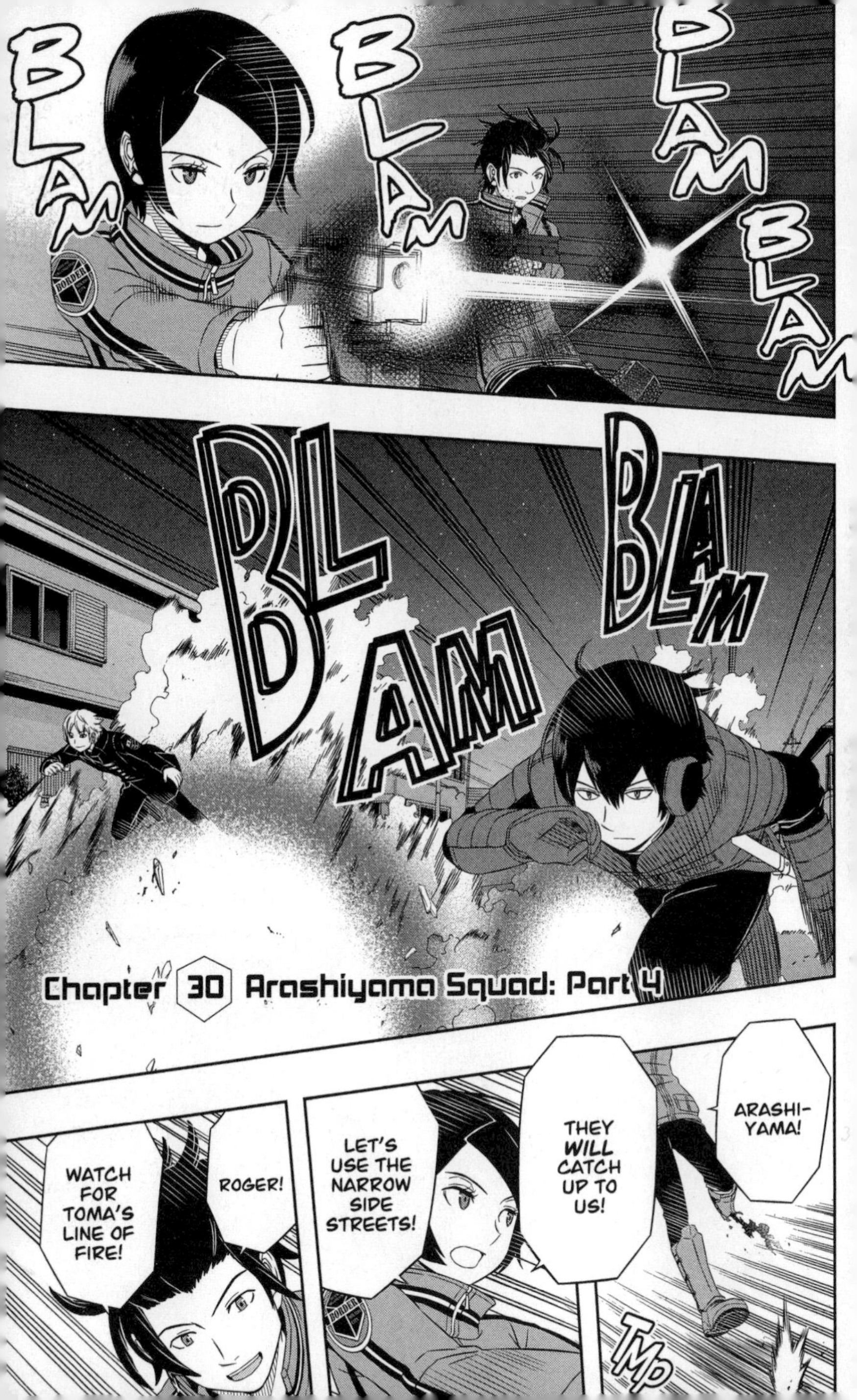
BLAM
BLAM
BLAM
BLAM
BLAM
BLAM
Chapter 30 Arashiyama Squad: Part 4
ARASHI-YAMA!
THEY WILL CATCH UP TO US!
TMP
LET'S USE THE NARROW SIDE STREETS!
ROGER!
WATCH FOR TOMA'S LINE OF FIRE!

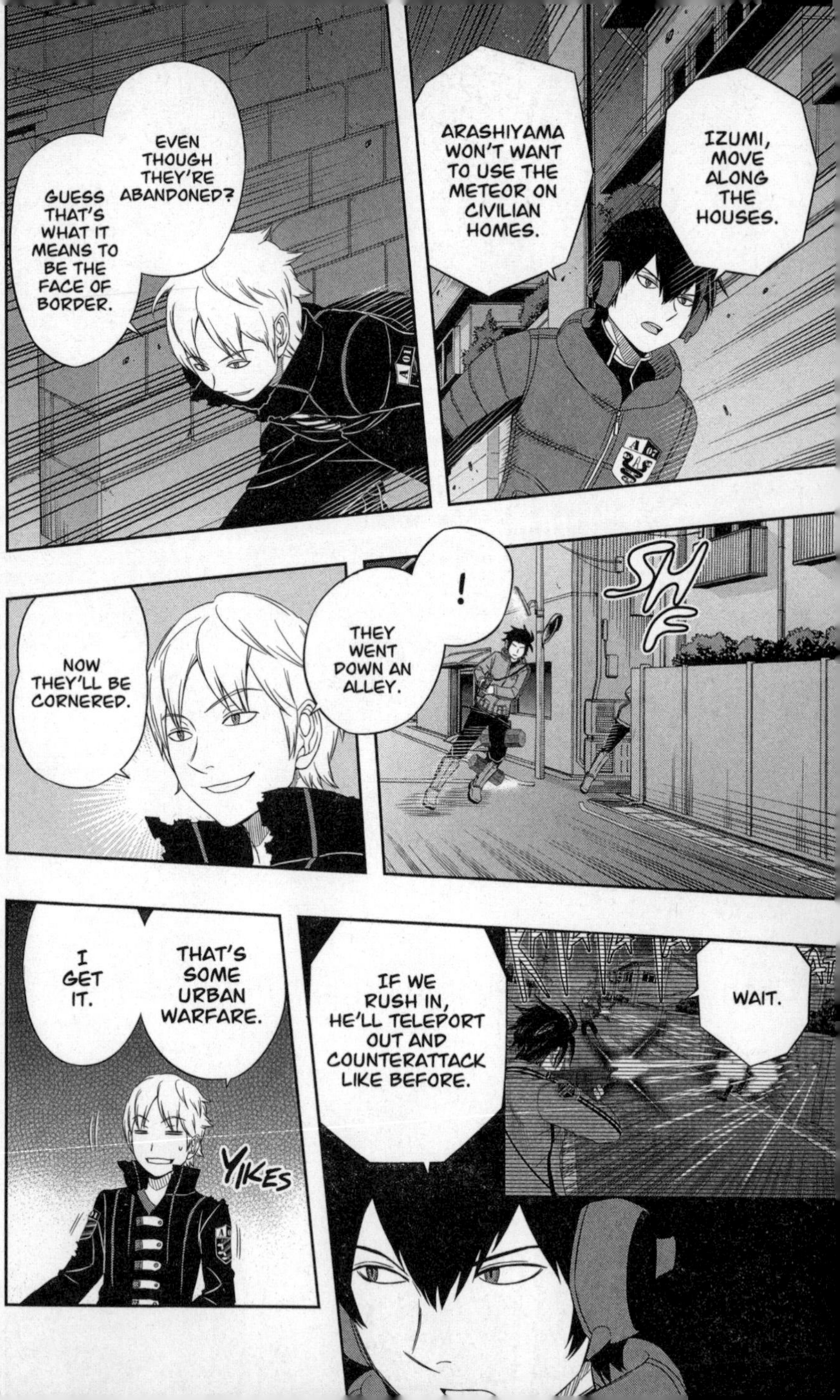
IZUMI, MOVE ALONG THE HOUSES.
ARASHIYAMA WON'T WANT TO USE THE METEOR ON CIVILIAN HOMES.
EVEN THOUGH THEY'RE ABANDONED?
GUESS THAT'S WHAT IT MEANS TO BE THE FACE OF BORDER.
SHF
!
THEY WENT DOWN AN ALLEY.
NOW THEY'LL BE CORNERED.
WAIT.
IF WE RUSH IN, HE'LL TELEPORT OUT AND COUNTERATTACK LIKE BEFORE.
THAT'S SOME URBAN WARFARE.
I GET IT.
YIKES

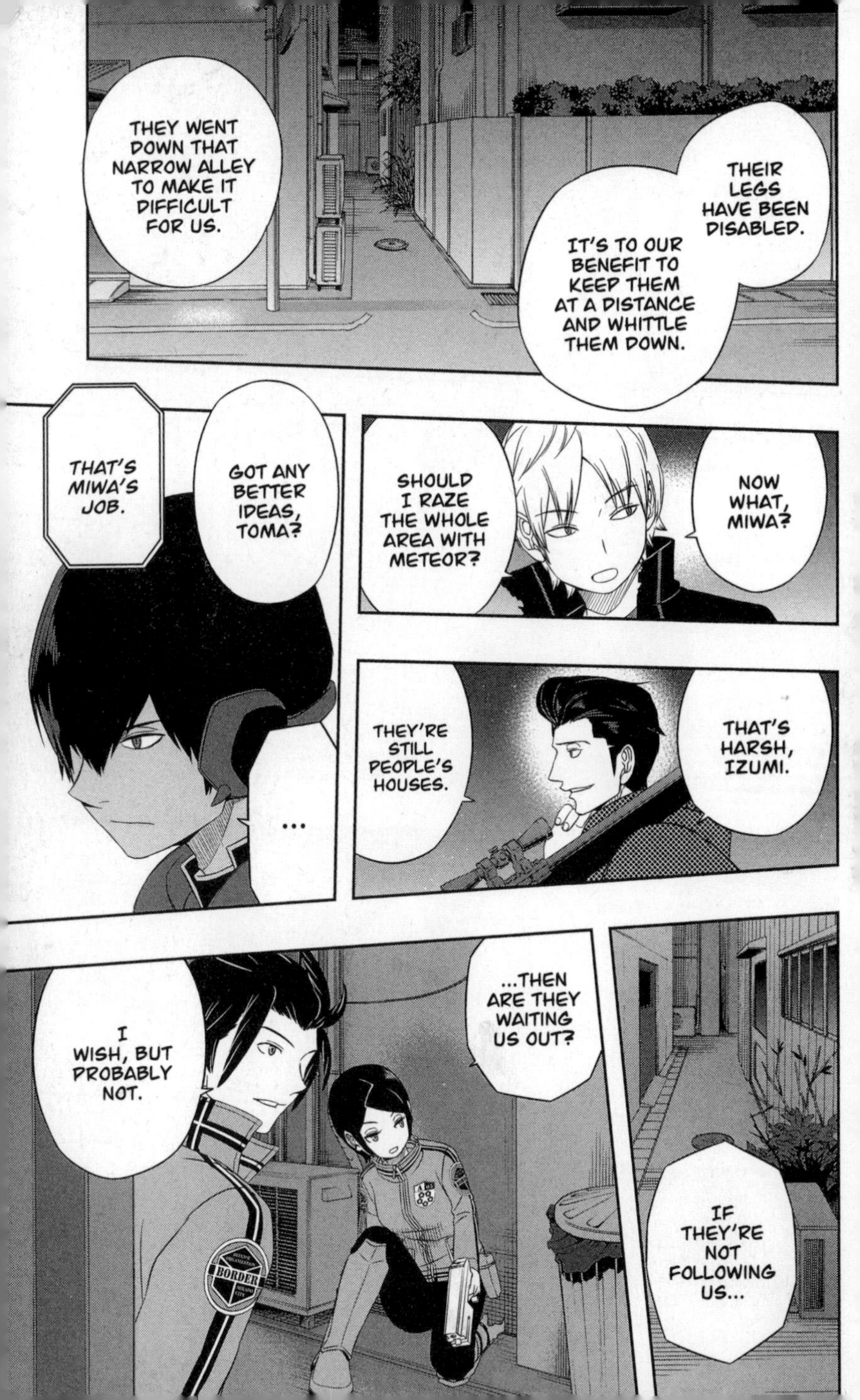
THEIR LEGS HAVE BEEN DISABLED.
IT'S TO OUR BENEFIT TO KEEP THEM AT A DISTANCE AND WHITTLE THEM DOWN.
THEY WENT DOWN THAT NARROW ALLEY TO MAKE IT DIFFICULT FOR US.
NOW WHAT, MIWA?
SHOULD I RAZE THE WHOLE AREA WITH METEOR?
THAT'S HARSH, IZUMI.
THEY'RE STILL PEOPLE'S HOUSES.
GOT ANY BETTER IDEAS, TOMA?
THAT'S MIWA'S JOB.
...
IF THEY'RE NOT FOLLOWING US...
...THEN ARE THEY WAITING US OUT?
I WISH, BUT PROBABLY NOT.

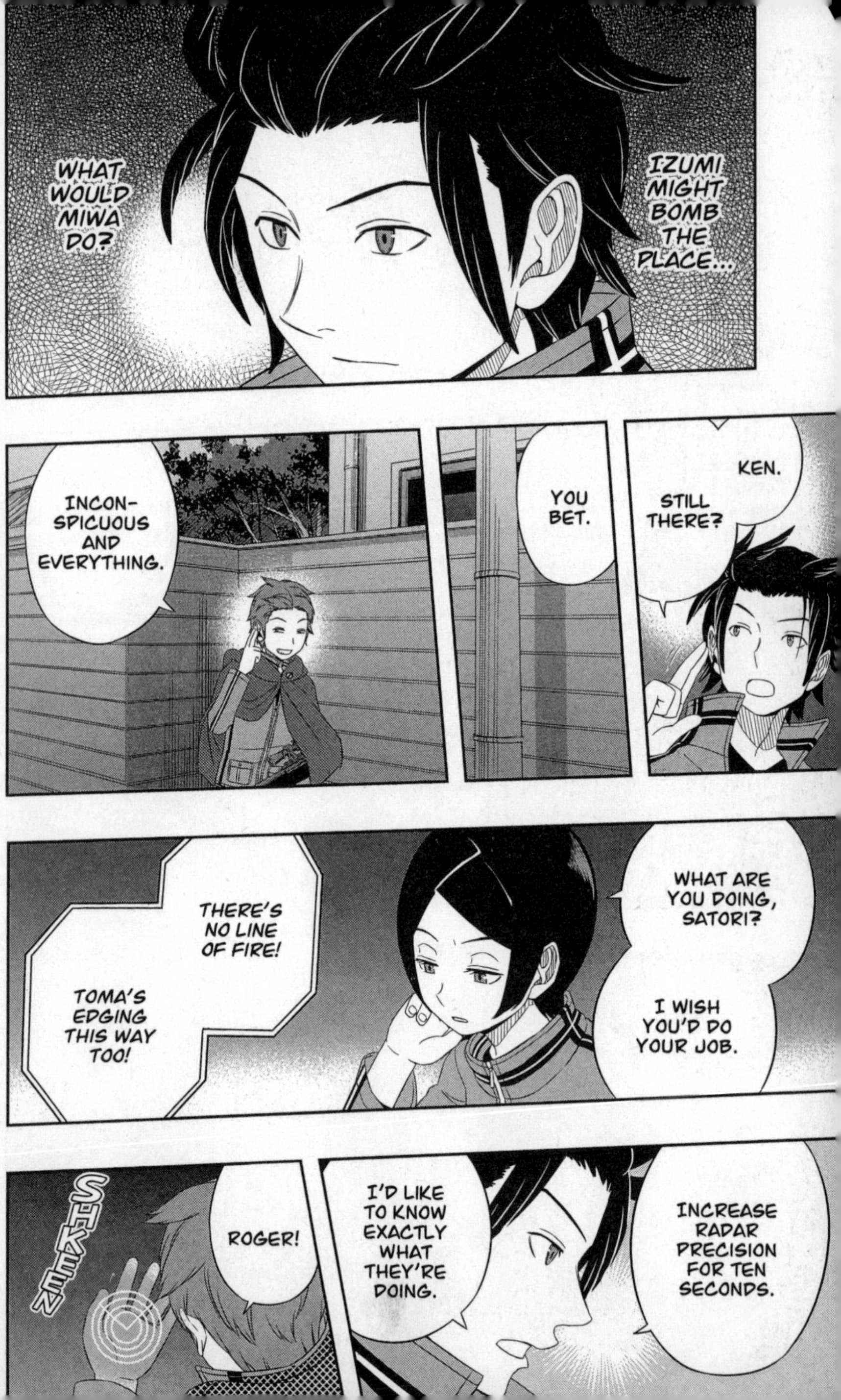
IZUMI MIGHT BOMB THE PLACE...
WHAT WOULD MIWA DO?
KEN.
STILL THERE?
YOU BET.
INCON-SPICUOUS AND EVERYTHING.
WHAT ARE YOU DOING, SATORI?
I WISH YOU'D DO YOUR JOB.
THERE'S NO LINE OF FIRE!
TOMA'S EDGING THIS WAY TOO!
INCREASE RADAR PRECISION FOR TEN SECONDS.
I'D LIKE TO KNOW EXACTLY WHAT THEY'RE DOING.
ROGER!
SHKEEN

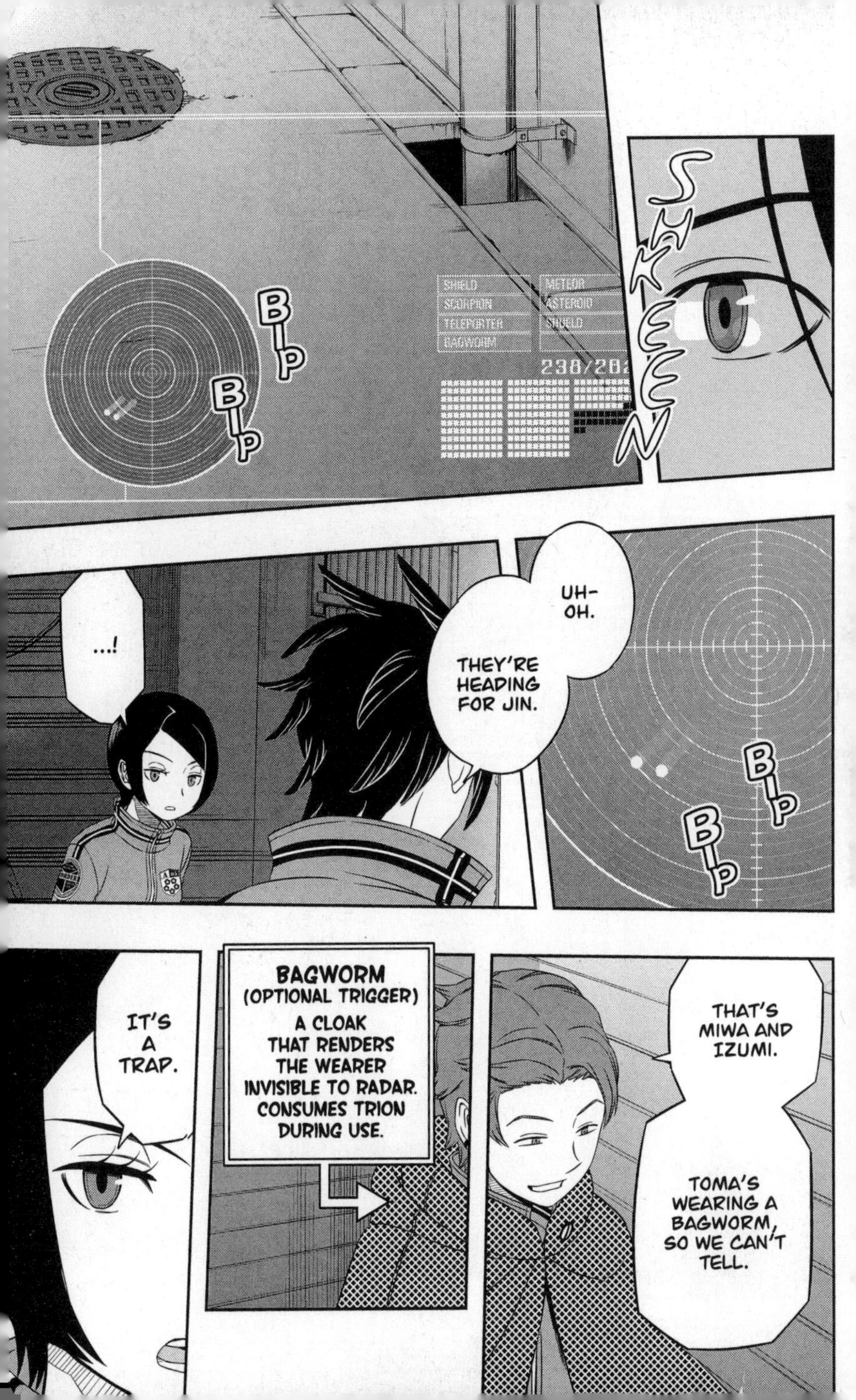
SHKEEN
SHIELD
SCORPION
TELEPORTER
BAGWORM
METEOR
ASTEROID
SHIELD
BIP
BIP
UH-OH.
THEY'RE HEADING FOR JIN.
BIP
BIP
...!
THAT'S MIWA AND IZUMI.
TOMA'S WEARING A BAGWORM, SO WE CAN'T TELL.
BAGWORM (OPTIONAL TRIGGER) A CLOAK THAT RENDERS THE WEARER INVISIBLE TO RADAR. CONSUMES TRION DURING USE.
IT'S A TRAP.

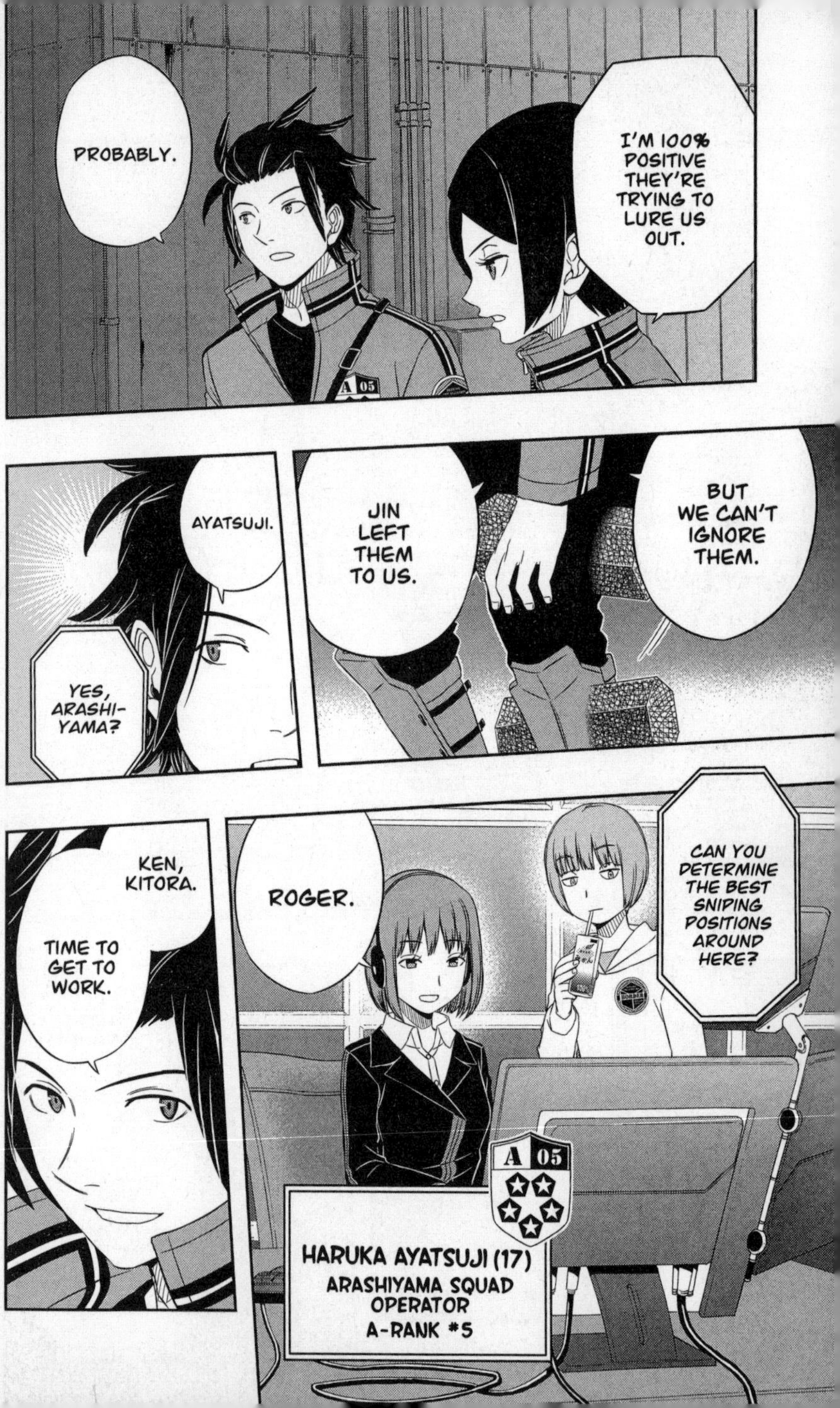
I'M 100% POSITIVE THEY'RE TRYING TO LURE US OUT.
PROBABLY.
BUT WE CAN'T IGNORE THEM.
JIN LEFT THEM TO US.
AYATSUJI.
YES, ARASHIYAMA?
CAN YOU DETERMINE THE BEST SNIPING POSITIONS AROUND HERE?
ROGER.
A 05
HARUKA AYATSUJI (17)
ARASHIYAMA SQUAD
OPERATOR
A-RANK #5
KEN, KITORA.
TIME TO GET TO WORK.

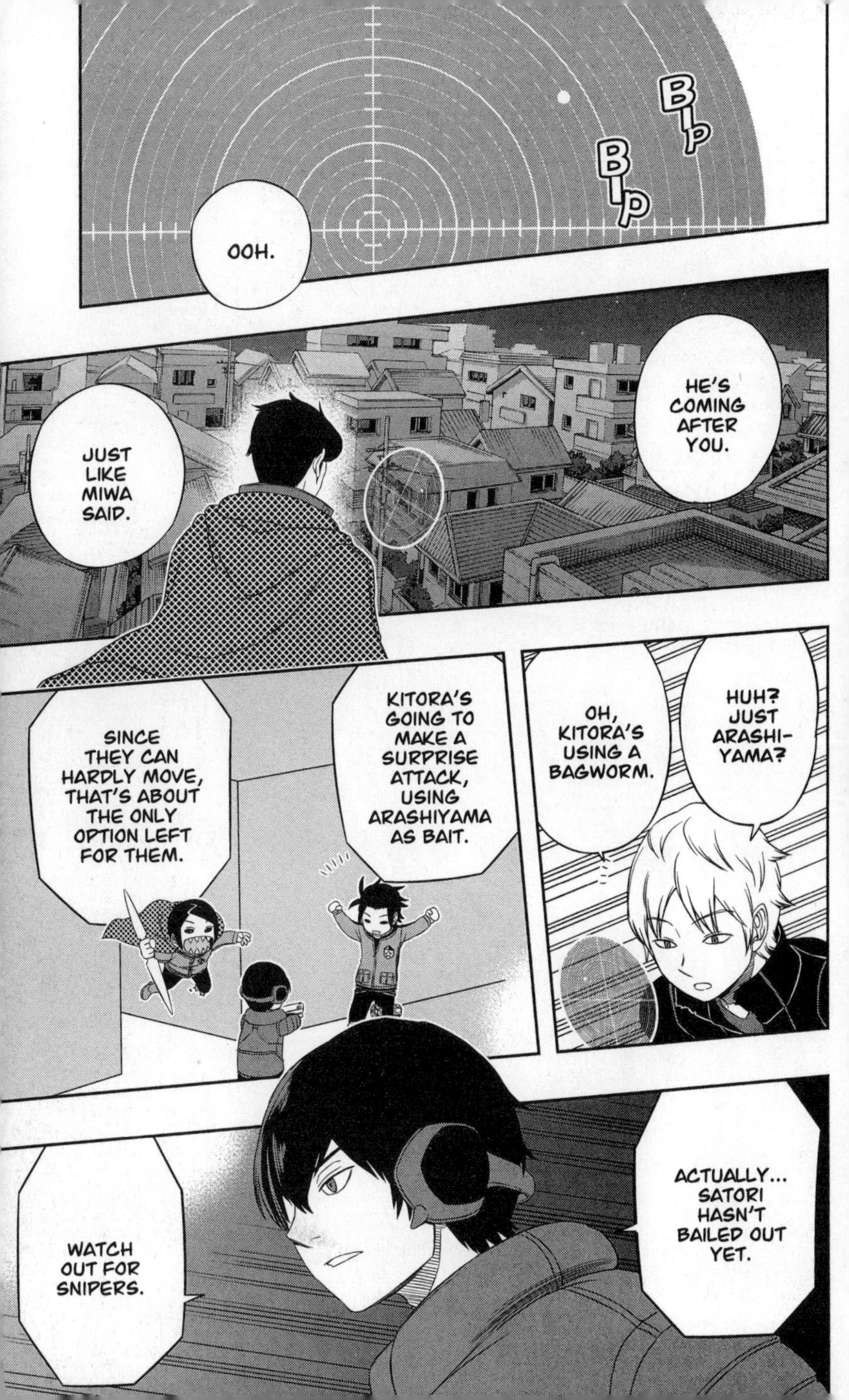
BIP
BIP
OOH.
HE'S COMING AFTER YOU.
JUST LIKE MIWA SAID.
HUH? JUST ARASHI-YAMA?
OH, KITORA'S USING A BAGWORM.
KITORA'S GOING TO MAKE A SURPRISE ATTACK, USING ARASHIYAMA AS BAIT.
SINCE THEY CAN HARDLY MOVE, THAT'S ABOUT THE ONLY OPTION LEFT FOR THEM.
ACTUALLY... SATORI HASN'T BAILED OUT YET.
WATCH OUT FOR SNIPERS.

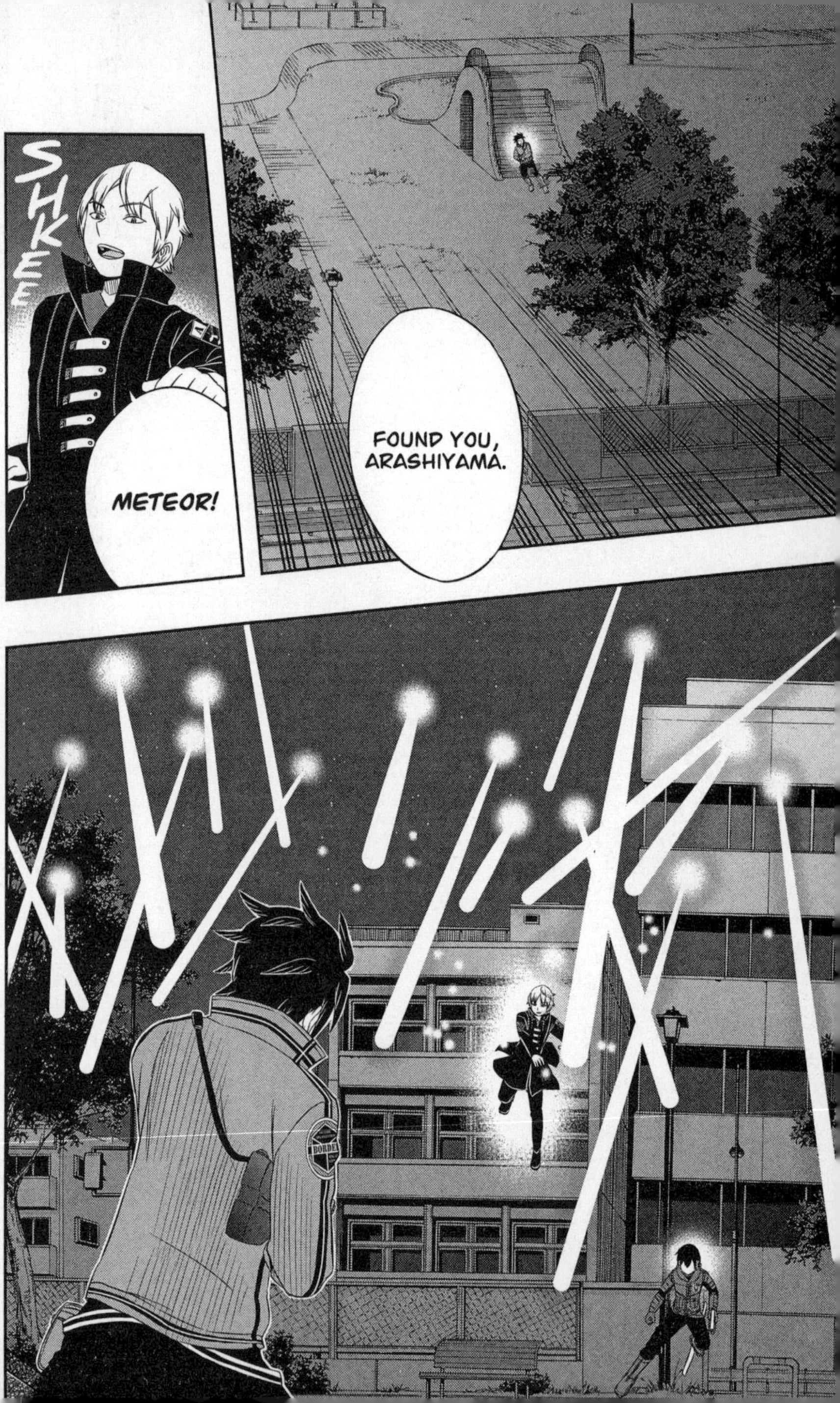
FOUND YOU, ARASHIYAMA.
SHKEE
METEOR!

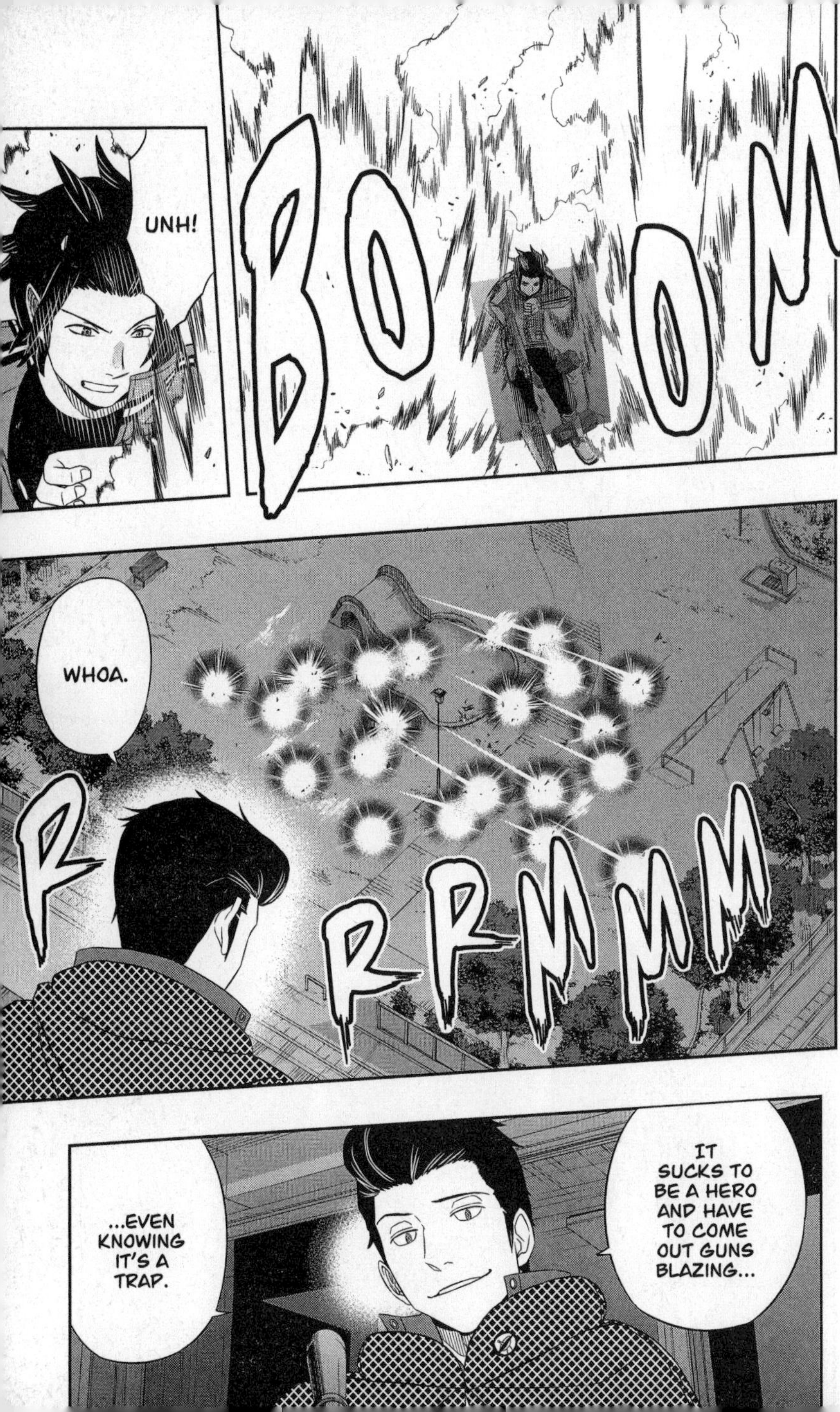
BOOM
UNH!
WHOA.
RRRMMM
IT SUCKS TO BE A HERO AND HAVE TO COME OUT GUNS BLAZING...
...EVEN KNOWING IT'S A TRAP.

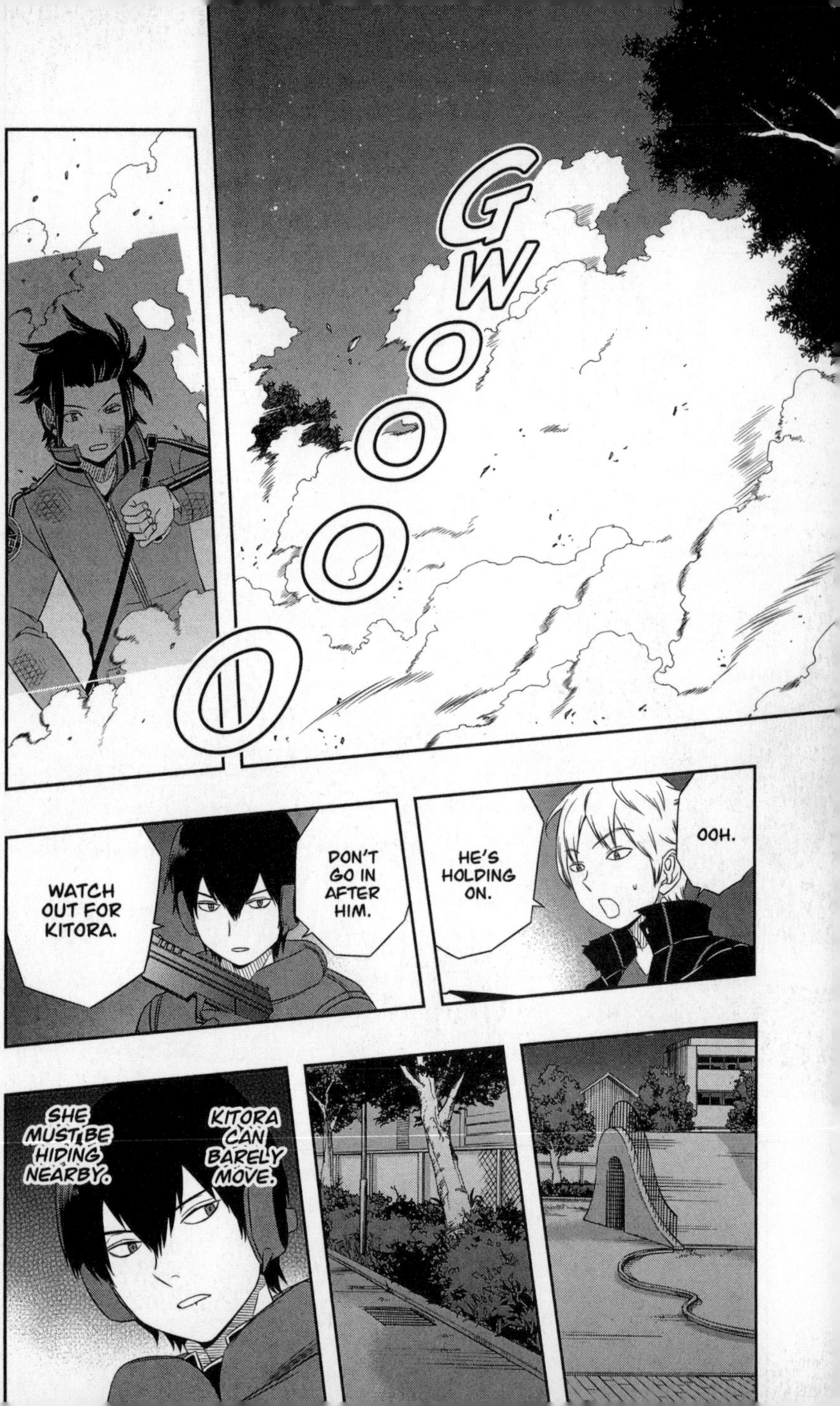
GWOOOO
OOH.
HE'S HOLDING ON.
DON'T GO IN AFTER HIM.
WATCH OUT FOR KITORA.
KITORA CAN BARELY MOVE.
SHE MUST BE HIDING NEARBY.

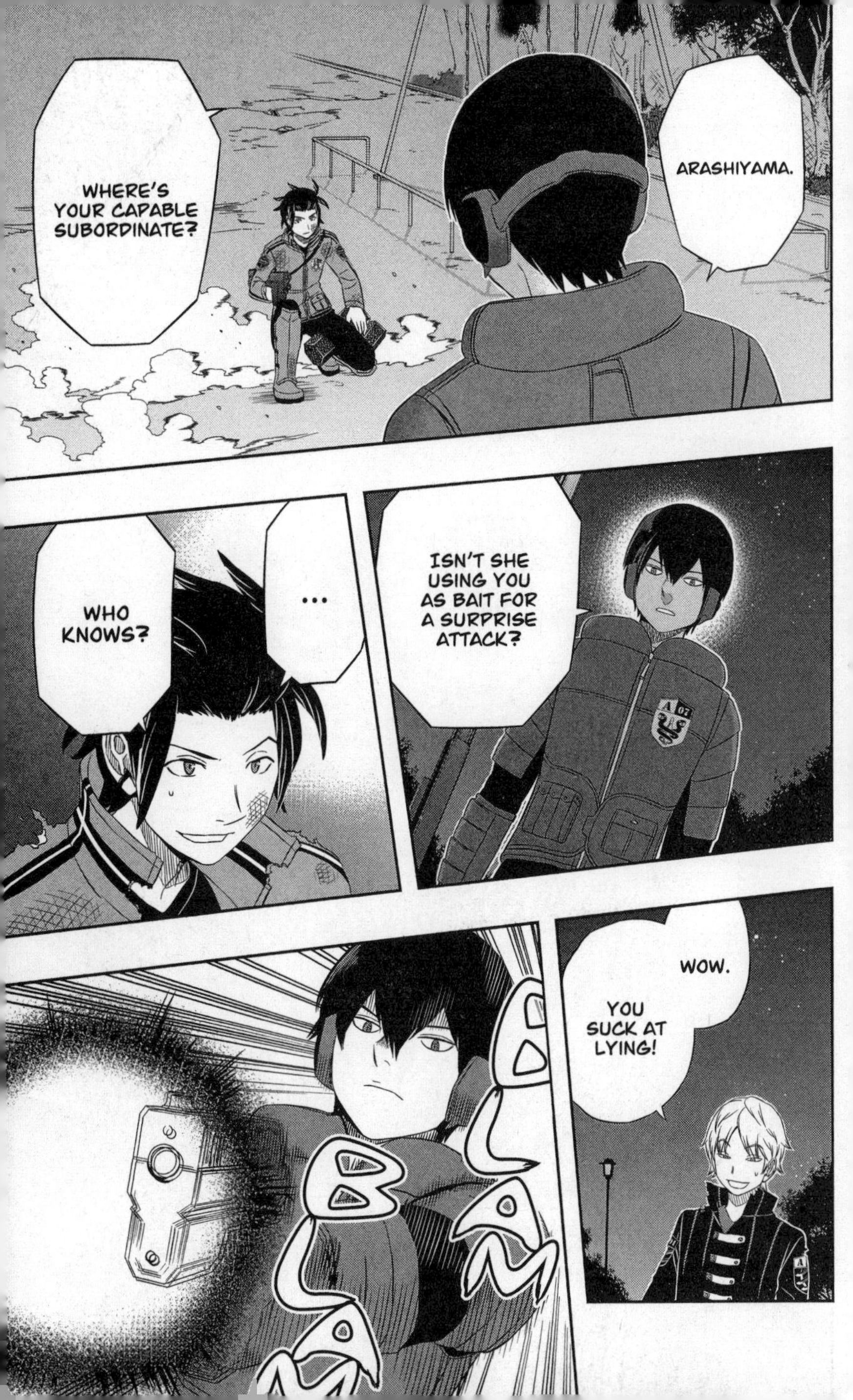
ARASHIYAMA.
WHERE'S YOUR CAPABLE SUBORDINATE?
ISN'T SHE USING YOU AS BAIT FOR A SURPRISE ATTACK?
...
WHO KNOWS?
WOW.
YOU SUCK AT LYING!
BLAM
BLAM

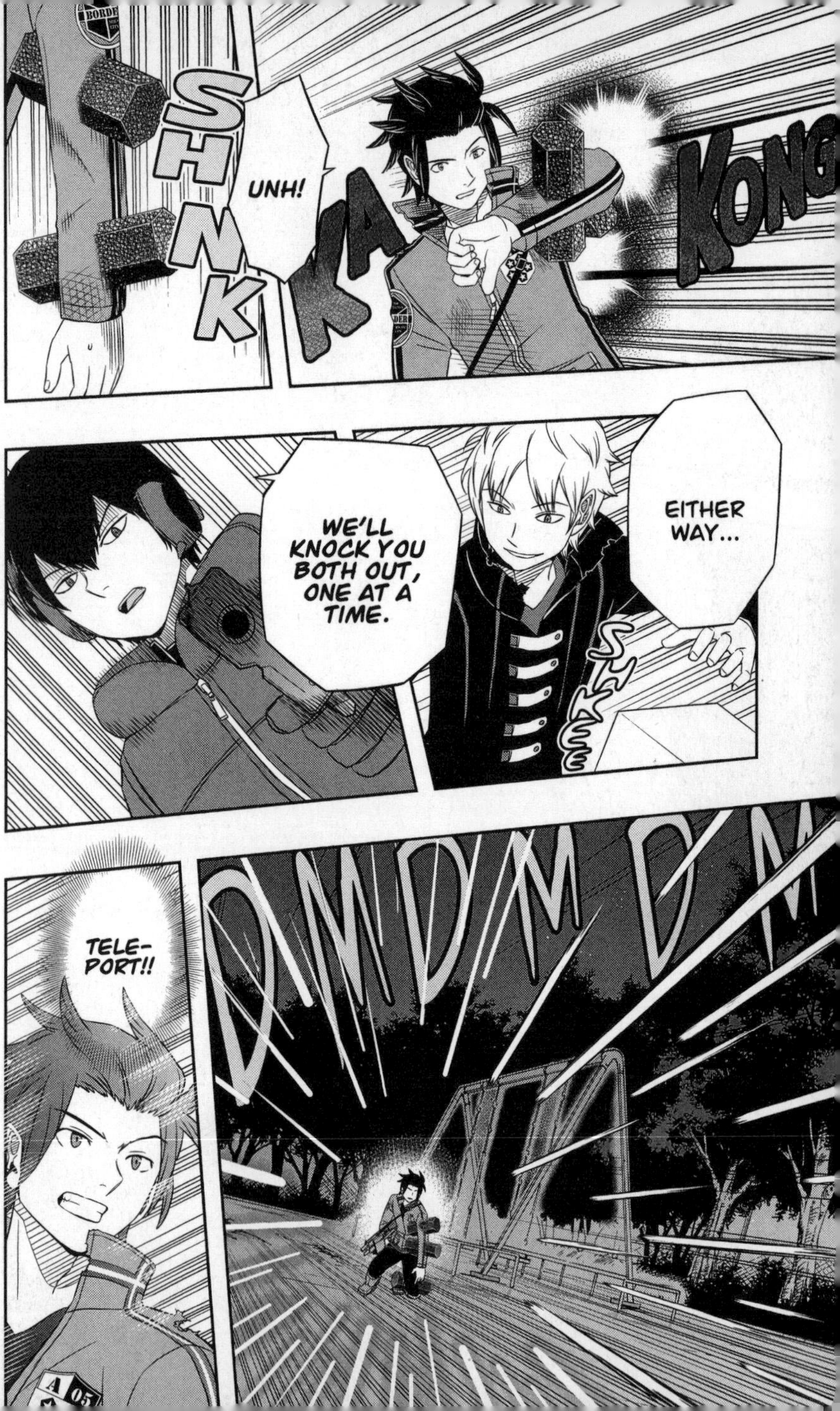
KONG
KA
UNH!
SHNK
EITHER WAY...
SHKEE
WE'LL KNOCK YOU BOTH OUT, ONE AT A TIME.
DMDMDMDM
TELE-PORT!!

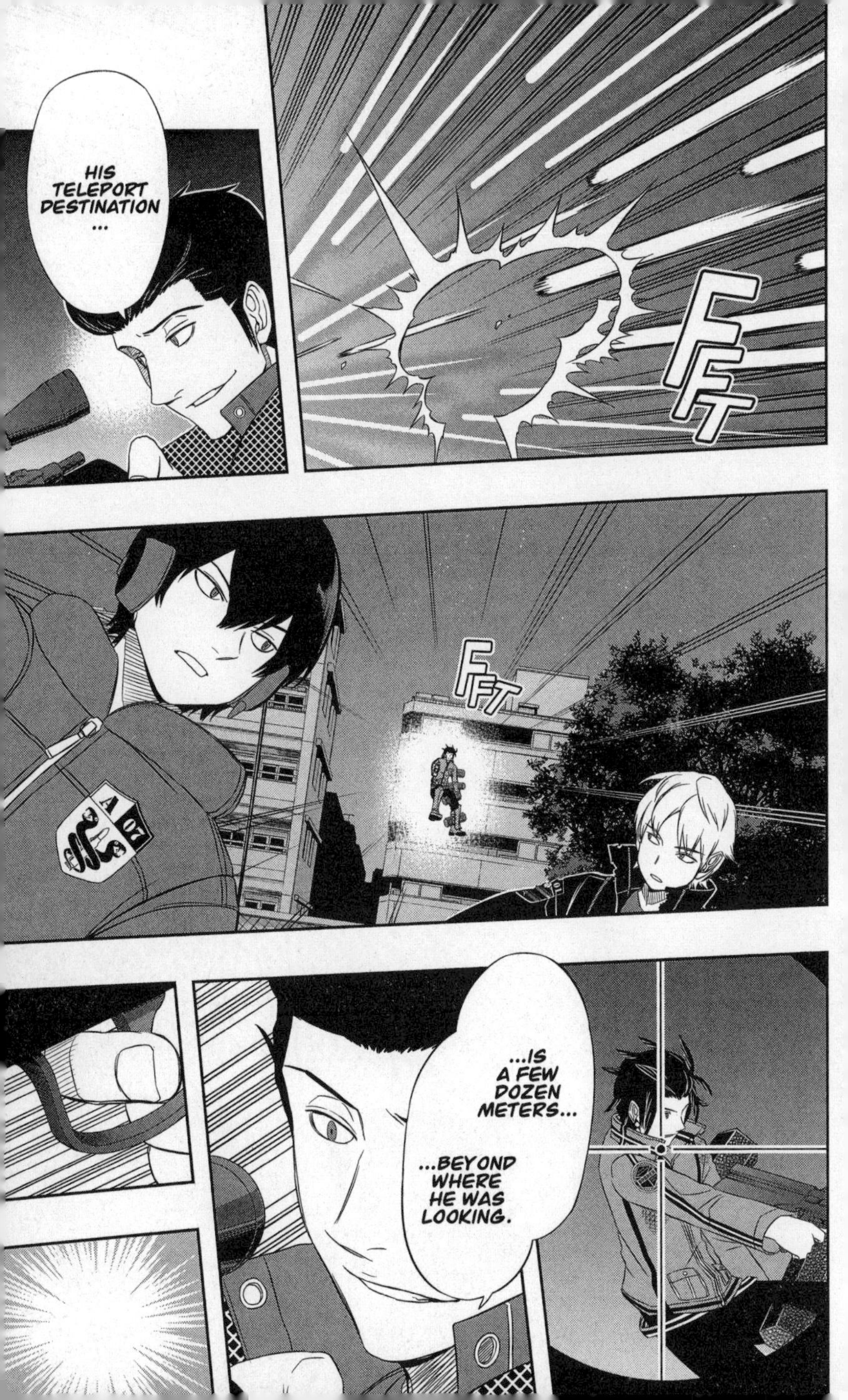
FFFT
HIS TELEPORT DESTINATION ...
FFFT
...IS A FEW DOZEN METERS...
...BEYOND WHERE HE WAS LOOKING.

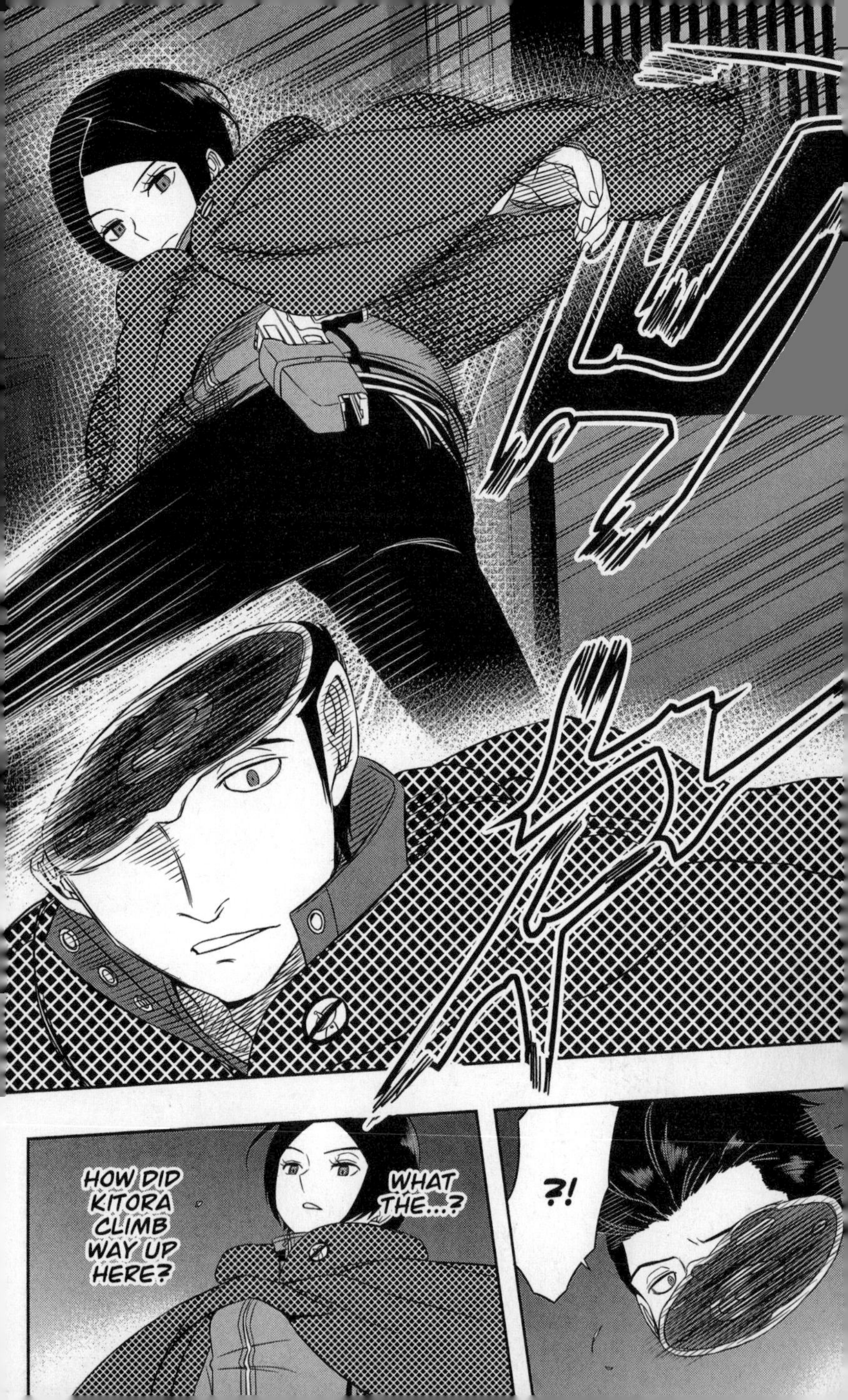
?!
WHAT THE...?
HOW DID KITORA CLIMB WAY UP HERE?

READ THIS WAY

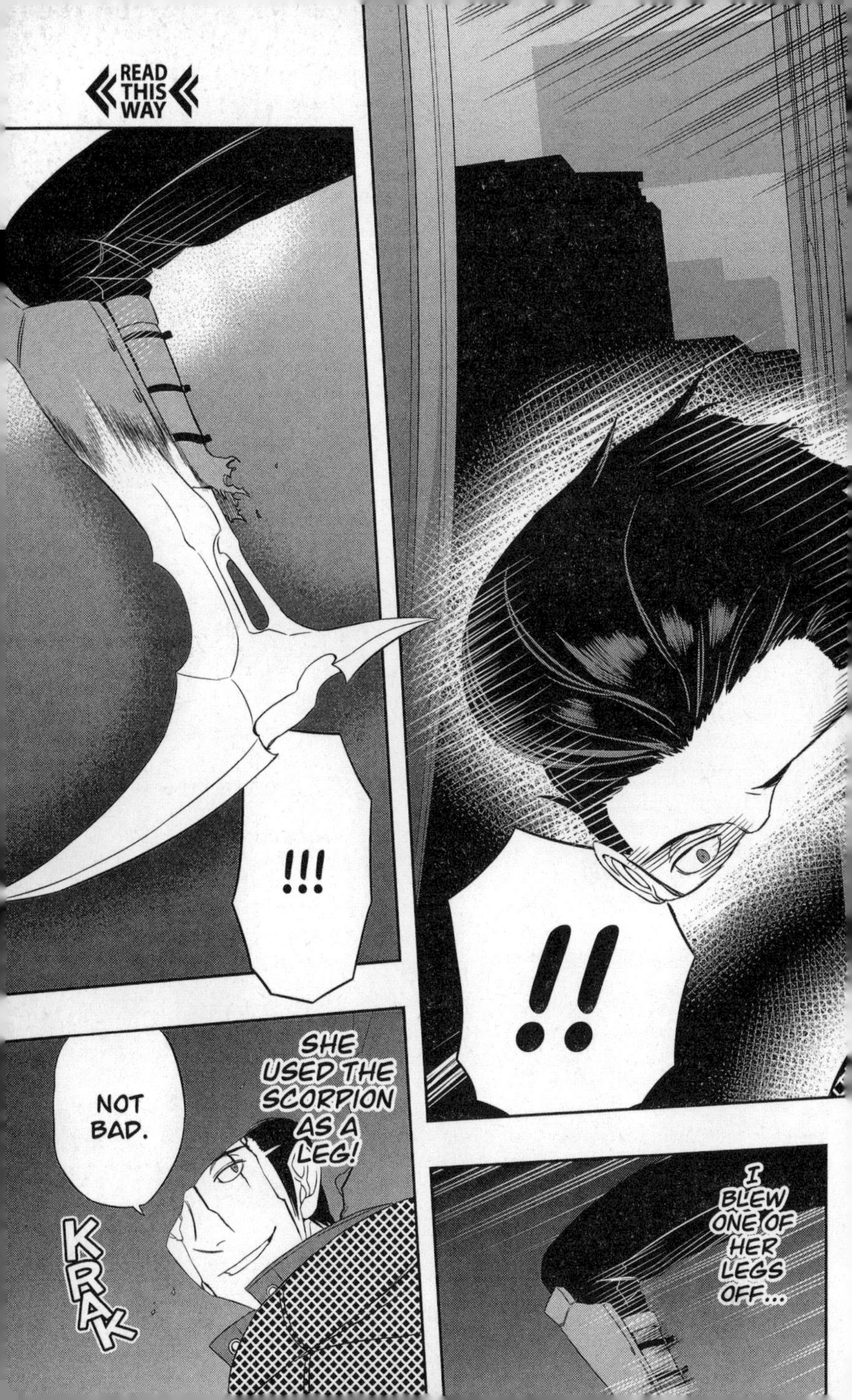
!!
!!!
I BLEW ONE OF HER LEGS OFF...
SHE USED THE SCORPION AS A LEG!
NOT BAD.
KRAK

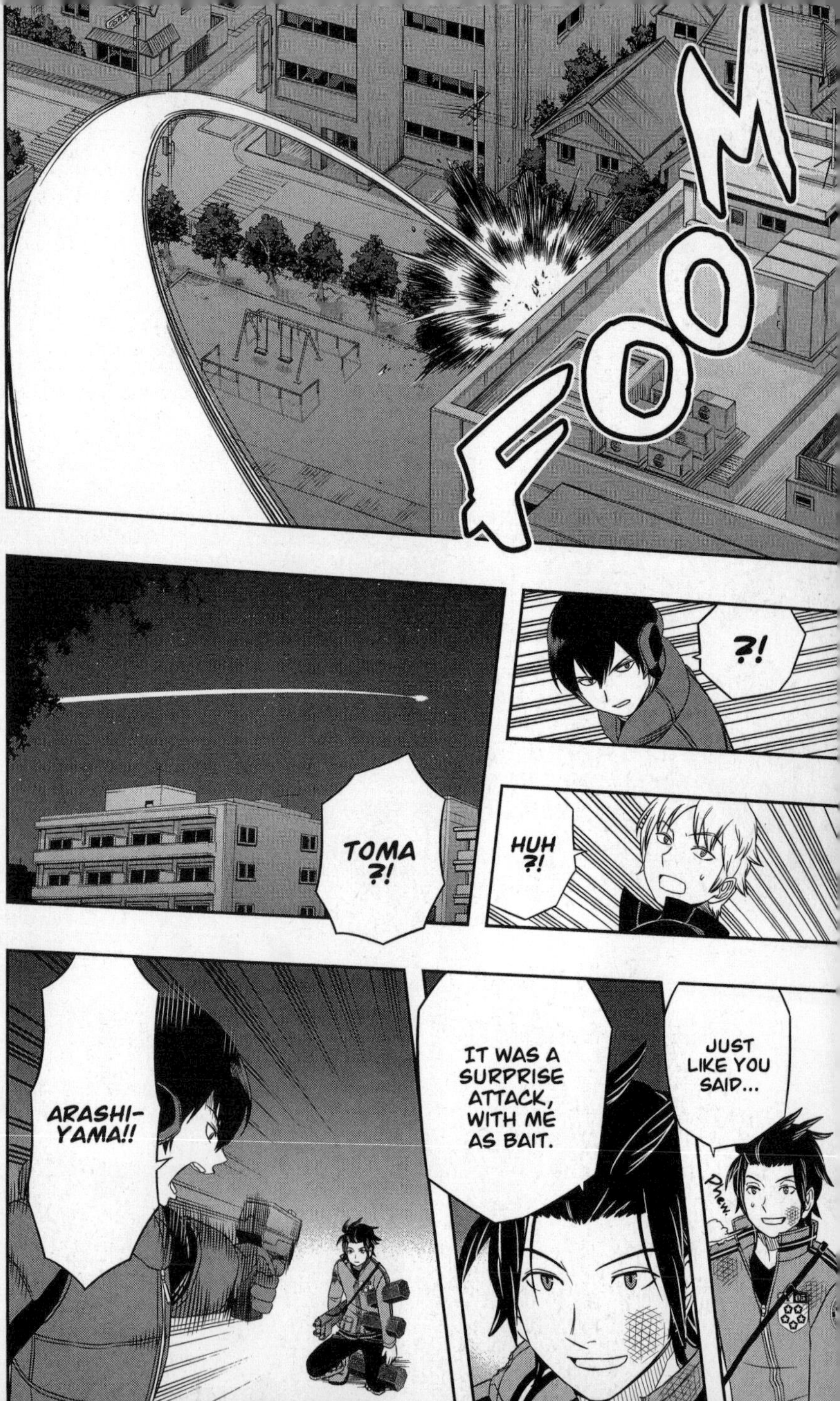
FOOOM
?!
HUH ?!
TOMA ?!
JUST LIKE YOU SAID...
Phew.
IT WAS A SURPRISE ATTACK, WITH ME AS BAIT.
ARASHI-YAMA!!

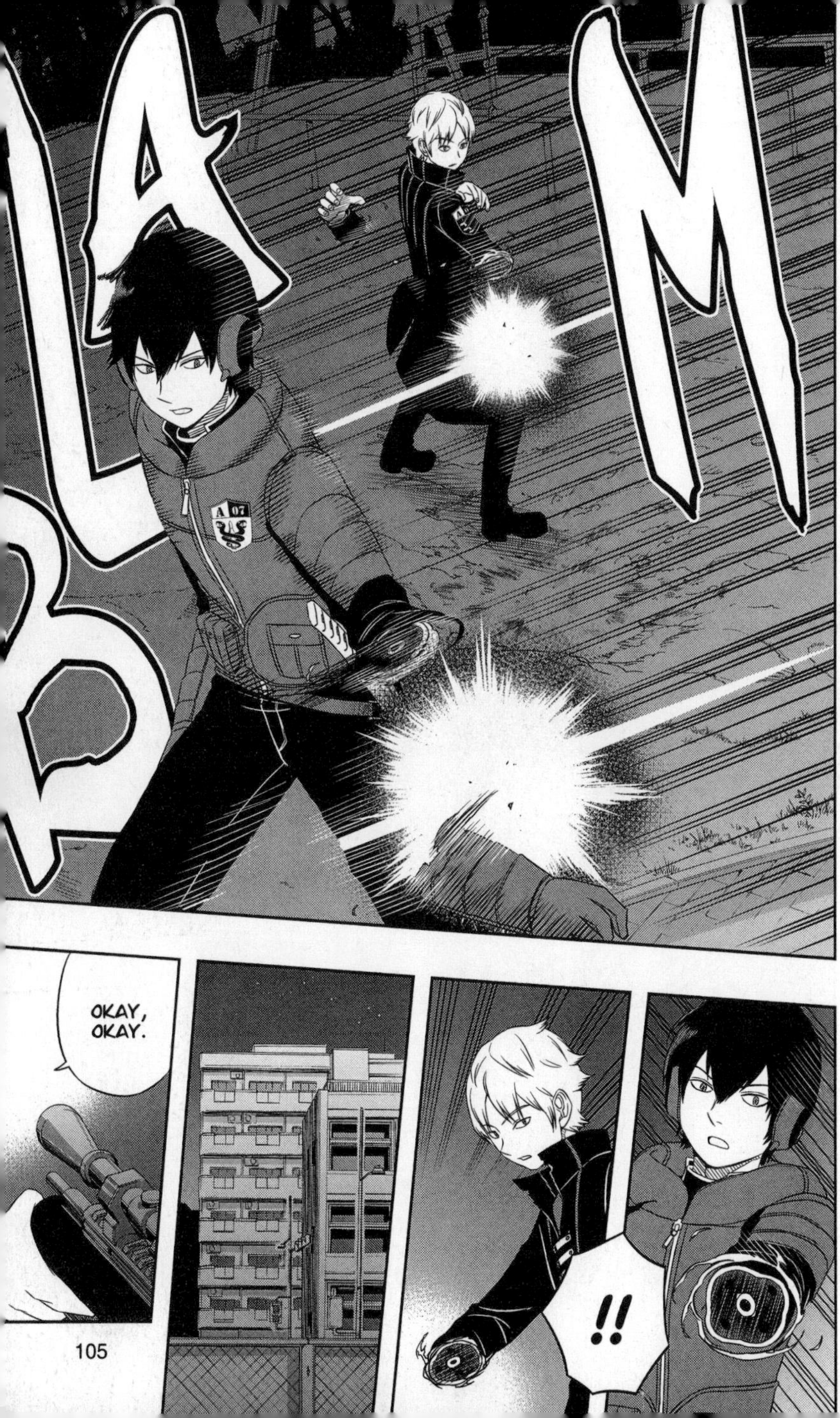
BLAM
!!
OKAY, OKAY.

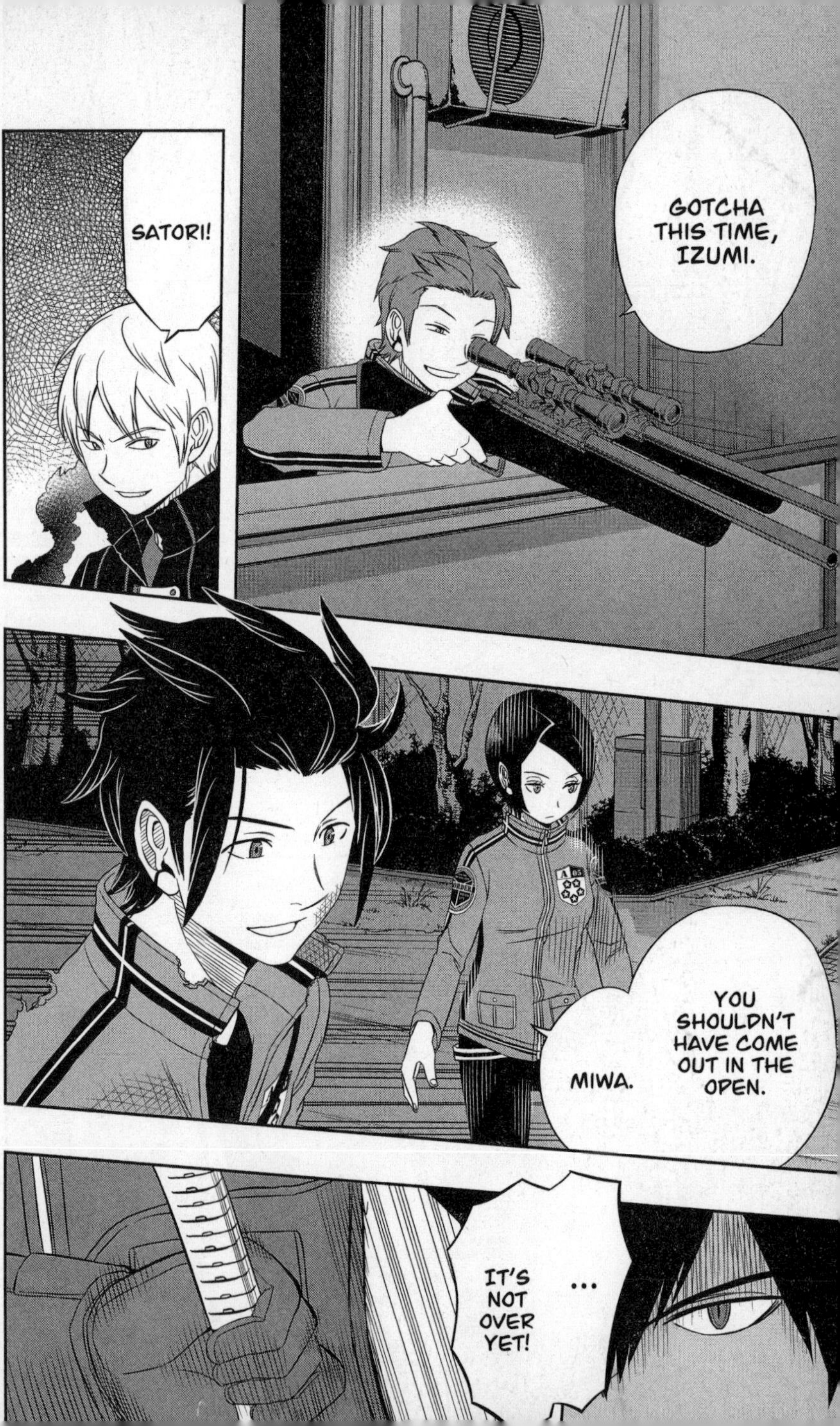
GOTCHA THIS TIME, IZUMI.
SATORI!
YOU SHOULDN'T HAVE COME OUT IN THE OPEN.
MIWA.
...
IT'S NOT OVER YET!

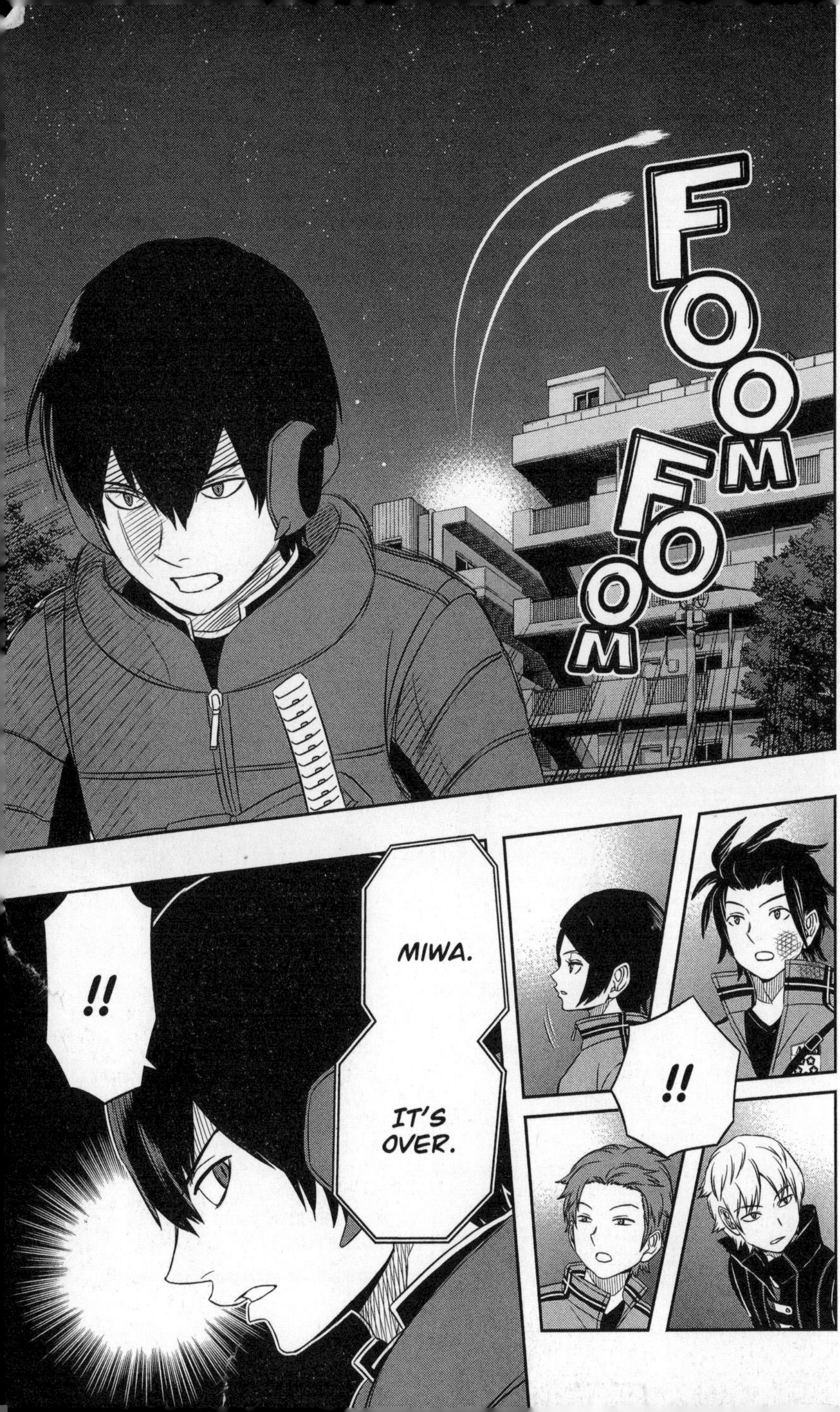
FOOOM
FOOOM
!!
MIWA.
IT'S OVER.
!!

Gunner Triggers

Mid-range shooting Triggers. Consumes Trion to propel bullets, so they're less powerful than blades. Consumes more Trion overall.

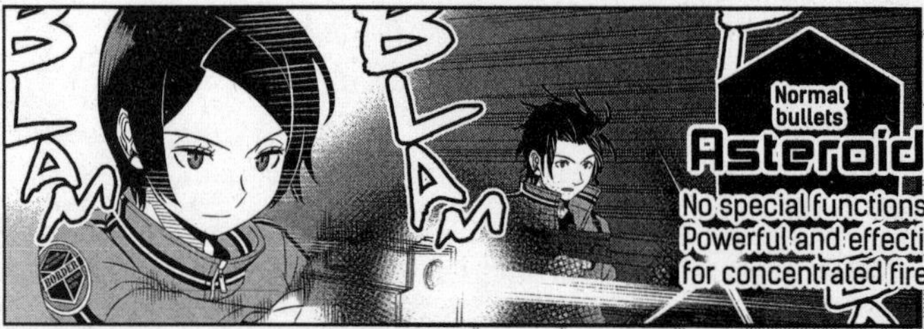
BLAM
BLAM

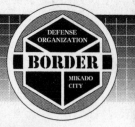

Normal bullets
Asteroid
No special functions. Powerful and effective for concentrated fire.

Special Bullets
Bullets with additional functions. Slightly less powerful.

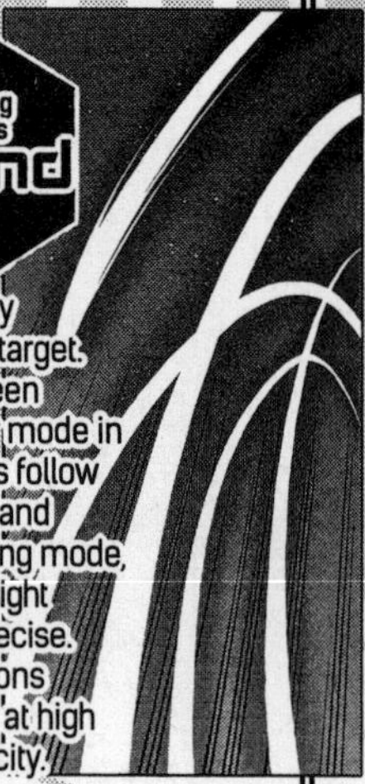

Homing bullets
Hound
Automatically pursues the target. Select between Trion-seeker mode in which bullets follow Trion bodies and guided homing mode, directed by sight and more precise. These functions are disabled at high muzzle velocity.

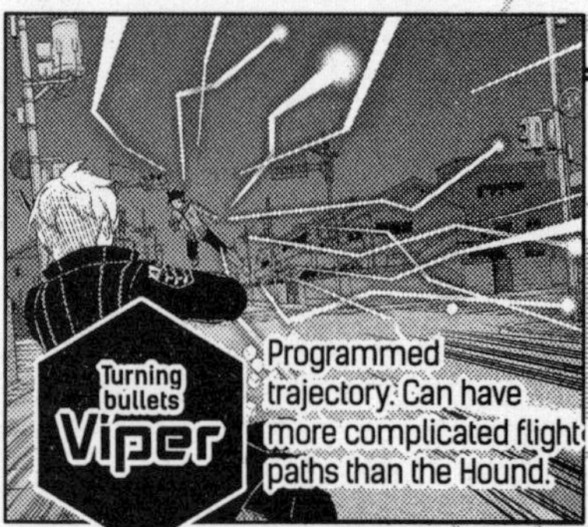

Turning bullets
Viper
Programmed trajectory. Can have more complicated flight paths than the Hound.

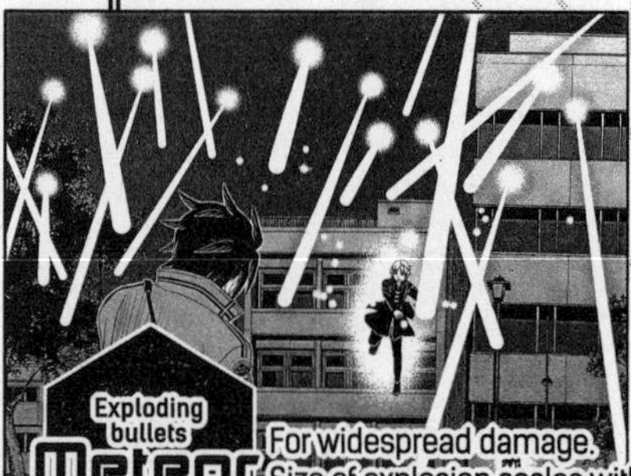

Exploding bullets
Meteor
For widespread damage. Size of explosion scales with the amount of Trion used.

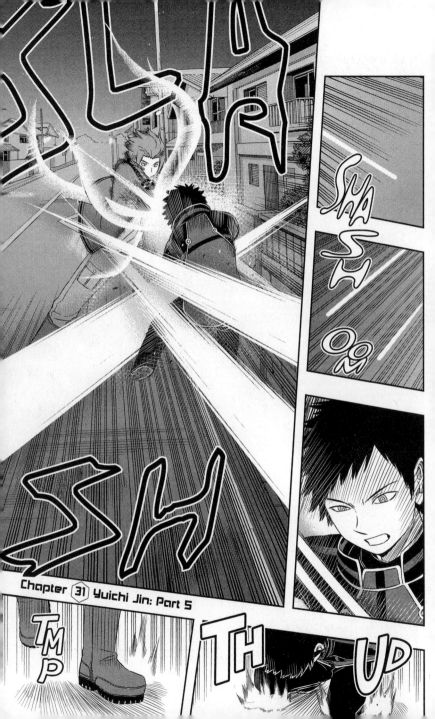

Chapter 31 Yuichi Jin: Part 5

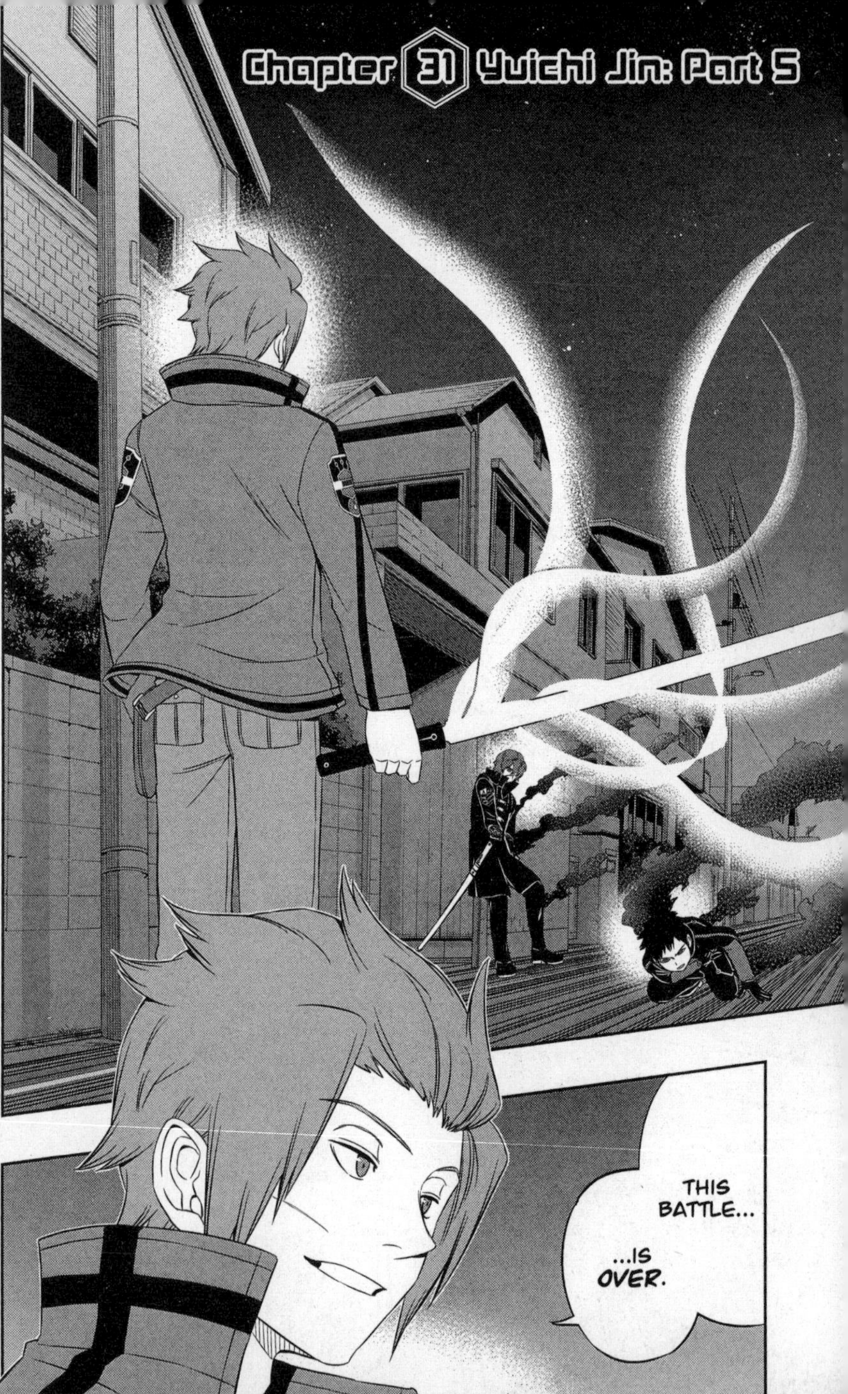
Chapter 31 Yuichi Jin: Part 5
THIS BATTLE...
...IS OVER.

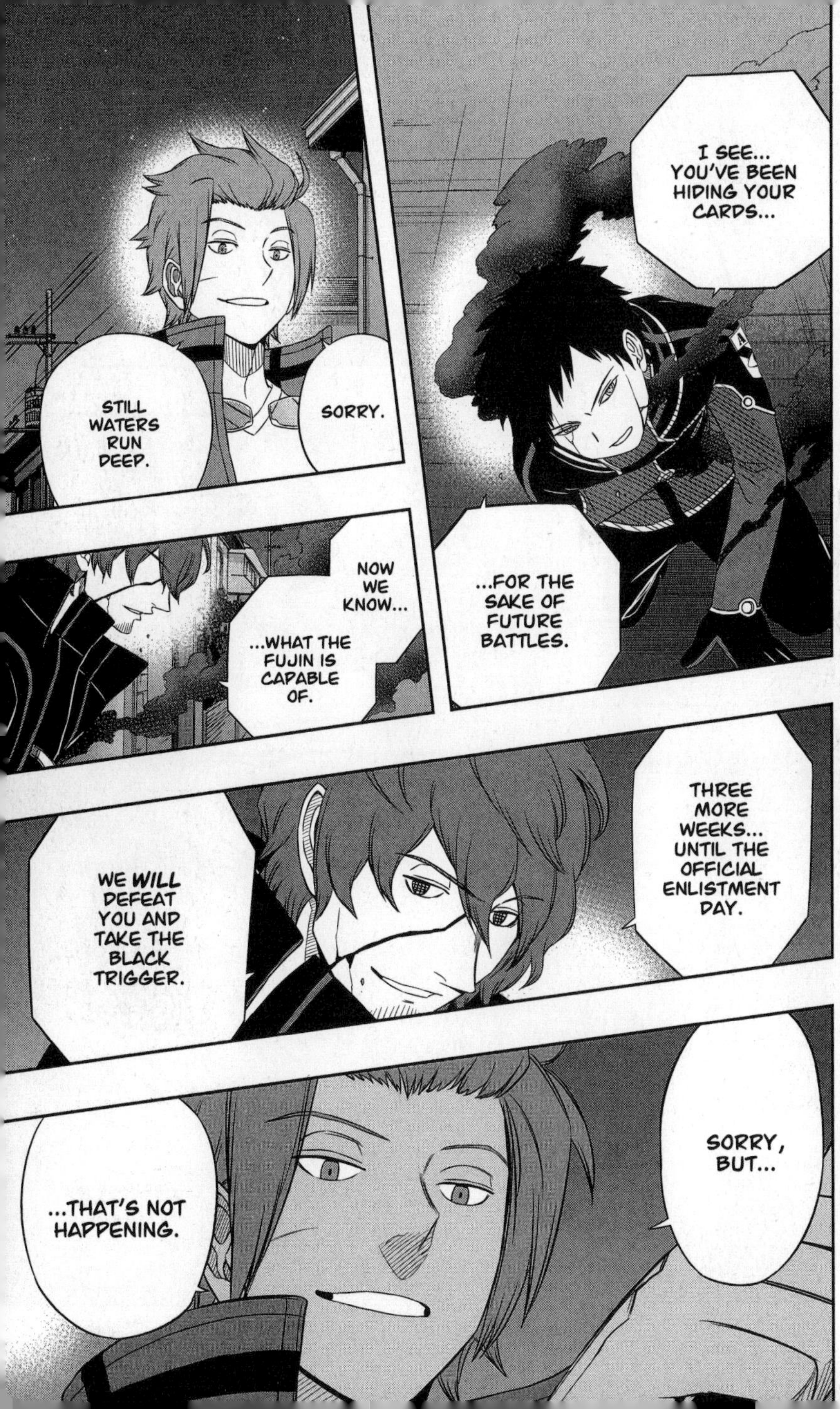
I SEE... YOU'VE BEEN HIDING YOUR CARDS...
...FOR THE SAKE OF FUTURE BATTLES.
SORRY.
STILL WATERS RUN DEEP.
NOW WE KNOW...
...WHAT THE FUJIN IS CAPABLE OF.
THREE MORE WEEKS... UNTIL THE OFFICIAL ENLISTMENT DAY.
WE WILL DEFEAT YOU AND TAKE THE BLACK TRIGGER.
SORRY, BUT...
...THAT'S NOT HAPPENING.

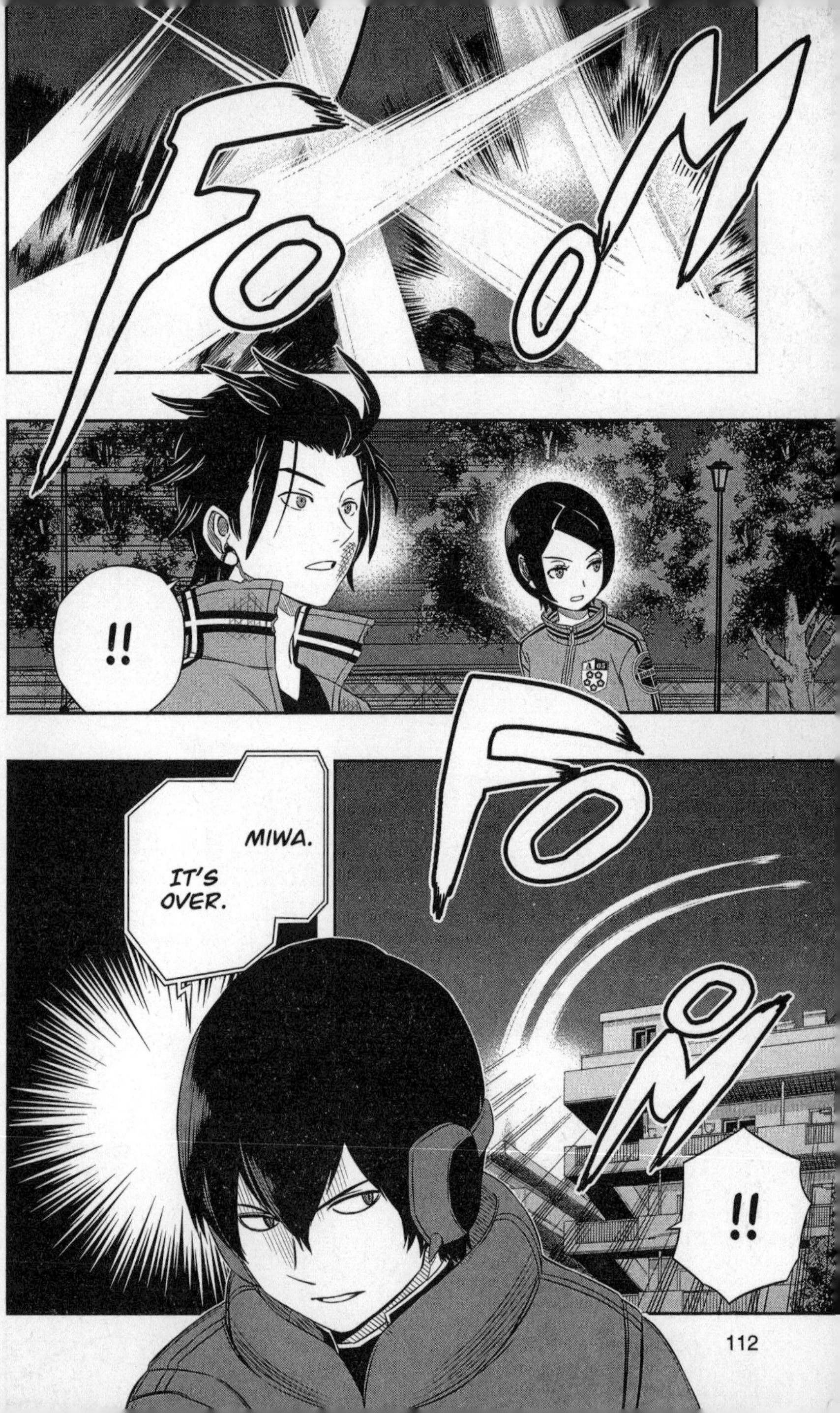
FOOM
!!
FOOM
MIWA.
IT'S OVER.
!!

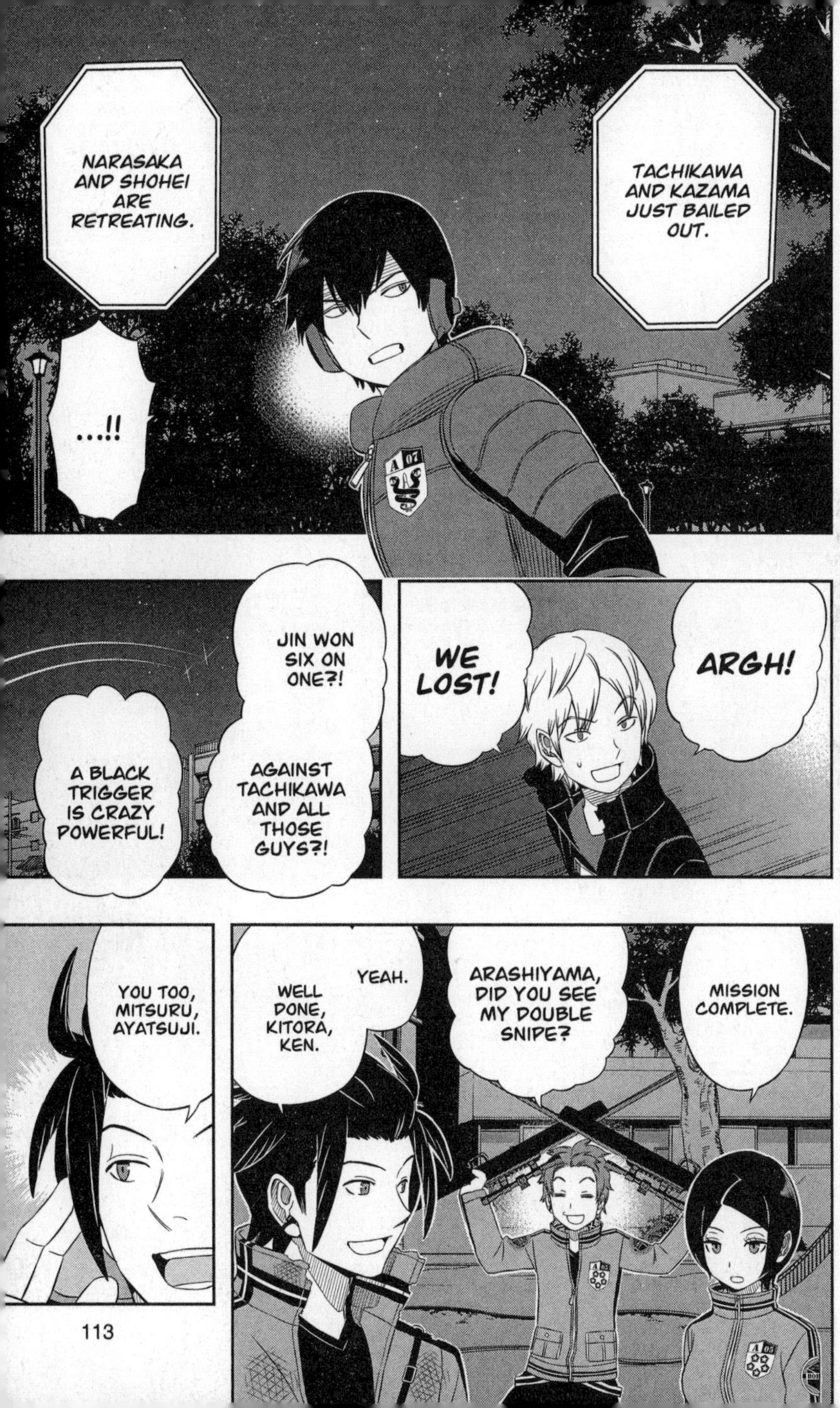
TACHIKAWA AND KAZAMA JUST BAILED OUT.
NARASAKA AND SHOHEI ARE RETREATING.
...!!
ARGH!
WE LOST!
JIN WON SIX ON ONE?!
AGAINST TACHIKAWA AND ALL THOSE GUYS?!
A BLACK TRIGGER IS CRAZY POWERFUL!
MISSION COMPLETE.
ARASHIYAMA, DID YOU SEE MY DOUBLE SNIPE?
YEAH.
WELL DONE, KITORA, KEN.
YOU TOO, MITSURU, AYATSUJI.

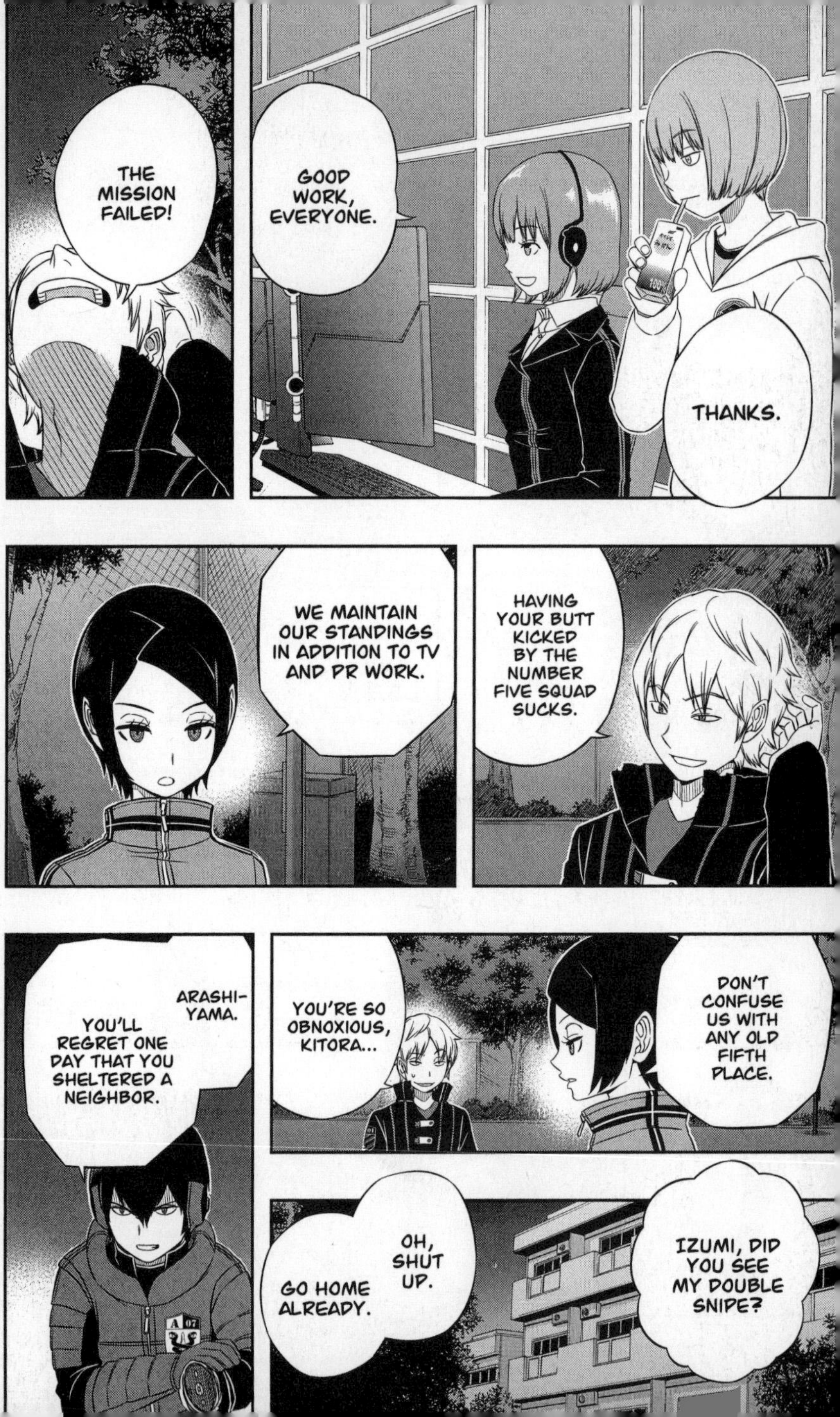
GOOD WORK, EVERYONE.
THANKS.
THE MISSION FAILED!
HAVING YOUR BUTT KICKED BY THE NUMBER FIVE SQUAD SUCKS.
WE MAINTAIN OUR STANDINGS IN ADDITION TO TV AND PR WORK.
DON'T CONFUSE US WITH ANY OLD FIFTH PLACE.
YOU'RE SO OBNOXIOUS, KITORA...
IZUMI, DID YOU SEE MY DOUBLE SNIPE?
OH, SHUT UP.
GO HOME ALREADY.
ARASHI-YAMA.
YOU'LL REGRET ONE DAY THAT YOU SHELTERED A NEIGHBOR.

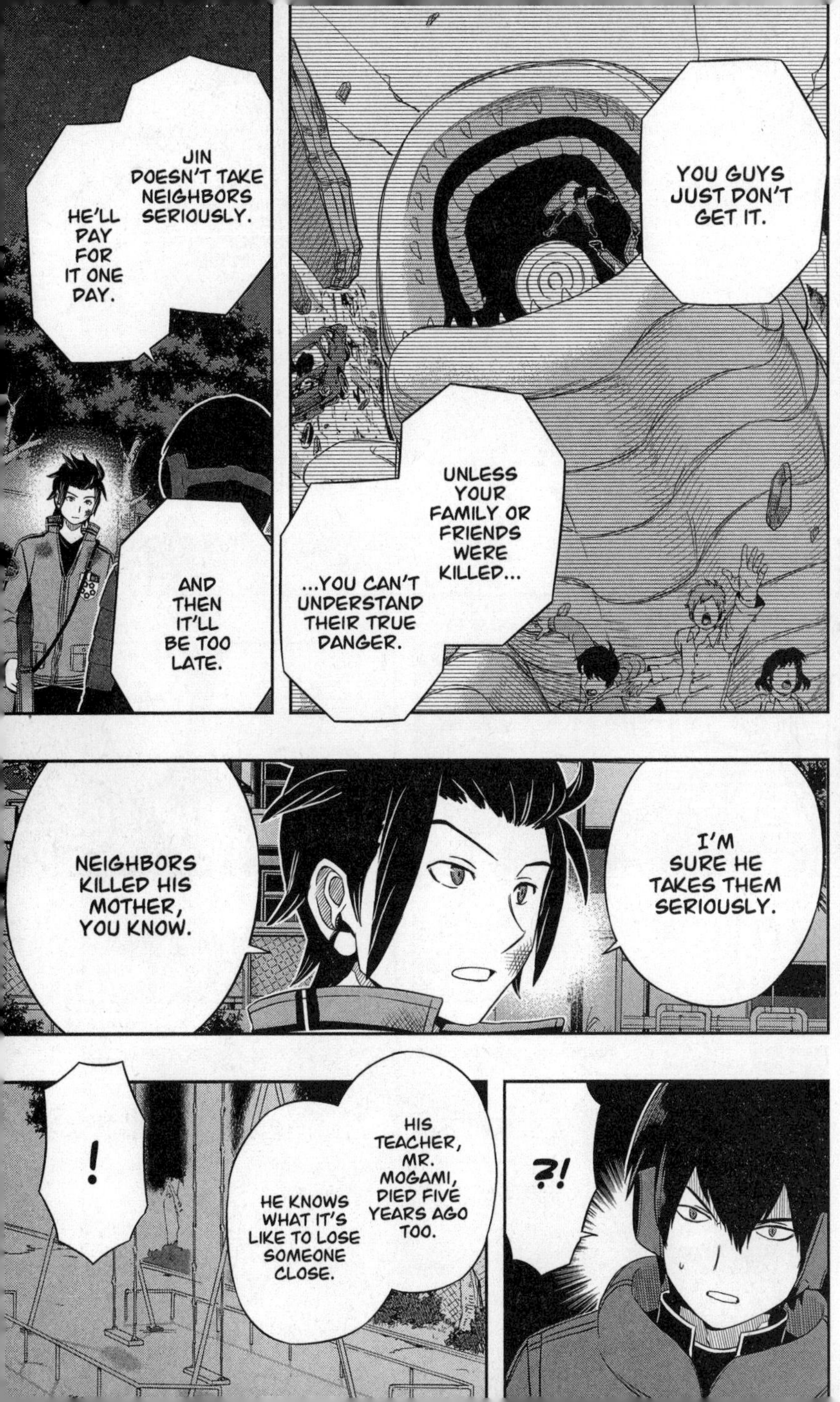
YOU GUYS JUST DON'T GET IT.
UNLESS YOUR FAMILY OR FRIENDS WERE KILLED...
...YOU CAN'T UNDERSTAND THEIR TRUE DANGER.
JIN DOESN'T TAKE NEIGHBORS SERIOUSLY.
HE'LL PAY FOR IT ONE DAY.
AND THEN IT'LL BE TOO LATE.
I'M SURE HE TAKES THEM SERIOUSLY.
NEIGHBORS KILLED HIS MOTHER, YOU KNOW.
?!
HIS TEACHER, MR. MOGAMI, DIED FIVE YEARS AGO TOO.
HE KNOWS WHAT IT'S LIKE TO LOSE SOMEONE CLOSE.
!

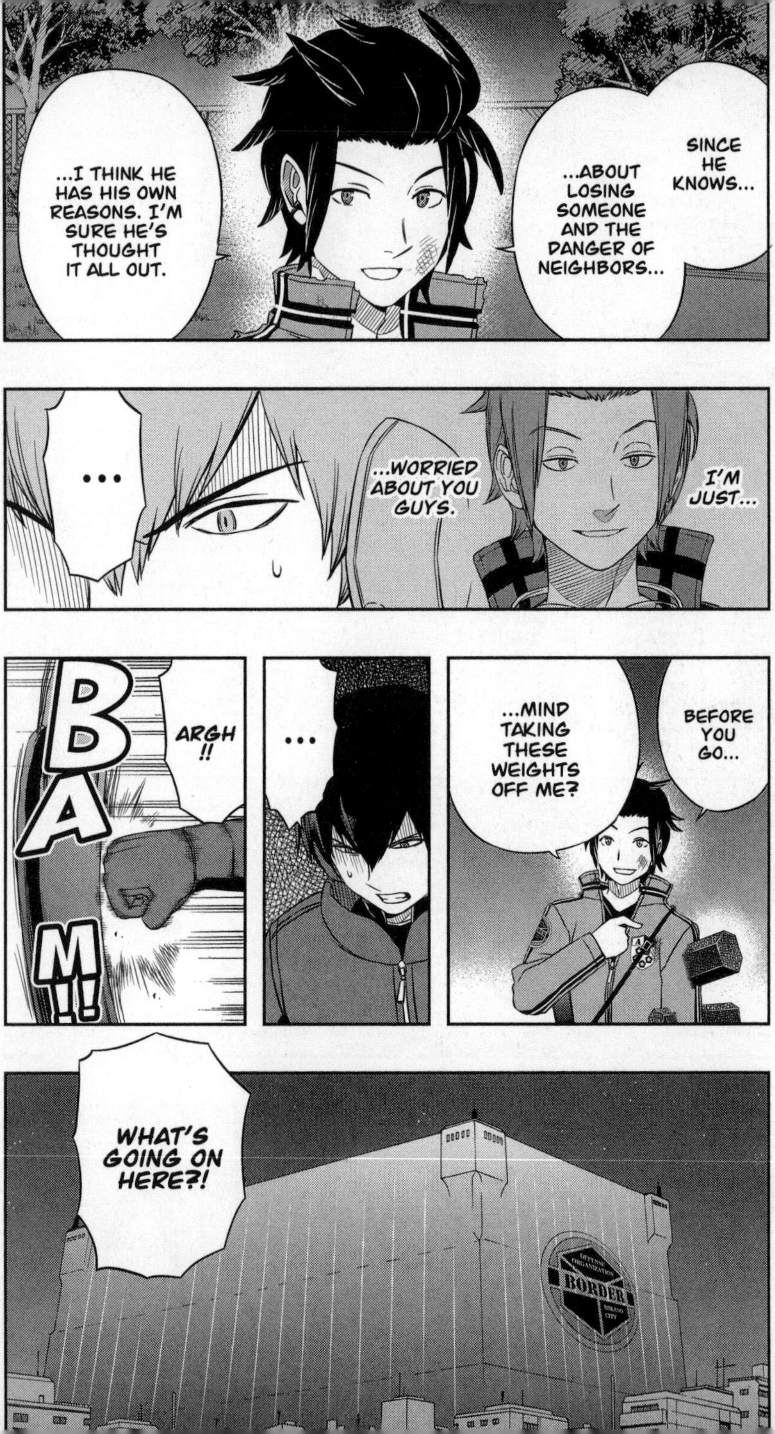
SINCE HE KNOWS...
...ABOUT LOSING SOMEONE AND THE DANGER OF NEIGHBORS...
...I THINK HE HAS HIS OWN REASONS. I'M SURE HE'S THOUGHT IT ALL OUT.
I'M JUST...
...WORRIED ABOUT YOU GUYS.
...
BEFORE YOU GO...
...MIND TAKING THESE WEIGHTS OFF ME?
...
ARGH!!
BAM!!
WHAT'S GOING ON HERE?!
BORDER

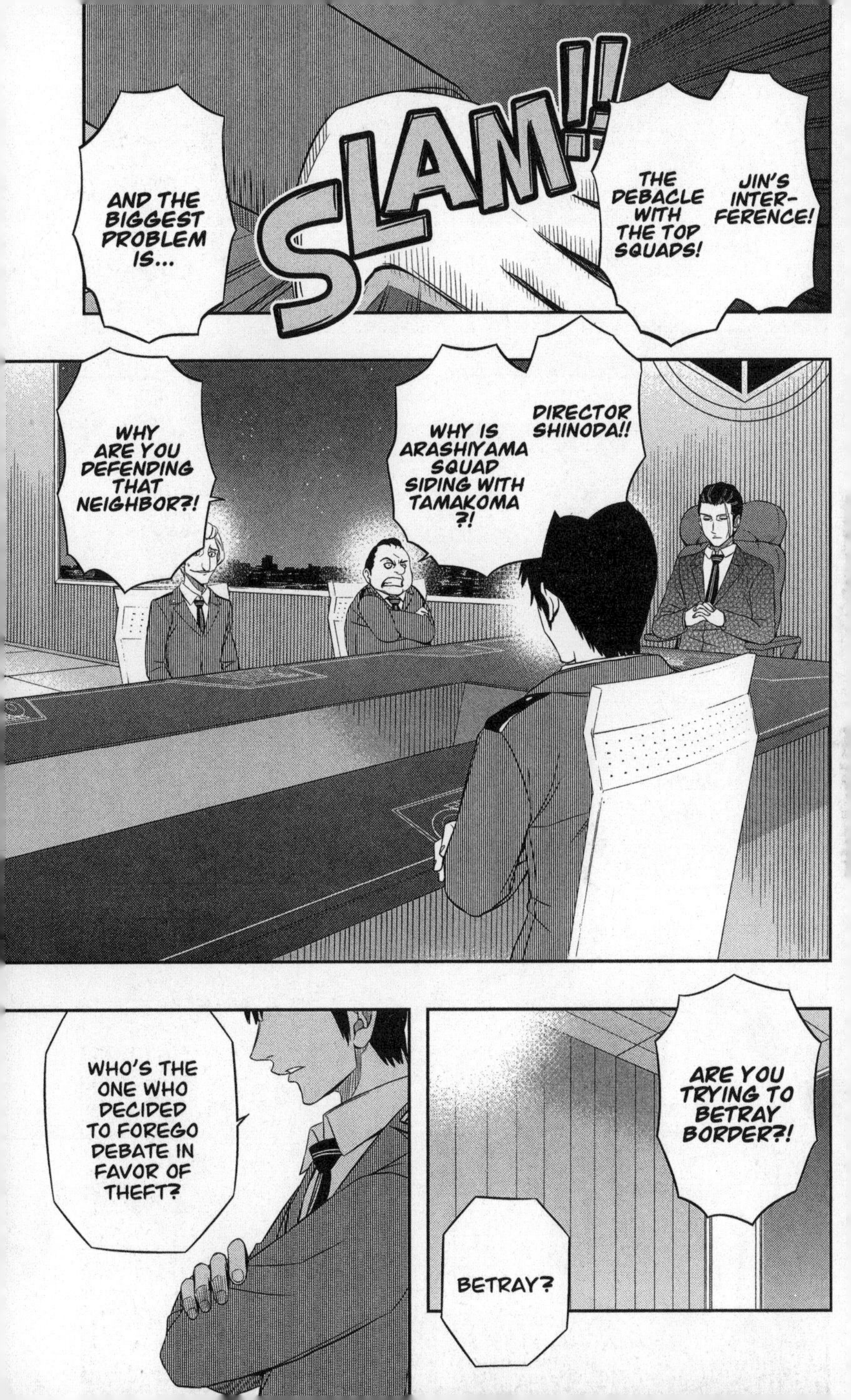
JIN'S INTERFERENCE!
THE DEBACLE WITH THE TOP SQUADS!
SLAM!!
AND THE BIGGEST PROBLEM IS...
DIRECTOR SHINODA!!
WHY IS ARASHIYAMA SQUAD SIDING WITH TAMAKOMA?!
WHY ARE YOU DEFENDING THAT NEIGHBOR?!
ARE YOU TRYING TO BETRAY BORDER?!
BETRAY?
WHO'S THE ONE WHO DECIDED TO FOREGO DEBATE IN FAVOR OF THEFT?

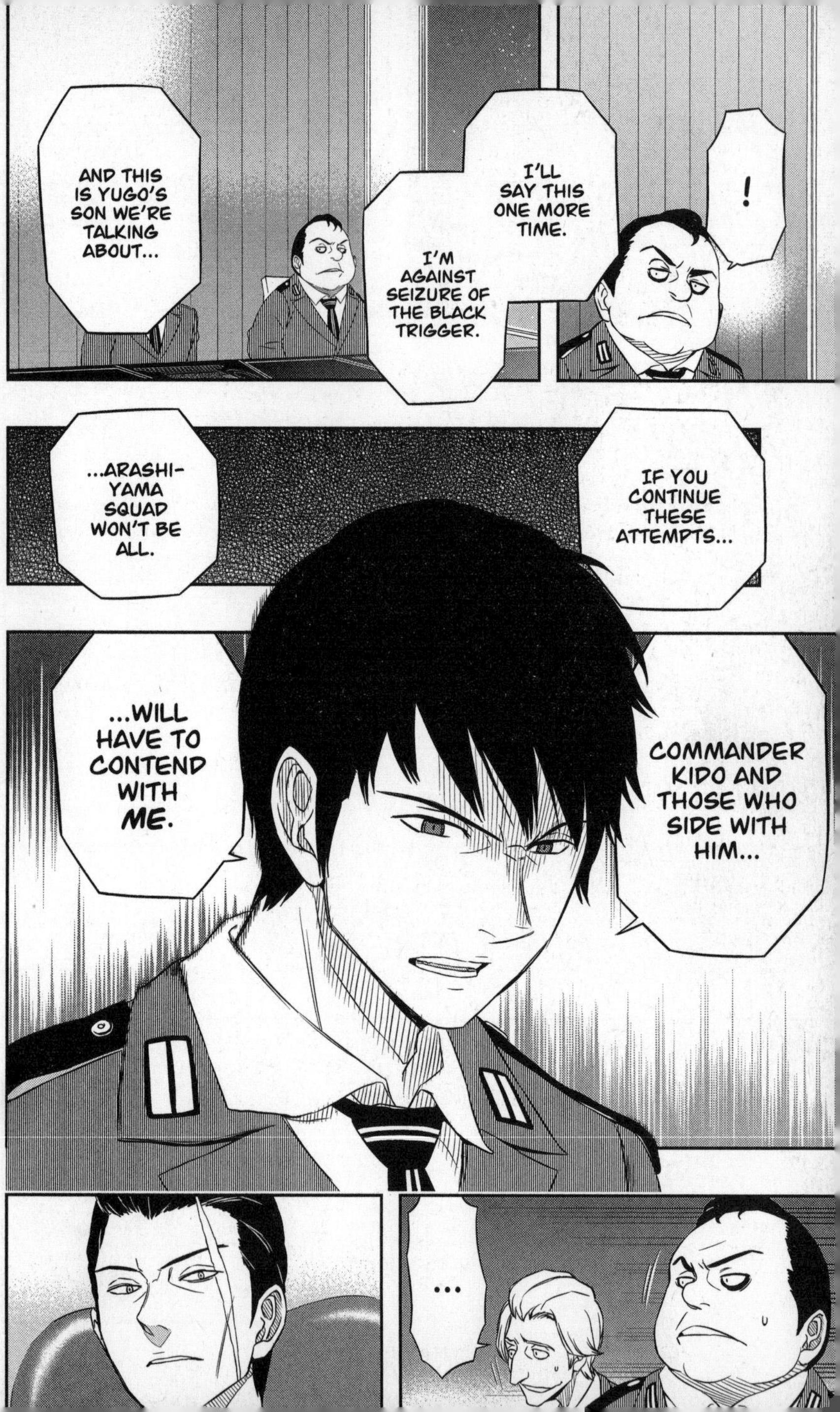
!
I'LL SAY THIS ONE MORE TIME.
I'M AGAINST SEIZURE OF THE BLACK TRIGGER.
AND THIS IS YUGO'S SON WE'RE TALKING ABOUT...
IF YOU CONTINUE THESE ATTEMPTS...
...ARASHI-YAMA SQUAD WON'T BE ALL.
COMMANDER KIDO AND THOSE WHO SIDE WITH HIM...
...WILL HAVE TO CONTEND WITH ME.
...

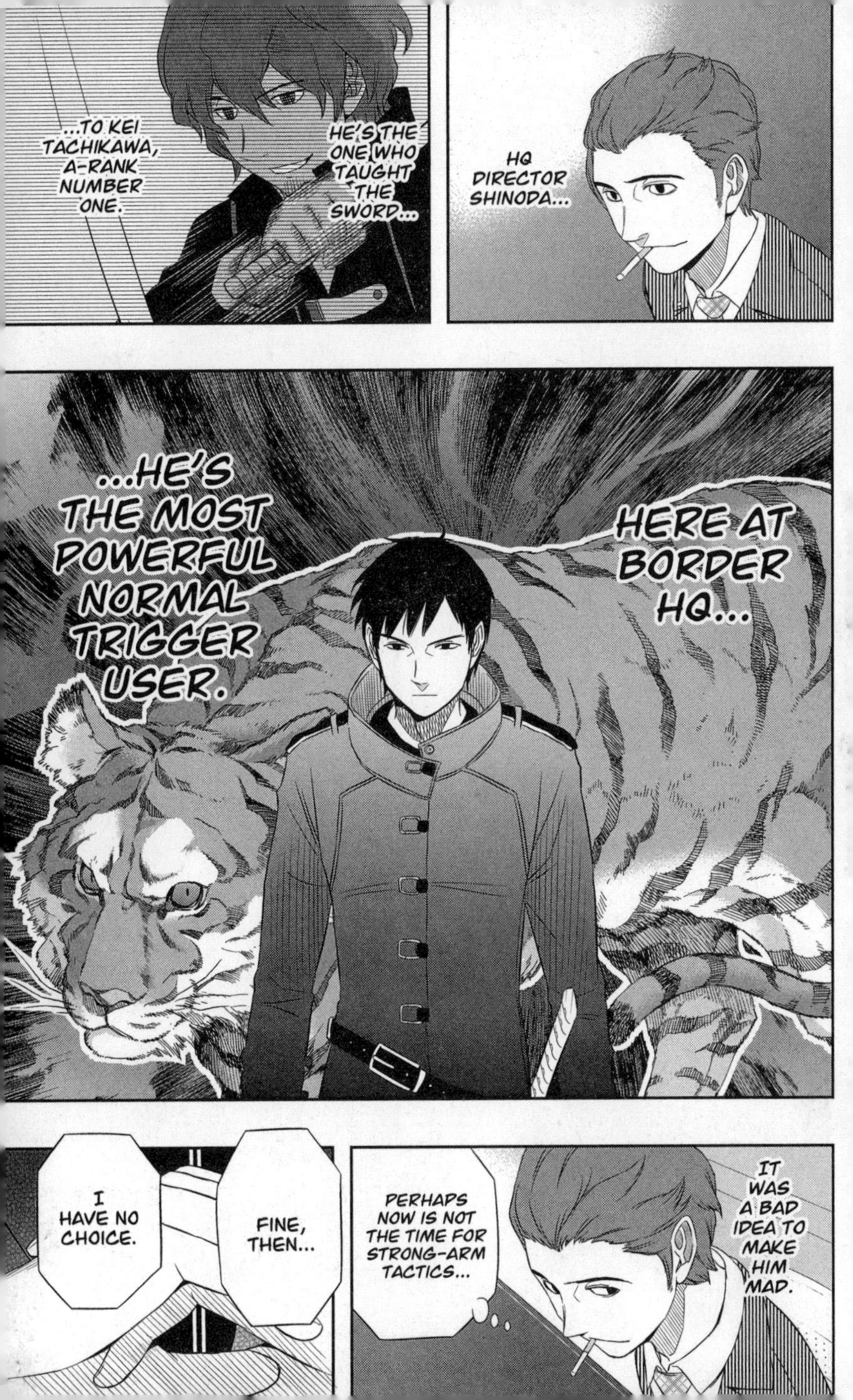
HQ DIRECTOR SHINODA...
HE'S THE ONE WHO TAUGHT THE SWORD...
...TO KEI TACHIKAWA, A-RANK NUMBER ONE.
HERE AT BORDER HQ...
...HE'S THE MOST POWERFUL NORMAL TRIGGER USER.
IT WAS A BAD IDEA TO MAKE HIM MAD.
PERHAPS NOW IS NOT THE TIME FOR STRONG-ARM TACTICS...
FINE, THEN...
I HAVE NO CHOICE.

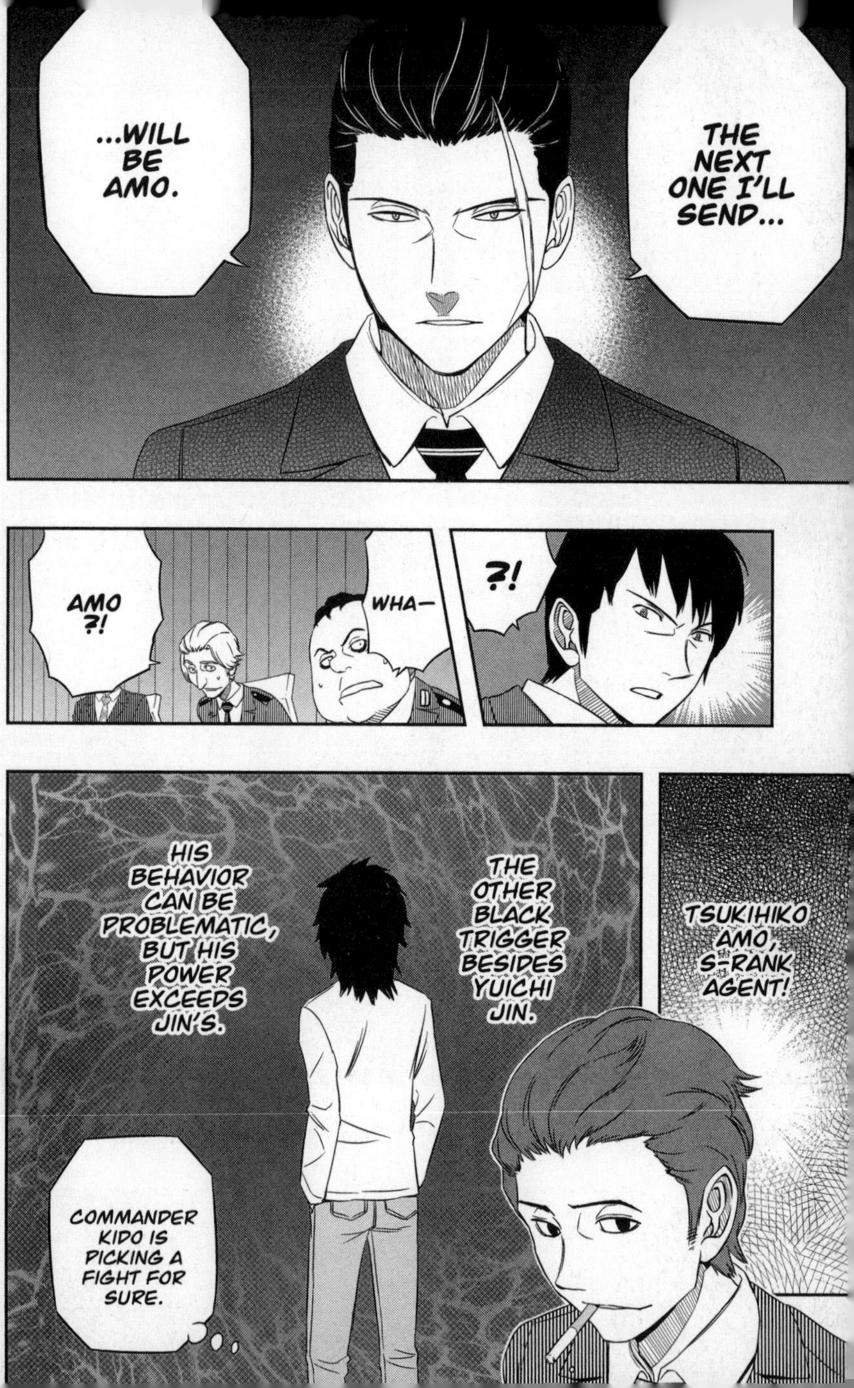
THE NEXT ONE I'LL SEND...
...WILL BE AMO.
?!
WHA—
AMO ?!
TSUKIHIKO AMO, S-RANK AGENT!
THE OTHER BLACK TRIGGER BESIDES YUICHI JIN.
HIS BEHAVIOR CAN BE PROBLEMATIC, BUT HIS POWER EXCEEDS JIN'S.
COMMANDER KIDO IS PICKING A FIGHT FOR SURE.

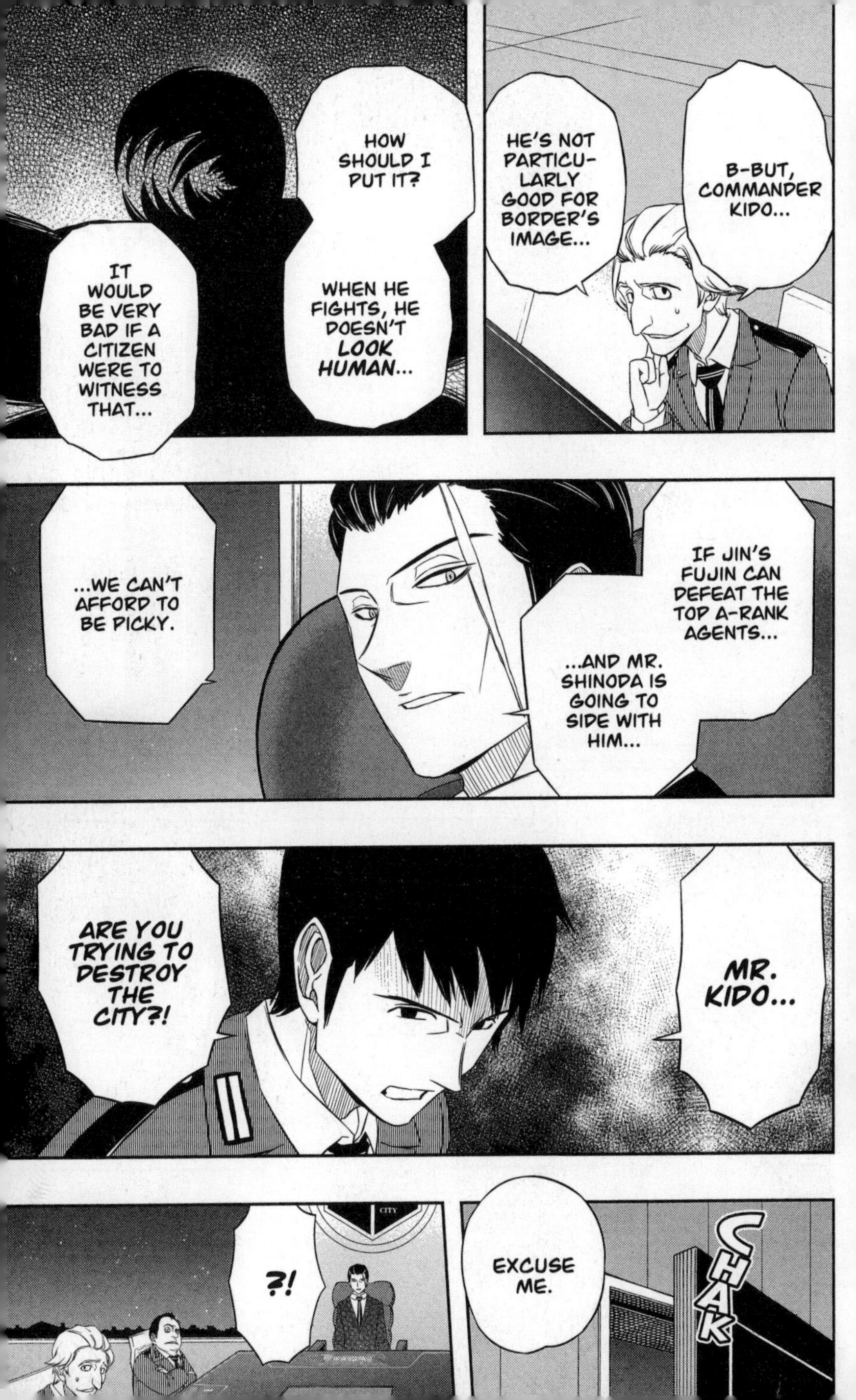
B-BUT, COMMANDER KIDO...
HE'S NOT PARTICULARLY GOOD FOR BORDER'S IMAGE...
HOW SHOULD I PUT IT?
WHEN HE FIGHTS, HE DOESN'T LOOK HUMAN...
IT WOULD BE VERY BAD IF A CITIZEN WERE TO WITNESS THAT...
IF JIN'S FUJIN CAN DEFEAT THE TOP A-RANK AGENTS...
...AND MR. SHINODA IS GOING TO SIDE WITH HIM...
...WE CAN'T AFFORD TO BE PICKY.
MR. KIDO...
ARE YOU TRYING TO DESTROY THE CITY?!
CHAK
EXCUSE ME.
?!

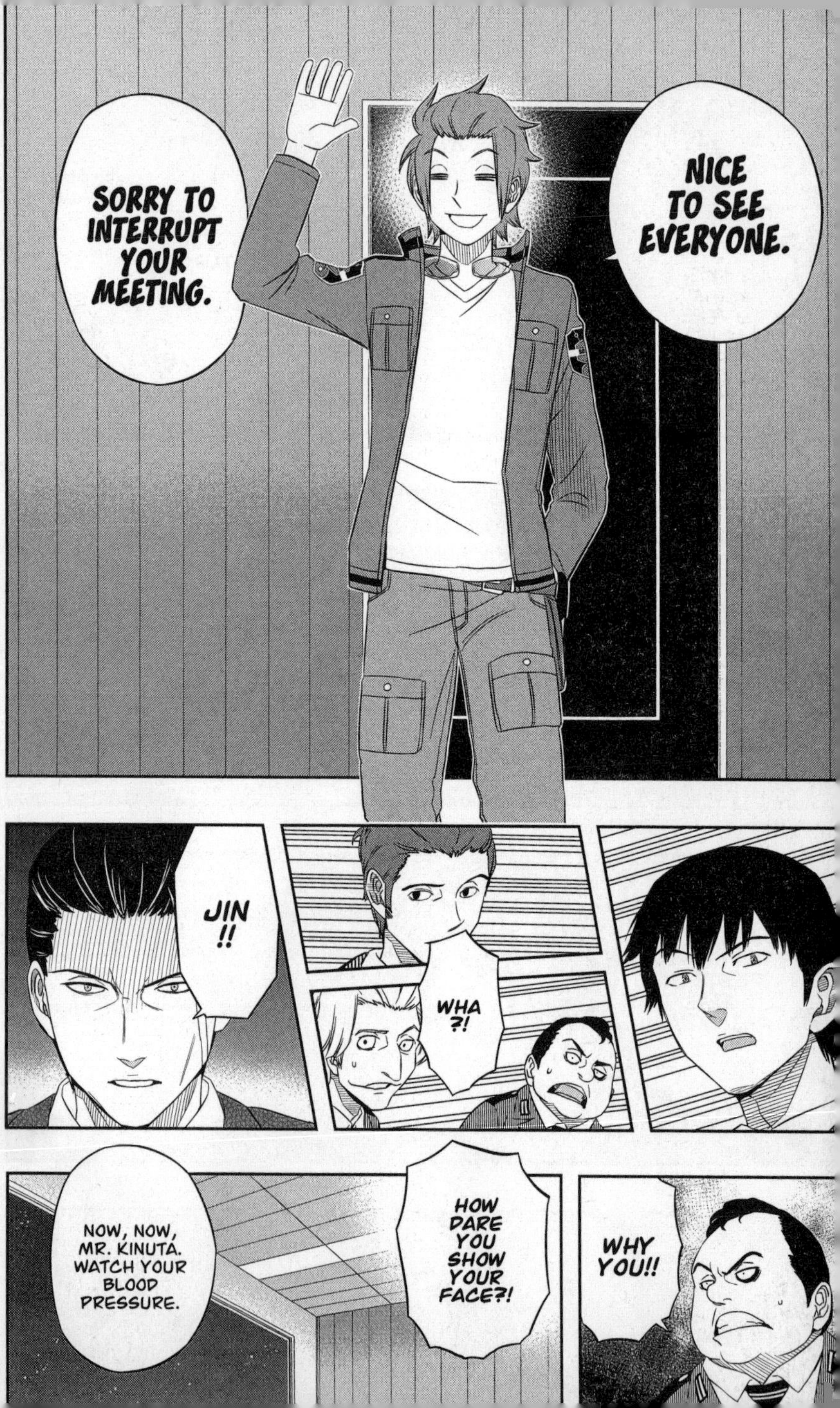
NICE TO SEE EVERYONE.
SORRY TO INTERRUPT YOUR MEETING.
WHA ?!
JIN !!
WHY YOU!!
HOW DARE YOU SHOW YOUR FACE?!
NOW, NOW, MR. KINUTA. WATCH YOUR BLOOD PRESSURE.

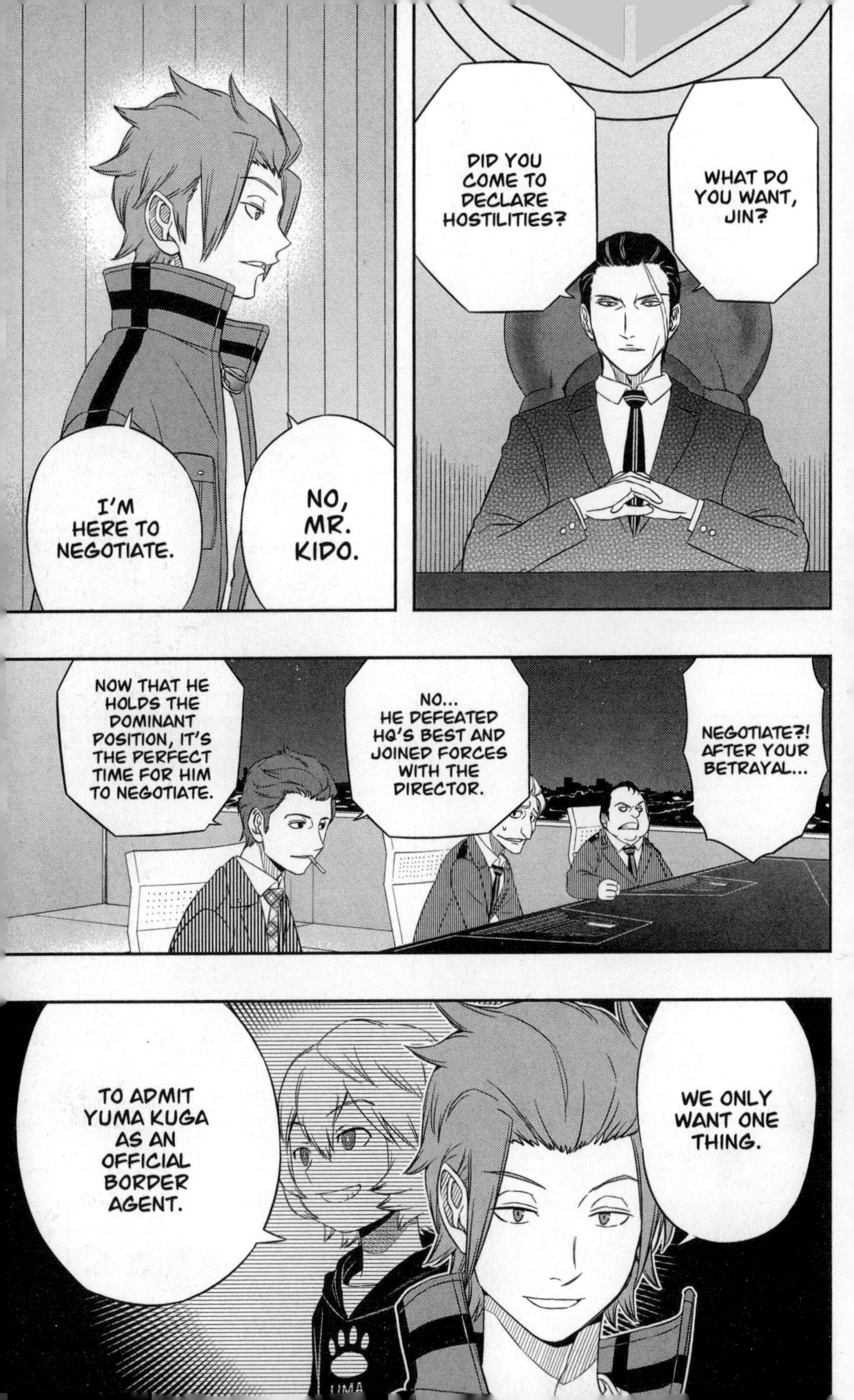
WHAT DO YOU WANT, JIN?
DID YOU COME TO DECLARE HOSTILITIES?
NO, MR. KIDO.
I'M HERE TO NEGOTIATE.
NEGOTIATE?! AFTER YOUR BETRAYAL...
NO... HE DEFEATED HQ'S BEST AND JOINED FORCES WITH THE DIRECTOR.
NOW THAT HE HOLDS THE DOMINANT POSITION, IT'S THE PERFECT TIME FOR HIM TO NEGOTIATE.
WE ONLY WANT ONE THING.
TO ADMIT YUMA KUGA AS AN OFFICIAL BORDER AGENT.

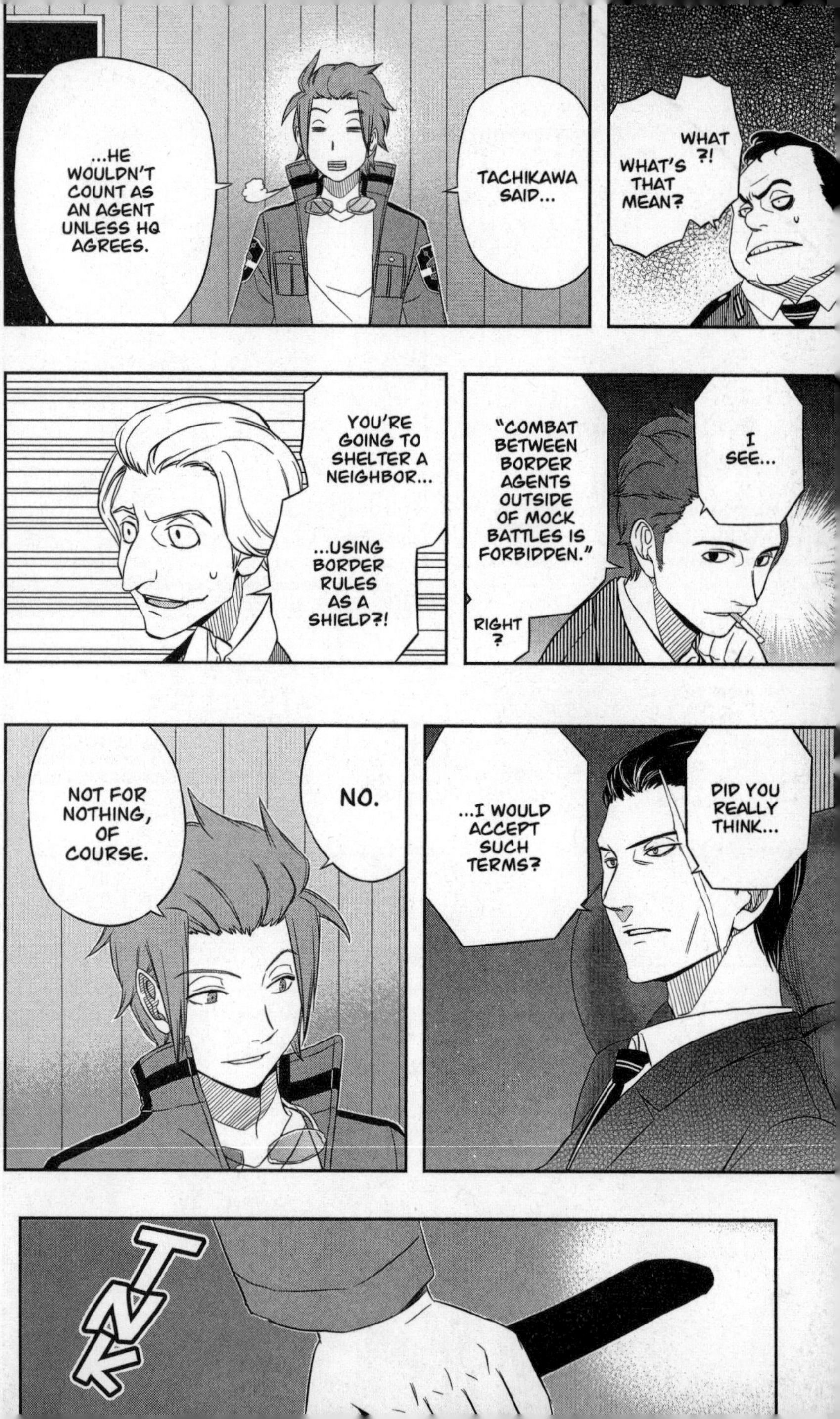
WHAT ?!
WHAT'S THAT MEAN?
TACHIKAWA SAID...
...HE WOULDN'T COUNT AS AN AGENT UNLESS HQ AGREES.
I SEE...
"COMBAT BETWEEN BORDER AGENTS OUTSIDE OF MOCK BATTLES IS FORBIDDEN."
RIGHT?
YOU'RE GOING TO SHELTER A NEIGHBOR...
...USING BORDER RULES AS A SHIELD?!
DID YOU REALLY THINK...
...I WOULD ACCEPT SUCH TERMS?
NO.
NOT FOR NOTHING, OF COURSE.
TINK

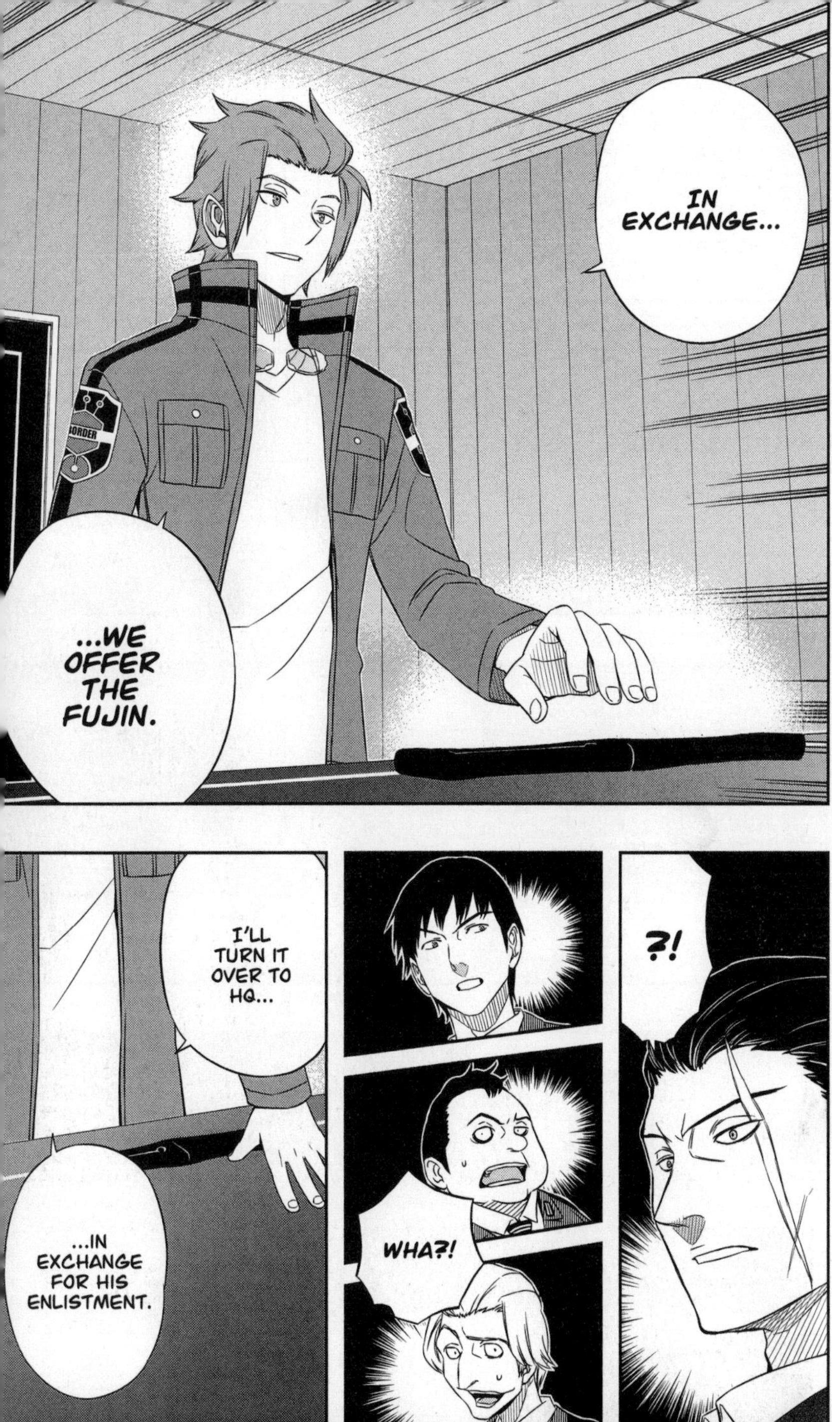
IN EXCHANGE...
...WE OFFER THE FUJIN.
?!
WHA?!
I'LL TURN IT OVER TO HQ...
...IN EXCHANGE FOR HIS ENLISTMENT.

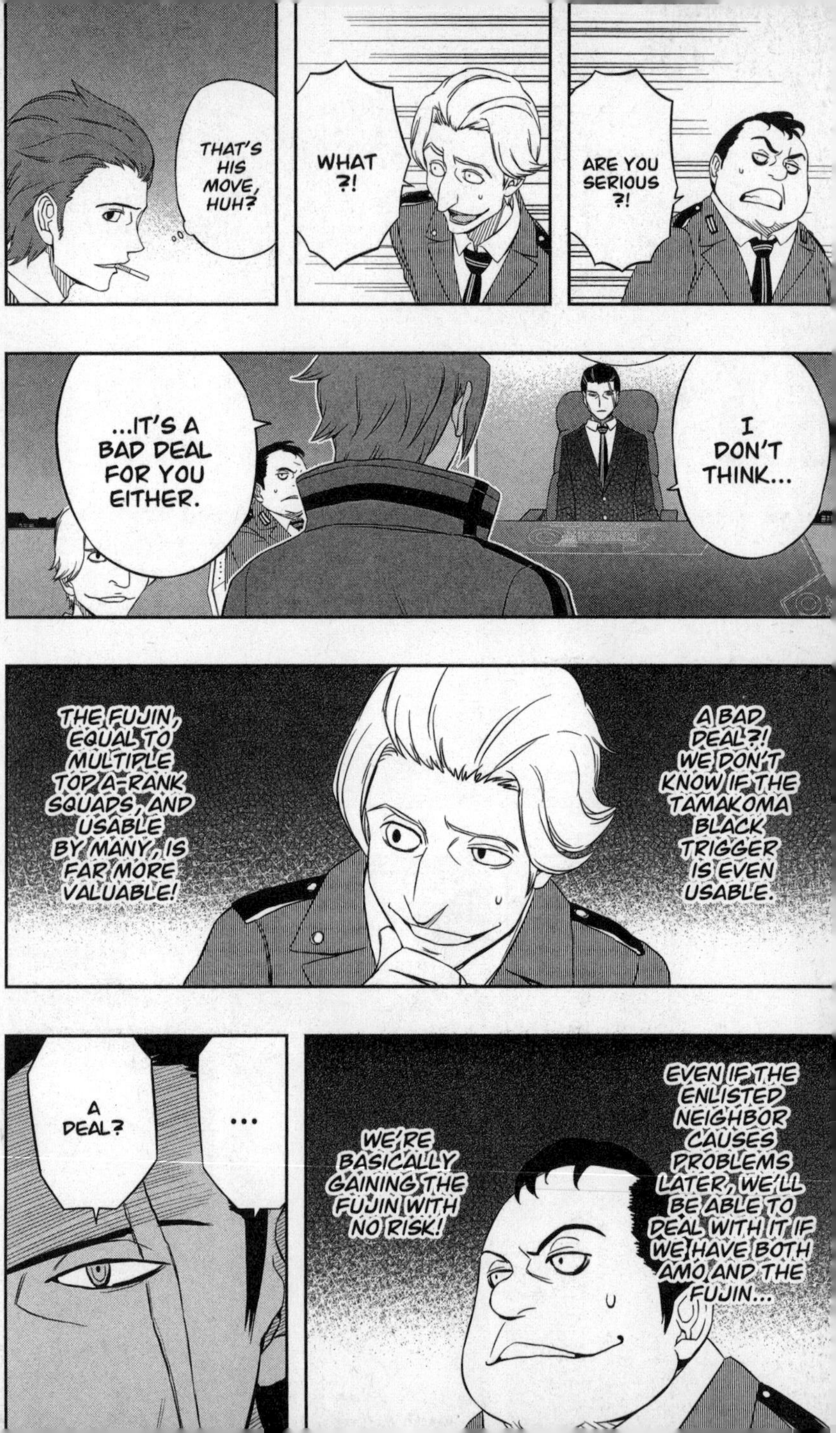
ARE YOU SERIOUS?!
WHAT?!
THAT'S HIS MOVE, HUH?
I DON'T THINK...
...IT'S A BAD DEAL FOR YOU EITHER.
A BAD DEAL?! WE DON'T KNOW IF THE TAMAKOMA BLACK TRIGGER IS EVEN USABLE.
THE FUJIN, EQUAL TO MULTIPLE TOP A-RANK SQUADS, AND USABLE BY MANY, IS FAR MORE VALUABLE!
EVEN IF THE ENLISTED NEIGHBOR CAUSES PROBLEMS LATER, WE'LL BE ABLE TO DEAL WITH IT IF WE HAVE BOTH AMO AND THE FUJIN...
WE'RE BASICALLY GAINING THE FUJIN WITH NO RISK!
...
A DEAL?

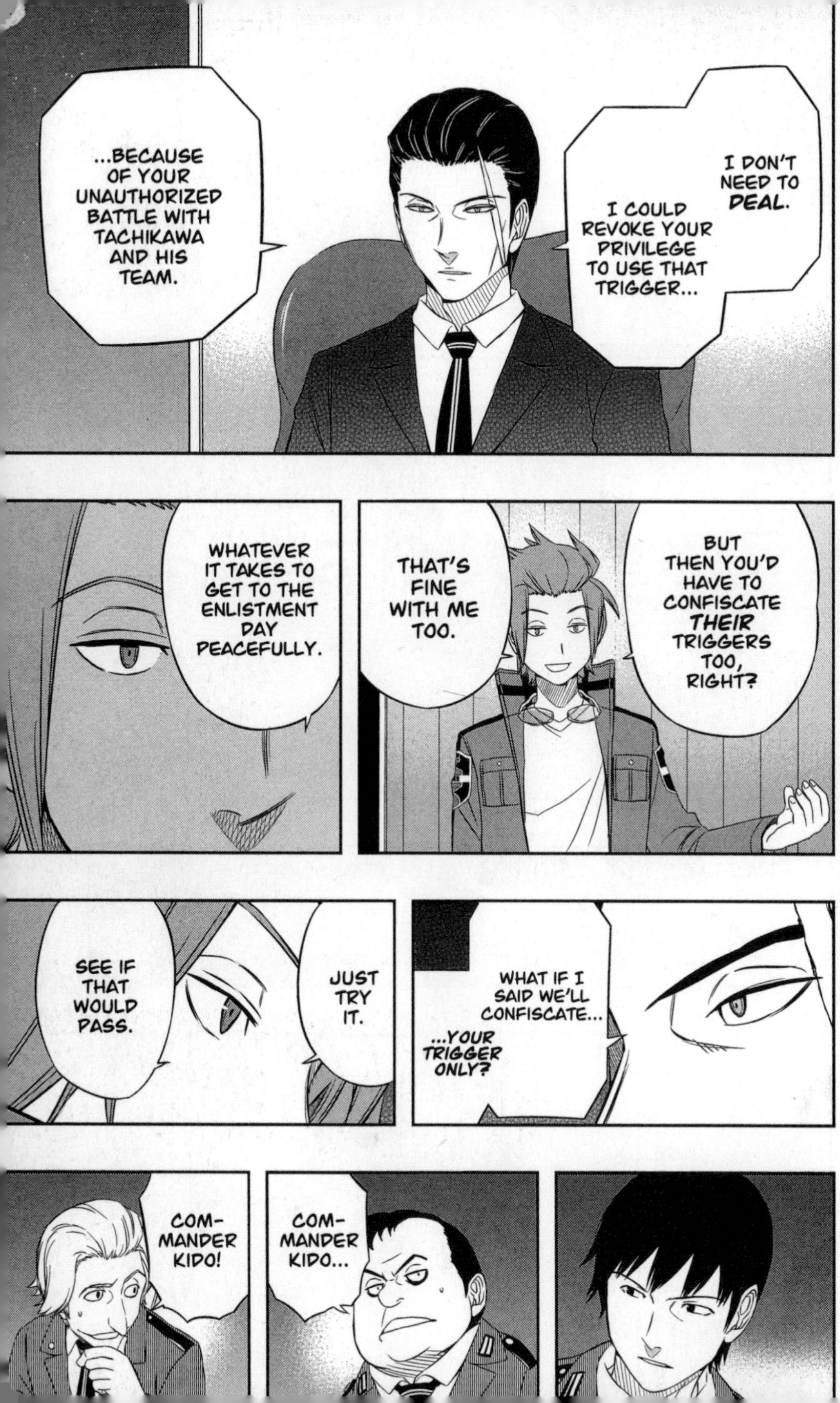
I DON'T NEED TO DEAL.
I COULD REVOKE YOUR PRIVILEGE TO USE THAT TRIGGER...
...BECAUSE OF YOUR UNAUTHORIZED BATTLE WITH TACHIKAWA AND HIS TEAM.
BUT THEN YOU'D HAVE TO CONFISCATE THEIR TRIGGERS TOO, RIGHT?
THAT'S FINE WITH ME TOO.
WHATEVER IT TAKES TO GET TO THE ENLISTMENT DAY PEACEFULLY.
WHAT IF I SAID WE'LL CONFISCATE...
...YOUR TRIGGER ONLY?
JUST TRY IT.
SEE IF THAT WOULD PASS.
COM-MANDER KIDO...
COM-MANDER KIDO!

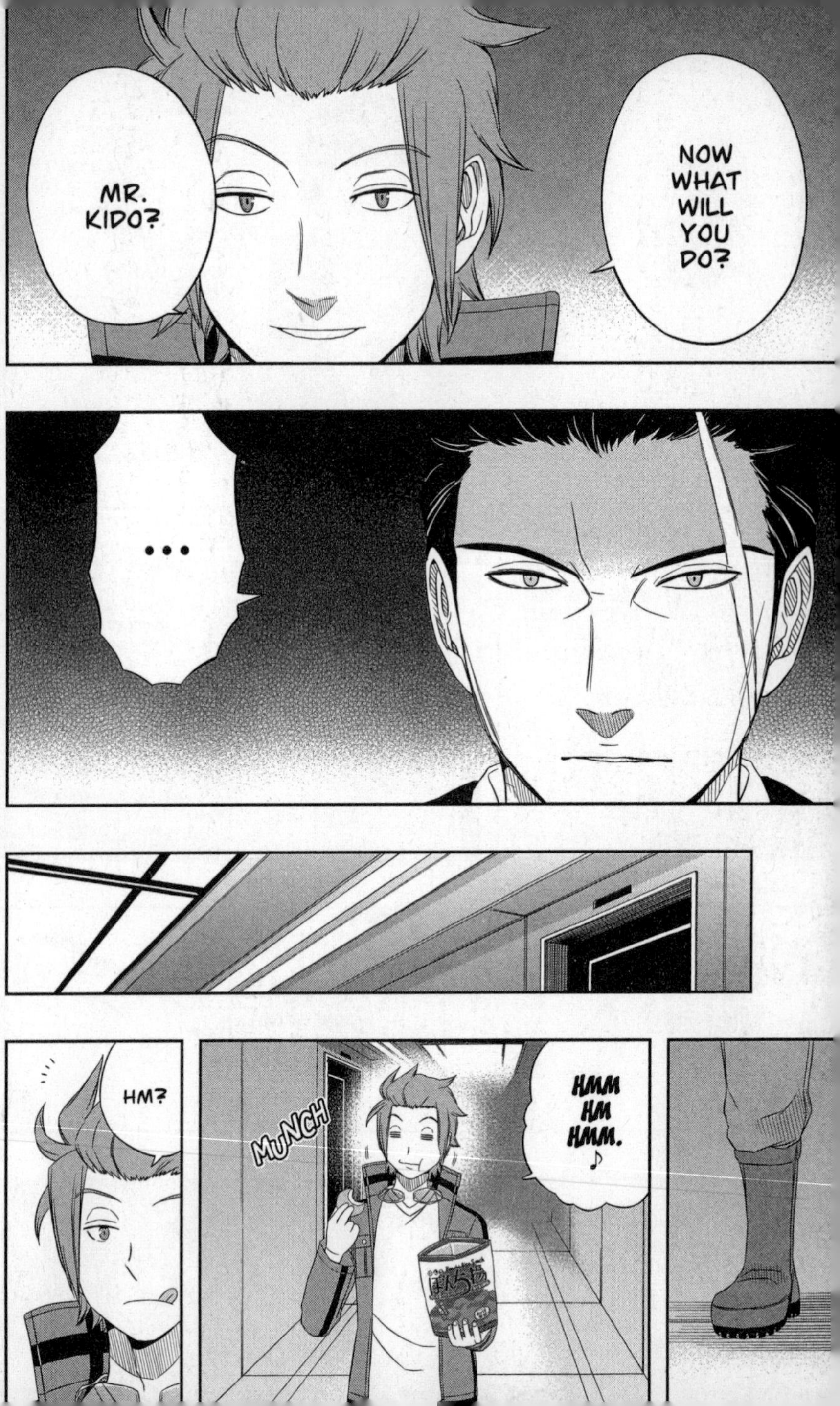
NOW WHAT WILL YOU DO?
MR. KIDO?
...
HMM HM HMM. ♪
MUNCH
HM?

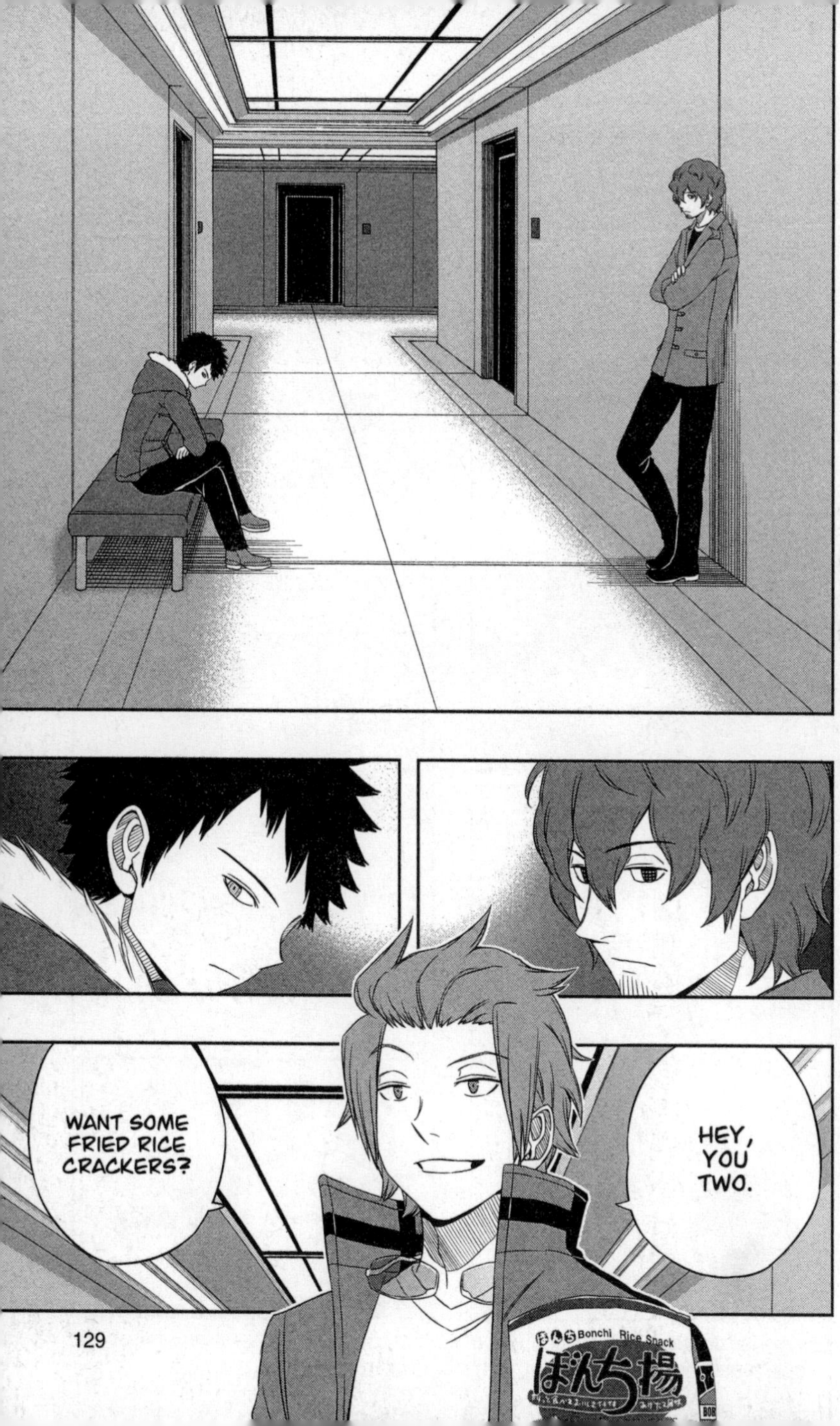
HEY, YOU TWO.
WANT SOME FRIED RICE CRACKERS?
Bonchi Rice Snack
ぼんち揚

Making Emblems

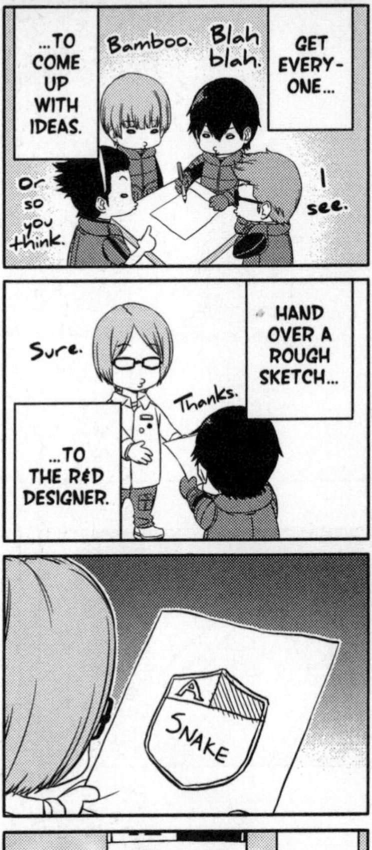
GET EVERY-ONE...
Blah blah.
Bamboo.
...TO COME UP WITH IDEAS.
I see.
Or so you think.
HAND OVER A ROUGH SKETCH...
Thanks.
Sure.
...TO THE R&D DESIGNER.
A
SNAKE
IT'S DONE.
Yup.
Just like we said..
Bamboo ...
Nice.

Good Luck, Capt. Miwa

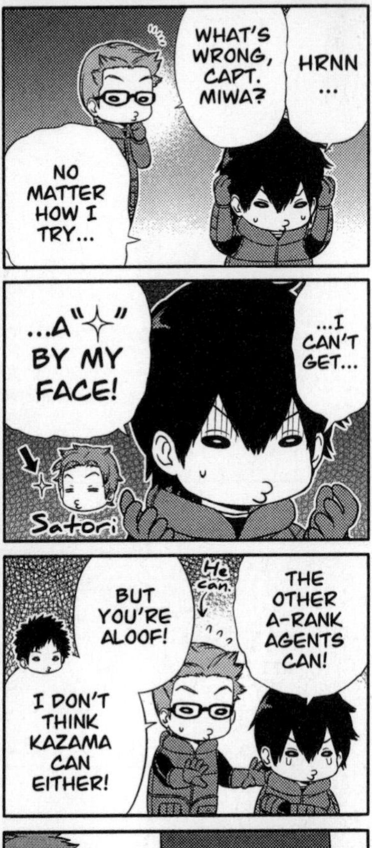
HRNN ...
WHAT'S WRONG, CAPT. MIWA?
NO MATTER HOW I TRY...
...I CAN'T GET...
...A "✧" BY MY FACE!
Satori
THE OTHER A-RANK AGENTS CAN!
He can.
BUT YOU'RE ALOOF!
I DON'T THINK KAZAMA CAN EITHER!

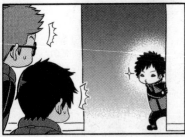

■ A bonus comic strip I did for *Jump NEXT!* The one on the right was to answer a fan question, "Who comes up with the squad emblems?"

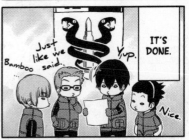

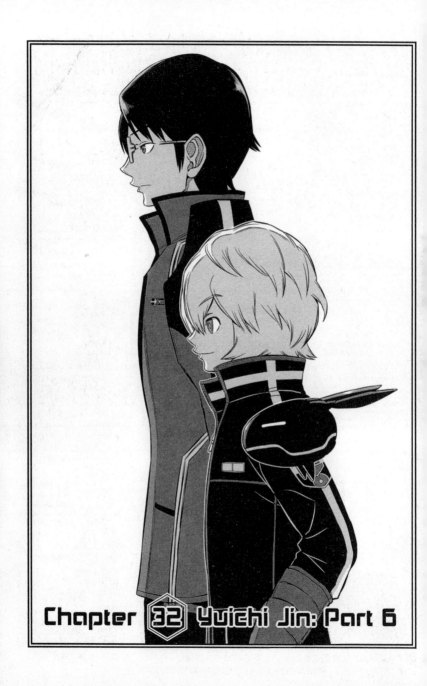

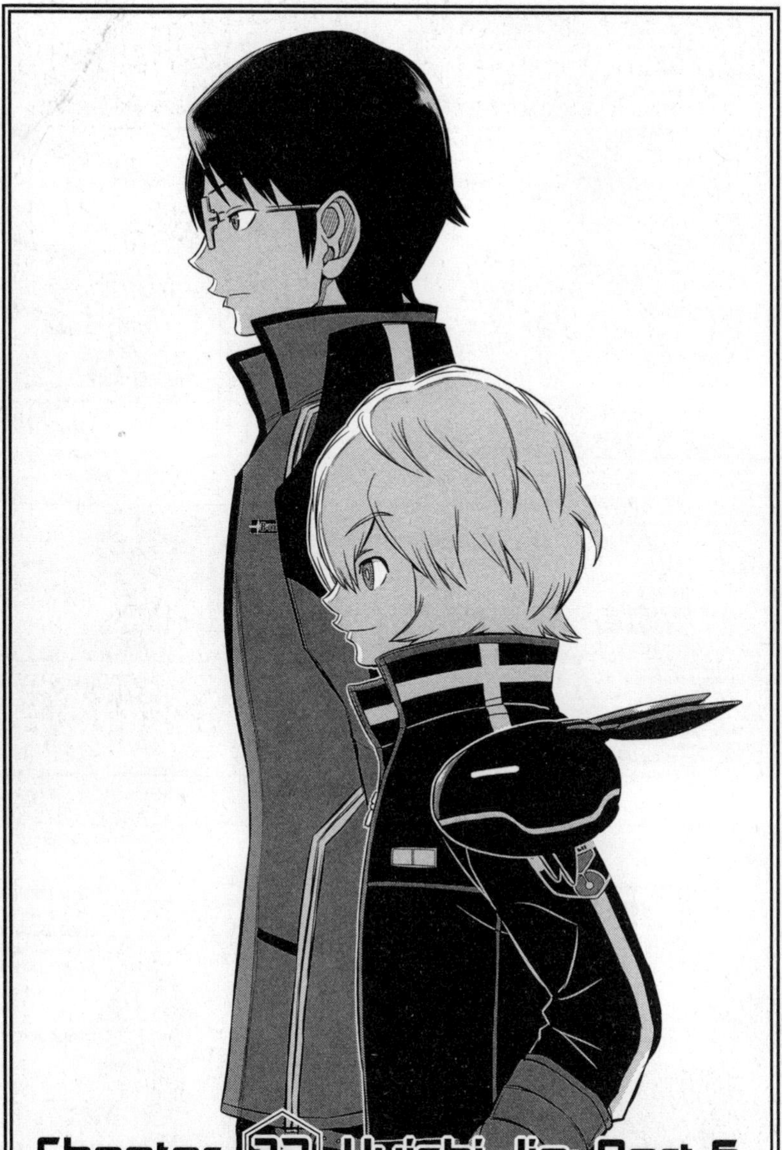
Chapter 32 Yuichi Jin: Part 6

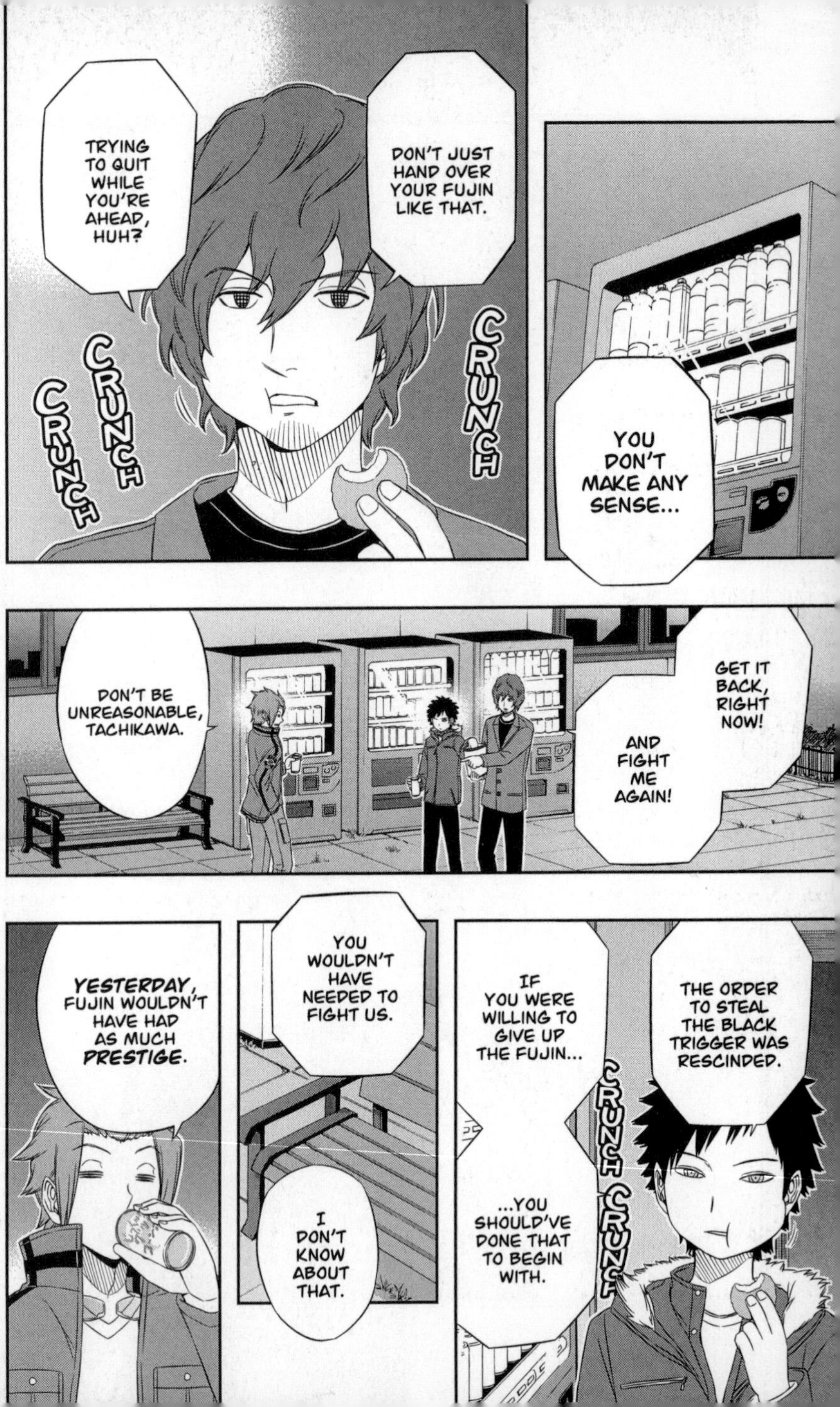
YOU DON'T MAKE ANY SENSE...
DON'T JUST HAND OVER YOUR FUJIN LIKE THAT.
TRYING TO QUIT WHILE YOU'RE AHEAD, HUH?
CRUNCH
CRUNCH
CRUNCH
GET IT BACK, RIGHT NOW!
AND FIGHT ME AGAIN!
DON'T BE UNREASONABLE, TACHIKAWA.
THE ORDER TO STEAL THE BLACK TRIGGER WAS RESCINDED.
CRUNCH CRUNCH
IF YOU WERE WILLING TO GIVE UP THE FUJIN...
...YOU SHOULD'VE DONE THAT TO BEGIN WITH.
YOU WOULDN'T HAVE NEEDED TO FIGHT US.
I DON'T KNOW ABOUT THAT.
YESTERDAY, FUJIN WOULDN'T HAVE HAD AS MUCH PRESTIGE.

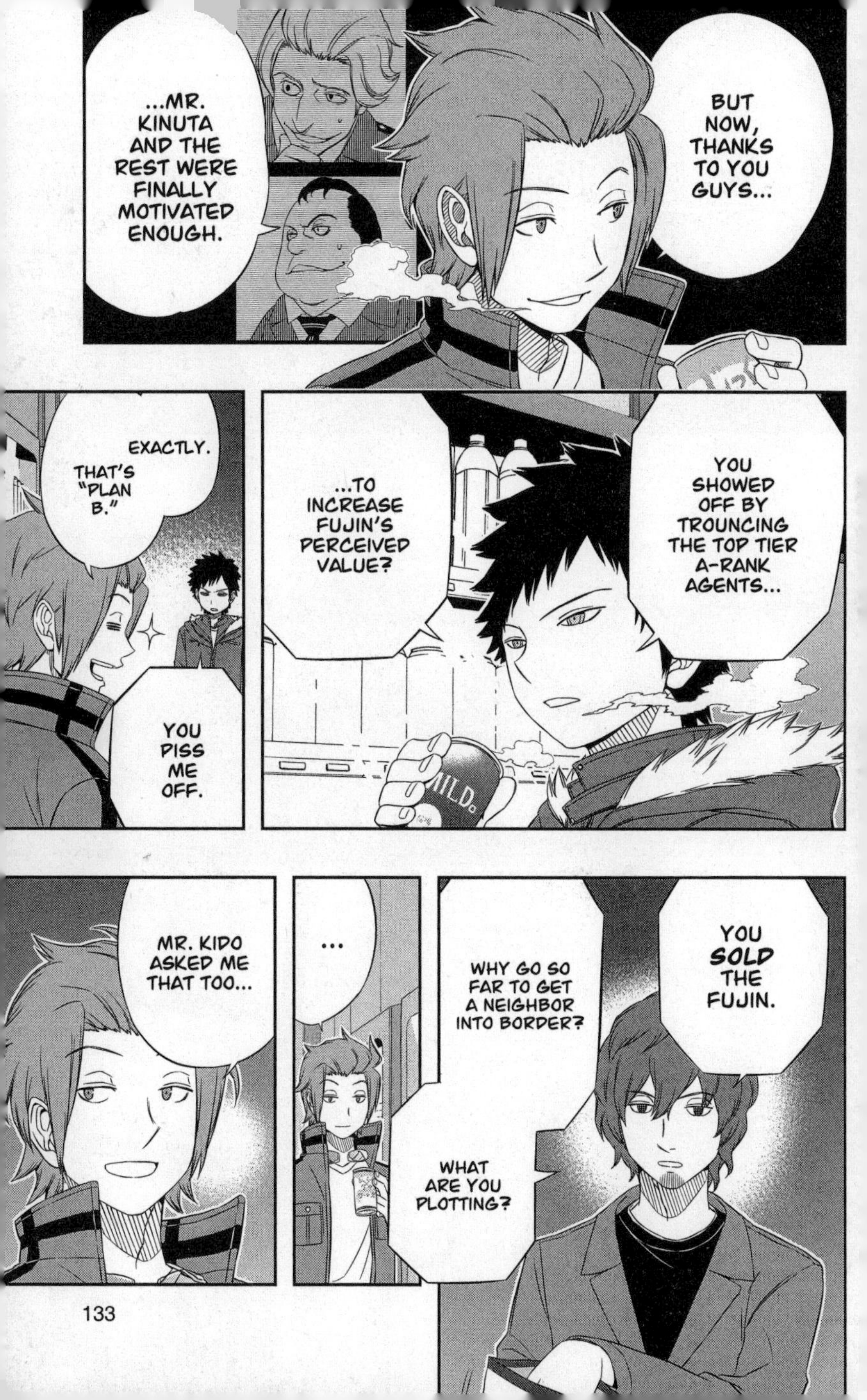
BUT NOW, THANKS TO YOU GUYS...
...MR. KINUTA AND THE REST WERE FINALLY MOTIVATED ENOUGH.
YOU SHOWED OFF BY TROUNCING THE TOP TIER A-RANK AGENTS...
...TO INCREASE FUJIN'S PERCEIVED VALUE?
EXACTLY. THAT'S "PLAN B."
YOU PISS ME OFF.
YOU **SOLD** THE FUJIN.
WHY GO SO FAR TO GET A NEIGHBOR INTO BORDER?
WHAT ARE YOU PLOTTING?
...
MR. KIDO ASKED ME THAT TOO...

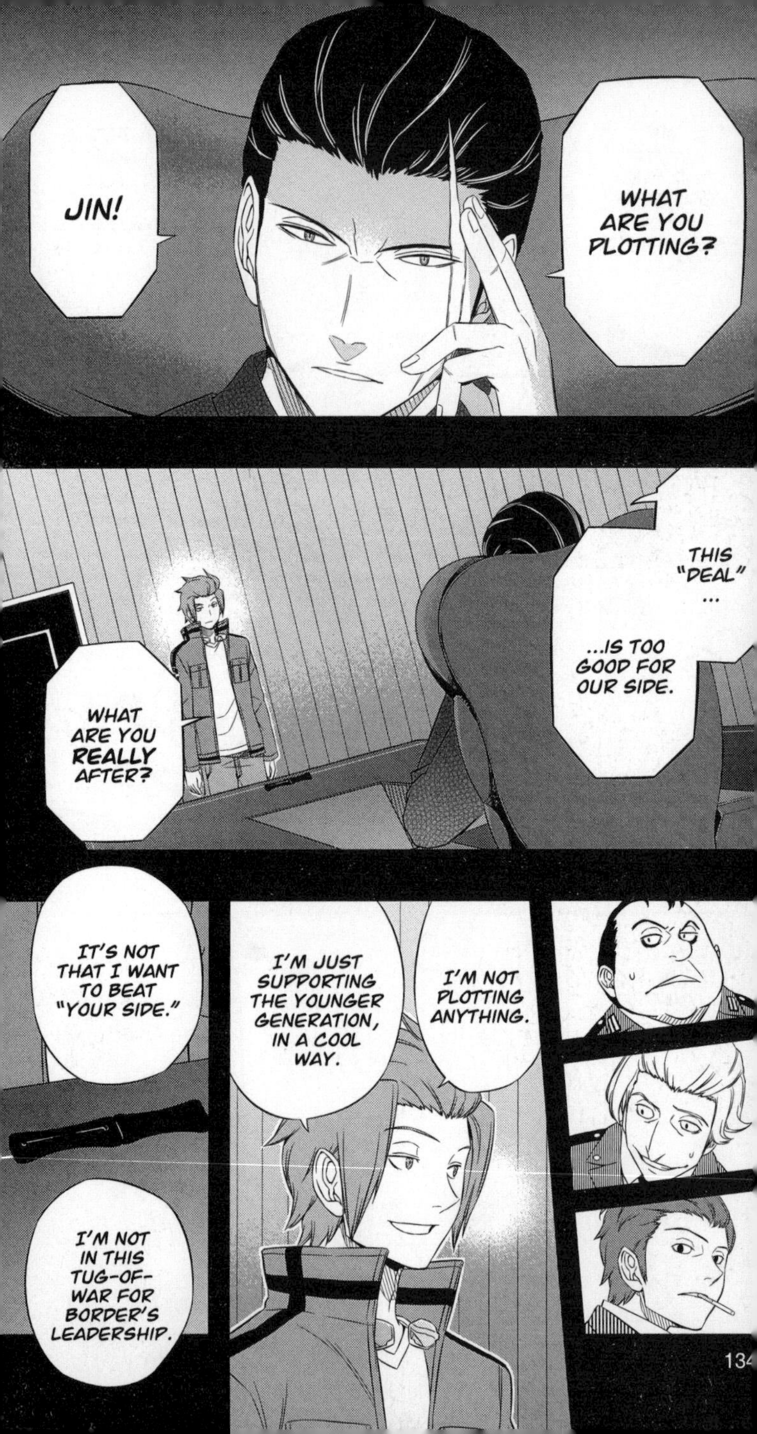
WHAT ARE YOU PLOTTING?
JIN!
THIS "DEAL"...
...IS TOO GOOD FOR OUR SIDE.
WHAT ARE YOU REALLY AFTER?
I'M NOT PLOTTING ANYTHING.
I'M JUST SUPPORTING THE YOUNGER GENERATION, IN A COOL WAY.
IT'S NOT THAT I WANT TO BEAT "YOUR SIDE."
I'M NOT IN THIS TUG-OF-WAR FOR BORDER'S LEADERSHIP.

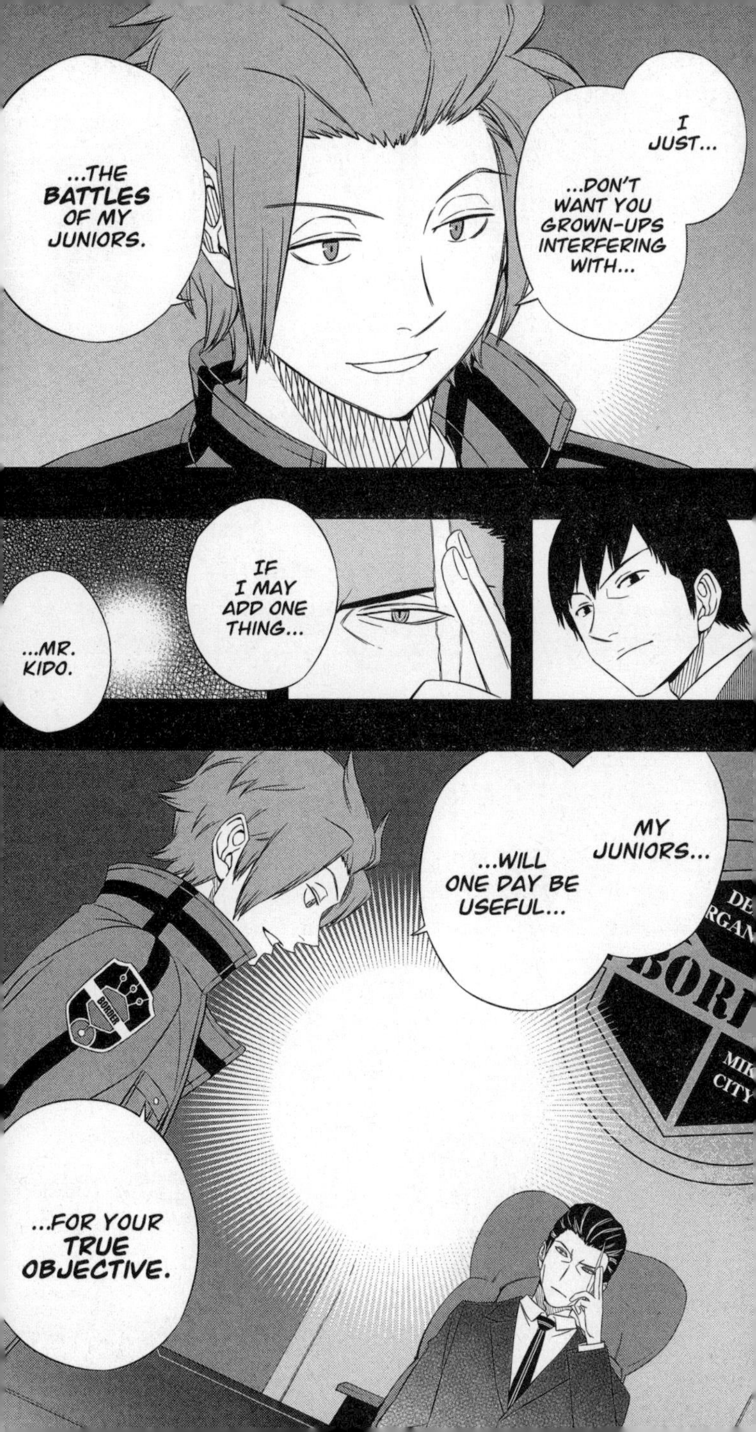
I JUST...
...DON'T WANT YOU GROWN-UPS INTERFERING WITH...
...THE BATTLES OF MY JUNIORS.
IF I MAY ADD ONE THING...
...MR. KIDO.
MY JUNIORS...
...WILL ONE DAY BE USEFUL...
...FOR YOUR TRUE OBJECTIVE.

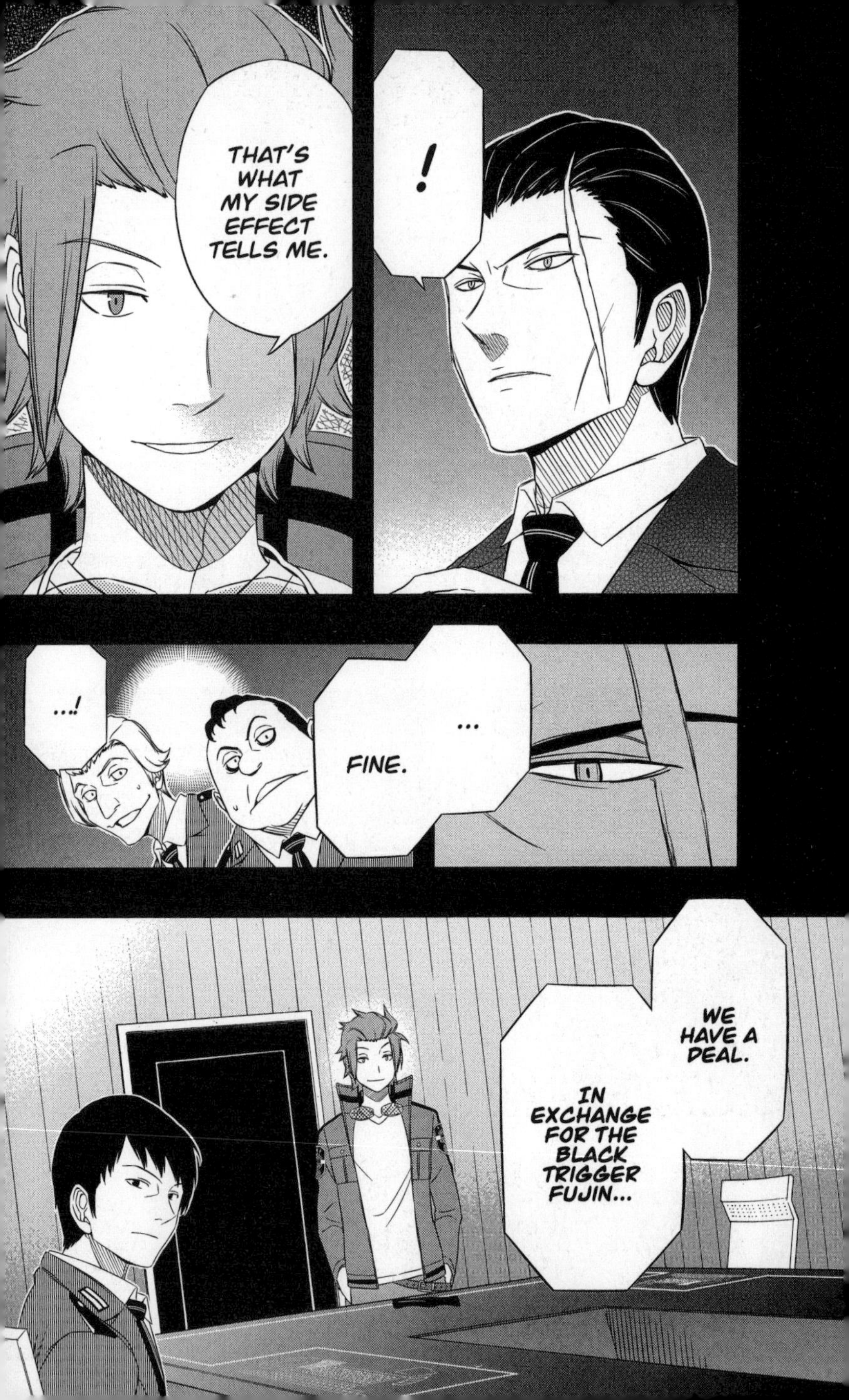
!
THAT'S WHAT MY SIDE EFFECT TELLS ME.
... FINE.
...!
WE HAVE A DEAL.
IN EXCHANGE FOR THE BLACK TRIGGER FUJIN...

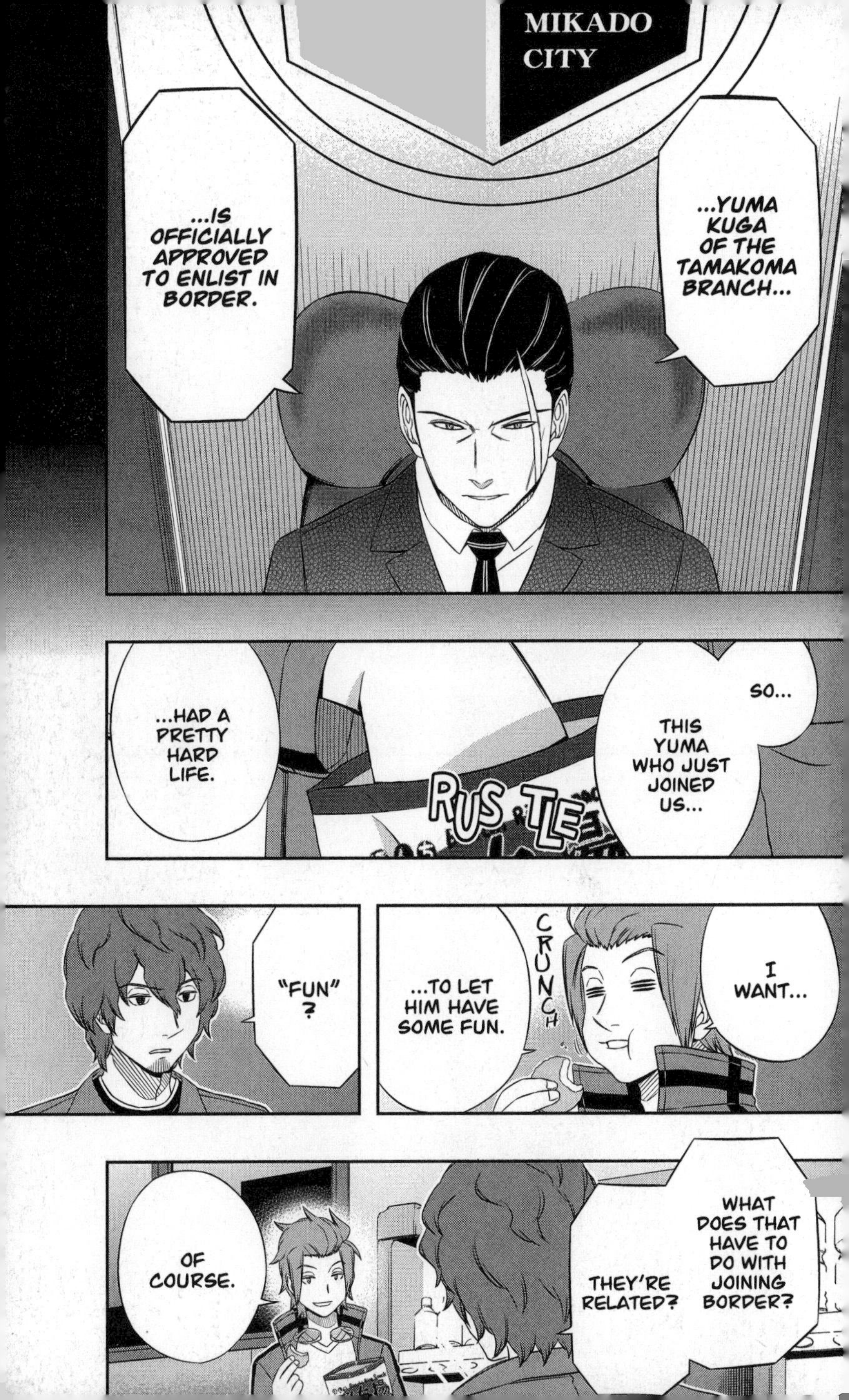
MIKADO CITY
...YUMA KUGA OF THE TAMAKOMA BRANCH...
...IS OFFICIALLY APPROVED TO ENLIST IN BORDER.
SO...
THIS YUMA WHO JUST JOINED US...
RUSTLE
...HAD A PRETTY HARD LIFE.
I WANT...
CRUNCH
...TO LET HIM HAVE SOME FUN.
“FUN”?
WHAT DOES THAT HAVE TO DO WITH JOINING BORDER?
THEY'RE RELATED?
OF COURSE.

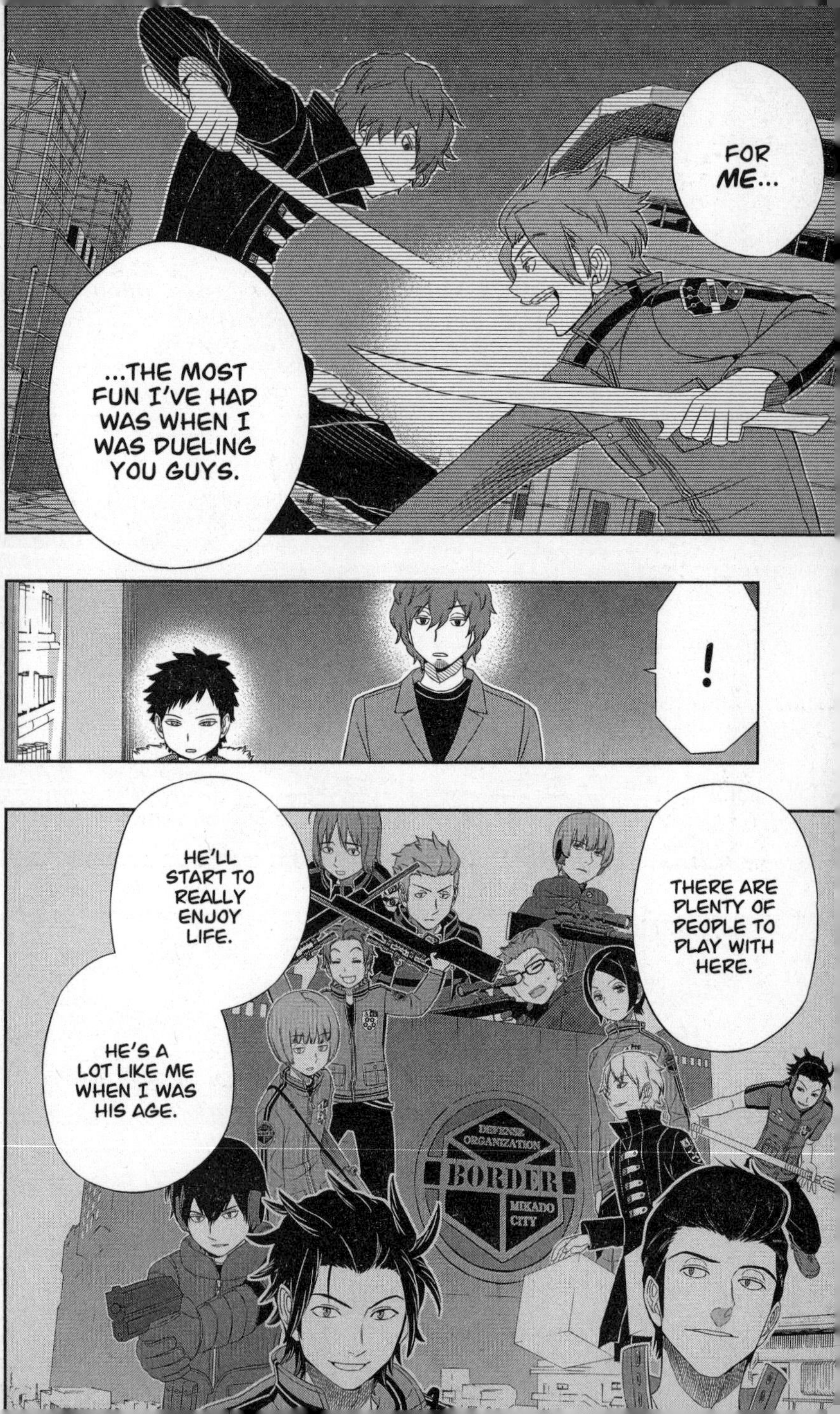
FOR ME...
...THE MOST FUN I'VE HAD WAS WHEN I WAS DUELING YOU GUYS.
!
THERE ARE PLENTY OF PEOPLE TO PLAY WITH HERE.
HE'LL START TO REALLY ENJOY LIFE.
HE'S A LOT LIKE ME WHEN I WAS HIS AGE.
DEFENSE ORGANIZATION
BORDER
MIKADO CITY

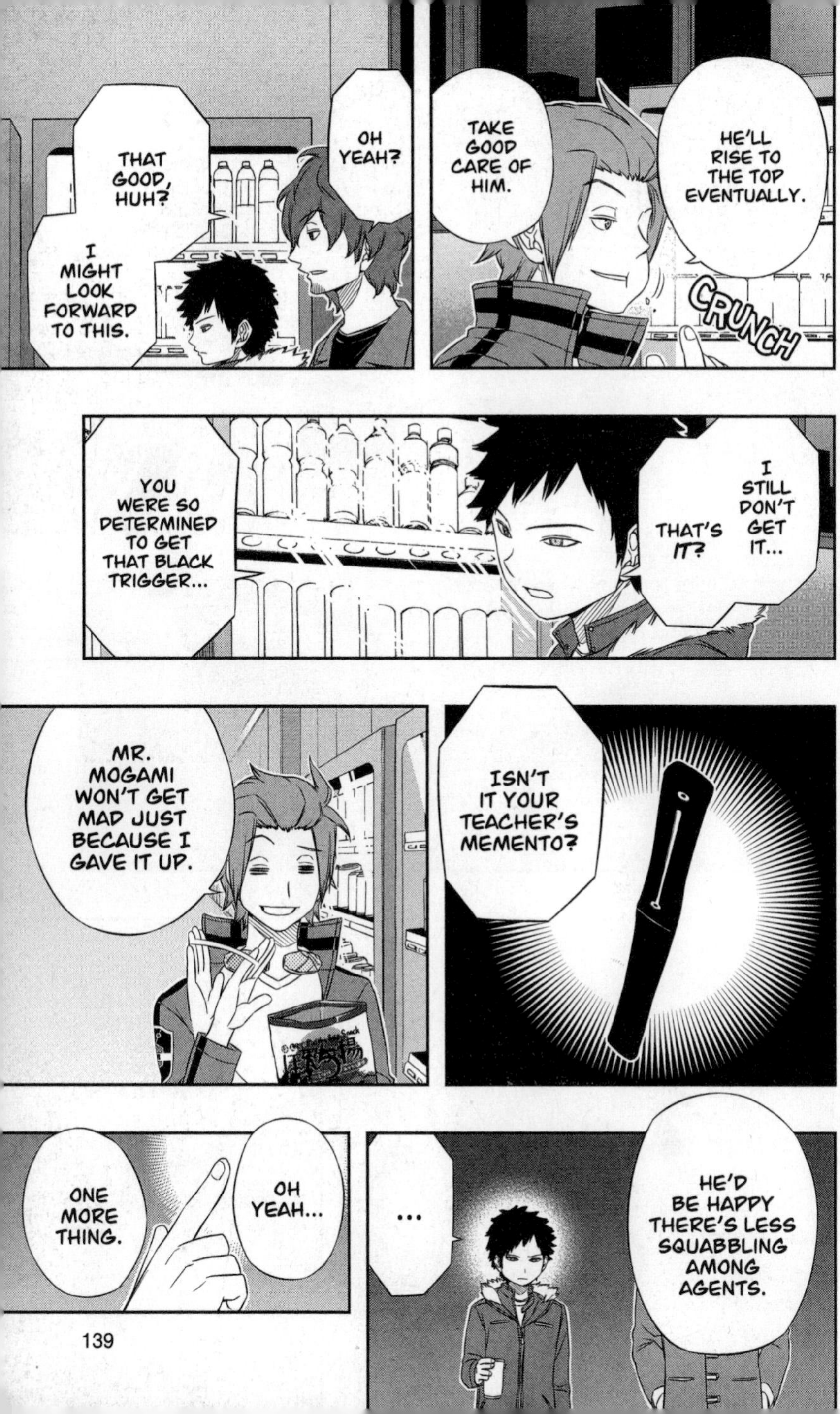
HE'LL RISE TO THE TOP EVENTUALLY.
TAKE GOOD CARE OF HIM.
CRUNCH
OH YEAH?
THAT GOOD, HUH?
I MIGHT LOOK FORWARD TO THIS.
I STILL DON'T GET IT...
THAT'S *IT*?
YOU WERE SO DETERMINED TO GET THAT BLACK TRIGGER...
ISN'T IT YOUR TEACHER'S MEMENTO?
MR. MOGAMI WON'T GET MAD JUST BECAUSE I GAVE IT UP.
HE'D BE HAPPY THERE'S LESS SQUABBLING AMONG AGENTS.
...
OH YEAH...
ONE MORE THING.

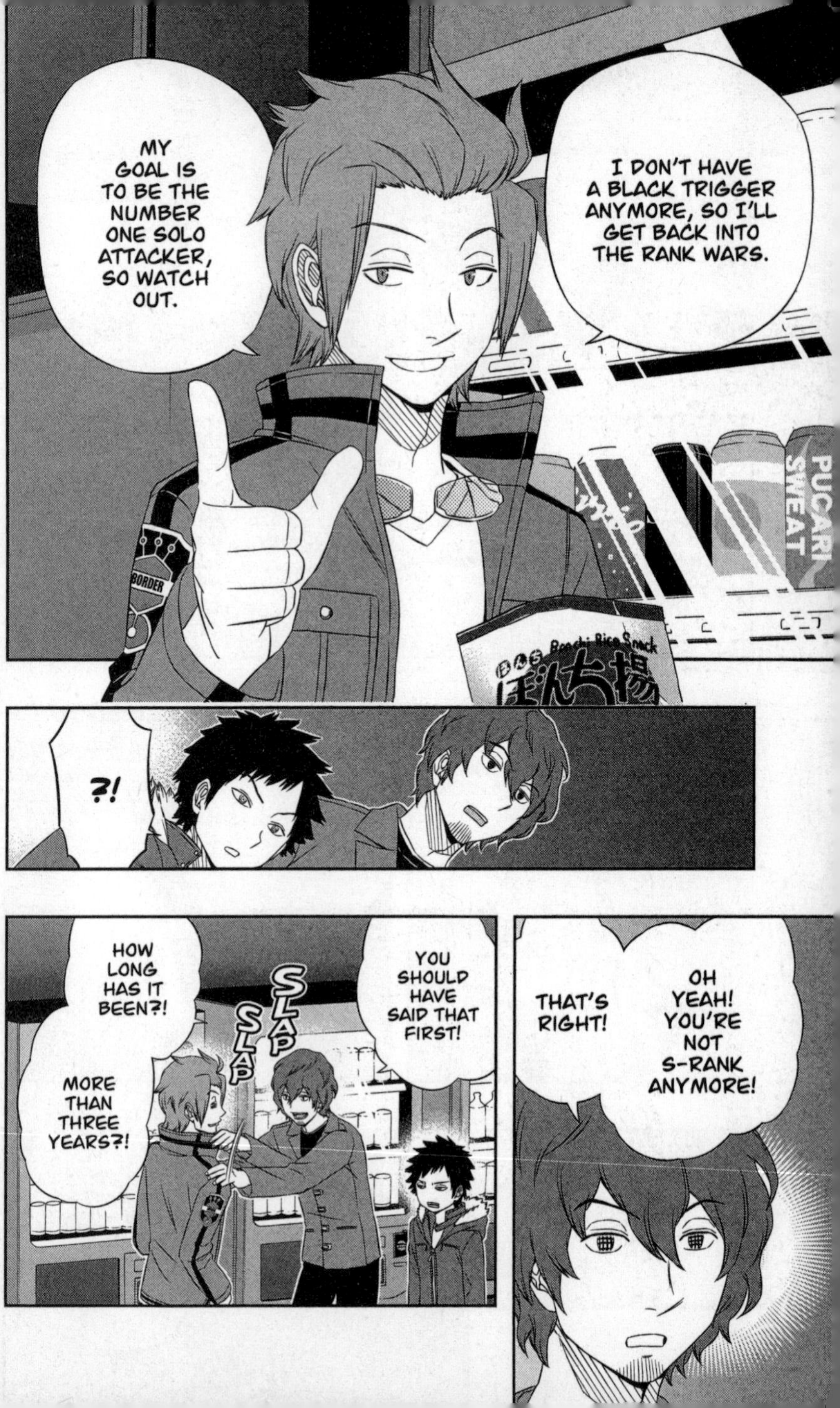
I DON'T HAVE A BLACK TRIGGER ANYMORE, SO I'LL GET BACK INTO THE RANK WARS.
MY GOAL IS TO BE THE NUMBER ONE SOLO ATTACKER, SO WATCH OUT.
PUCARI SWEAT
BORDER
Bonchi Rice Snack
ぼんち揚
?!
OH YEAH! YOU'RE NOT S-RANK ANYMORE!
THAT'S RIGHT!
YOU SHOULD HAVE SAID THAT FIRST!
SLAP
SLAP
HOW LONG HAS IT BEEN?!
MORE THAN THREE YEARS?!

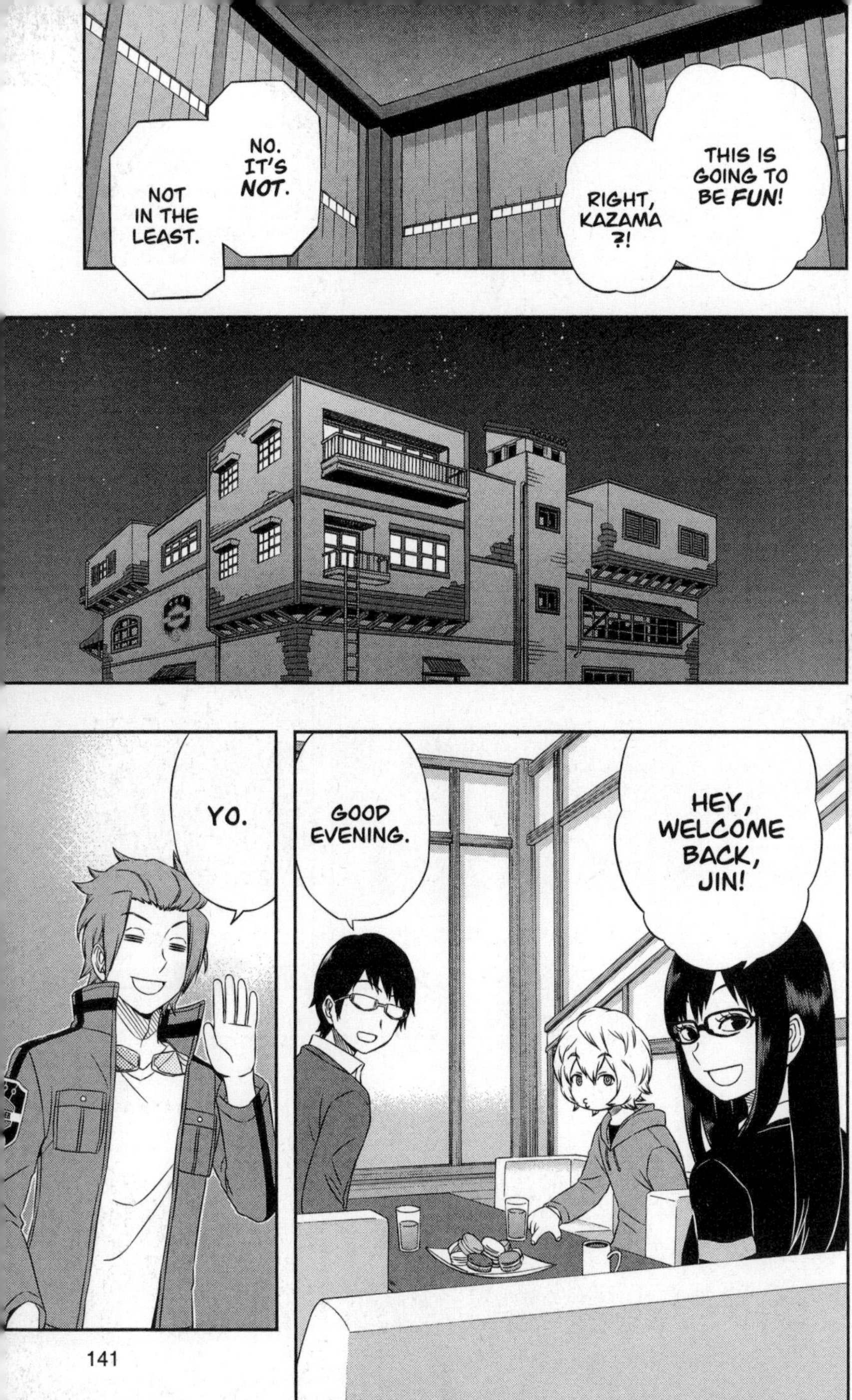
THIS IS GOING TO BE FUN!
RIGHT, KAZAMA?!
NO. IT'S NOT.
NOT IN THE LEAST.
HEY, WELCOME BACK, JIN!
GOOD EVENING.
YO.

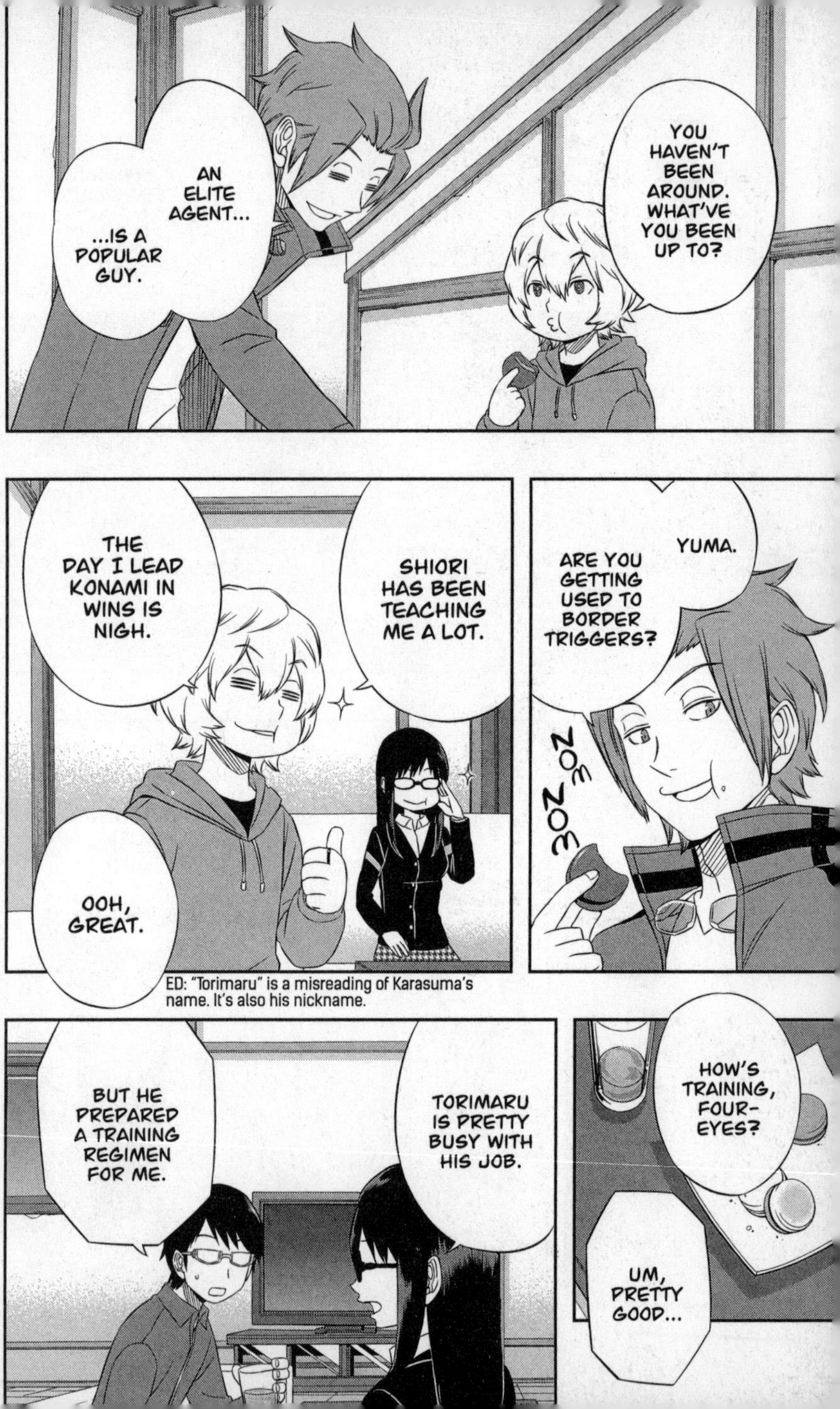
YOU HAVEN'T BEEN AROUND. WHAT'VE YOU BEEN UP TO?
AN ELITE AGENT...
...IS A POPULAR GUY.
YUMA.
ARE YOU GETTING USED TO BORDER TRIGGERS?
NOM NOM
SHIORI HAS BEEN TEACHING ME A LOT.
THE DAY I LEAD KONAMI IN WINS IS NIGH.
OOH, GREAT.
HOW'S TRAINING, FOUR-EYES?
UM, PRETTY GOOD...
TORIMARU IS PRETTY BUSY WITH HIS JOB.
BUT HE PREPARED A TRAINING REGIMEN FOR ME.

ED: "Torimaru" is a misreading of Karasuma's name. It's also his nickname.

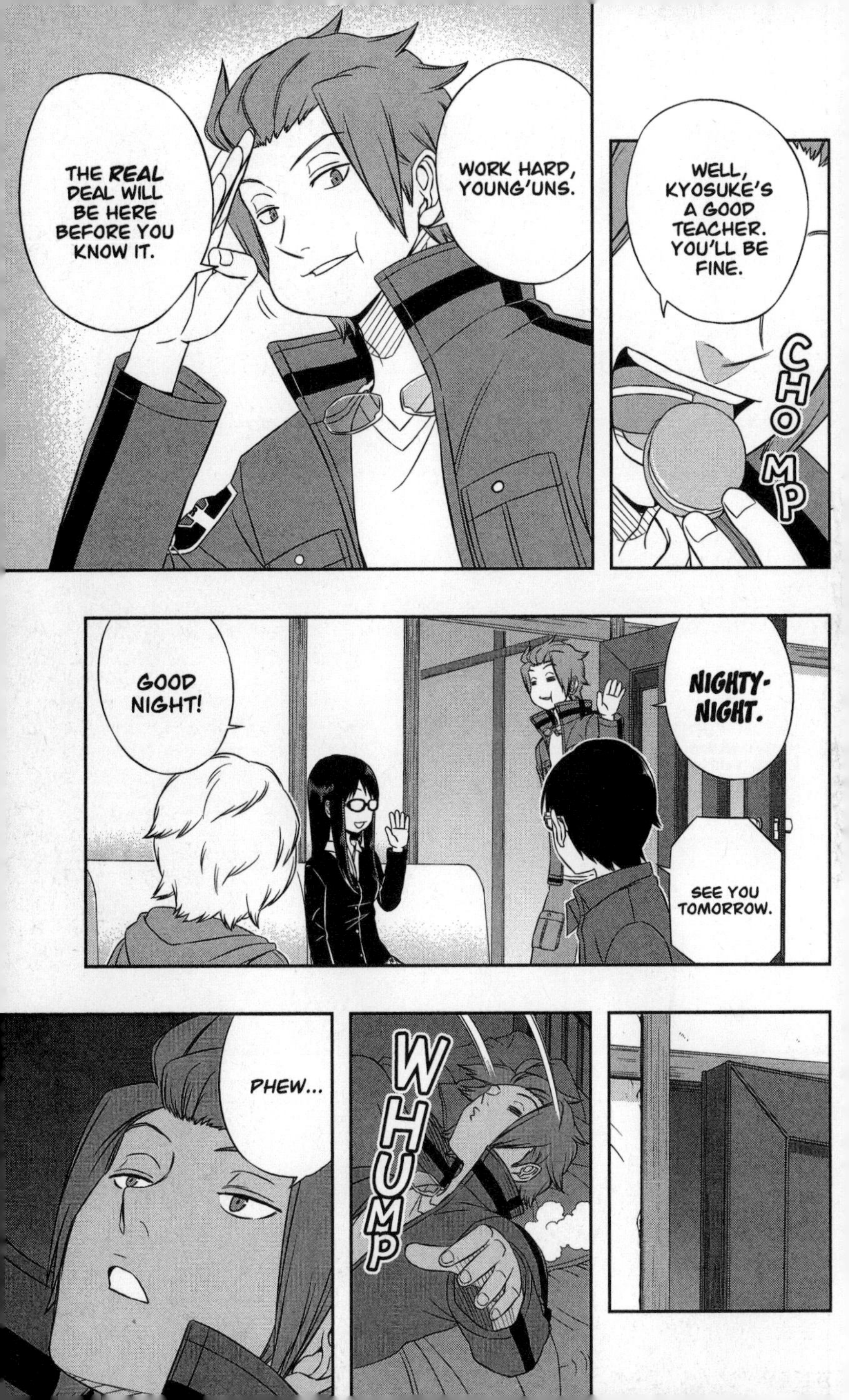
WELL, KYOSUKE'S A GOOD TEACHER. YOU'LL BE FINE.
CHOMP
WORK HARD, YOUNG'UNS.
THE REAL DEAL WILL BE HERE BEFORE YOU KNOW IT.
NIGHTY-NIGHT.
SEE YOU TOMORROW.
GOOD NIGHT!
WHUMP
PHEW...

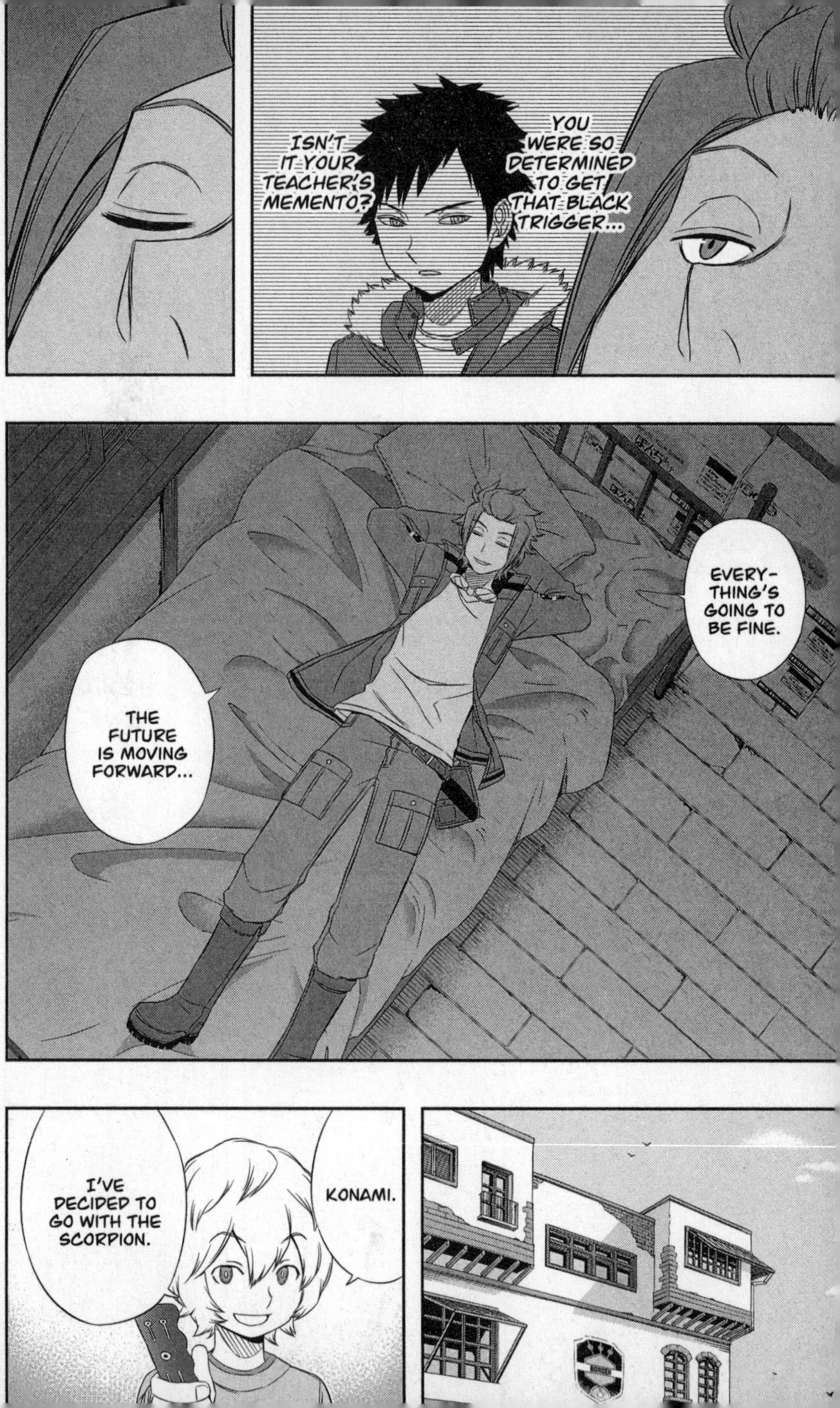
YOU WERE SO DETERMINED TO GET THAT BLACK TRIGGER...
ISN'T IT YOUR TEACHER'S MEMENTO?
EVERY-THING'S GOING TO BE FINE.
THE FUTURE IS MOVING FORWARD...
KONAMI.
I'VE DECIDED TO GO WITH THE SCORPION.

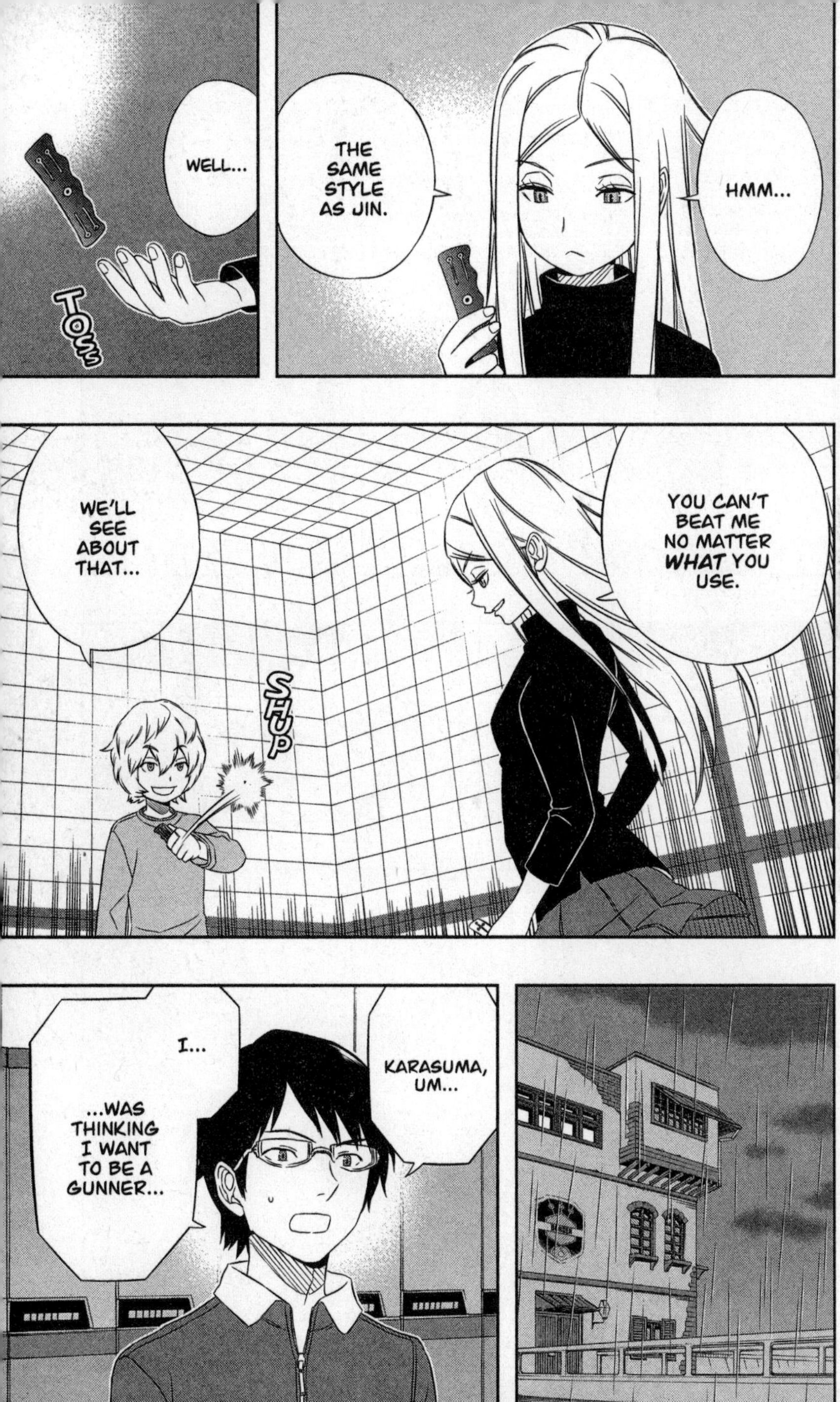
HMM...
THE SAME STYLE AS JIN.
WELL...
TOSS
YOU CAN'T BEAT ME NO MATTER WHAT YOU USE.
WE'LL SEE ABOUT THAT...
SHUP
KARASUMA, UM...
I...
...WAS THINKING I WANT TO BE A GUNNER...

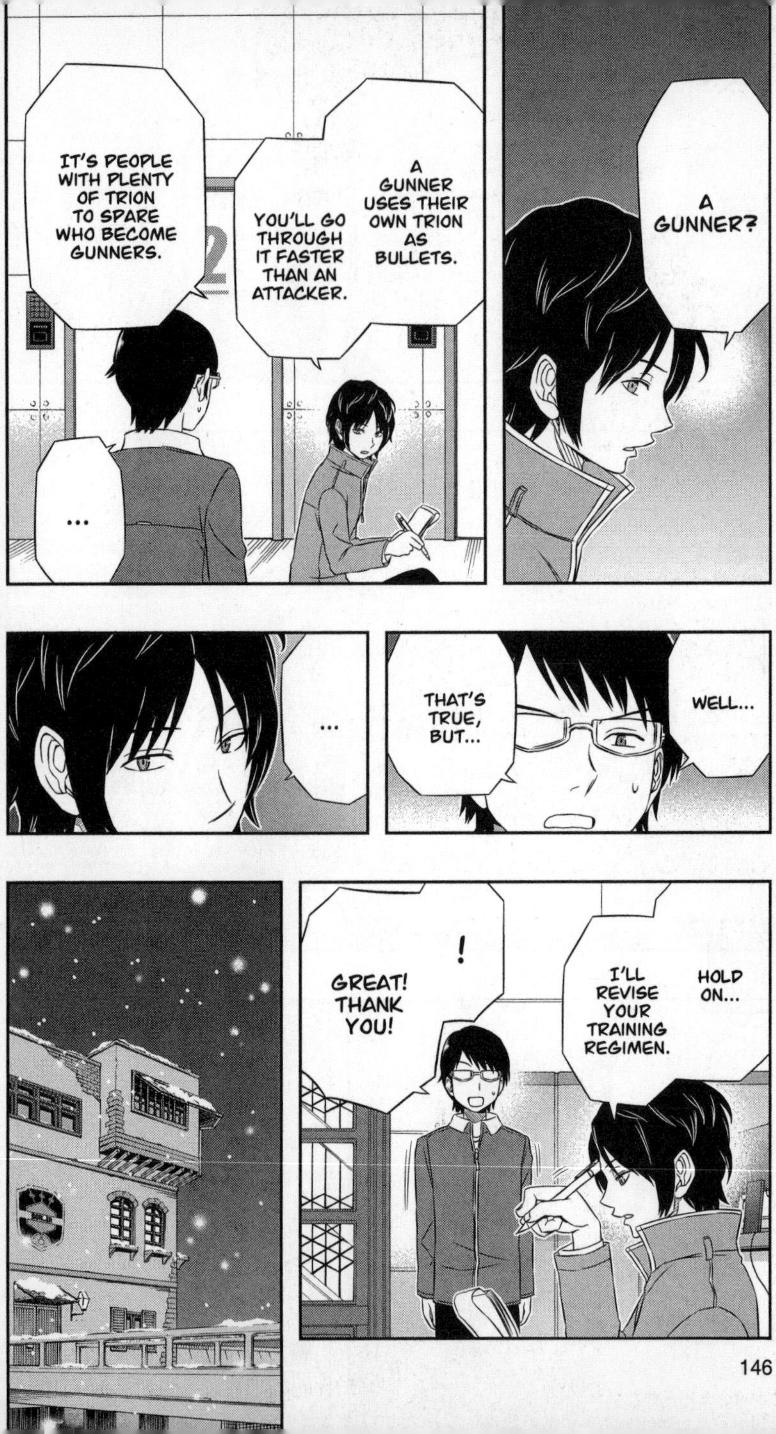
A GUNNER?
A GUNNER USES THEIR OWN TRION AS BULLETS.
YOU'LL GO THROUGH IT FASTER THAN AN ATTACKER.
IT'S PEOPLE WITH PLENTY OF TRION TO SPARE WHO BECOME GUNNERS.
...
WELL...
THAT'S TRUE, BUT...
...
HOLD ON...
I'LL REVISE YOUR TRAINING REGIMEN.
!
GREAT! THANK YOU!

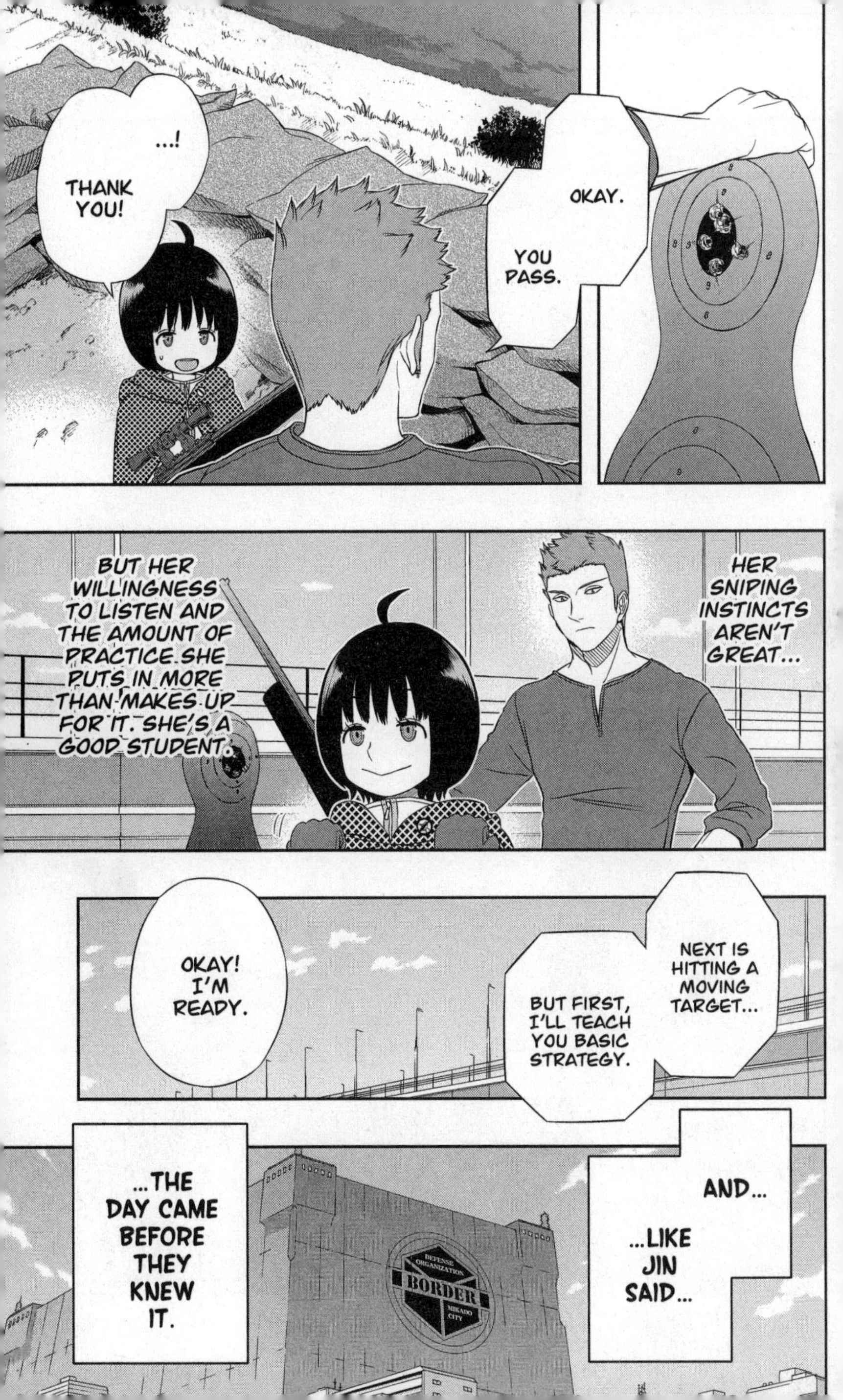
OKAY.
YOU PASS.
...!
THANK YOU!
HER SNIPING INSTINCTS AREN'T GREAT...
BUT HER WILLINGNESS TO LISTEN AND THE AMOUNT OF PRACTICE SHE PUTS IN MORE THAN MAKES UP FOR IT. SHE'S A GOOD STUDENT.
NEXT IS HITTING A MOVING TARGET...
BUT FIRST, I'LL TEACH YOU BASIC STRATEGY.
OKAY! I'M READY.
AND...
...LIKE JIN SAID...
...THE DAY CAME BEFORE THEY KNEW IT.
DEFENSE ORGANIZATION
BORDER
MIKADO CITY

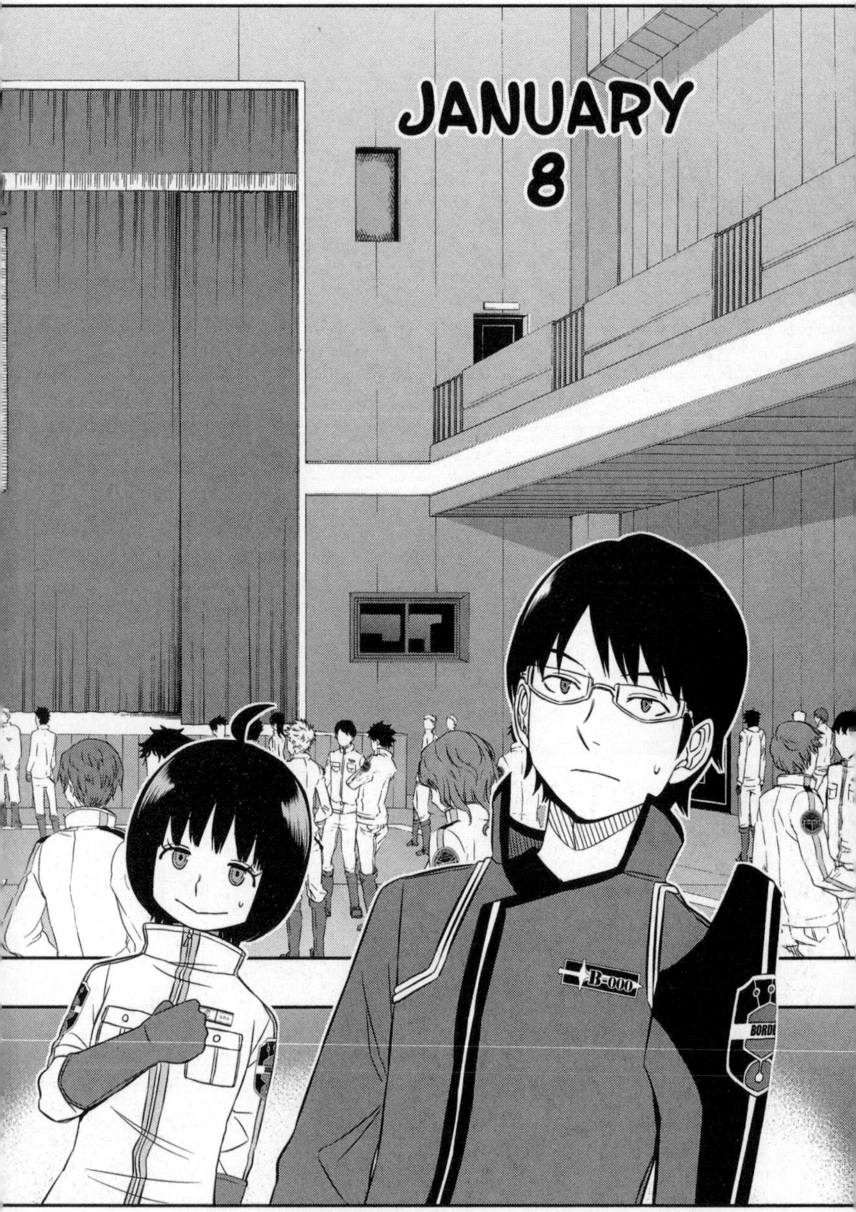
JANUARY 8
B-000
BORDE

READ THIS WAY

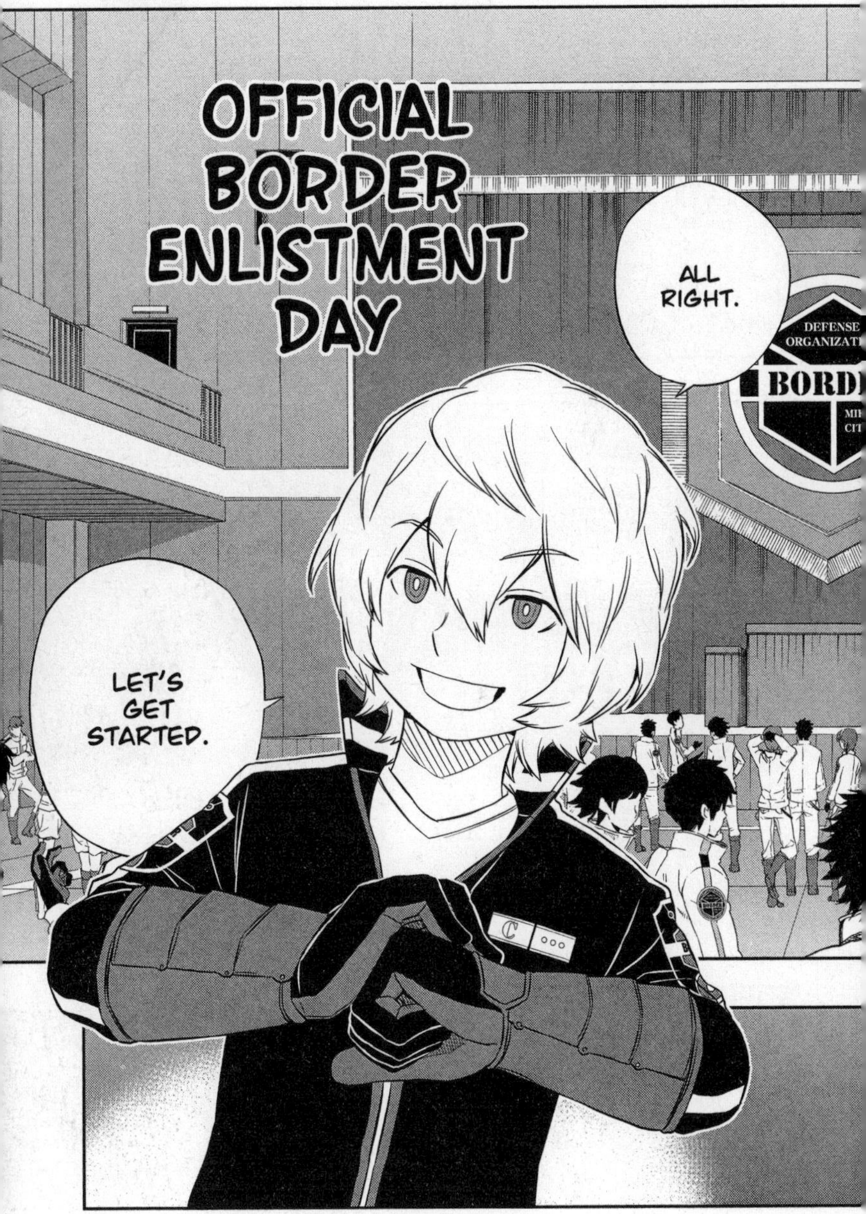
OFFICIAL BORDER ENLISTMENT DAY
ALL RIGHT.
DEFENSE ORGANIZAT
BORD
LET'S GET STARTED.

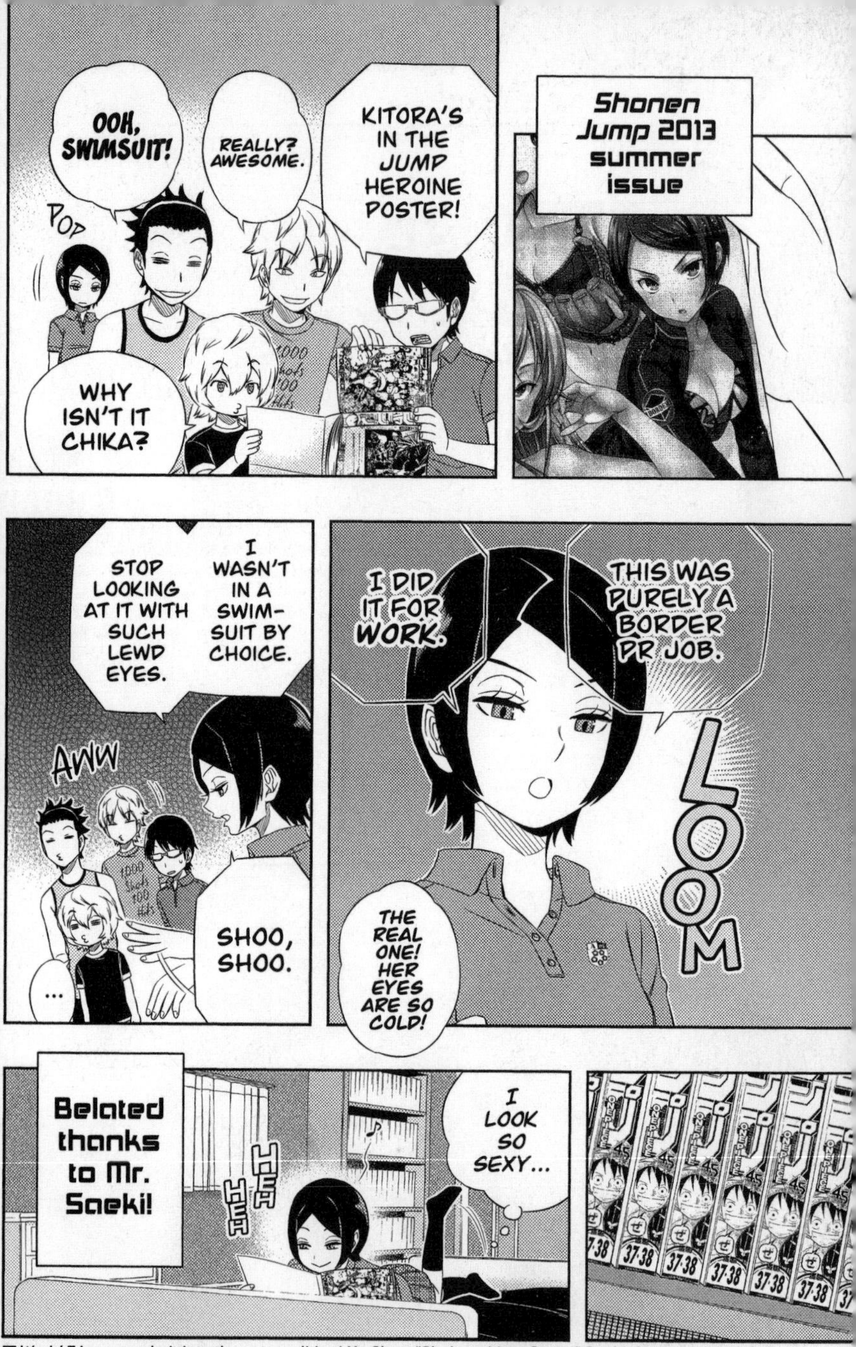
Shonen Jump 2013 summer issue
KITORA'S IN THE JUMP HEROINE POSTER!
REALLY? AWESOME.
OOH, SWIMSUIT!
POP
WHY ISN'T IT CHIKA?
THIS WAS PURELY A BORDER PR JOB.
I DID IT FOR WORK.
LOOM
THE REAL ONE! HER EYES ARE SO COLD!
I WASN'T IN A SWIM-SUIT BY CHOICE.
STOP LOOKING AT IT WITH SUCH LEWD EYES.
AWW
SHOO, SHOO.
...
I LOOK SO SEXY...
HEH HEH
Belated thanks to Mr. Saeki!

■ *World Trigger* made it into the extra edition! Mr. Shun "Shokugeki no Soma" Saeki drew a poster of all the *Jump* heroines. My editor volunteered Kitora because of her chest size. Izumi and Yoneya are hanging out with Osamu here, so this must take place a bit into the future.

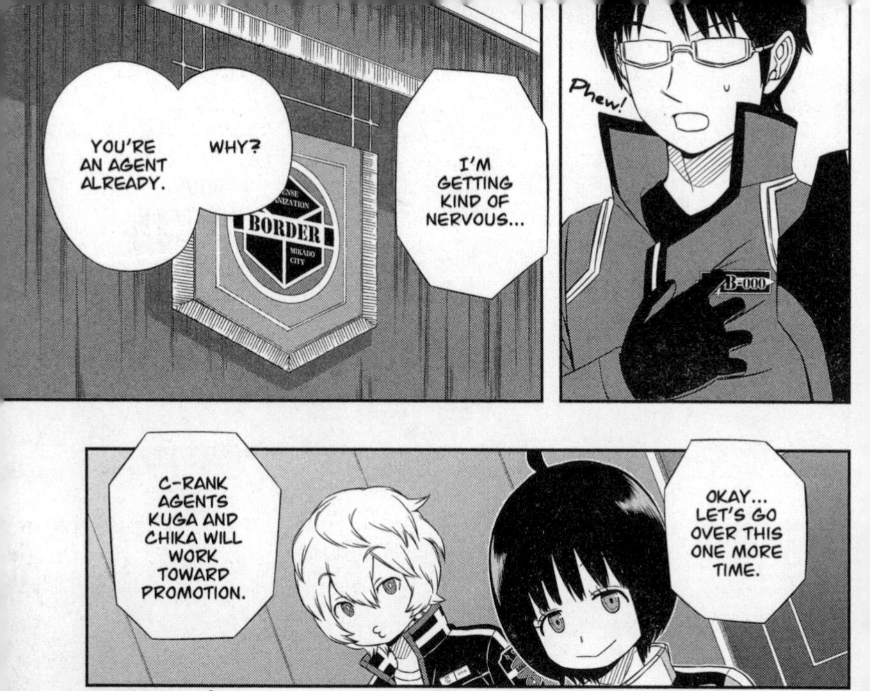
Phew!
I'M GETTING KIND OF NERVOUS...
WHY?
YOU'RE AN AGENT ALREADY.
BORDER
MIKADO CITY
B-000
OKAY... LET'S GO OVER THIS ONE MORE TIME.
C-RANK AGENTS KUGA AND CHIKA WILL WORK TOWARD PROMOTION.

Chapter 33 Yuma Kuga: Part 5

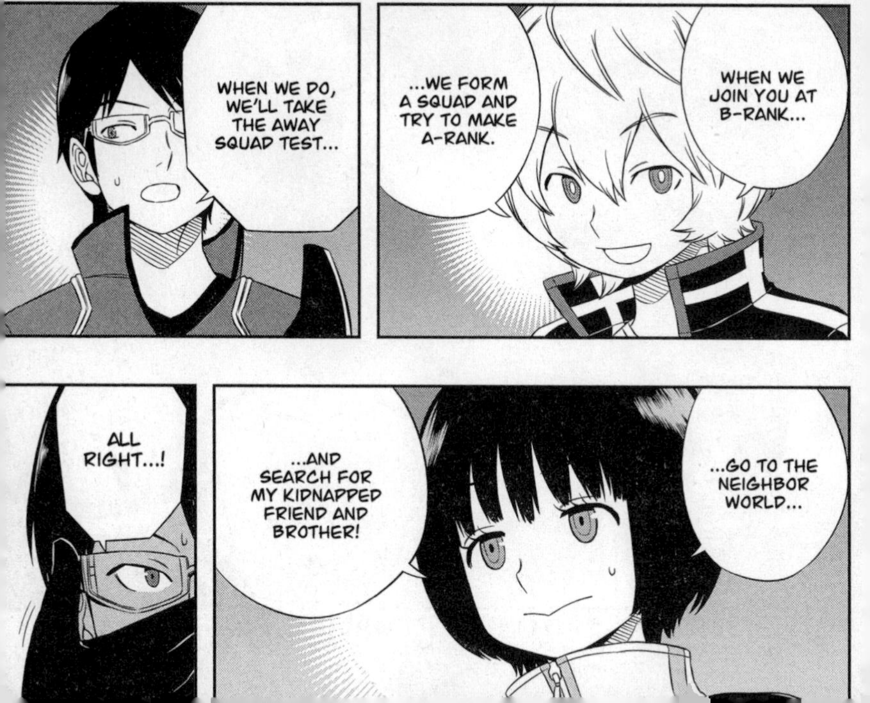
WHEN WE JOIN YOU AT B-RANK...
...WE FORM A SQUAD AND TRY TO MAKE A-RANK.
WHEN WE DO, WE'LL TAKE THE AWAY SQUAD TEST...
...GO TO THE NEIGHBOR WORLD...
...AND SEARCH FOR MY KIDNAPPED FRIEND AND BROTHER!
ALL RIGHT...!

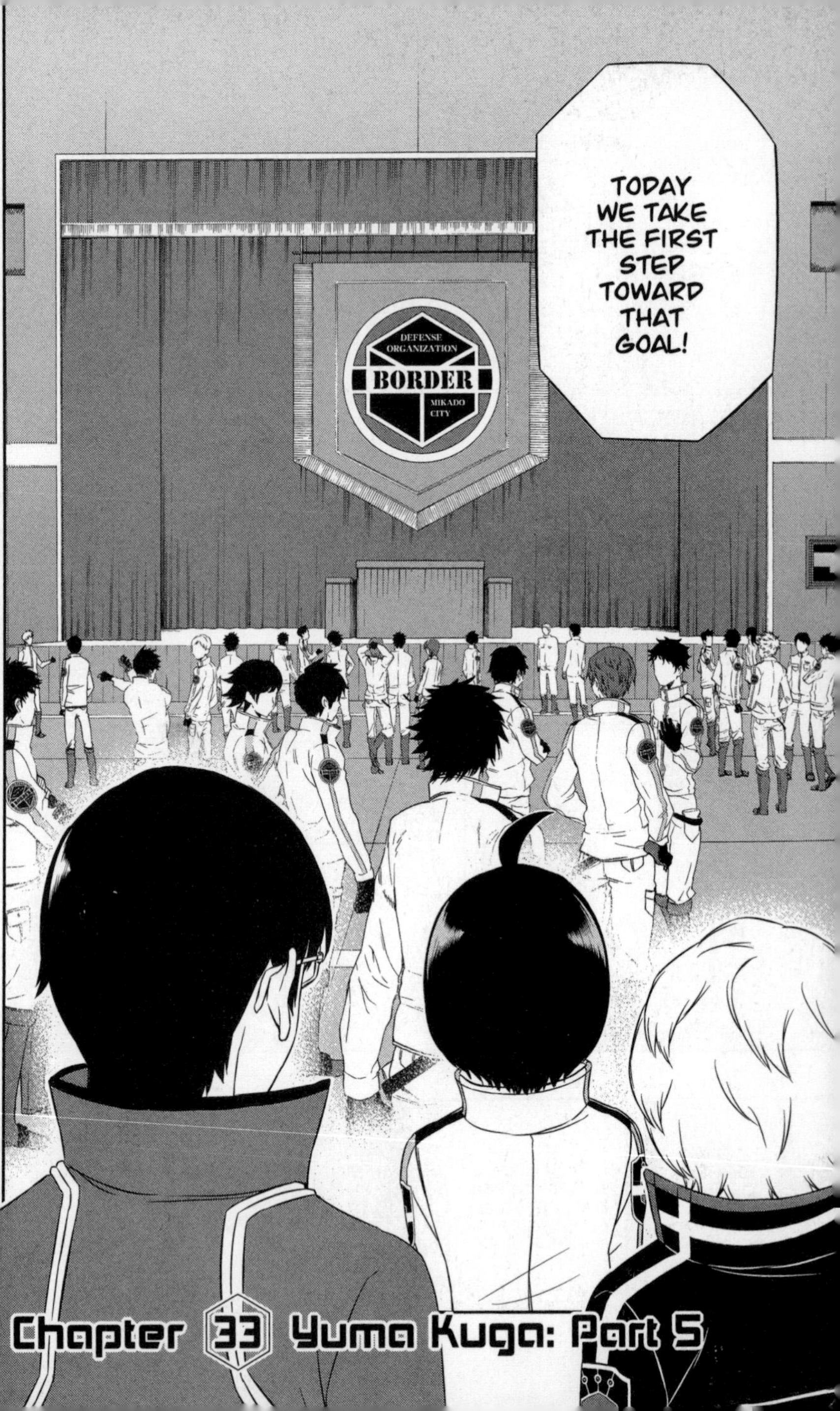
TODAY WE TAKE THE FIRST STEP TOWARD THAT GOAL!
DEFENSE ORGANIZATION
BORDER
MIKADO CITY
Chapter 33 Yuma Kuga: Part 5

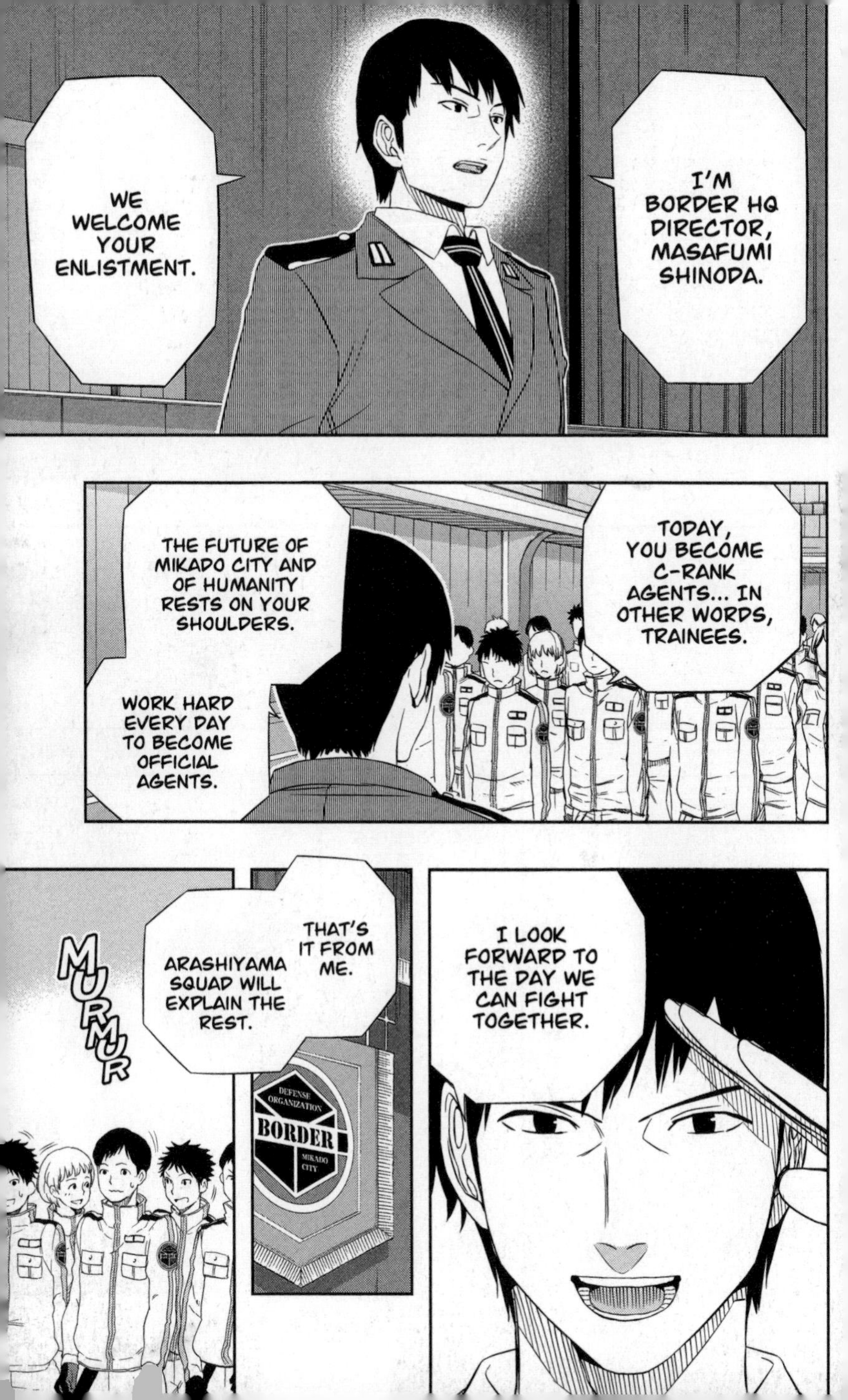
I'M BORDER HQ DIRECTOR, MASAFUMI SHINODA.
WE WELCOME YOUR ENLISTMENT.
TODAY, YOU BECOME C-RANK AGENTS... IN OTHER WORDS, TRAINEES.
THE FUTURE OF MIKADO CITY AND OF HUMANITY RESTS ON YOUR SHOULDERS.
WORK HARD EVERY DAY TO BECOME OFFICIAL AGENTS.
I LOOK FORWARD TO THE DAY WE CAN FIGHT TOGETHER.
THAT'S IT FROM ME.
ARASHIYAMA SQUAD WILL EXPLAIN THE REST.
DEFENSE ORGANIZATION
BORDER
MIKADO CITY
MURMUR

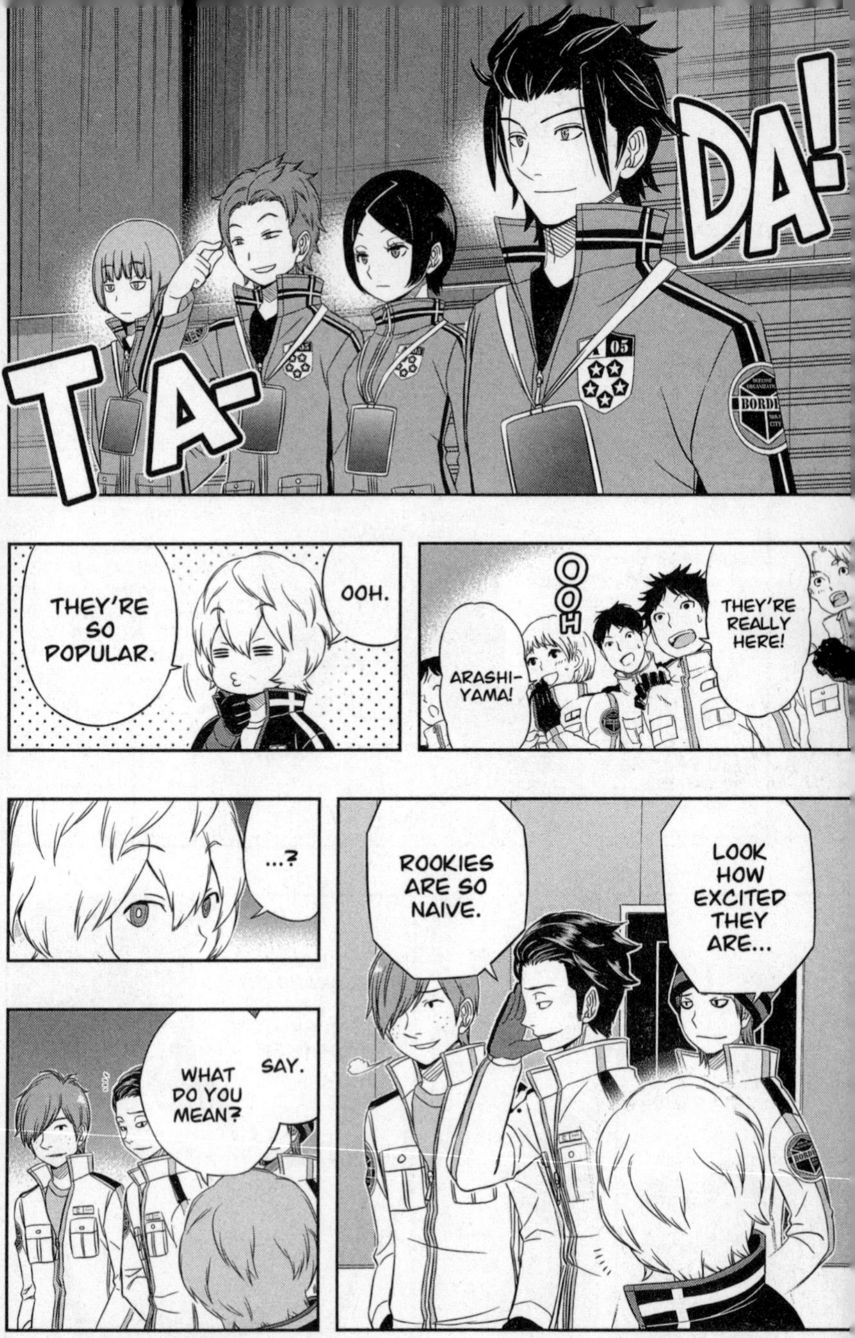
TA-DA!
THEY'RE REALLY HERE!
OOH
ARASHI-YAMA!
OOH.
THEY'RE SO POPULAR.
LOOK HOW EXCITED THEY ARE...
ROOKIES ARE SO NAIVE.
...?
SAY.
WHAT DO YOU MEAN?

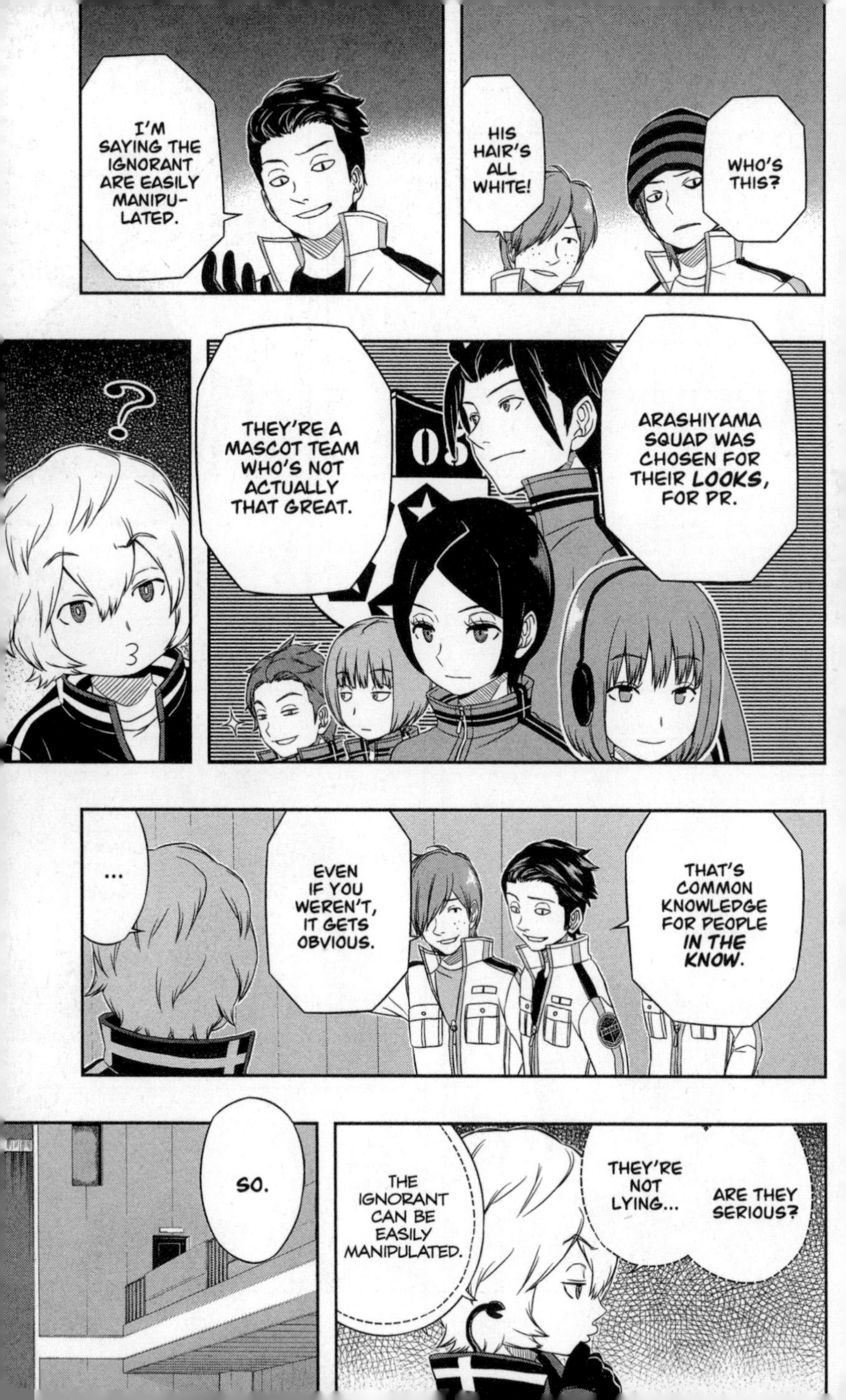
WHO'S THIS?
HIS HAIR'S ALL WHITE!
I'M SAYING THE IGNORANT ARE EASILY MANIPU-LATED.
ARASHIYAMA SQUAD WAS CHOSEN FOR THEIR LOOKS, FOR PR.
THEY'RE A MASCOT TEAM WHO'S NOT ACTUALLY THAT GREAT.
?
THAT'S COMMON KNOWLEDGE FOR PEOPLE IN THE KNOW.
EVEN IF YOU WEREN'T, IT GETS OBVIOUS.
...
ARE THEY SERIOUS?
THEY'RE NOT LYING...
THE IGNORANT CAN BE EASILY MANIPULATED.
SO.

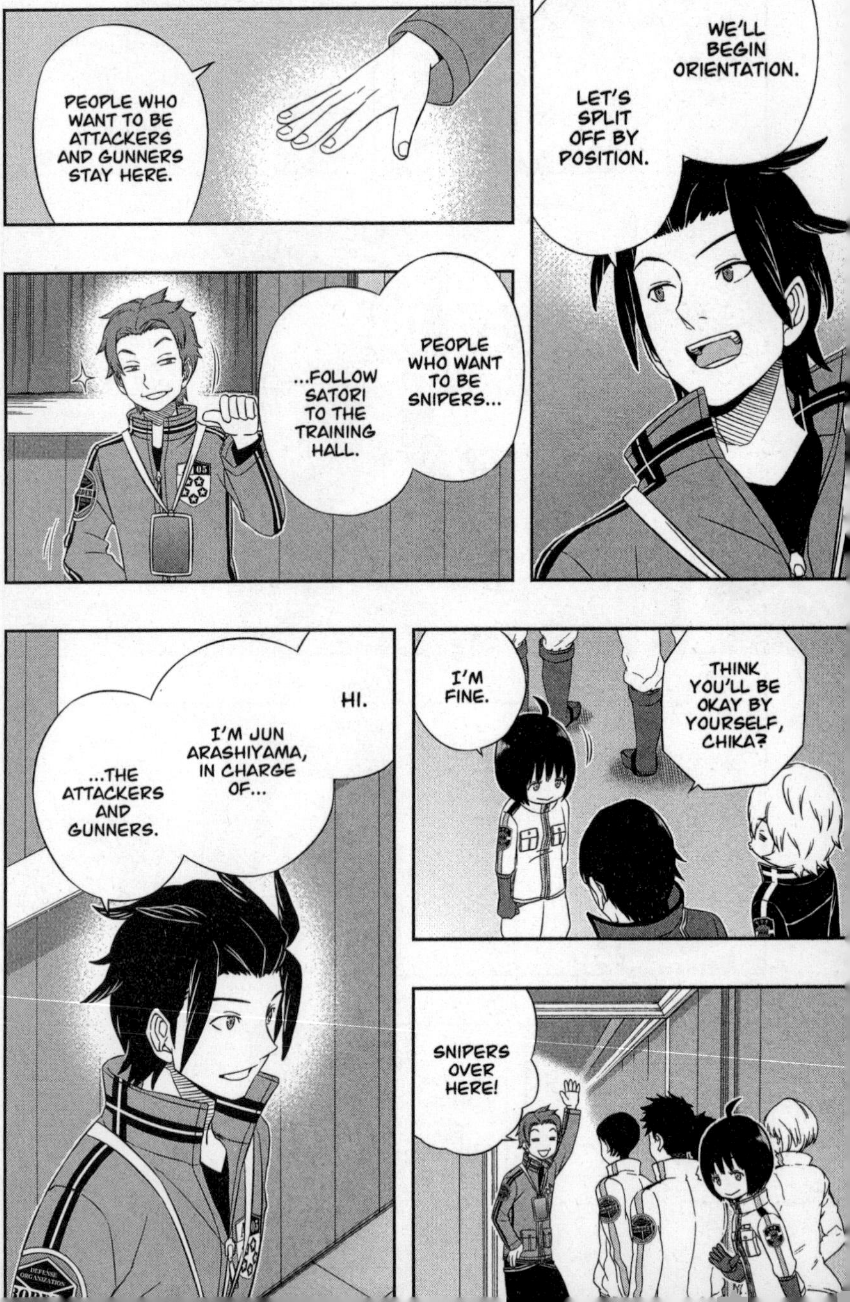
WE'LL BEGIN ORIENTATION.
LET'S SPLIT OFF BY POSITION.
PEOPLE WHO WANT TO BE ATTACKERS AND GUNNERS STAY HERE.
PEOPLE WHO WANT TO BE SNIPERS...
...FOLLOW SATORI TO THE TRAINING HALL.
THINK YOU'LL BE OKAY BY YOURSELF, CHIKA?
I'M FINE.
SNIPERS OVER HERE!
HI.
I'M JUN ARASHIYAMA, IN CHARGE OF...
...THE ATTACKERS AND GUNNERS.

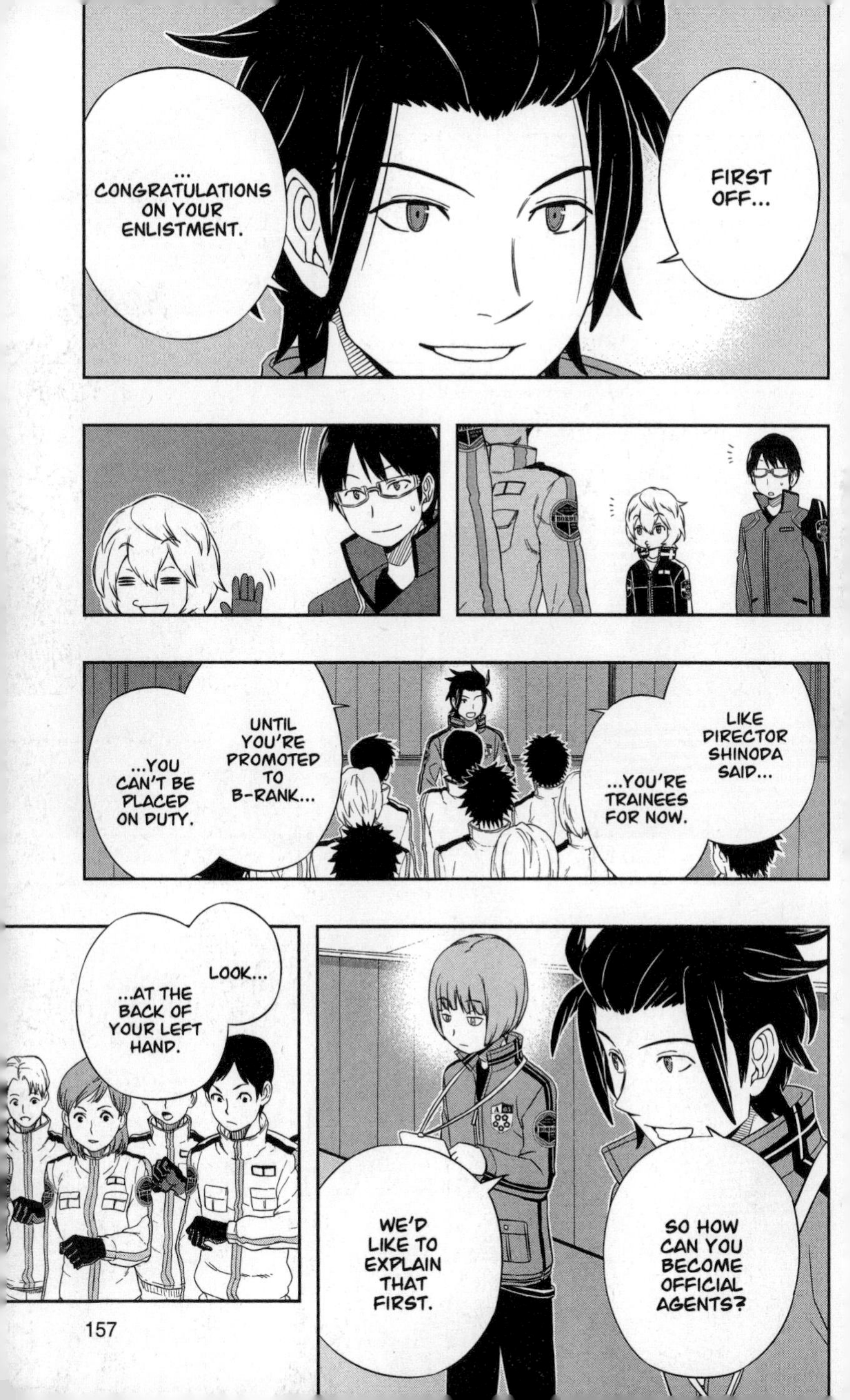
FIRST OFF...
...CONGRATULATIONS ON YOUR ENLISTMENT.
LIKE DIRECTOR SHINODA SAID...
...YOU'RE TRAINEES FOR NOW.
UNTIL YOU'RE PROMOTED TO B-RANK...
...YOU CAN'T BE PLACED ON DUTY.
SO HOW CAN YOU BECOME OFFICIAL AGENTS?
WE'D LIKE TO EXPLAIN THAT FIRST.
LOOK...
...AT THE BACK OF YOUR LEFT HAND.

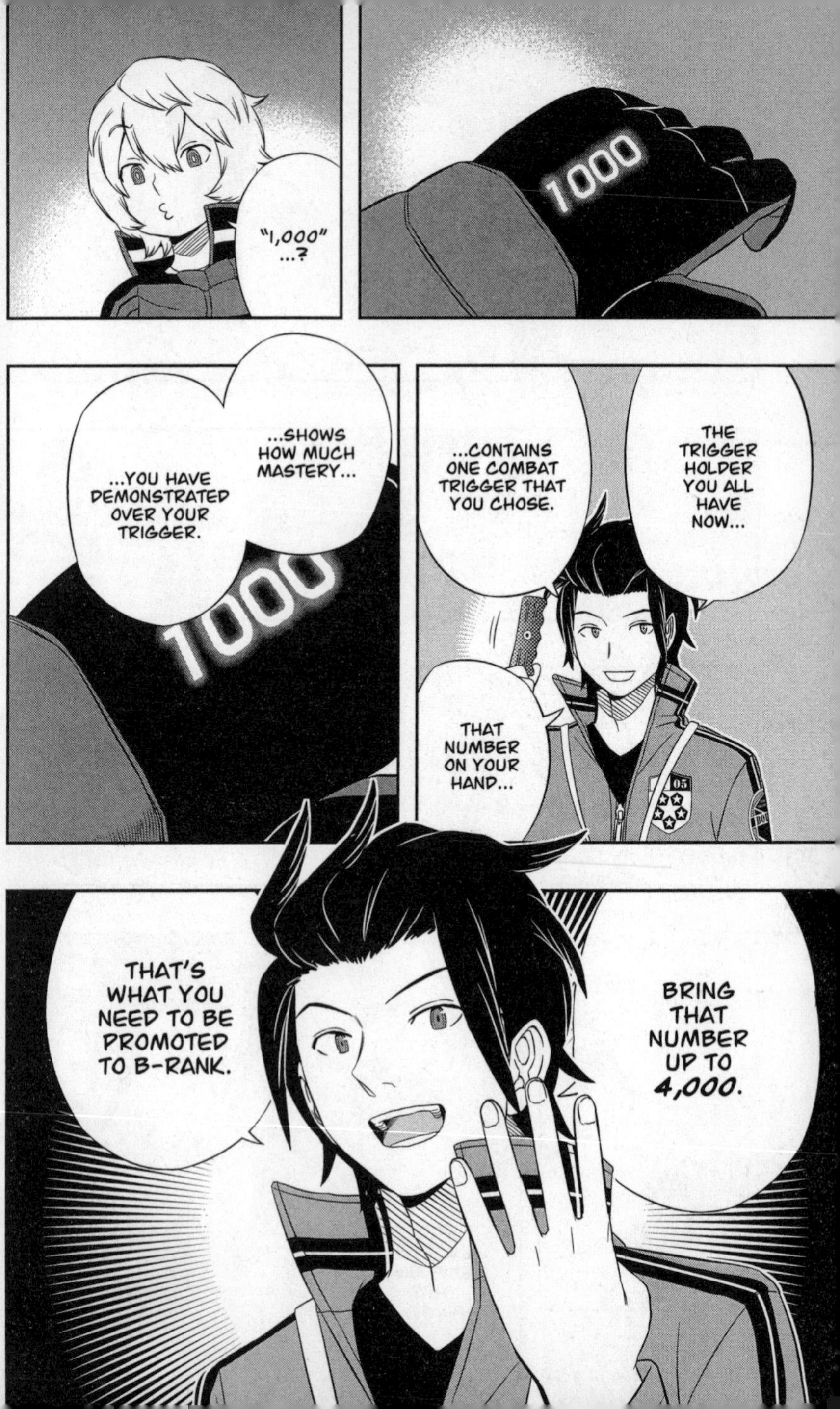
1000
"1,000" ...?
THE TRIGGER HOLDER YOU ALL HAVE NOW...
...CONTAINS ONE COMBAT TRIGGER THAT YOU CHOSE.
THAT NUMBER ON YOUR HAND...
...SHOWS HOW MUCH MASTERY...
...YOU HAVE DEMONSTRATED OVER YOUR TRIGGER.
1000
BRING THAT NUMBER UP TO 4,000.
THAT'S WHAT YOU NEED TO BE PROMOTED TO B-RANK.

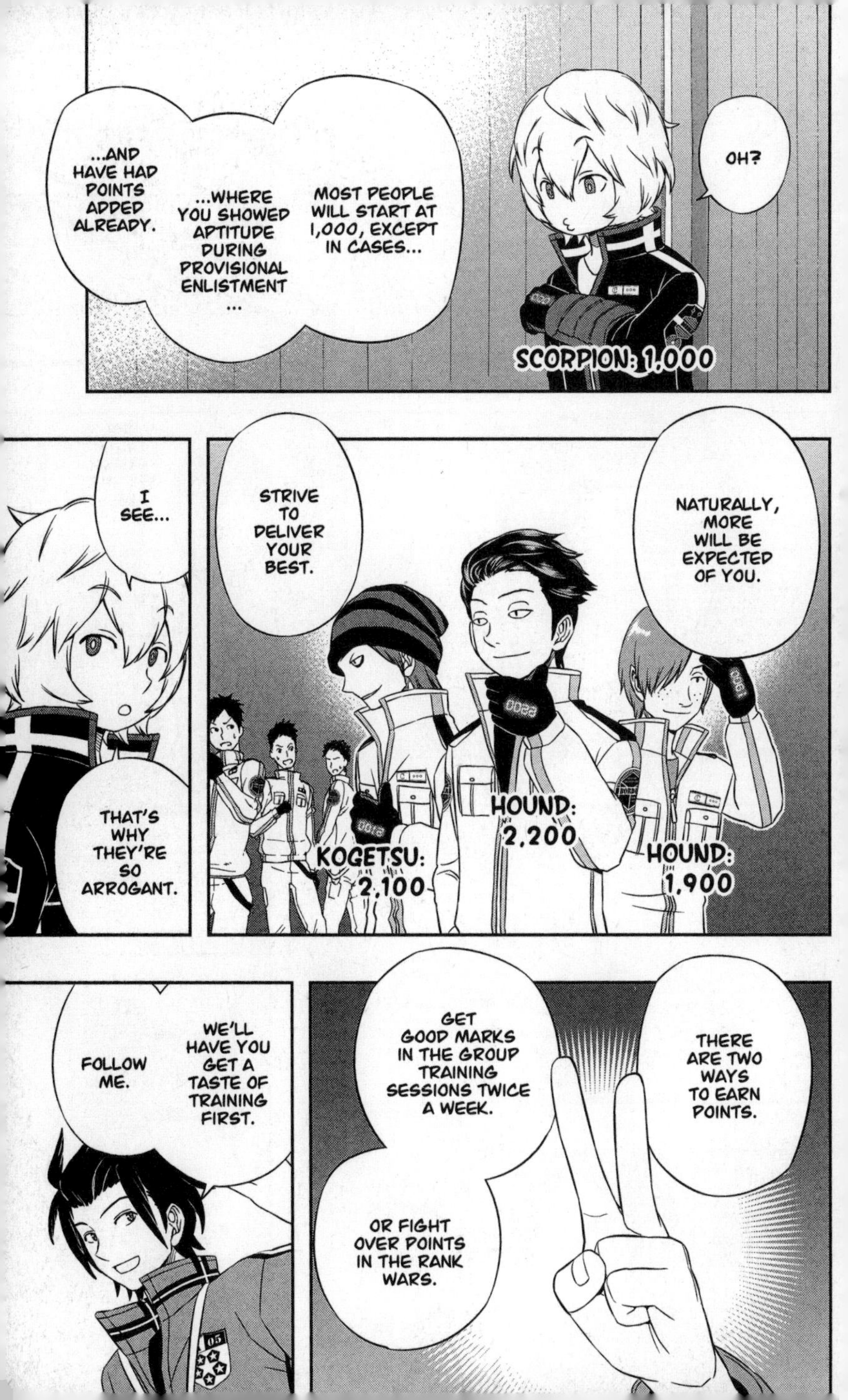
OH?
MOST PEOPLE WILL START AT 1,000, EXCEPT IN CASES...
...WHERE YOU SHOWED APTITUDE DURING PROVISIONAL ENLISTMENT ...
...AND HAVE HAD POINTS ADDED ALREADY.
SCORPION: 1,000
NATURALLY, MORE WILL BE EXPECTED OF YOU.
STRIVE TO DELIVER YOUR BEST.
HOUND: 1,900
HOUND: 2,200
KOGETSU: 2,100
I SEE...
THAT'S WHY THEY'RE SO ARROGANT.
THERE ARE TWO WAYS TO EARN POINTS.
GET GOOD MARKS IN THE GROUP TRAINING SESSIONS TWICE A WEEK.
OR FIGHT OVER POINTS IN THE RANK WARS.
WE'LL HAVE YOU GET A TASTE OF TRAINING FIRST.
FOLLOW ME.

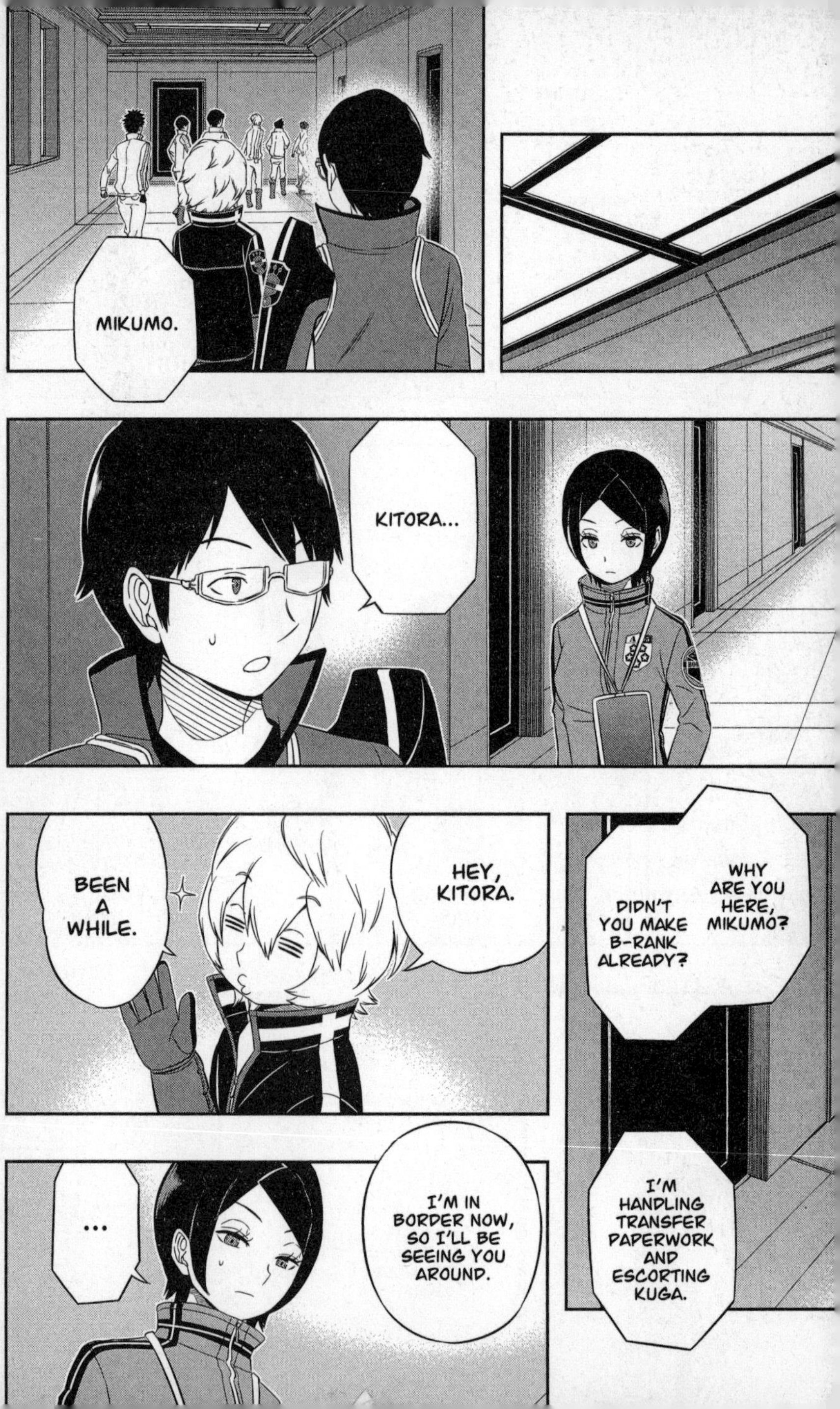
MIKUMO.
KITORA...
WHY ARE YOU HERE, MIKUMO?
DIDN'T YOU MAKE B-RANK ALREADY?
I'M HANDLING TRANSFER PAPERWORK AND ESCORTING KUGA.
HEY, KITORA.
BEEN A WHILE.
I'M IN BORDER NOW, SO I'LL BE SEEING YOU AROUND.
...

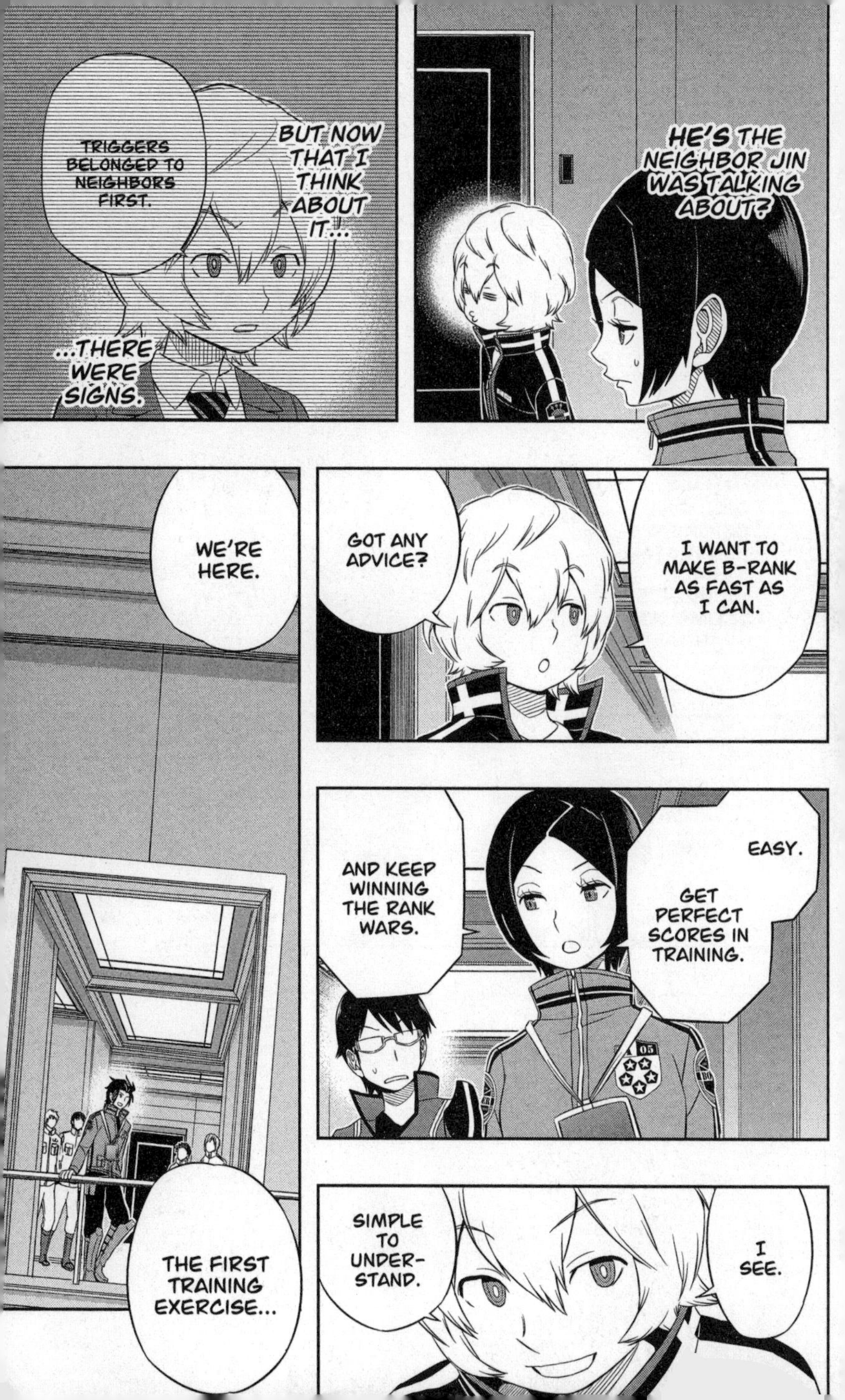
HE'S THE NEIGHBOR JIN WAS TALKING ABOUT?
BUT NOW THAT I THINK ABOUT IT...
TRIGGERS BELONGED TO NEIGHBORS FIRST.
...THERE WERE SIGNS.
I WANT TO MAKE B-RANK AS FAST AS I CAN.
GOT ANY ADVICE?
EASY.
GET PERFECT SCORES IN TRAINING.
AND KEEP WINNING THE RANK WARS.
I SEE.
SIMPLE TO UNDER-STAND.
WE'RE HERE.
THE FIRST TRAINING EXERCISE...

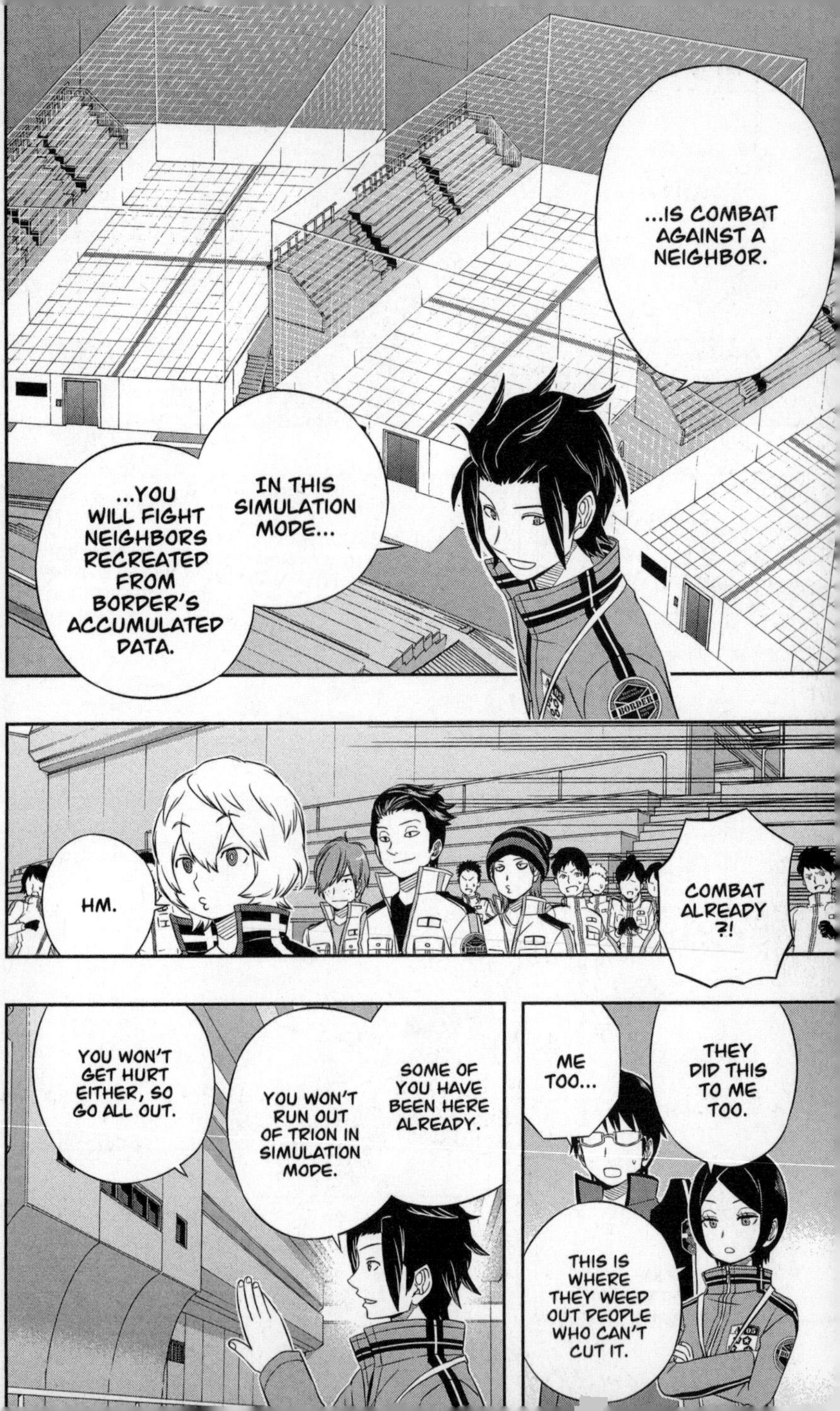
...IS COMBAT AGAINST A NEIGHBOR.
IN THIS SIMULATION MODE...
...YOU WILL FIGHT NEIGHBORS RECREATED FROM BORDER'S ACCUMULATED DATA.
COMBAT ALREADY ?!
HM.
THEY DID THIS TO ME TOO.
ME TOO...
THIS IS WHERE THEY WEED OUT PEOPLE WHO CAN'T CUT IT.
SOME OF YOU HAVE BEEN HERE ALREADY.
YOU WON'T RUN OUT OF TRION IN SIMULATION MODE.
YOU WON'T GET HURT EITHER, SO GO ALL OUT.

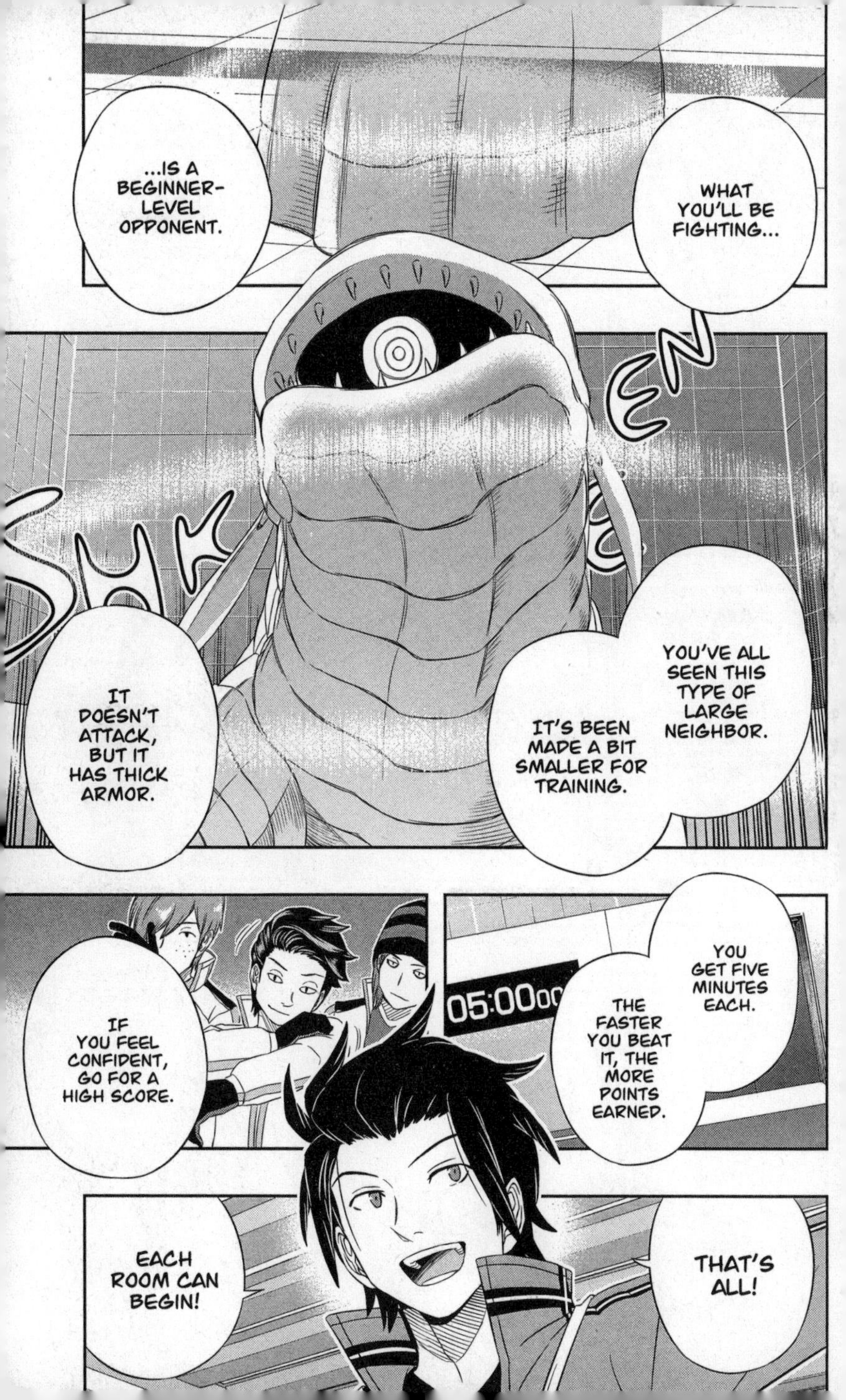
WHAT YOU'LL BE FIGHTING...
...IS A BEGINNER-LEVEL OPPONENT.
YOU'VE ALL SEEN THIS TYPE OF LARGE NEIGHBOR.
IT'S BEEN MADE A BIT SMALLER FOR TRAINING.
IT DOESN'T ATTACK, BUT IT HAS THICK ARMOR.
YOU GET FIVE MINUTES EACH.
THE FASTER YOU BEAT IT, THE MORE POINTS EARNED.
05:00
IF YOU FEEL CONFIDENT, GO FOR A HIGH SCORE.
THAT'S ALL!
EACH ROOM CAN BEGIN!

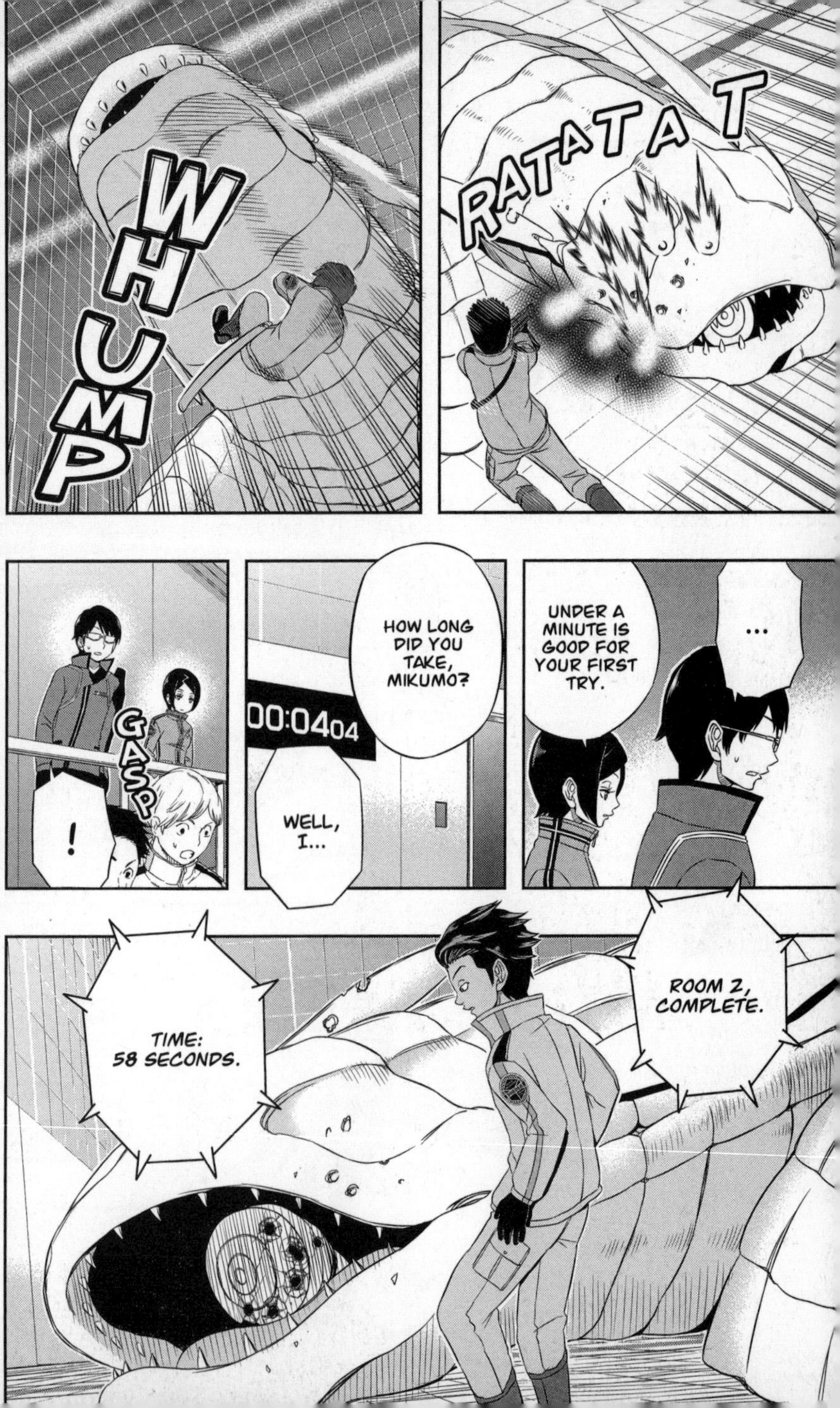
RATATAT
WHUMP
...
UNDER A MINUTE IS GOOD FOR YOUR FIRST TRY.
HOW LONG DID YOU TAKE, MIKUMO?
00:0404
WELL, I...
GASP
!
ROOM 2, COMPLETE.
TIME: 58 SECONDS.

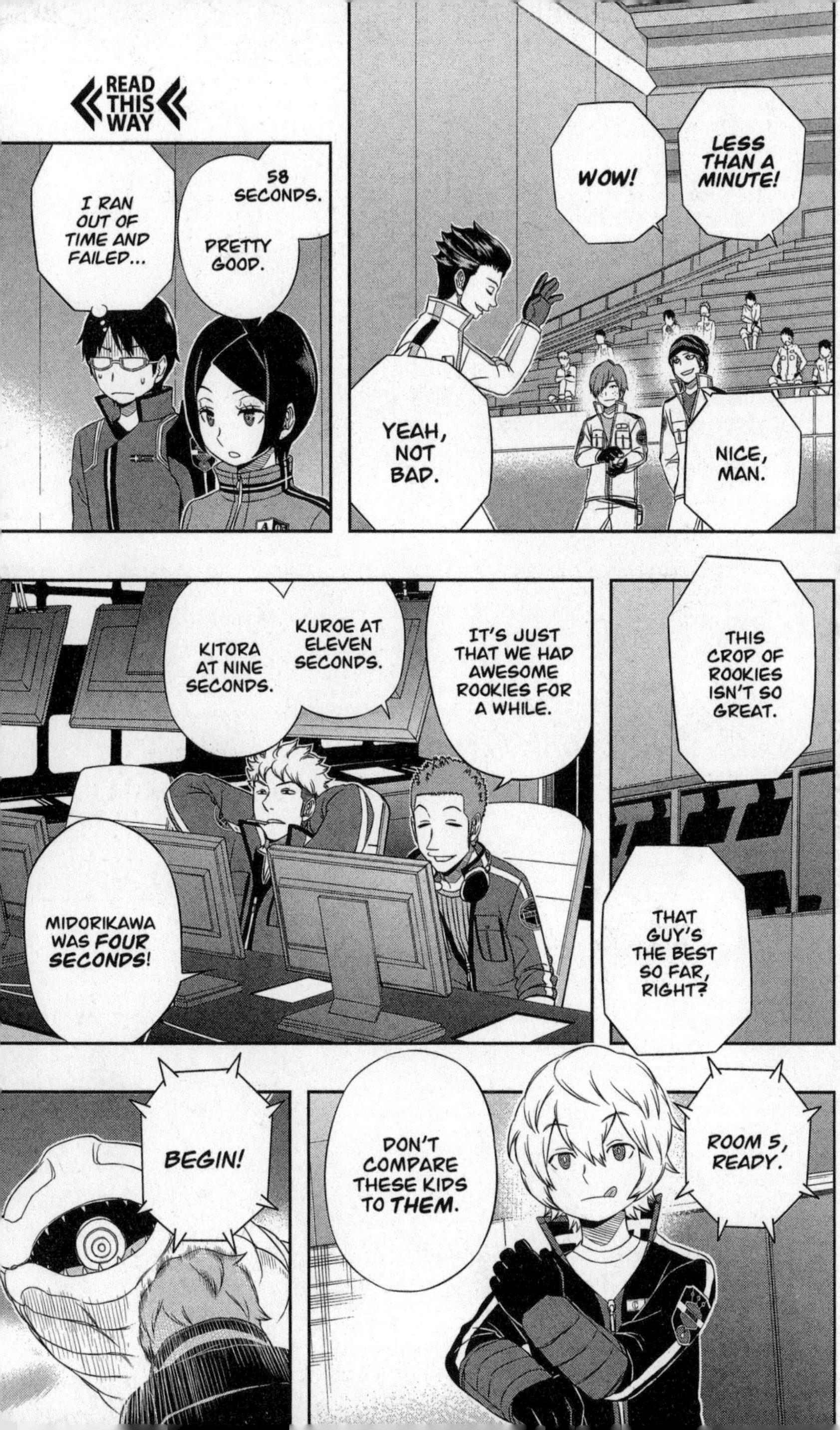

READ THIS WAY
LESS THAN A MINUTE!
WOW!
NICE, MAN.
YEAH, NOT BAD.
58 SECONDS. PRETTY GOOD.
I RAN OUT OF TIME AND FAILED...
THIS CROP OF ROOKIES ISN'T SO GREAT.
THAT GUY'S THE BEST SO FAR, RIGHT?
IT'S JUST THAT WE HAD AWESOME ROOKIES FOR A WHILE.
KUROE AT ELEVEN SECONDS.
KITORA AT NINE SECONDS.
MIDORIKAWA WAS FOUR SECONDS!
ROOM 5, READY.
DON'T COMPARE THESE KIDS TO THEM.
BEGIN!

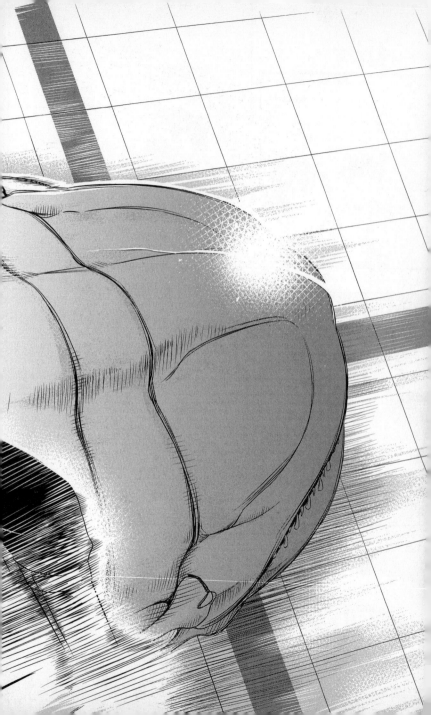

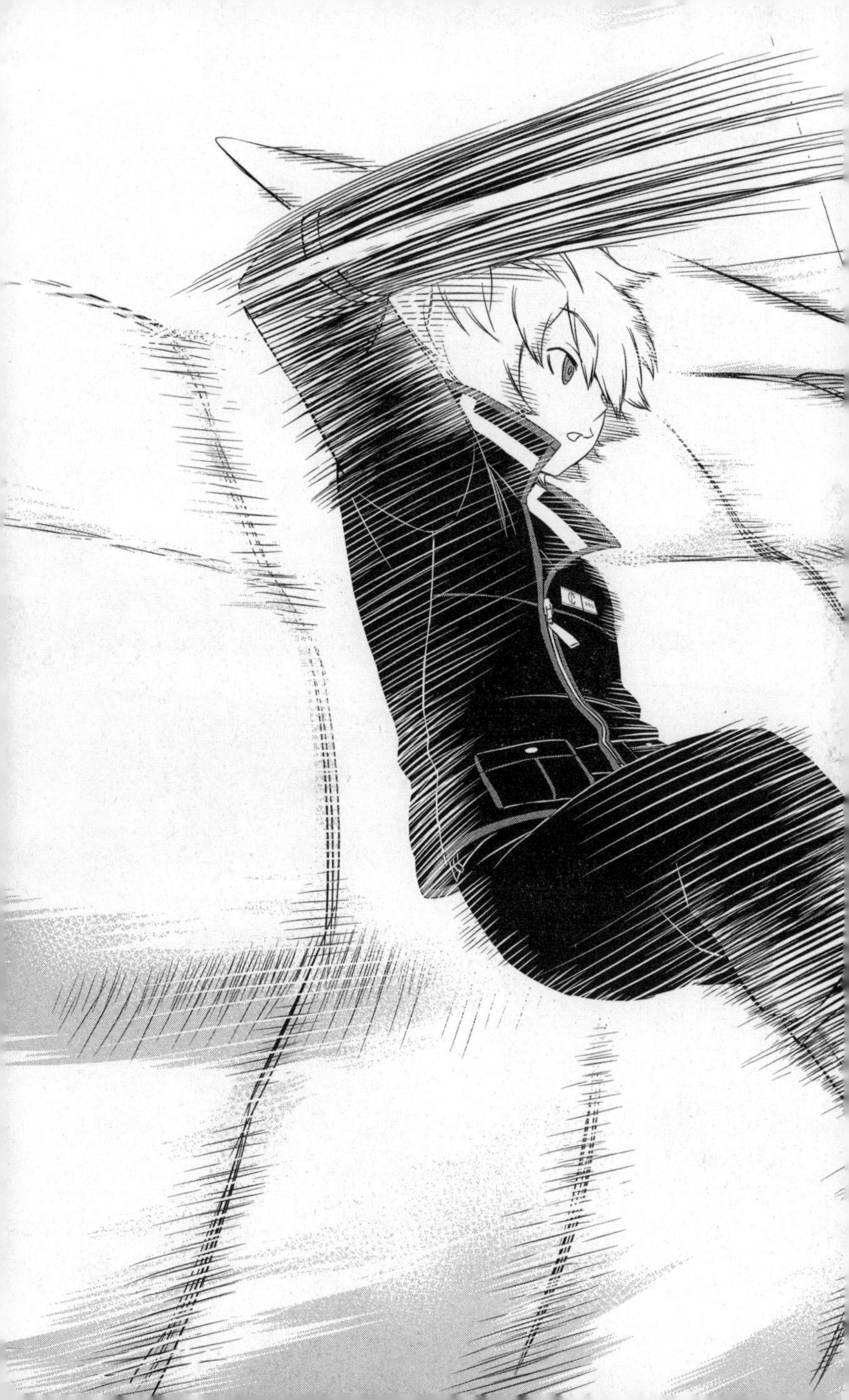

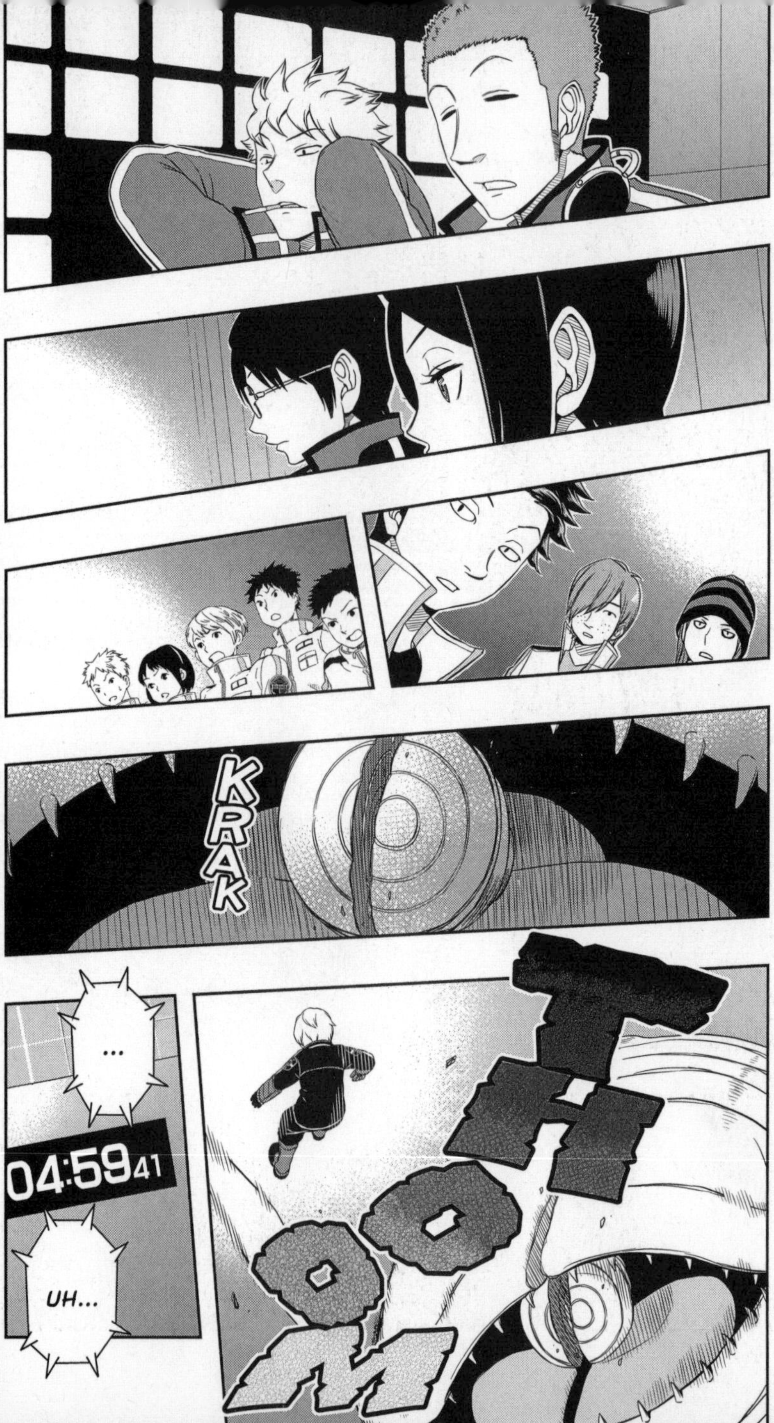
KRAK
FOOM
...
04:59 41
UH...

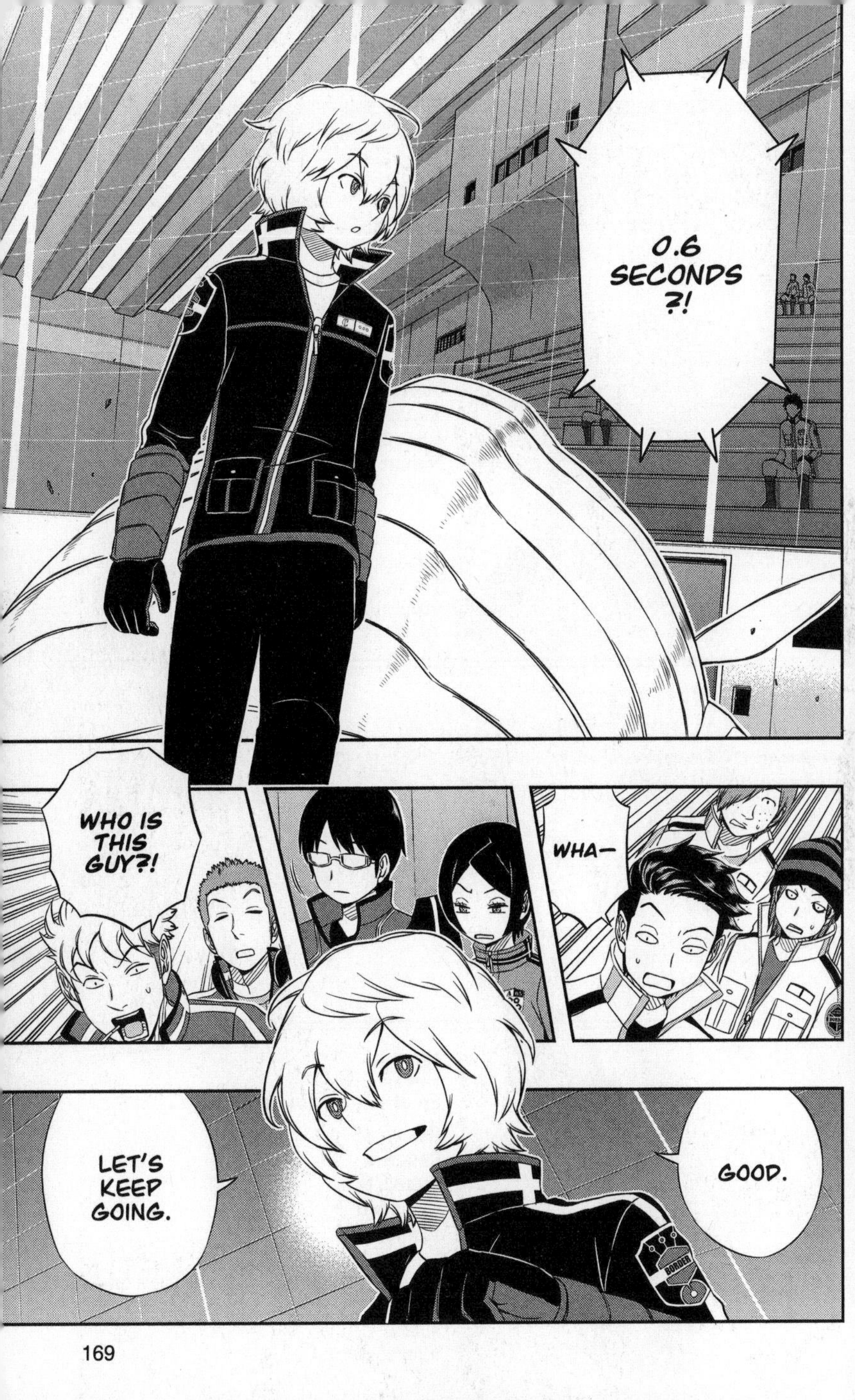
0.6 SECONDS ?!
WHA-
WHO IS THIS GUY?!
GOOD.
LET'S KEEP GOING.

Sniper Triggers

Long-range Triggers. They consume a lot of Trion at once, so raid fire is not possible.

Egret
Standard model, emphasis on range

Power: B
Range: S
Speed: A
Reload: C
Weight: C

Excellent range and bullet speed, pretty good power. Because of its balance, this is the Sniper Trigger used most in Rank Wars. All-purpose.

Lightning
Emphasis on muzzle velocity

Power: C
Range: B
Speed: SS
Reload: B
Weight: B

Light with passable reload time. Higher muzzle velocity means it's easier to hit a target, but less power means shields can block it. Pepper the enemy with bullets.

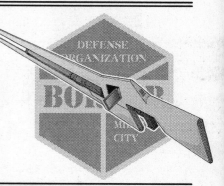

Ibis
Emphasis on power

Power: SS
Range: A
Speed: B
Reload: D
Weight: D

Heavyweight rifle with an emphasis on one-hit kills. It's a little overkill for combat against people, so it's mainly used against Trion soldiers.

Chapter 34 Chika Amatori: Part 3

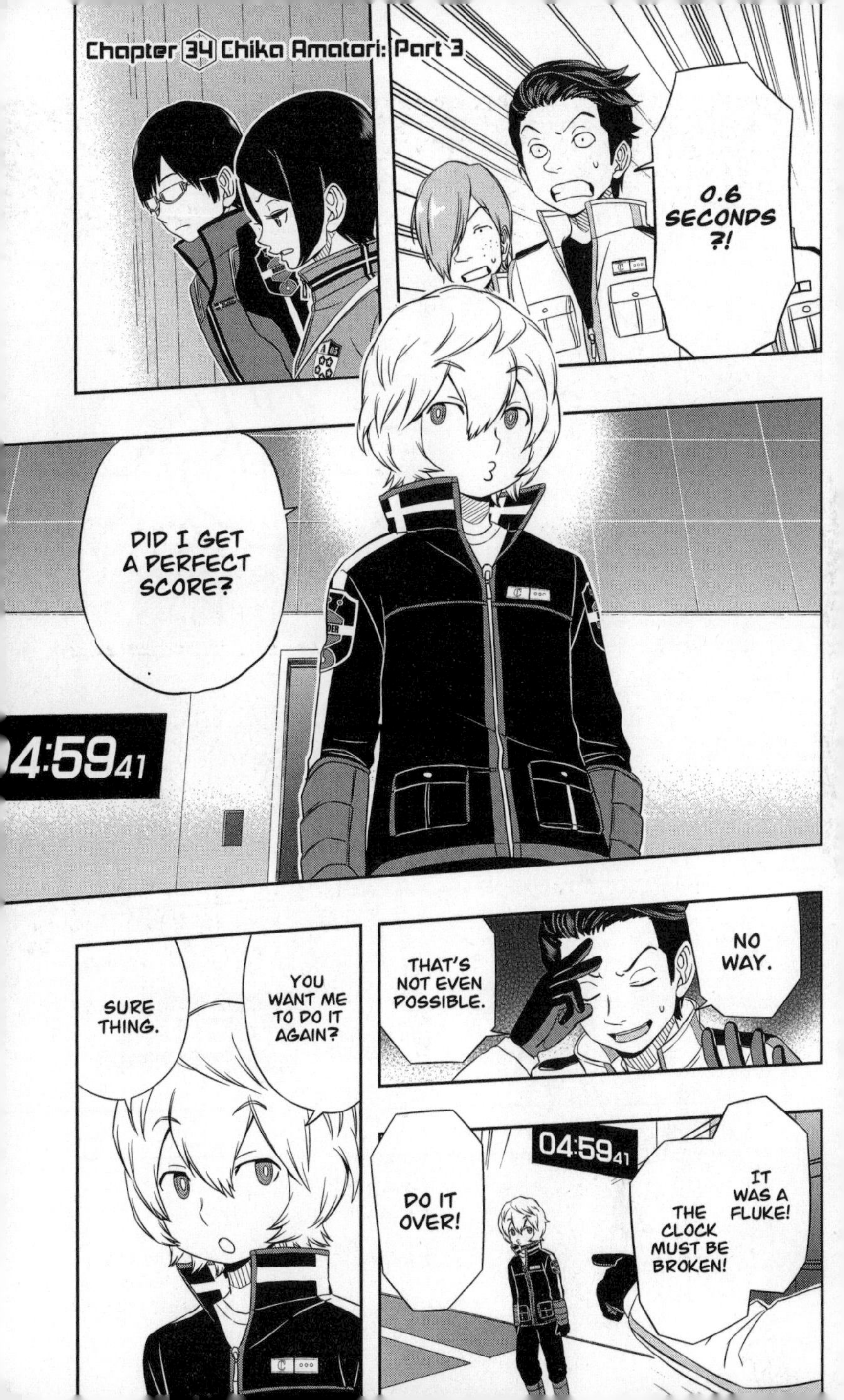
0.6 SECONDS ?!
DID I GET A PERFECT SCORE?
04:59 41
NO WAY.
THAT'S NOT EVEN POSSIBLE.
04:59 41
IT WAS A FLUKE!
THE CLOCK MUST BE BROKEN!
DO IT OVER!
YOU WANT ME TO DO IT AGAIN?
SURE THING.

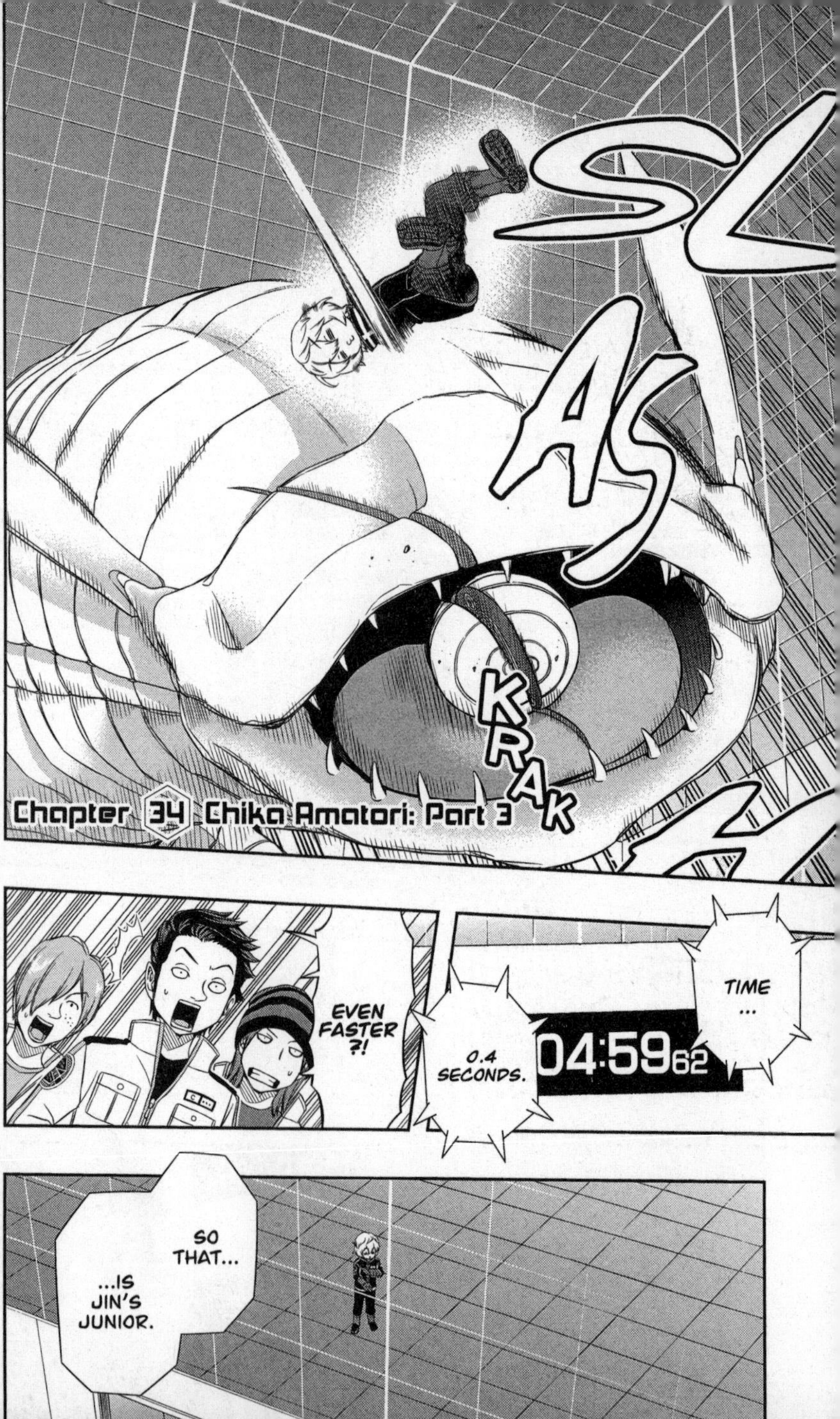
SLASH
KRAK
Chapter 34 Chika Amatori: Part 3
TIME ...
0.4 SECONDS.
04:59 62
EVEN FASTER ?!
SO THAT...
...IS JIN'S JUNIOR.

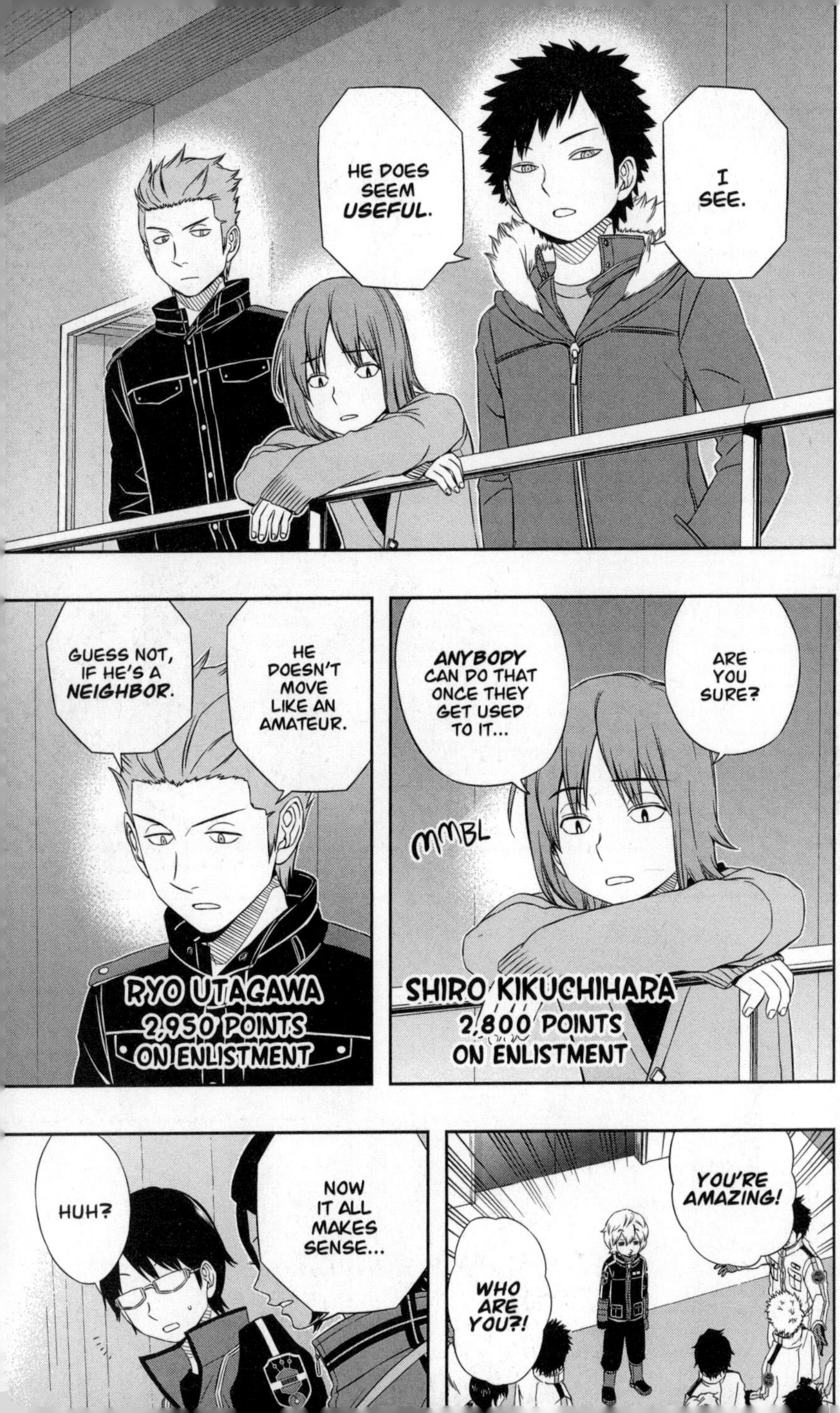
I SEE.
HE DOES SEEM USEFUL.
ARE YOU SURE?
ANYBODY CAN DO THAT ONCE THEY GET USED TO IT...
MMBL
SHIRO KIKUCHIHARA
2,800 POINTS ON ENLISTMENT
HE DOESN'T MOVE LIKE AN AMATEUR.
GUESS NOT, IF HE'S A NEIGHBOR.
RYO UTAGAWA
2,950 POINTS ON ENLISTMENT
YOU'RE AMAZING!
WHO ARE YOU?!
NOW IT ALL MAKES SENSE...
HUH?

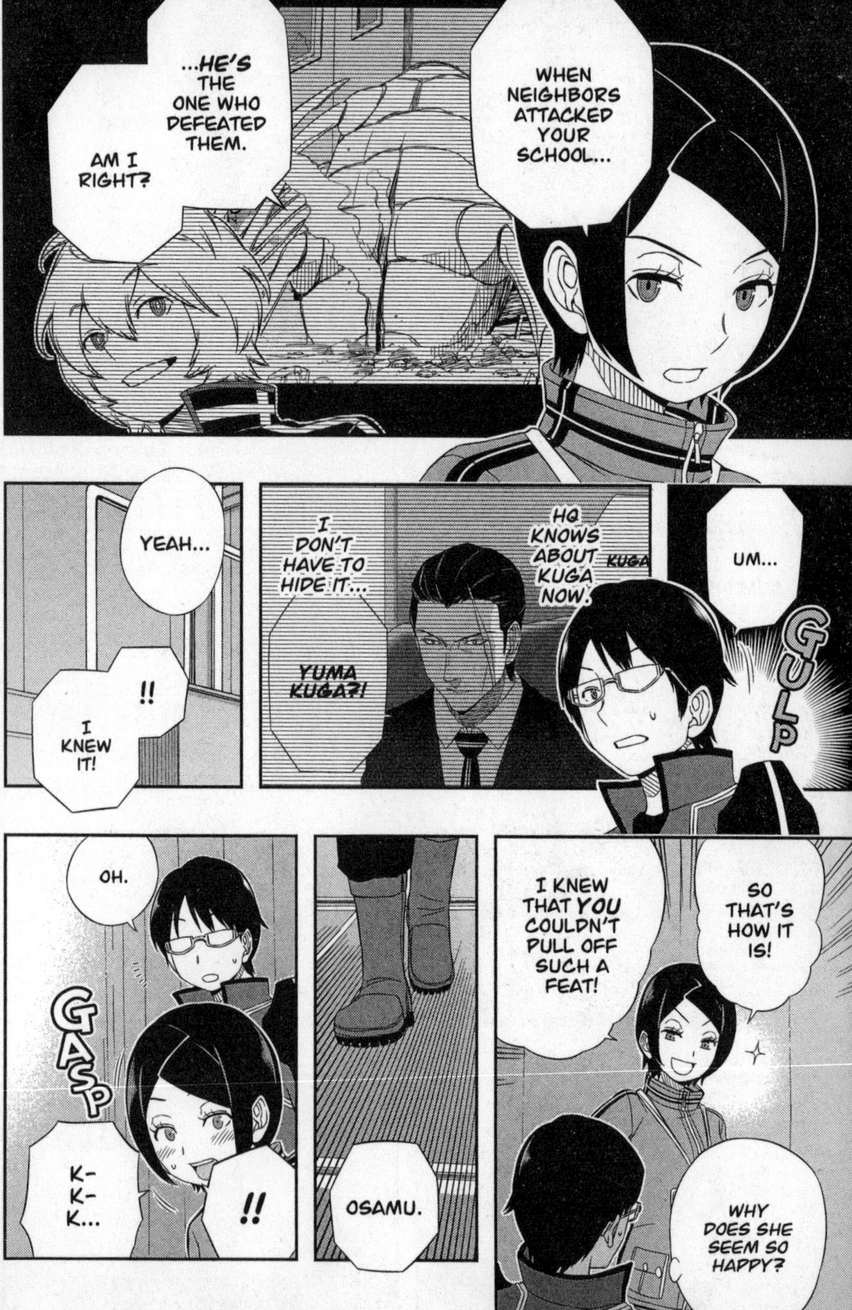
WHEN NEIGHBORS ATTACKED YOUR SCHOOL...
...HE'S THE ONE WHO DEFEATED THEM.
AM I RIGHT?
UM...
GULP
HQ KNOWS ABOUT KUGA NOW.
KUGA
I DON'T HAVE TO HIDE IT...
YUMA KUGA?!
YEAH...
!!
I KNEW IT!
SO THAT'S HOW IT IS!
I KNEW THAT YOU COULDN'T PULL OFF SUCH A FEAT!
WHY DOES SHE SEEM SO HAPPY?
OSAMU.
OH.
GASP
!!
K-K-K...

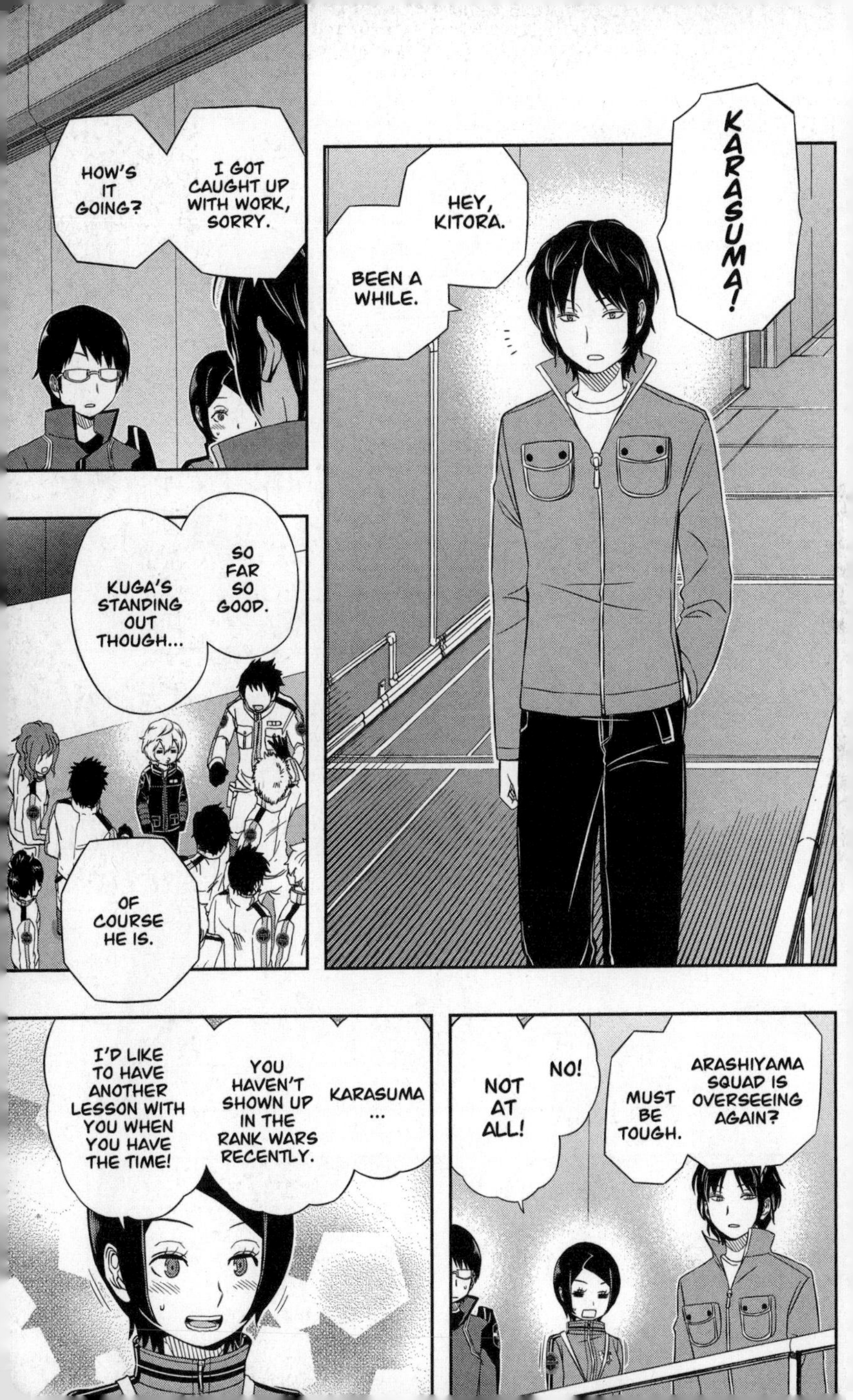
KARASUMA!
HEY, KITORA.
BEEN A WHILE.
I GOT CAUGHT UP WITH WORK, SORRY.
HOW'S IT GOING?
SO FAR SO GOOD.
KUGA'S STANDING OUT THOUGH...
OF COURSE HE IS.
ARASHIYAMA SQUAD IS OVERSEEING AGAIN?
MUST BE TOUGH.
NO!
NOT AT ALL!
KARASUMA...
YOU HAVEN'T SHOWN UP IN THE RANK WARS RECENTLY.
I'D LIKE TO HAVE ANOTHER LESSON WITH YOU WHEN YOU HAVE THE TIME!

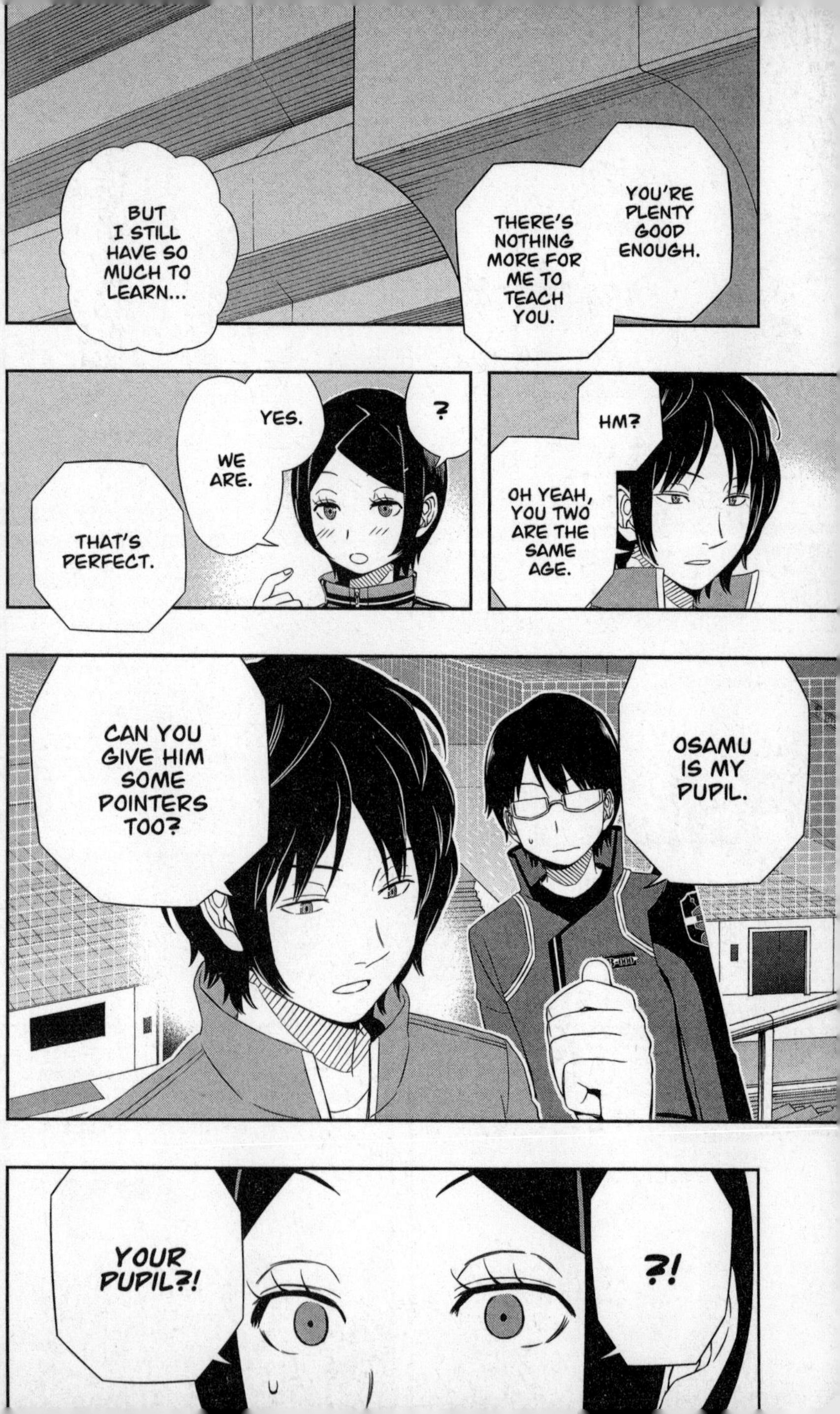
YOU'RE PLENTY GOOD ENOUGH.
THERE'S NOTHING MORE FOR ME TO TEACH YOU.
BUT I STILL HAVE SO MUCH TO LEARN...
HM?
OH YEAH, YOU TWO ARE THE SAME AGE.
?
YES.
WE ARE.
THAT'S PERFECT.
OSAMU IS MY PUPIL.
CAN YOU GIVE HIM SOME POINTERS TOO?
?!
YOUR PUPIL?!

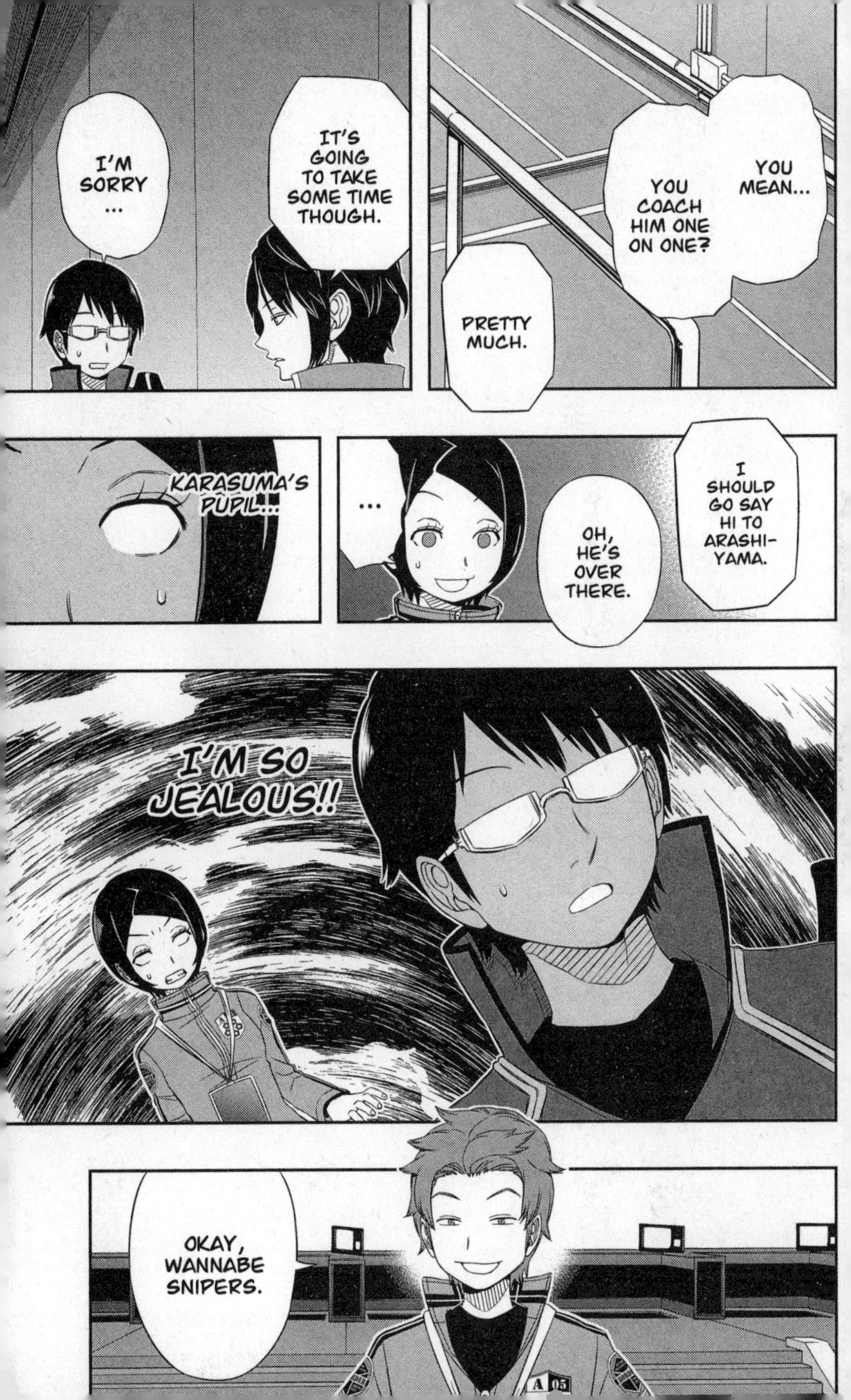
YOU MEAN...
YOU COACH HIM ONE ON ONE?
PRETTY MUCH.
IT'S GOING TO TAKE SOME TIME THOUGH.
I'M SORRY ...
I SHOULD GO SAY HI TO ARASHI-YAMA.
OH, HE'S OVER THERE.
...
KARASUMA'S PUPIL...
I'M SO JEALOUS!!
OKAY, WANNABE SNIPERS.

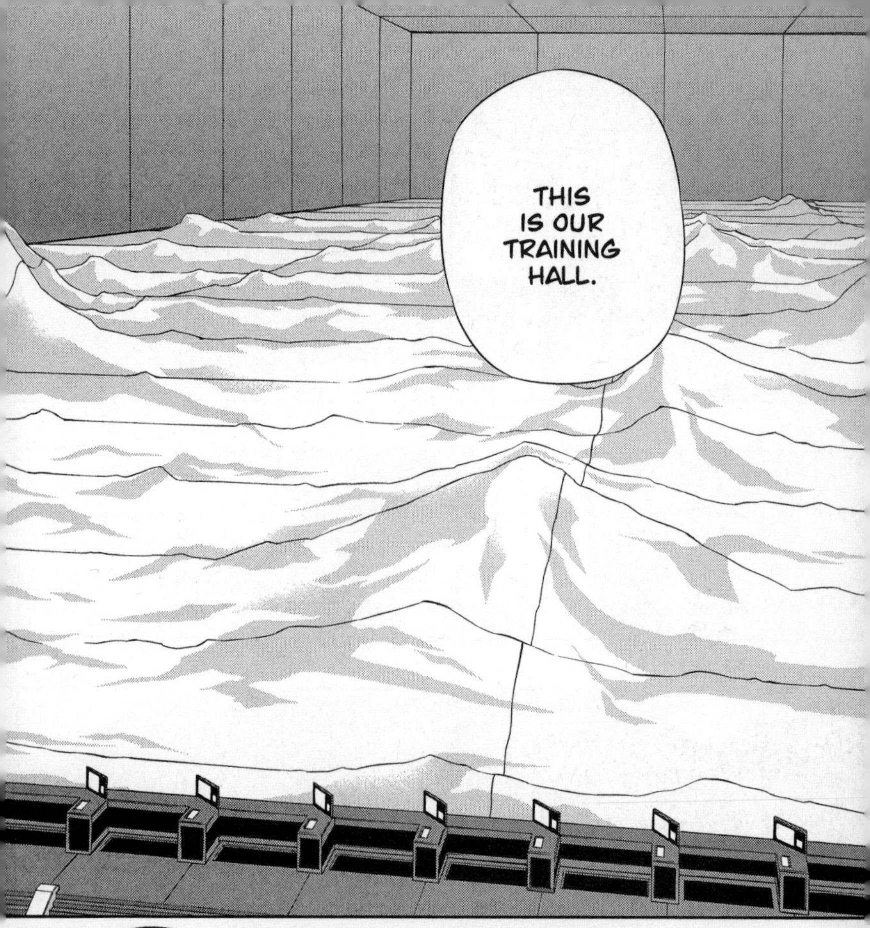
THIS IS OUR TRAINING HALL.
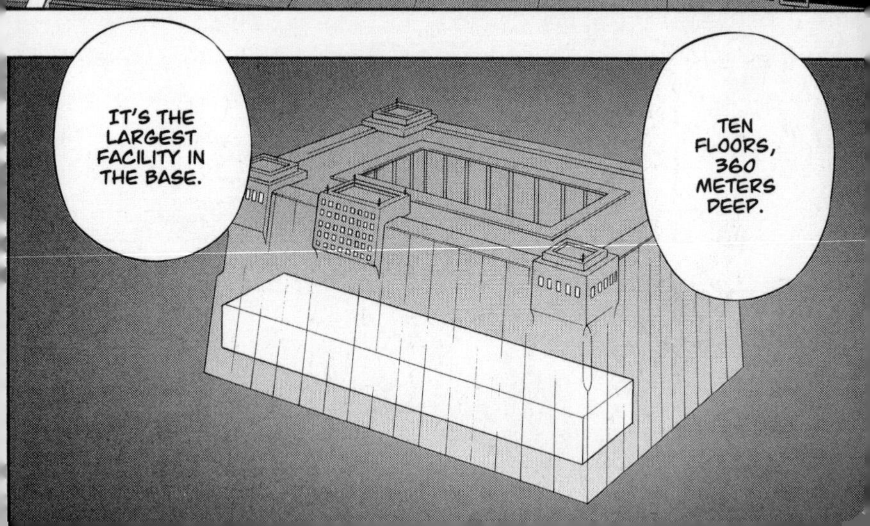
TEN FLOORS, 360 METERS DEEP.
IT'S THE LARGEST FACILITY IN THE BASE.

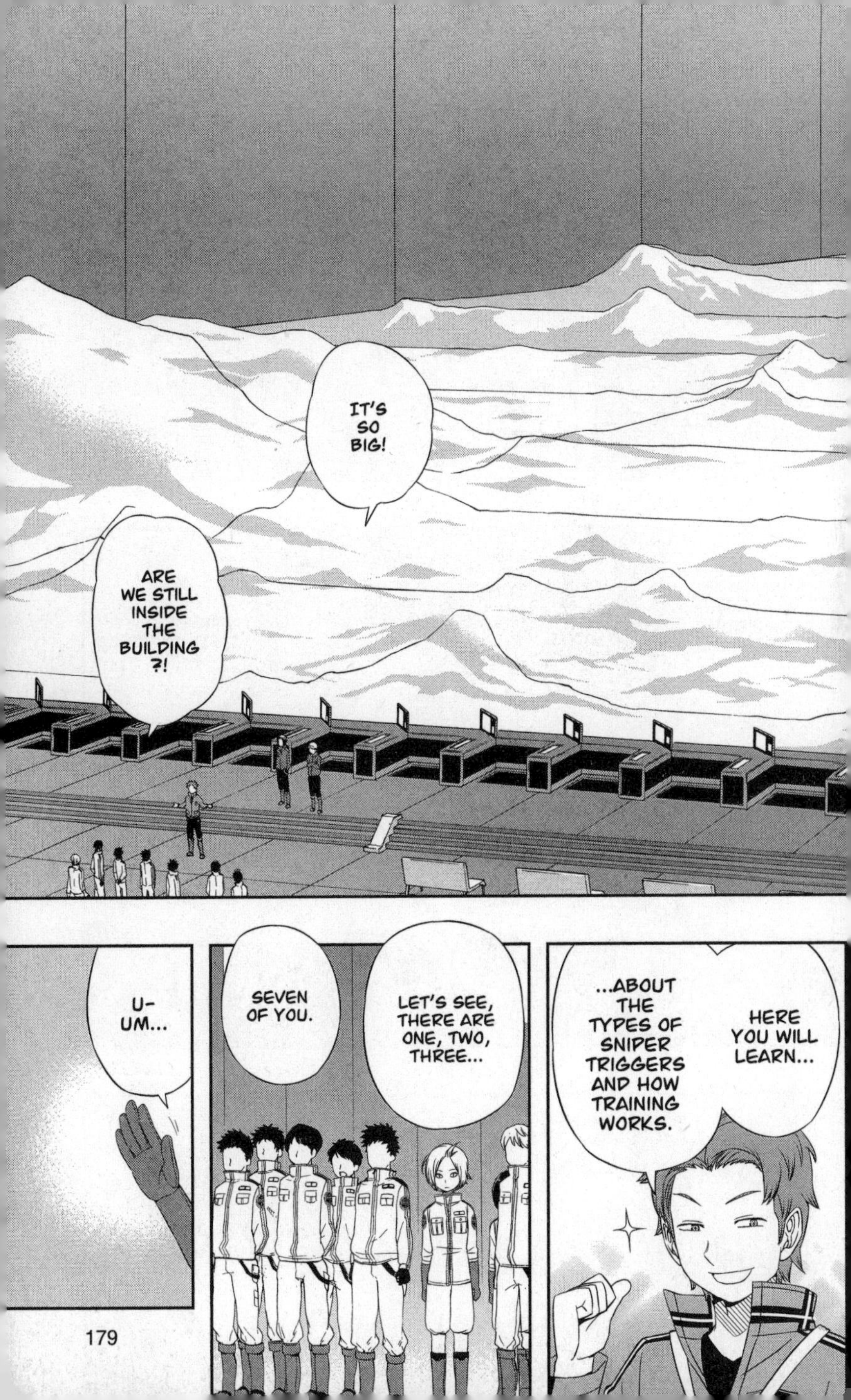
IT'S SO BIG!
ARE WE STILL INSIDE THE BUILDING?!
HERE YOU WILL LEARN...
...ABOUT THE TYPES OF SNIPER TRIGGERS AND HOW TRAINING WORKS.
LET'S SEE, THERE ARE ONE, TWO, THREE...
SEVEN OF YOU.
U-UM...

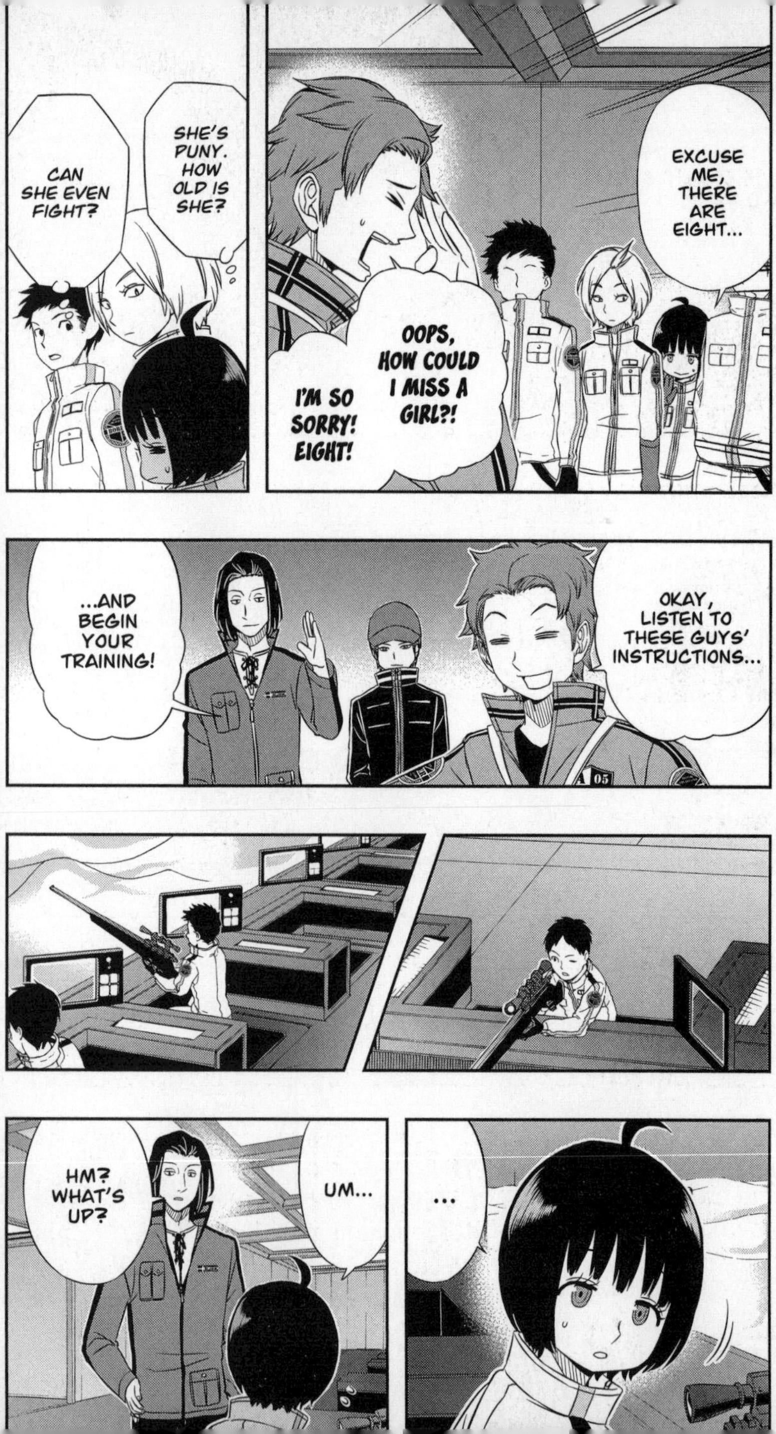
EXCUSE ME, THERE ARE EIGHT...
OOPS, HOW COULD I MISS A GIRL?!
I'M SO SORRY! EIGHT!
SHE'S PUNY. HOW OLD IS SHE?
CAN SHE EVEN FIGHT?
OKAY, LISTEN TO THESE GUYS' INSTRUCTIONS...
...AND BEGIN YOUR TRAINING!
...
UM...
HM? WHAT'S UP?

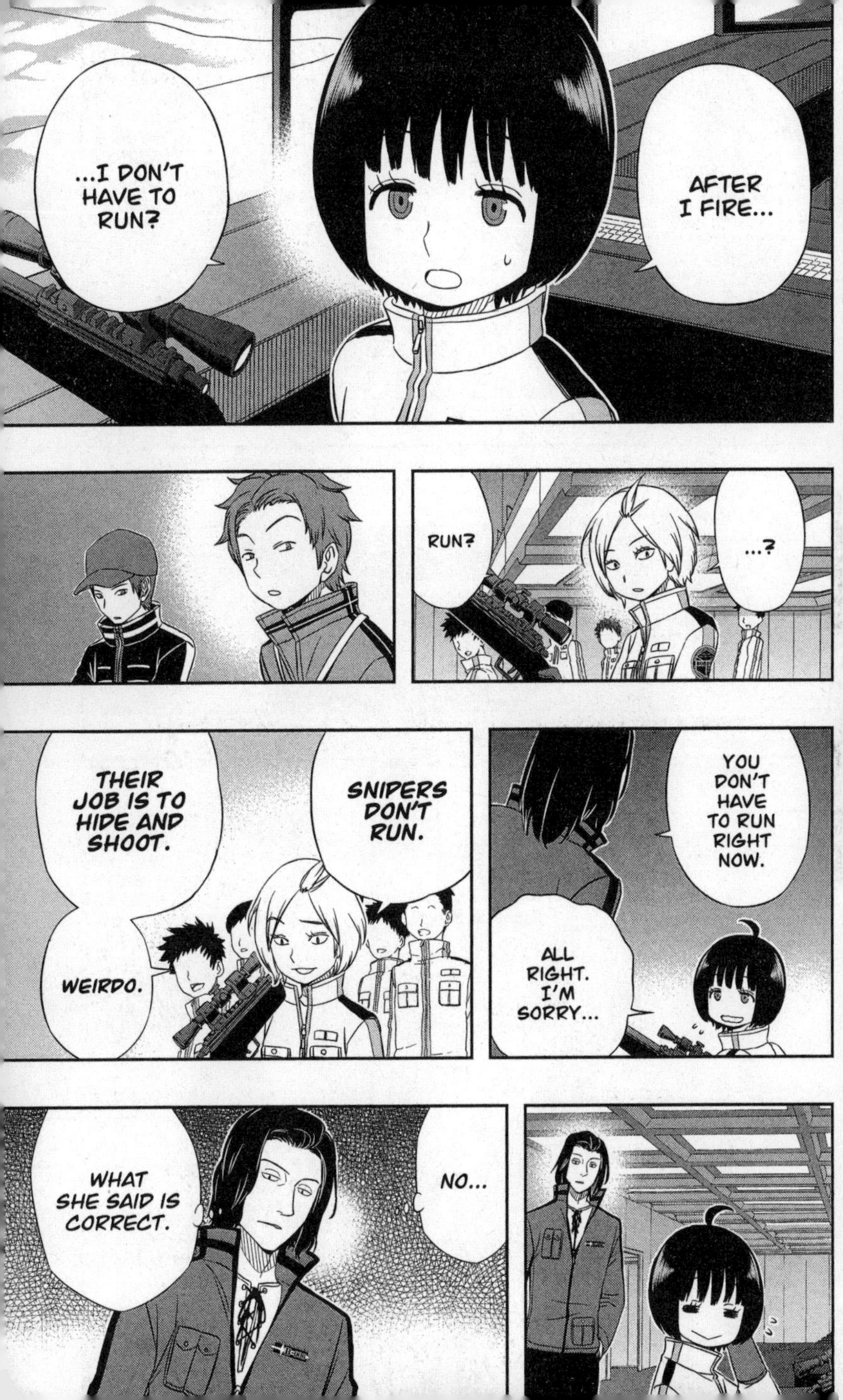
AFTER I FIRE...
...I DON'T HAVE TO RUN?
...?
RUN?
YOU DON'T HAVE TO RUN RIGHT NOW.
ALL RIGHT. I'M SORRY...
SNIPERS DON'T RUN.
THEIR JOB IS TO HIDE AND SHOOT.
WEIRDO.
NO...
WHAT SHE SAID IS CORRECT.

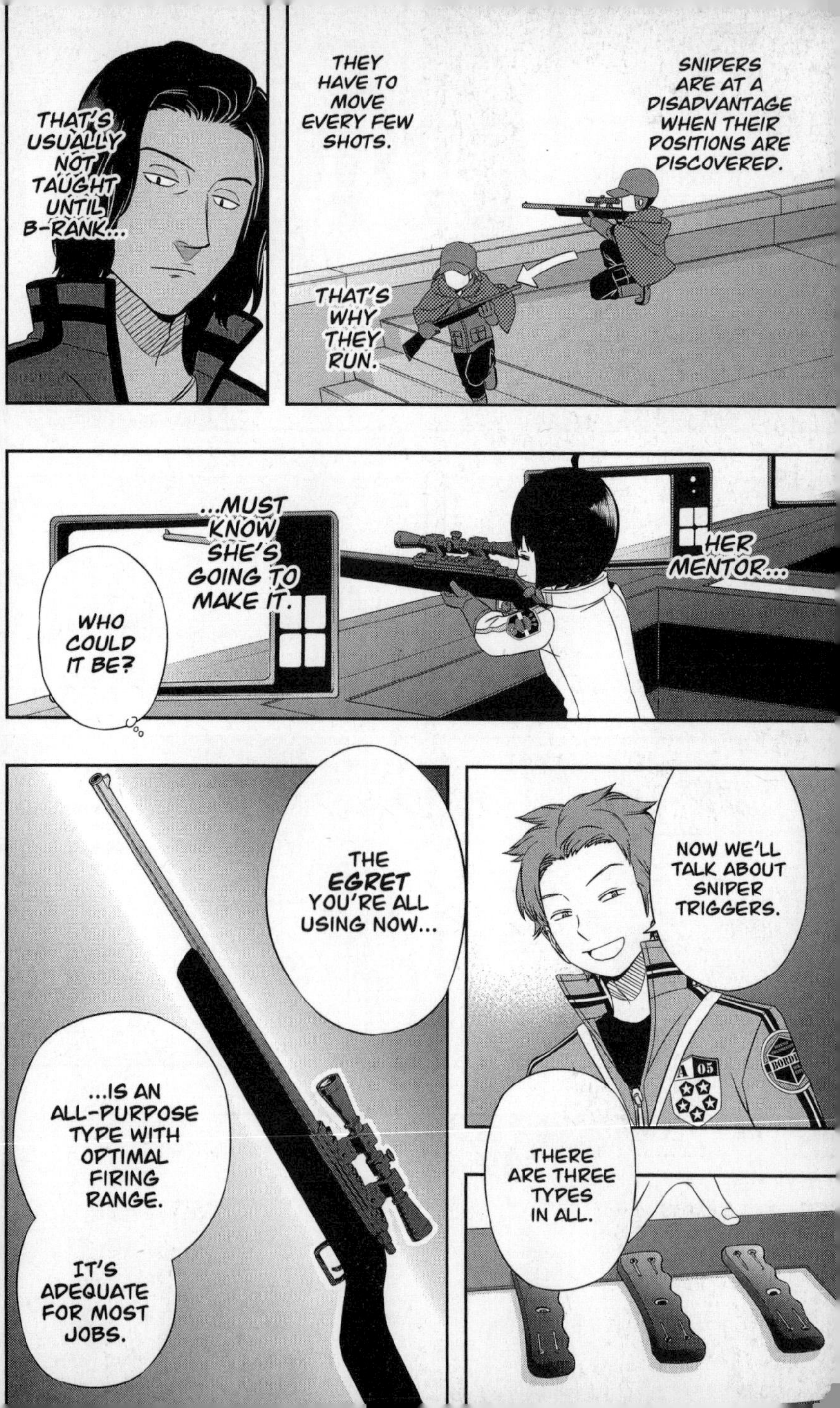
SNIPERS ARE AT A DISADVANTAGE WHEN THEIR POSITIONS ARE DISCOVERED.
THEY HAVE TO MOVE EVERY FEW SHOTS.
THAT'S WHY THEY RUN.
THAT'S USUALLY NOT TAUGHT UNTIL B-RANK...
HER MENTOR...
...MUST KNOW SHE'S GOING TO MAKE IT.
WHO COULD IT BE?
NOW WE'LL TALK ABOUT SNIPER TRIGGERS.
THERE ARE THREE TYPES IN ALL.
THE EGRET YOU'RE ALL USING NOW...
...IS AN ALL-PURPOSE TYPE WITH OPTIMAL FIRING RANGE.
IT'S ADEQUATE FOR MOST JOBS.

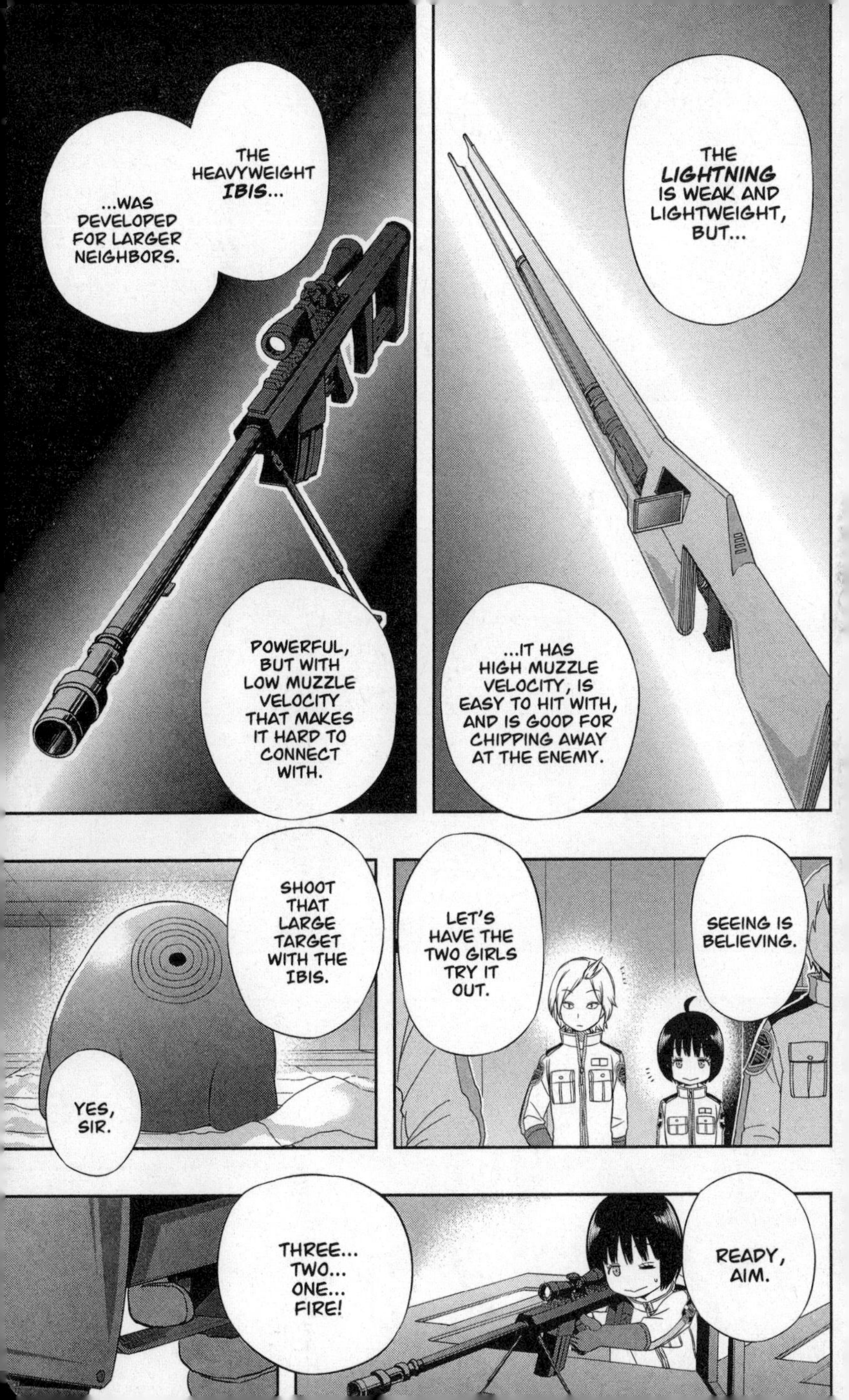
THE LIGHTNING IS WEAK AND LIGHTWEIGHT, BUT...
...IT HAS HIGH MUZZLE VELOCITY, IS EASY TO HIT WITH, AND IS GOOD FOR CHIPPING AWAY AT THE ENEMY.
THE HEAVYWEIGHT IBIS...
...WAS DEVELOPED FOR LARGER NEIGHBORS.
POWERFUL, BUT WITH LOW MUZZLE VELOCITY THAT MAKES IT HARD TO CONNECT WITH.
SEEING IS BELIEVING.
LET'S HAVE THE TWO GIRLS TRY IT OUT.
SHOOT THAT LARGE TARGET WITH THE IBIS.
YES, SIR.
READY, AIM.
THREE... TWO... ONE... FIRE!

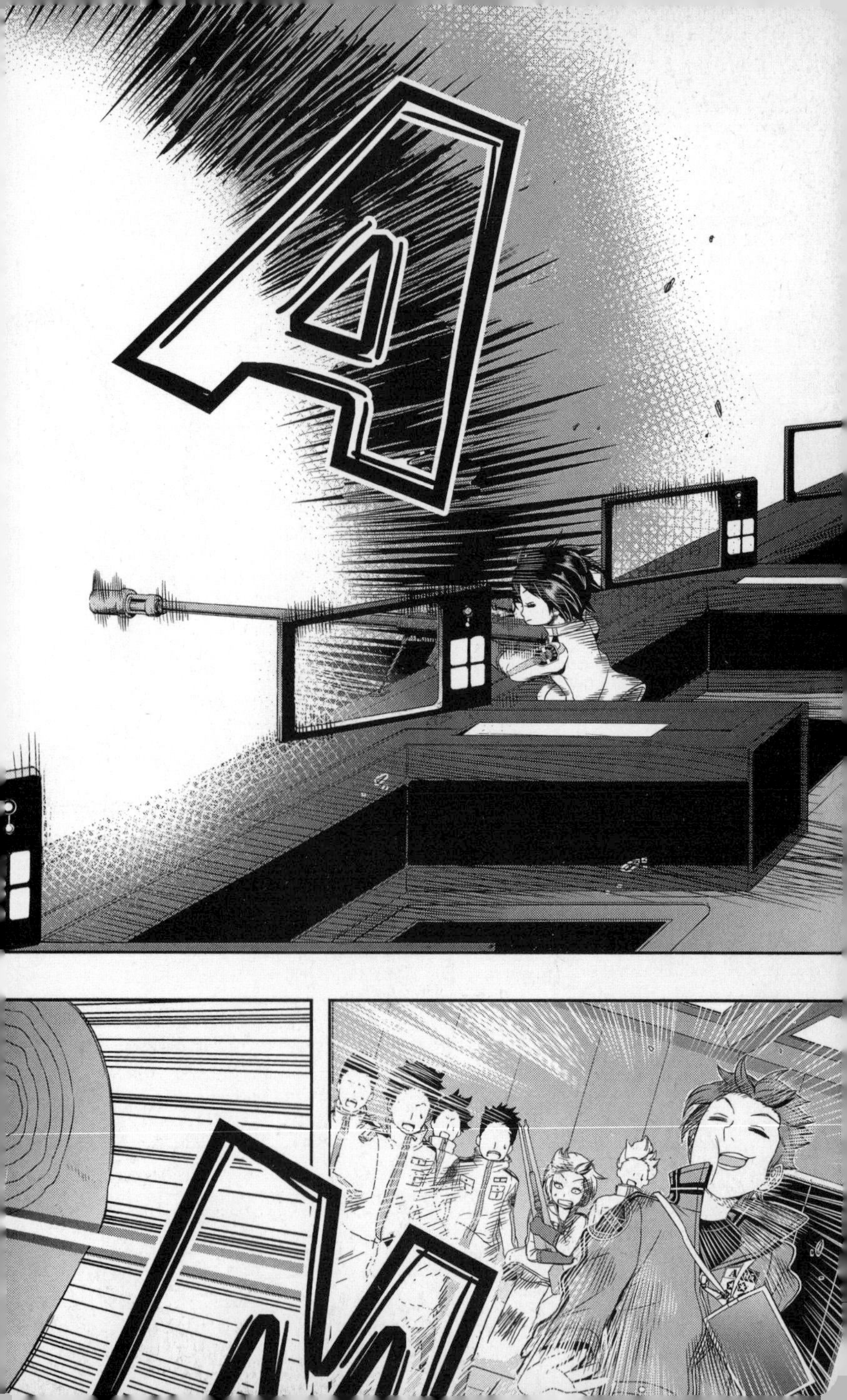
A
M

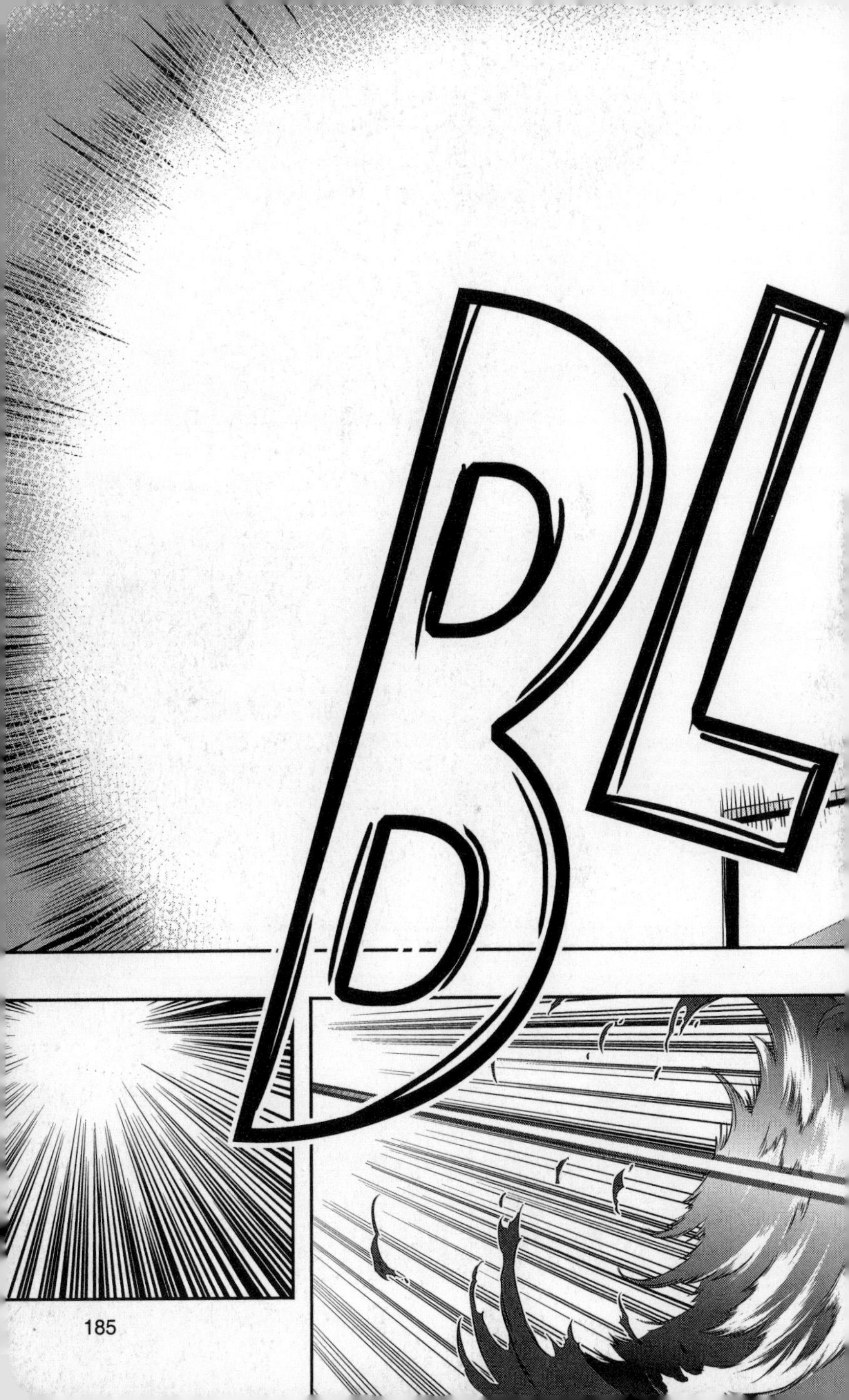
BL

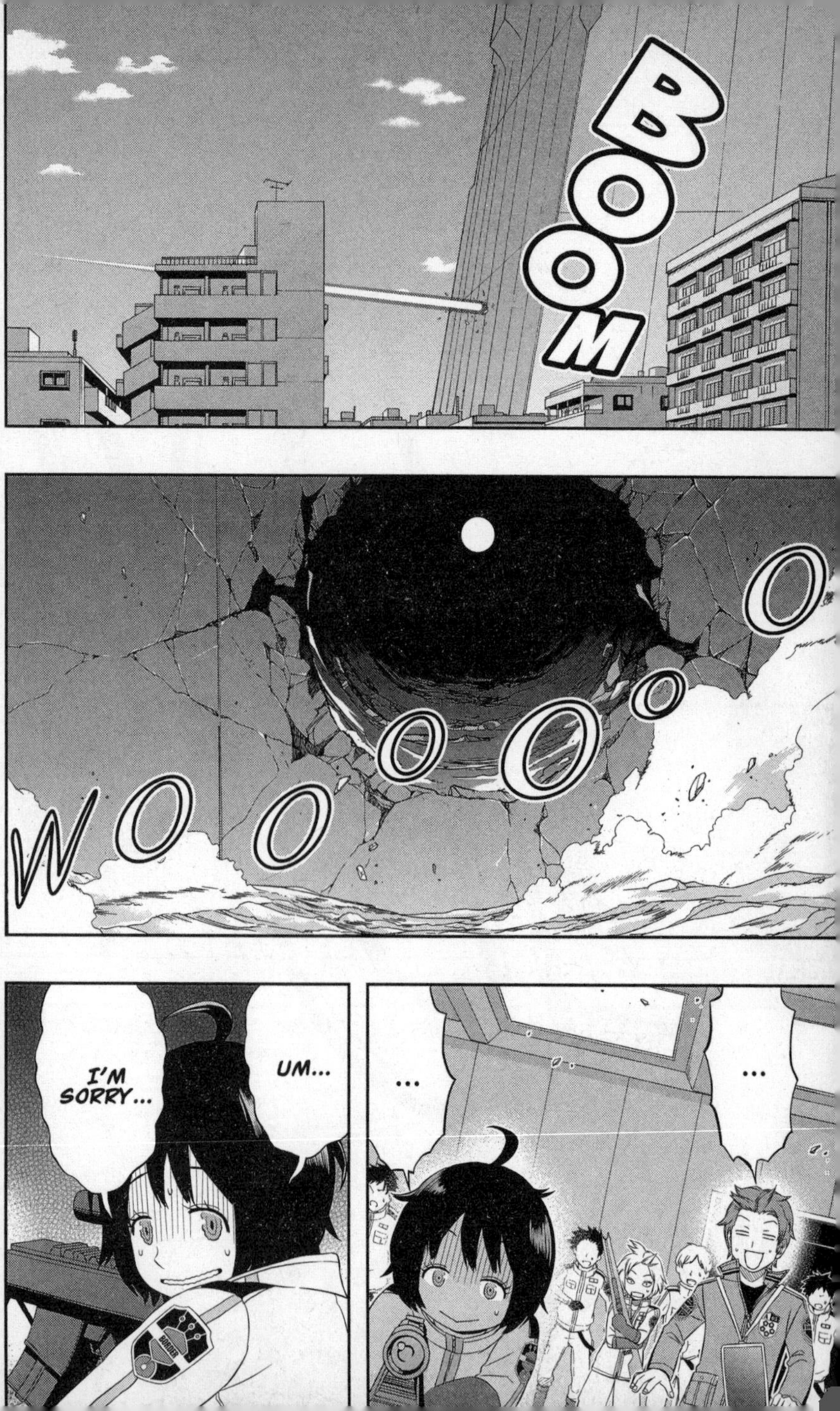
BOOM
WOOOOOOO
...
...
UM...
I'M SORRY...

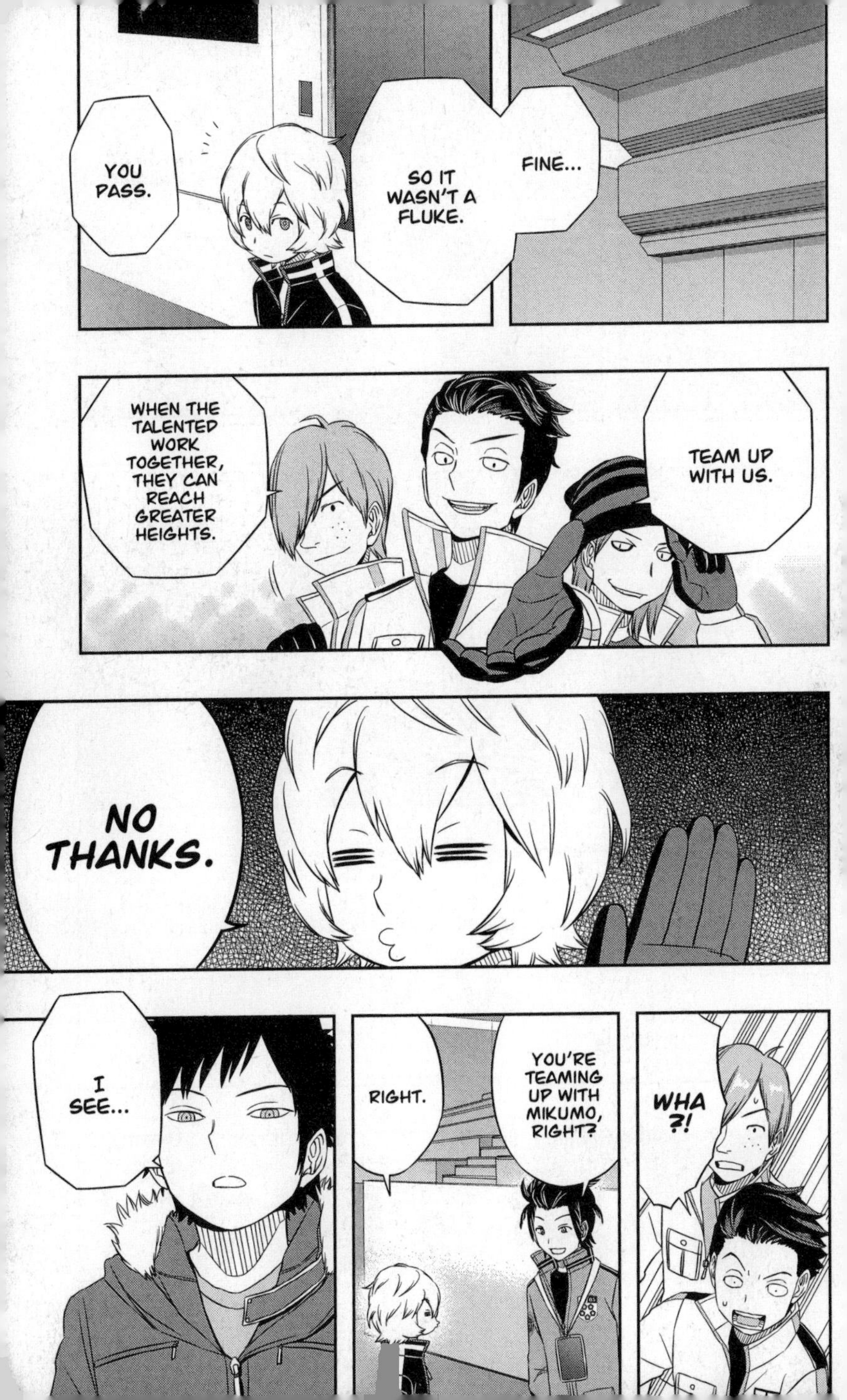
FINE...
SO IT WASN'T A FLUKE.
YOU PASS.
TEAM UP WITH US.
WHEN THE TALENTED WORK TOGETHER, THEY CAN REACH GREATER HEIGHTS.
NO THANKS.
WHA?!
YOU'RE TEAMING UP WITH MIKUMO, RIGHT?
RIGHT.
I SEE...

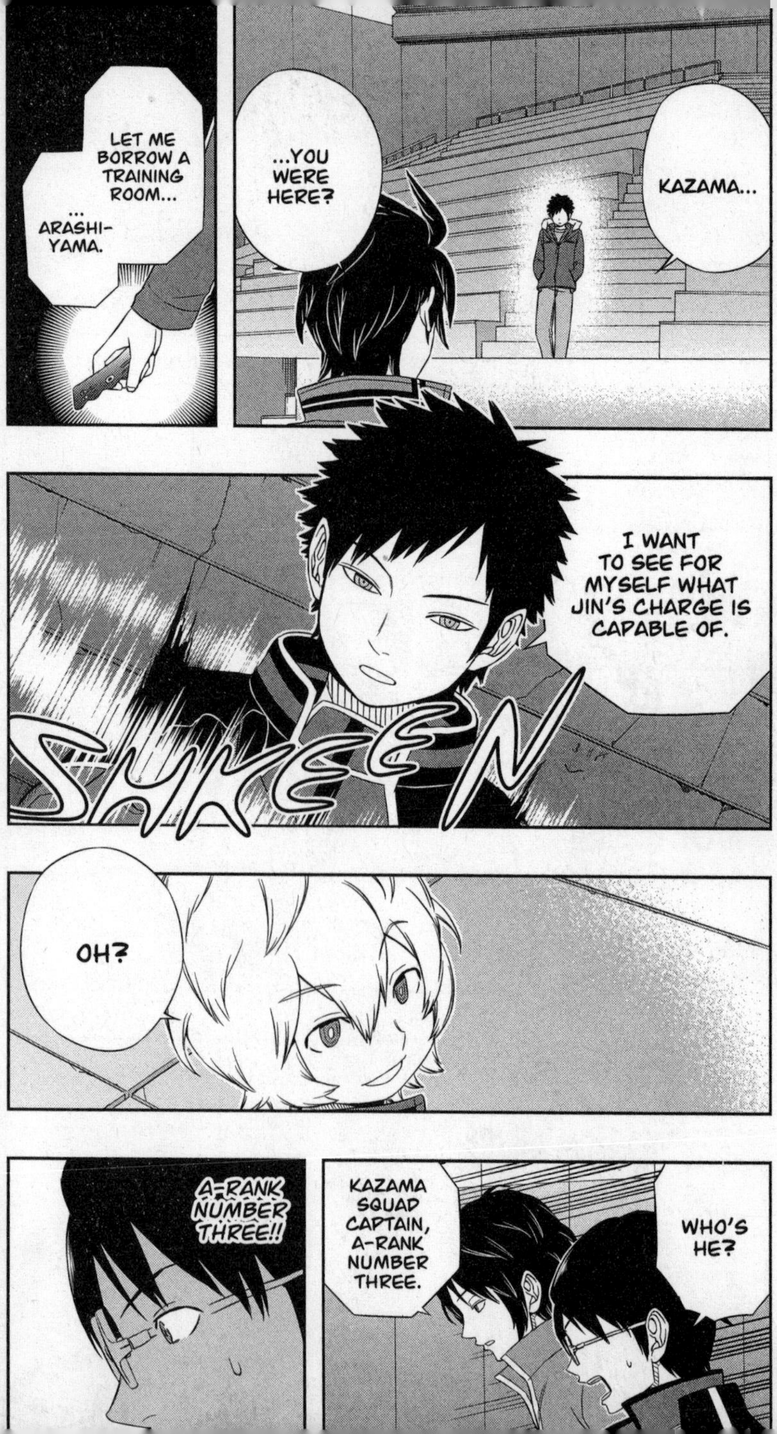
KAZAMA...
...YOU WERE HERE?
LET ME BORROW A TRAINING ROOM...
... ARASHI-YAMA.
I WANT TO SEE FOR MYSELF WHAT JIN'S CHARGE IS CAPABLE OF.
SHKEEN
OH?
WHO'S HE?
KAZAMA SQUAD CAPTAIN, A-RANK NUMBER THREE.
A-RANK NUMBER THREE!!

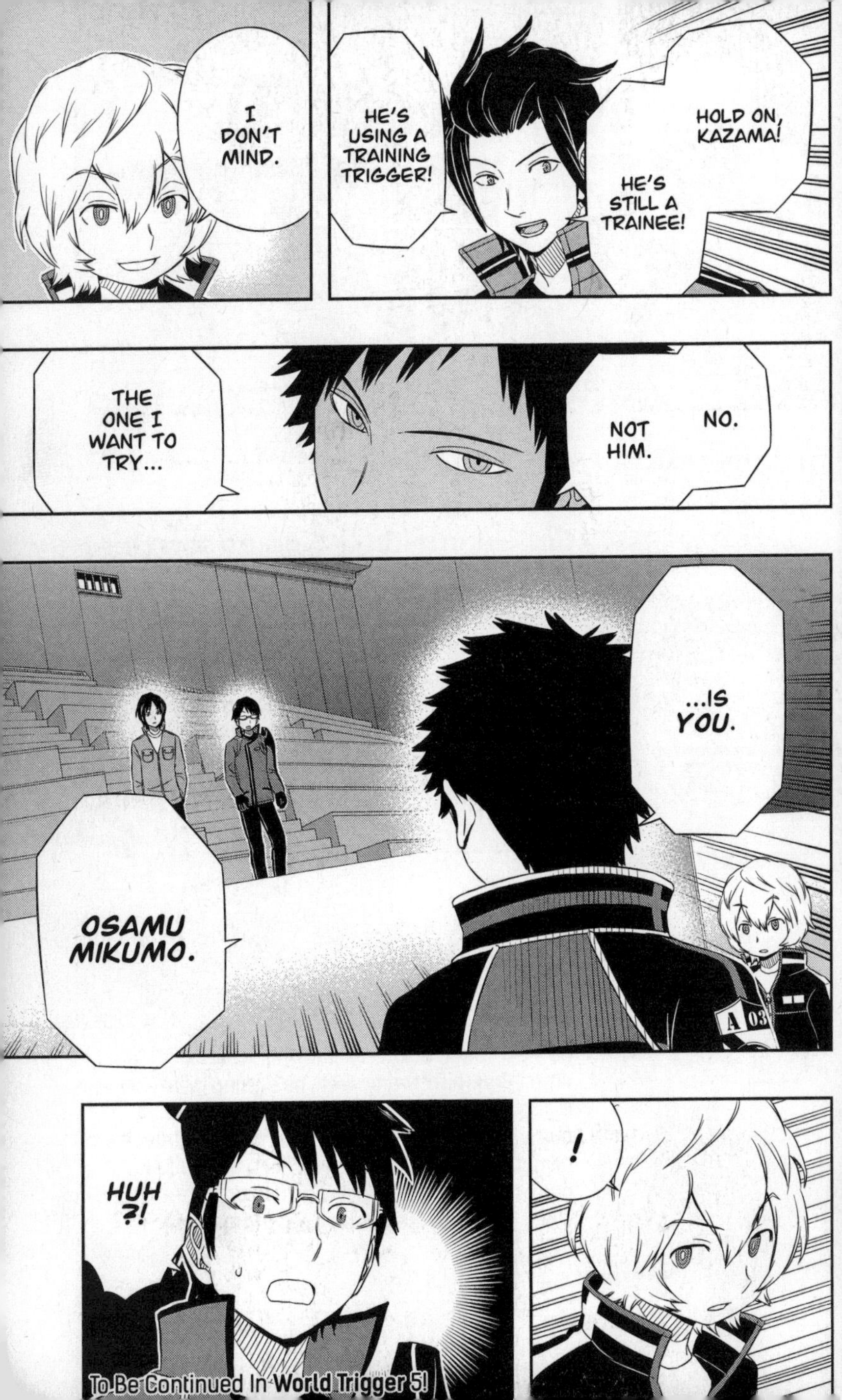
HOLD ON, KAZAMA!
HE'S STILL A TRAINEE!
HE'S USING A TRAINING TRIGGER!
I DON'T MIND.
NO.
NOT HIM.
THE ONE I WANT TO TRY...
...IS YOU.
OSAMU MIKUMO.
!
HUH ?!
To Be Continued In World Trigger 5!

WORLD TRIGGER

Bonus Character Pages

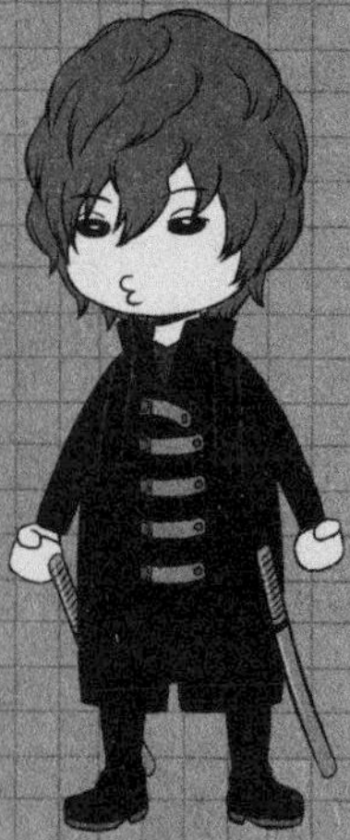

TACHIKAWA

Two-Sword-Style Goatee Wielder

He's ranked number one at Border among those with crosshatch eyes. He's a tough cookie who's not embarrassed about wearing a black trench coat and carrying two swords despite being over 20. He lives for combat, and unlike Yoneya, also has a talent for command. But I don't think he's good at anything other than fighting. Barely taking enough classes to stay in college.

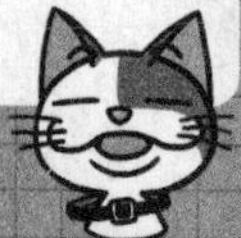

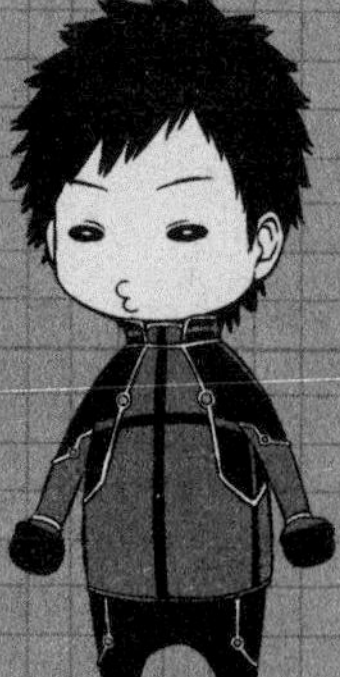

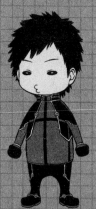

KAZAMA

A-Rank 21-Year-Old

He's 5'2", but it seems like he shrinks every time I draw him. Pretty soon, he's going to be indistinguishable from Yotaro and he'll be eating dinner at Tamakoma. He's not concerned about his height, and he's ready to fight using the cards he's been dealt. His uniform is a pain to draw, and I die every time his squad is featured prominently.

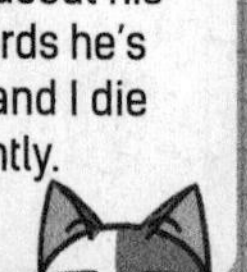